The Transformation of the Classical Heritage

Peter Brown, General Editor

Theodosian Empresses

KENNETH G. HOLUM

THEODOSIAN

Women and Imperial

EMPRESSES

Dominion in
Late Antiquity

UNIVERSITY OF CALIFORNIA PRESS

Berkeley   *Los Angeles*   *London*

University of California Press
Berkeley and Los Angeles, California

University of California Press, Ltd.
London, England

©1982 by
The Regents of the University of California

Printed in the United States of America

1 2 3 4 5 6 7 8 9

First Paperback Printing 1989

Library of Congress Cataloging in Publication Data

Holum, Kenneth G.
 Theodosian empresses.

 Originally presented as the author's thesis
(Ph.D.)—University of Chicago.
 Bibliography: p.
 Includes index.
 1. Roman empresses—Biography. 2. Rome—Nobility
—Biography. 3. Rome—History—Theodosians, 379-455.
I. Title. DG322.H64 1982 937'.02 81-43690
ISBN 0-520-06801-7   AACR2

For Ann,

φιλίας ἕνεκεν

CONTENTS

LIST OF ILLUSTRATIONS

LIST OF ABBREVIATIONS

AASS	*Acta sanctorum*
ACO	*Acta conciliorum oecumenicorum.* Ed. E. Schwartz
CIL	*Corpus inscriptionum latinarum*
CSCO: SS	*Corpus scriptorum christianorum orientalium, Scriptores syri*
CSEL	*Corpus scriptorum ecclesiasticorum latinorum*
DACL	*Dictionnaire d'archéologie chrétienne et de liturgie*
DHGE	*Dictionnaire d'histoire et de géographie ecclésiastiques*
DTC	*Dictionnaire de théologie catholique*
FHG	*Fragmenta historicorum graecorum.* Ed. C. Müller
IG	*Inscriptiones graecae*
ILS	*Inscriptiones latinae selectae.* Ed. H. Dessau
MGH: AA	*Monumenta Germaniae historica, Auctores antiquissimi*
PG	*Patrologiae cursus completus, Series graeca.* Ed. J.-P. Migne
PL	*Patrologiae cursus completus, Series latina.* Ed. J.-P. Migne
PLRE	A.H.M. Jones, J.R. Martindale, and J. Morris. *The Prosopography of the Later Roman Empire,* vols. I and II. Cambridge, 1971 and 1980
PO	*Patrologia orientalis*
POxy	*The Oxyrhynchus Papyri*
RAC	*Real-Lexicon für Antike und Christentum*
RE	A. Pauly, G. Wissowa, and W. Kroll, eds. *Real-Encyclopädie der classischen Altertumswissenschaft*
RIC	*Roman Imperial Coinage*
ROC	*Revue de l'Orient chrétien*

SEG   *Supplementum epigraphicum graecum*
St. Pal. Pap. *Studien zur Palaeographie und Papyruskunde*
TU   *Texte und Untersuchungen*

N.B. Abbreviated journal titles appear in expanded form in the bibliography. Abbreviations for ancient authors and their works generally follow the lists in *PLRE,* I, xi–xx; II, xiii–xxx.

ACKNOWLEDGMENTS

This book began eight years ago as a University of Chicago Ph.D. dissertation. My teacher, the late Stewart Irvin Oost, suggested the topic, and his colleague Walter Kaegi shared in the task of supervision. In the intervening years it has become also a Dumbarton Oaks book. Proximity has enabled me to work regularly in the Dumbarton Oaks library. William Loerke and Giles Constable, successive directors of Dumbarton Oaks, and its librarian Irene Vaslef and her staff have been most helpful throughout. In 1976–77 the Trustees for Harvard University granted me a visiting fellowship at Dumbarton Oaks, a year of uninterrupted research in an unparalleled community of scholars. This is, finally, a University of Maryland book. My university's General Research Board provided funds for study in 1974 and 1978, and Horace Samuel Merrill, a colleague in the History Department, labored relentlessly to improve my prose.

I have learned from many friends, both personal and professional. John Nesbitt has offered an example of scholarly judgment and precision, Gary Vikan his expertise in Art History, and Sabine MacCormack her sensitivity to Late Antique spirituality. Alan Cameron provided an advance copy of an important article, permitting me to respond to it here. Hal Drake, a reader for the University of California Press, and Peter Brown saved me from weaknesses in presentation and from a number of inaccuracies. Craig Snider of the University of Maryland School of Architecture drew the plan of Theodosian Constantinople. Aileen Arnold typed a difficult manuscript, and Darlene King retyped parts of it.

My family—sister, brothers, my father's wife, and my own daughter—has shown regard for a distracted member far beyond the obligations of kinship. My father, a man of action with little taste for arcane pursuits, has warmly encouraged this one.

To all of these I express my gratitude, with the hope that their skill and generosity have proven fruitful. I reserve for myself full credit for my book's surviving faults.

K. G. H.
Silver Spring, Maryland
November 1, 1981

INTRODUCTION

In 434 the Roman empress Justa Grata Honoria, although not officially wed, became unmistakably pregnant. Eugenius, a man of low
degree who managed her estates, had also shared her bed. Despite
the man's humble rank, his liaison with an empress shook the foundations of the state. Circles in the western court at Ravenna, where
Honoria resided, assumed inevitably that she planned to raise her
paramour to imperial rank and to challenge the existing western
emperor, her brother Valentinian III. The latter therefore ordered
Eugenius executed and banished his wayward sister, sending her to
Constantinople, to the court of his eastern relative and colleague
Theodosius II. Presumably the woman gave birth there, but contemporary authors passed over that event and the child's fate in ominous
silence. When Honoria returned to Ravenna, for safekeeping Valentinian betrothed her to Herculanus Bassus, a man of distinction but
no imperial ambition.

Some years later (449–50), Honoria unsheathed a more potent
weapon against her brother. "Distressed terribly by her misfortune,"
she sent one of her eunuchs as an emissary to Attila, king of the Huns
and lord of a powerful confederacy of barbarian warriors. Promising
to pay him generously, and offering her ring as a pledge that she was
in earnest, she pleaded that the Hun king assist her in avenging the
death of Eugenius. Once again Valentinian learned of her intrigues,
but this time he responded more forcefully, depriving his sister of the
"scepter of empire." Ready to pick a quarrel with the western
Empire, Attila dispatched to Ravenna ambassadors who insisted that
Honoria had committed no wrong and announced Attila's intention
to make her his bride. He would revenge her, moreover, if she did
not receive back the "scepter of empire," which Valentinian had
taken away. Unnamed "men of the western court" framed a brusque
reply. "Honoria has been promised to another," they declared, "and
cannot marry you. Nor does she have any claim to the scepter, for the
rule of the Roman Empire belongs not to females but to men!"[1]

1. Prisc. frg. 15. For full discussion see K. Holum, "Justa Grata Honoria and
the Scepter of Empire (Priscus frg. 15)" (forthcoming).

1

Attila invaded Gaul soon after this, and the Roman victory of Châlons (451) barely preserved the Empire from the Hun menace. Thus Justa Grata Honoria made her way into history. Writing a decade or two later, and reflecting no doubt the opinion of his contemporaries, the historian Priscus of Panium interpreted Attila's invasion as the fruit of Honoria's "distress." In effect she entered that gallery of prodigious Greek and Roman women—Helen of Troy and the rest—whose inability to exercise proper restraint threatened peace and the established social order.

This interpretation will not do. A woman's lust is not enough to account for the Hun attack.[2] Still, history will reveal some of its secrets to those who *cherchent la femme,* as Priscus suspected, and in a liberal age scholars have learned to treat Honoria and her sisters with greater sensitivity. Sixty years ago J.B. Bury demonstrated that she was no "improper and rather absurd young lady" but another of those political women whose perils and accomplishments lend color to the history of the Theodosian era.[3]

Theodosius the Great, his sons, and his grandsons reigned 379–455, a critical period of Late Antiquity. Their contemporaries witnessed the division of the Empire into East and West. Barbarians spilled across the ancient frontiers, forcing permanent mobilization and an over-reliance on generals which threatened the independence of the monarchy. In the provinces Christian monks and bishops accelerated the drive against tenacious pagan cults, even as variant interpretations of dogma undermined the ideal unity of church and Empire. At last the wealthy and powerful Roman aristocracy embraced the new faith wholeheartedly, permitting men of theological bent to articulate the political ideology of Byzantium. On the Bosporus a new Rome emerged to carry the lamp of civilization into the Middle Ages. In the government's response to these developments, imperial mothers, wives, daughters, and sisters participated as never before. Honoria was one of these women, as Bury recognized, and her "distress" was symptomatic of a general phenomenon.

Since Bury's time, study of Theodosian women has concentrated on the West—on Galla Placidia, the mother of Valentinian III and

2. O.J. Maenchen-Helfen goes too far, however, when he disregards the "melodramatic story of the vicious Princess Honoria" because it "has all the earmarks of Byzantine court gossip": *The World of the Huns* (Berkeley-Los Angeles-London, 1973), p. 130.
3. J.B. Bury, "Justa Grata Honoria," *JRS* 9 (1919), 1–13.

Justa Grata Honoria.[4] But the phenomenon Honoria represented came from the East, and to understand it thoroughly the historian dare not limit himself to perils and accomplishments but must probe more deeply.

This probing reveals that Theodosius the Great, Honoria's ancestor and founder of the dynasty's power, addressed the crises of the age in a characteristically dynastic fashion. He believed that his personal qualities and those of his kin, not abstract principles of law and ideology, would best strengthen and preserve the state. He knew instinctively that the power he held could best be made effective through the concrete channels of friendship and blood. This dynastic impetus led naturally to the enhancement of imperial women, a process which can be traced in detail in the careers of Flaccilla, Eudoxia, Pulcheria, and Eudocia, three generations of Theodosian empresses who reigned in the East. These were indeed a colorful lot, and their careers merit detailed investigation. For through these careers, beyond the sheer human interest which permitted these women to make their way into history, the historian can discern a mor: profound development. Ultimately, these women did achieve auth entic imperial dominion.

This study, therefore, is about female *basileía*, the imperial dominion of women. It concerns a major creative impulse of Late Antiquity, that which produced the Byzantine notion of *basileía* and through it the European ideology of sacral kingship. It suggests that this impulse may be traced in part to a previously unsuspected origin: to the dynastic proclivities of Theodosius the Great and their manifestation in the careers of Theodosian empresses who reigned in the East.

Apparent paradoxes in Honoria's case raise important questions. If women did not share in the rule of the Empire, what was the "scepter" she forfeited? Why did she hold it in the first place? How could her liaison with Eugenius present such grave dangers, and why

4. V. A. Sirago, *Galla Placidia e la trasformazione politica dell'Occidente* (Louvain, 1961); S. I. Oost, *Galla Placidia Augusta* (Chicago and London, 1968). Despite the importance of such empresses, they have received very little attention from analytical scholarship. For a recent exception see Averil Cameron, "The Empress Sophia," *Byzantion* 45 (1975), 5–21. Empresses of the Roman principate are likewise an inviting subject for research. For indications of the rich material available see, e.g., Mary G. Williams, "Studies in the Lives of Roman Empresses I: Julia Domna," *American Journal of Archaeology* ser. 2, 6 (1902), 259–305, and W. Trillmich, *Familienpropaganda der Kaiser Caligula und Claudius: Agrippina Maior und Antonia Augusta auf Münzen*, Deutsches Archäologisches Institut: Antike Münzen und geschnittene Steine vol. VIII (Berlin, 1978).

would Attila, a skillful politician who was well acquainted with Roman institutions, exploit her "distress" to construct a *casus belli?* Is it possible that the "men of the western court" were wrong, that Honoria did rule the Empire legitimately and thus had a case against her brother?

This book proceeds from three assumptions which will clarify the Honoria episode and the careers of Theodosian empresses. First, the Roman monarchy, its Late Antique version included, was more than a juristic and constitutional phenomenon. An emperor's power depended less on his ability to issue commands and laws, an ability no woman could share, than on his subjects' willingness to obey. To create that willingness, the government developed a set of ideas about imperial power and invited response to its ideology through the channels of official propaganda. In this effort a woman's sex presented no insuperable barrier to her participation. Hence the "men of the western court" expressed too limited a view of Honoria's "scepter of empire," no doubt for political advantage. Modern concentration on Roman genius in administration and law has likewise obscured the truth.[5] Creating consent was (and is) an act of sovereignty. Any conception of *sovereignty* that ignores this fact, whether ancient or modern, fails to make sense both of the Roman monarchy and of the woman's function within it.

The reader would do well to bear in mind also the way Priscus interpreted Honoria's "distress." Traditional prejudices like those of Priscus sometimes prevented even contemporary authors from understanding empresses and from speaking candidly. Fortunately, official sources—documents from the imperial chancery, the coinage of the empresses, monuments of imperial sculpture, in some cases even the sermons and controversial writings of church fathers who expressed the official line—provide a corrective. This plentiful material proves that the interpretation of Priscus, like the formidable reply of those "men of the western court," needs reevaluation.

Also crucial is an awareness that the Theodosian era with which this book deals was one of pervasive anxiety. Previously the traditional

5. Years ago, A. Alföldi expressed this historiographical problem concisely: "Man vergass, dass schon bei dem Vorspiel der Monarchie ein ganz anderer Hebel als der juristische das Emporsteigen der führenden Staatsmänner über die Bürgergemeinschaft bewerkstelligen half . . . ," "Insignien und Tracht der römischen Kaiser," *Mitteilungen des Deutschen Archäologischen Instituts, Römische Abteilung* 50 (1935), 68 = *Die monarchische Repräsentation im römischen Kaiserreiche* (Darmstadt, 1970), p. 186.

gods had permeated the world, suffusing it with comfort and order. Their decline left men in the cold, and other crises of the age aggravated this effect. When the barbarian Goths sacked Rome (August, 410), the main visible link with the past lost its power to inspire hope for a secure future. In this chilly atmosphere men's hopes and security depended more and more on a transcendent God, one who existed outside the world and beyond history, but who made Himself known through other visible links such as the relics of martyrs and saints, the spectacular achievements of His living holy men, His command of the forces of nature—or through the dominion of emperors and empresses. In this age, heaven's will genuinely mattered. Anxious men looked for a sign that a new order was breaking in, and expected it at any moment. Such a sign came in 394, when the dynasty's founder faced an earlier Eugenius, the homonym of Honoria's lover.

CHAPTER ONE

Theodosius the Great and His Women

On the morning of September 6, 394, in the ultimate confrontation of a Christian emperor with the forces of traditional paganism, Theodosius the Great sent his troops against the army of the usurper Eugenius.[1] The outcome was to settle the future of the Theodosian dynasty and its women.

On the eve of the battle Theodosius had been trapped. Descending from the Julian Alps above Aquileia, where the road from the East first looked out upon Italy, he had found Eugenius and his troops drawn up near the river Frigidus blocking passage into the plain below. To prevent retreat, another enemy force moved in from cover behind the emperor's column. Thousands of his Gothic vanguard perished in an attempt to break out forward. In the rocks above, statues of Jupiter raised golden thunderbolts against the soldiers of Theodosius, and the image of Hercules paraded among the enemy formations.[2] During the night, the officer who commanded the forces to the emperor's rear betrayed Eugenius, but even so, Theodosius declined to postpone the offensive. He knew that withdrawal would confirm the ability of the traditional gods to protect their worshipers and deliver a victory.[3] In the morning the emperor attacked again, and a raging wind blew up at his back. In the words of an awestruck contemporary:

It tore the shields from the hands of the faithless and flung every spear and missile they cast back into the army of the sinner. Brought low by their own

---

1. O. Seeck and G. Veith, "Die Schlacht am Frigidus," *Klio* 13 (1913), 451–67; for the ideological setting H. Bloch, "The Pagan Revival in the West at the End of the Fourth Century," *The Conflict between Paganism and Christianity in the Fourth Century*, ed. A. Momigliano (Oxford, 1963), pp. 193–218; J. Straub, *RAC*, VI, fasc. 46 (1965), 864–75, "Eugenius"; contrast now J. Szidat, "Die Usurpation des Eugenius," *Historia* 28 (1979), 487–508.
2. Aug. *De civ. Dei* 5. 26, Thdt. *HE* 5. 24. 4, 17.
3. This escaped the rationalist Seeck (Seeck and Veith, "Schlacht," p. 465), who concluded that Theodosius, like Constantine at the Saxa Rubra, chose battle

weapons, they gave ground to the attacking winds even before their adversaries reached them. Yet these wounds to their bodies were no more severe than those to their spirits, for they lost heart when they found that God was fighting against them.[4]

The wind propelled Theodosius onto the plain and to complete victory. Eugenius was captured and beheaded. The general Arbogast, who had raised Eugenius to imperial rank and engineered his dispositions on the Frigidus, took his own life, as did Virius Flavianus Nicomachus, doyen of the pagan aristocracy of Italy and inspiration of the reactionary movement.

On the Frigidus a miraculous wind, or so it appeared, inflicted heaven's judgment upon the enemies of faith. At the same time this wind set a divine capstone on Theodosius' achievement—the crafting of an unassailable edifice of imperial power. The edifice thus brought to completion bore the personal stamp of its maker. Its architecture, patched together laboriously from often discordant elements, nonetheless displayed a unifying theme. Theodosius made it clear throughout that the integrity of the Empire depended on himself and his family, including its women. He followed, in short, the dynastic principle.

The Dynastic Impetus

Theodosius himself was a westerner and a military man.[5] Eighteen years before the Frigidus encounter, he had withdrawn, in danger of his life, from a command on the Danube frontier and returned to his family estates near Cauca in northwestern Spain. His father, also named Theodosius, a brilliant general who had served faithfully in numerous campaigns, was executed in Africa early in 376, the victim of rivals whose influence also threatened his son.[6] But the younger

---

"weder aus strategischen noch aus politischen Gründen . . . sondern nur aus abergläubischen." Equally misleading is Szidat's view ("Usurpation," p. 504) that "die Schlacht am Frigidus lässt sich . . . kaum als eine religiöse Auseinandersetzung interpretieren."

4. Amb. *Explan. psalm.* 36. 25. 2–4 (*CSEL*, LXIV, 91), no doubt based on eyewitness accounts.

5. In general A. Lippold, *Theodosius der Grosse und seine Zeit* (Stuttgart, 1968), and in detail *idem, RE,* suppl. XIII (1973), 837–961, "Theodosius I."

6. A. Demandt, "Die Feldzüge des älteren Theodosius," *Hermes* 100 (1972), 81–113, and the same scholar's "Der Tod des älteren Theodosius," *Historia* 18 (1969), 598–626, esp. 600–607 for the probability that Gratian bore responsibility for the execution.

man had already revealed talents which would make him indispensable. In August, 378, when the Visigoths and their allies destroyed the eastern emperor Valens and a large part of his army near Adrianople in Thrace, the crisis demanded a tested and capable commander. To restore order in the Danube provinces and secure the defenses of Constantinople, the western emperor Gratian brought Theodosius back from exile and made him co-emperor at Sirmium on January 19, 379.

The new dynasty was not so easily founded. Theodosius urgently required victory, in the later Roman monarchy the ultimate claim to emperorship and guarantee that an emperor would survive.[7] But victory seemed beyond his grasp, because a decade earlier Valens had given up sixteen crack regiments of the eastern field army to his western colleague and older brother Valentinian I, and the loss of sixteen additional regiments at Adrianople had reduced even the paper forces of the new emperor to perhaps three-fifths of their original level.[8] Sheer lack of troops forced Theodosius in his first years to seek reconciliation with the Visigoths and other barbarians.

In October, 382, he directed his general Saturninus to conclude a treaty with the enemy chiefs allowing them to settle peacefully on Roman lands south of the Danube, under obligation of service with their followers as allies (*foederati*) of the Empire. Many traditionalists resisted this policy as barbarization and accused its perpetrator of cowardice and inertia for not annihilating Rome's enemies,[9] but the orator Themistius, himself a traditionalist and a pagan, argued for the court that an emperor might claim victories of a different order: "the victories of reason and of philanthropy, which consist not of

---

7. J. Gagé, "ΣΤΑΥΡΟΣ ΝΙΚΟΠΟΙΟΣ," *Revue d'histoire et de philosophie religieuses* 13 (1933), 370–400; more generally, A. Grabar, *L'empereur dans l'art byzantin* (Paris, 1936), pp. 31–84; O. Treitinger, *Die oströmische Kaiser- und Reichsidee* (Jena, 1938), pp. 168–85; J. Straub, *Vom Herrscherideal in der Spätantike* (Stuttgart, 1939), pp. 7–75. Thus Valens rashly accepted battle at Adrianople before Gratian arrived to avoid sharing with his colleague "a victory already nearly won": Amm. 31. 12. 7. For a case study cf. K. Holum, "Pulcheria's Crusade and the Ideology of Imperial Victory," *GRBS* 18 (1977), 153–72, and *infra*, pp. 102–10.

8. D. Hoffmann, *Das spätrömische Bewegungsheer und die Notitia dignitatum*, Epigraphische Studien VII; 1–2 (Düsseldorf, 1969), pp. 425–50.

9. J. Straub, "Die Wirking der Niederlage bei Adrianopel auf die Diskussion über das Germanenproblem in der spätrömischen Literatur," *Philologus* 95 (1943), 255–86; M. Pavan, *La politica gotica di Teodosio nella pubblicistica del suo tempo* (Rome, 1964).

destroying those who have harmed us but of improving them."[10] In the next several years, moreover, solid benefits were to emerge. Reconciliation provided the opportunity to stabilize the Danube frontier and to recruit Gothic volunteers for service in the Roman army under Roman standards and officers. The emperor's "philanthropy" reached these volunteers in the welcome form of rations, making them his dependents and thus highly suitable for use in dynastic wars.[11] By 388 Theodosius had amassed the strength to march against the western usurper Maximus, who had overthrown Gratian. The defeat of Maximus (July, 388) permitted incorporation of some first-line western regiments into the eastern army—a characteristic move which reflected greater commitment to dynastic needs than to the security of the Empire as a whole.[12] When Theodosius set out a second time toward Italy in 394 to face Eugenius, Arbogast, and the pagan reaction, he had grounded his victory claims in military strength and could enter battle on roughly equal terms.

Resistance to Theodosian Gothic policy and its dynastic implications was bound to surface among the top generals, the two *magistri militum praesentales* who commanded the field army "in the emperor's presence" and their subordinates, the *magistri* of regional army groups stationed some distance from the emperor. In 379 the *magister* Julius, one of the subordinate generals, had massacred all Gothic recruits serving under his command, a superfluous act of savagery committed, symptomatically, without imperial authority.[13] To avert such threats to reconciliation and to his own control of the army, Theodosius favored officers of German or other non-Roman extraction—whose race would discourage collusion with traditionalists— and men bound by kinship with the imperial house. One man suited the requirements admirably. Flavius Stilicho, son of a Vandal by a

10. *Or.* 16. 211a. On Themistius the "théoricien de l'Empire romain oriental" see esp. G. Dagron, "L'Empire romain d'Orient au IVe siècle et les traditions politiques de l'hellénisme," *Travaux et mémoires* 3 (1968), 1–242.

11. Passages like Pacat. *Pan.* 32. 4–5 and Zos. 4. 30. 1–2, 31. 1 (from Eunapius) tend to refute the theory of Hoffmann, *Bewegungsheer*, pp. 503–4, that the massive influx of Germans into Roman units came only after 388 and that most of these Germans were of western origin. Cf. the observations of E. Demougeot, "Modalités d'établissement des fédérés barbares de Gratien et de Théodose," *Mélanges d'histoire ancienne offerts à William Seston* (Paris, 1974), pp. 143–60.

12. Hoffmann, *Bewegungsheer*, pp. 469–519, esp. pp. 485–86 on the "selbstsüchtige Familienpolitik" of Theodosius.

13. Amm. 31. 16. 8, Zos. 4. 26. 2–9.

Roman woman, married the emperor's niece Serena *ca.* 384 and from then on accompanied him on all his campaigns, reaching the rank of *magister* in time to share command in the war against Arbogast and Eugenius.[14] In addition, Theodosius reorganized the structure of the high command in the East. After the defeat of Maximus, he established five independent army groups (including two "in the presence"), each commanded by a *magister* responsible only to the emperor.[15] This arrangement prevented concentration of military power in the hands of one of the *magistri praesentales* and a consequent threat to the independence of the dynasty.

Theodosius also acquired a dynastic city. In 379, when he had just begun to work out his Gothic policy and reconstruct the eastern army, the orator Themistius appeared before him in Thessalonica to bring the vote of Constantinople confirming Gratian's choice of colleague. Themistius used this occasion to urge that Theodosius in turn choose a megalopolis, and that of the two available he adopt Constantine's city. Like Theodosius, Constantinople owed its advancement not to kinship with the existing imperial house but to "surpassing virtue and proof of strength and courage." In all haste Theodosius should enter "the patron city of the entire East," confirm the gifts of his predecessors, and begin drawing from the senate of Constantinople the men he needed to govern the Empire and its provinces—a privilege Rome itself had enjoyed from the beginning. "Then finally," Themistius concluded, "will *your* city indeed be Second Rome."[16]

Theodosius celebrated his formal arrival (*adventus*) in Constantinople on November 24, 380, and during long periods of residence consummated the union of dynasty and city proposed by Themistius.[17] From 380 the people of Constantinople regularly confronted the emperor or his officials in the thoroughfares, public squares, and churches of the city. The imperial presence enforced the notion that in Constantinople the *voces populi* represented the sovereign Roman people, sometimes assailing the shortcomings of the government but

14. A. Demandt, *RE,* suppl. XII (1970), 726, "Magister Militum," listing Butherichus, Ellebichus, Gildo, Modares, Richomeres, and Stilicho; cf. appropriate entries in *PLRE,* I, and on Stilicho, *infra,* pp. 49, 59–60, 66, 87.

15. See now D. Hoffmann, "Der Oberbefehl des spätrömischen Heeres im 4. Jahrhundert n. Chr.," *Actes du IXe congrès international d'études sur les frontières romaines, Mamaïa, 6–13 Septembre 1972* (Bucuresti-Cologne-Vienna, 1974), pp. 387–97.

16. *Or.* 14. 182a–84a.

17. G. Dagron, *Naissance d'une capitale* (Paris, 1974), p. 85, speaks correctly of "une deuxième consécration de la ville."

more often extolling imperial victories and the emperor's claims to power.[18] These *voces* characterized especially the ceremonial of the hippodrome, where Theodosius presided over chariot races[19] and received accolades as master of victory, no matter which of the circus factions had produced the winning driver.[20]

Naturally, imperial oratory cultivated the desired response. In 384 Themistius praised Theodosius for easing the burden of taxation and for provisioning the city so efficiently that the abundance of grain attracted numerous new inhabitants. Rapid construction crowded the available space to the limit of Constantine's wall and beyond, creating in effect a magnificent city of Theodosius, comparable to Constantine's own.[21] Naturally also, Theodosius selected a setting in this burgeoning city for the expression through official art of his claims to victory and legitimacy. By 384 architects had begun to lay out a new forum[22] on the *mesē*, the great colonnaded street that formed the city's axis (see fig. 1). In this forum they erected an equestrian statue of Theodosius with a remarkable verse inscription on its base, exalting the emperor in the traditional imagery of solar kingship:

> You rise from eastward, shining, a second Helios
> For mortals, Theodosius, serene amid the heavens
> With Ocean and boundless Earth beneath your feet.

18. *Ibid.*, pp. 299–304, 310; on the *voces populi* cf. esp. the *locus classicus CTh* 1. 16. 6 (331): ". . . We grant to all persons the privilege of praising by public acclamation the most just and vigilant judges, so that We may grant increased accessions of honor to them. On the contrary, the unjust and the evildoers must be accused by cries of complaints, in order that the force of Our censure may destroy them. For We shall carefully investigate whether such utterances are truthful and are not poured forth effusively and wontonly by clients. The praetorian prefects and the counts who have been stationed throughout the provinces shall refer to Our wisdom the utterances [*voces*] of Our provincials" (trans. Pharr).

19. As on the base of the obelisk of Theodosius; see G. Bruns, *Der Obelisk und seine Basis auf dem Hippodrom zu Konstantinopel*, Istanbuler Forschungen vol. VII (Istanbul, 1935), pp. 153–68, and cf. *infra*, p. 14.

20. Gagé, "ΣΤΑΥΡΟΣ ΝΙΚΟΠΟΙΟΣ," pp. 374–79; see now Alan Cameron, *Circus Factions: Blues and Greens at Rome and Byzantium* (Oxford, 1976), for organization of the factions, their function, and their social and political impact.

21. Them. *Or.* 18. 221a–23b.

22. See J. Kollwitz, *Oströmische Plastik der theodosianischen Zeit* (Berlin, 1941), pp. 3–16; G. Becatti, *La colonna coclide istoriata* (Rome, 1960), pp. 83–150; and R. Guilland, *Etudes de topographie de Constantinople byzantine,* Berliner byzantinische Arbeiten vol. XXXVII (Berlin and Amsterdam, 1969), pt. 2, pp. 56–59, on the *forum Tauri* or *Theodosii* and its monuments. Construction was in progress by 384 if the αὐλή . . . βασιλέως ἐπώνυμος of Them. *Or.* 18. 222c was this complex. Cf. *infra*, n. 30, for a similar effort to provide Constantinople with imperial monuments like those of Rome.

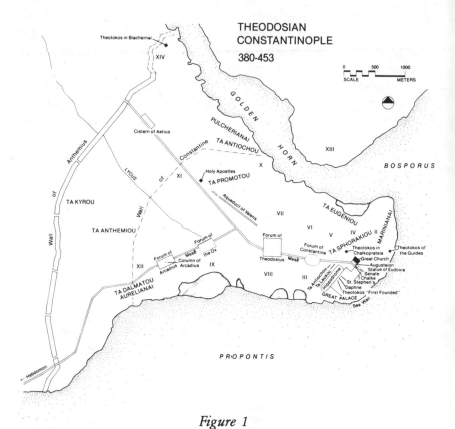

Figure 1
Theodosian Constantinople, 380–453
Place-names like *Aurelianai* and *ta Antiochou*
represent quarters of medieval Constantinople that received
nomenclature from the palatial *domūs* of members of the Theodosian
house or of officials in its service. The distribution of such names
across the urban landscape of Constantinople
indicates the manner in which the dynasty
dominated the imperial city.

Bright arrayed for war, your splendid mount
Lightly rein, great spirit, although he rage.[23]

Nearby a tall column went up, carved in spiral with reliefs commemorating the victories of Theodosius. This monument and its setting repeated Trajan's column and forum in Rome, showing that Theodosius, whose Spanish origins and military ambitions made Trajan an inescapable model,[24] indeed considered Constantinople to be Rome's double, a fitting seat for the new dynasty.

The emperor's presence in Constantinople implied the permanent residence there of the *comitatus,* the apparatus of central government with its assortment of *magistri militum* and other military and civilian officials.[25] Most powerful among the latter was the *praefectus praetorio per Orientem,* who headed the hierarchy of diocesan vicars and provincial governors charged with the administration of justice and collection of the revenues (*annonae*) that fed and supplied the army and civil service. From the time of Theodosius I, the broad responsibilities of the praetorian prefect and his constant access to the emperor made him virtually a prime minister. Other financial officers of the *comitatus* were the *comes rerum privatarum,* minister of the vast estates and private revenues of the emperor, and the *comes sacrarum largitionum,* whose subordinates collected money taxes and duties, supervised the mints and other imperial workshops, and paid out salaries and donatives to civil servants and troops. The *magister officiorum* regulated admissions to the emperor's presence and administered the bodies of clerks who handled the emperor's correspondence and files (*scrinia*), while the *quaestor sacri palatii* served as his chief legal adviser. Finally, since 359 emperors had ruled Constantinople through the *praefectus urbi constantinopolitanae,* the double of the prefect of Rome who presided over the eastern senate.

If Theodosius' city was to become Second Rome, Themistius had insisted, he ought to give high office to members of this body, the senate of Constantinople. After decades of recruiting, the senate now included many ambitious men who exhibited the traditional qualifications—large fortunes or family estates that produced gener-

---

23. *Anth. graec.* 16. 65; cf. Kollwitz, *Plastik,* pp. 6–11, and esp. E. Kantorowicz, "Oriens Augusti: Lever du Roi," *DOP* 17 (1963), 119–77, for the ideological context.
24. E.g., Them. *Or.* 16. 205a, 19. 229c, *Epit. de Caes.* 48. 8.
25. See esp. A.H.M. Jones, *The Later Roman Empire 284–602* (Oxford, 1964), I, 366–410.

ous incomes; a modicum of administrative experience, at a level conferring the required rank of *clarissimus;* and the ornaments of culture or "Hellenism" acquired through an education in Greek rhetoric.[26] Because "Hellenism" frequently extended from culture to religion, three generations into the Christian Empire numerous pagans still sat in the senate of Constantinople.[27]

Theodosius could not afford to ignore the claims of such men, so throughout his reign he allocated provincial governorships and the city prefecture to senators of Constantinople and other easterners, as Themistius had recommended. Themistius himself held the city prefecture briefly in 384, but two other appointments are more instructive. In 388, as Theodosius prepared to march westward against Maximus, he promoted a Lycian named Proculus to the city prefecture and simultaneously made Proculus' father, Flavius Eutolmius Tatianus, praetorian prefect of the East.[28] Both men had compiled distinguished records in lesser posts, and both were pagans. Tatianus possessed sufficient culture to compose a verse sequel to the *Iliad* which won praise from students and teachers of rhetoric.[29] During their prefectures, Proculus and Tatianus demonstrated the same commitment to dynastic legitimacy that Themistius had expressed on many occasions. In 390 Proculus erected the great obelisk of Theodosius in the hippodrome of Constantinople. A verse inscription on its base (which still survives) celebrated the emperor's spectacular "victory" over this intractable granite monolith (in successfully having it raised) and drew a parallel with his battlefield success over Maximus the "tyrant."[30] In the same year Tatianus carried similar propaganda to the provinces, ordering that statues of the legitimate emperors be dedicated in various cities of the East; L. Robert has identified examples in inscriptions from Antinoupolis in Egypt, from

26. *Ep. Constantii Augusti ad Senatum* 19c (Themistii *Orationes*, ed. G. Downey and A.F. Norman, III, 123–24); cf. Dagron, *Naissance*, pp. 119–210, the fullest recent treatment of the eastern senate.

27. For a sampling see P. Petit, "Les sénateurs de Constantinople dans l'oeuvre de Libanius," *Antiquité classique* 26 (1927), 347–82.

28. *PLRE*, I, 746–47, "Proculus 6," 876–78, "Tatianus 5."

29. Liban. *Ep.* 990. 2–3 (XI, 120–21 Foerster); Eudocia *Homerocentones* praef. 19–29 (ed. A. Ludwich, pp. 84–85).

30. Bruns, *Obelisk, passim;* esp. H. Wrede, "Zur Errichtung des Theodosius-Obelisken in Istanbul," *Istanbuler Mitteilungen* 16 (1966), 178–98, emphasizing that this obelisk paralleled a triumphal monument Constantius II had erected on the *spina* of the Circus Maximus when he visited Rome in 357 after his defeat of the usurper Magnentius.

Aphrodisias in Caria, and from Pamphylian Side.[31] During his absence in the West, Theodosius felt constrained to leave the great prefectures with men whose service and correct attitude toward the dynasty merited prolonged tenure of office and whose culture made them especially acceptable to their subordinates.

When such constraints did not apply, however, Theodosius made it clear that other qualifications weighed more heavily. Maternus Cynegius, for instance, became *comes sacrarum largitionum* in 383, then *quaestor* briefly, and finally a powerful and sinister praetorian prefect of the East from 384 until his death in 388.[32] The man was a Spaniard and apparently distant kin to the emperor. As John Matthews has demonstrated, Cynegius was only one of a tribe of relatives and familiar westerners whom Theodosius brought with him to the East and advanced to high office there.[33] Tatianus succeeded Cynegius, exceptionally, as praetorian prefect, and both he and his son retained their posts through the emperor's absence. But when Theodosius returned from the West a dramatic sequel proved the rule. Flavius Rufinus from southern Aquitaine had emerged in 388 as *magister officiorum*.[34] In 392 he managed the disgrace of Tatianus, whom he succeeded as praetorian prefect, and a year later engineered the execution of Proculus before his father's eyes. Despite the insinuations of detractors, the ambition of Rufinus and his violent character counted no more in this affair than the emperor's predisposition toward kinsmen and familiar westerners whose personal enthusiasms corresponded most closely to his own.[35]

Half a century later, the ecclesiastical historian Socrates identified the personal enthusiasm of Theodosius as Christian piety "inher-

---

31. L. Robert, *Epigrammes du Bas-Empire*, Hellenica vol. IV (Paris, 1948), pp. 47–53.

32. *PLRE*, I 235–36, "Maternus Cynegius 3"; J.F. Matthews, "A Pious Supporter of Theodosius I," *JThS* n.s. 18 (1967), 438–46.

33. Matthews, "Supporter"; also his *Western Aristocracies and the Imperial Court* (Oxford, 1975), pp. 107–15.

34. *PLRE*, I, 778, "Flavius Rufinus 18"; E. Demougeot, *De l'unité à la division de l'Empire romain 395–410* (Paris, 1951), pp. 119–26; *infra*, pp. 20, 52–53, 59–60.

35. Eun. frg. 59 (*FHG*, IV, 40); Zos. 4. 52; Claud. *In Ruf.* 1. 246–49; *Chron. pasch. a.* 393 (p. 565 Bonn); E. Stein, *Histoire du Bas-Empire*, ed. J.R. Palanque, I (Paris-Bruges, 1959), p. 212; contrast Dagron, *Naissance*, pp. 256–57, 288–89, suggesting that the joint prefecture of Tatianus and Proculus endangered the emperor's own authority, a hypothesis I find dubious when applied to this reign (cf., however, *infra*, p. 95).

ited from his forefathers."[36] His piety, Socrates asserted, was of the homoousian variety descended from the first ecumenical council of Nicaea (325) and its teaching that Christ was "of the same substance" as the Father. Though colored by retrospect, this judgment was correct. In the autumn of 380, when Theodosius fell dangerously ill at Thessalonica and faced the private crisis of death, his refuge was the purifying Christian sacrament of baptism, and he insisted on receiving it from a homoousian bishop.[37]

But even before his baptism, the private piety of Theodosius had manifested itself in a characteristically dynastic form. As Theodosius labored with the Gothic problem, he encountered another challenge to his power that was hardly more tractable. If his own Nicene orthodoxy had triumphed in the West (including, significantly, southern Aquitaine and Spain), the opposite doctrine of Arianism had struck root in many eastern churches, with its insistence that Christ's substance was "unlike" or, at most, "like" that of the Father. This was no metaphysical quibble. If it is true that when one asked in the alleyways and markets of Constantinople

for the correct change, and they lecture you on the Begotten and the Unbegotten; or for the price of bread, and they respond that the Father is greater and the Son inferior; or if the bath is warm enough, and they define the Son for you as being from nothing,[38]

then when the Roman *populus* gathered in the churches, thoroughfares, and hippodrome of the city, it would not respond as desired to the claims of a Nicene emperor. On February 28, 380, Theodosius directed the famous law or "constitution" *cunctos populos* from Thessalonica to the people of Constantinople. He declared his will that every Roman embrace the emperor's own confession of faith: "the single godhead of Father, Son, and Holy Spirit in equal majesty and the Holy Trinity." Those who refused would be struck by divine vengeance and also by "our own punishment, which we will inflict according to the will of Heaven."[39]

36. Soc. 5. 6. 3; cf. in general W. Ensslin, *Die Religionspolitik des Kaisers Theodosius des Grossen,* Sitzungsberichte der Bayerischen Akademie der Wissenschaften, Philosophisch-historische Klasse, Jahrgang 1953, Heft 2 (Munich, 1953); N.Q. King, *The Emperor Theodosius and the Establishment of Christianity* (London, 1961).
37. Soc. 5. 6. 3–6, Soz. 7. 4. 3; cf. Ensslin, *Religionspolitik,* pp. 17–21, for the chronology.
38. Greg. Nyss. *De deitate Filii et Spiritus Sancti, PG,* XLVI, 557; cf. Dagron, *Naissance,* pp. 379, 448, on this "théologie de la rue."
39. *CTh* 16. 1. 2.

With the hyperbole typical of imperial manifestos, those strong words concealed a more practical attitude. *Cunctos populos* did not specify a penalty. In general, Theodosius intended neither extermination of heretics nor forced conversions, but, as in his Gothic policy, reconciliation for the benefit of the dynasty.[40] Bishops and priests were at the crux of the matter. Dissidents would lose their churches, while those who replaced them, holy and eloquent men of the emperor's persuasion, would begin to attract the usual fanatic loyalty of the faithful for their spiritual patrons.[41] On November 26, 380, just two days after his advent in Constantinople, Theodosius drove out the Arian bishop Demophilus. The next day he arrayed a troop of soldiers to keep in check mobs of Demophilus' followers, as he introduced the homoousian Gregory Nazianzen as bishop into the Holy Apostles, the city's principal church.[42]

This show of force both underscored the emperor's seriousness in *cunctos populos* and involved him in paradox. As Wilhelm Ensslin observed, *cunctos populos* amounted to "a legislative decision in matters of doctrine."[43] Although the Nicene bishops, on whom the success of Theodosian orthodoxy depended, did, like most contemporaries, recognize the divine character of the emperor's authority,[44] they limited it when doctrine was concerned to convoking councils of bishops, ensuring the freedom and order of their deliberations, and

40. Greg. Naz. *De vita sua* 1282–95 (ed. Jungck), Soc. 5. 20. 4–6, Soz. 7. 12. 12; cf. King, *Establishment*, p. 95: "his bark was far worse than his bite."

41. Gregory of Nyssa makes the faithful of Antioch a bride, their bishop Meletius a bridegroom, and his mystical union with them one of "gladness and spiritual delights" brought tragically to an end when Meletius died in 381: "Rachel weeps not for her children but for her husband and will not be comforted," *Oratio funebris in Meletium*, ed. Spira, pp. 448–50 (vol. IX Jaeger-Langerbeck). The people of Constantinople likewise refused comfort when their bishop John Chrysostom was sent into exile in 404: *infra*, pp. 74–77.

42. Greg. Naz. *De vita sua* 1325–95 (ed. Jungck), Soc. 5. 7. 4–11, Marcell. com. *a*. 380 (*MGH: AA*, XI, 61).

43. *Religionspolitik*, p. 24. A.-M. Ritter, *Das Konzil von Konstantinopel und sein Symbol* (Göttingen, 1965), pp. 28–31, 221–28, attempts *contra* Ensslin to interpret *cunctos populos* as a "white paper" without the force of law (*Grundsatzprogramm*), a theory that hardly accords with the view of Theodosius himself on the validity of his constitutions: "perpensas serenitatis nostrae longa deliberatione constitutiones nec ignorare quemquam nec dissimulare permittimus"; *CTh* 1. 1. 2 (391). For other objections to Ritter's interpretation see, e.g., Lippold, *RE*, suppl. XIII (1973), 847, "Theodosius I," and most recently H. Anton, "Kaiserliches Selbstverständnis in der Religionsgesetzgebung der Spätantike und päpstliche Herrschaftsinterpretation im 5. Jahrhundert," *ZfKg* 88 (1977), 55 n. 73.

44. See esp. the *logos prosphonetikos* the assembled bishops addressed to Theodosius after the Council of Constantinople, 381: "We give thanks to God who

enforcing their collective decisions.[45] To escape the paradox and associate himself with the prestigious tradition of Constantine and Nicaea, Theodosius gathered more than one hundred and fifty bishops from throughout the East in Constantinople in May of 381, for another imperial council.[46] The emperor did not need to impose his will upon these bishops or interfere with their episcopal freedom, because the majority of those whom he had invited were of the dynastic faith.[47]

Obediently, the council confirmed Gregory Nazianzen as bishop of Constantinople, then, when Gregory resigned, accepted and enthroned another candidate of Theodosius, an elderly senator named Nectarius whose qualifications included popularity from lavish celebration of games for the people and lack of identification with any doctrinal position; hence the Arian followers of Demophilus would be less inclined to reject his patronage and that of his sponsor Theodosius.[48] Equally dynastic were the council's confession and the canons it approved in its final session on July 9, 381. The confession corresponded in substance with *cunctos populos* and especially with another Theodosius constitution, *nullus haereticis* of January 10, 381.[49] Canon 1 "anathematized" the same heresies that *nullus haereticis* had "abolished" some months earlier, while Canon 3 exalted the city of Constantine and Theodosius, declaring that its bishop

has proclaimed the emperorship of Your Piety," Mansi, III, 557, printed conveniently in Ritter, *Konzil*, p. 124 n. 2; in general, W. Ensslin, *Gottkaiser und Kaiser von Gottes Gnaden,* Sitzungsberichte der Bayerischen Akademie der Wissenschaften, Philosophisch-historische Klasse, Jahrgang 1943, Heft 6 (Munich, 1943), and J. Karayannopulos, "Der frühbyzantinische Kaiser," *BZ* 49 (1956), 372–74.

45. The *logos prosphonetikos* of 381 explicitly recognizes the powers to convoke and confirm; cf. also *infra*, pp. 162–63, 198, 212–13, and in general A. Michel, *Die Kaisermacht in der Ostkirche (843-1204)* (Darmstadt, 1959), pp. 56–78, and F. Dvornik, *Early Christian and Byzantine Political Philosophy* (Washington, D.C., 1966), II, 635–42, 762–850.

46. Ritter, *Konzil,* pp. 41–131, 230–37, a brilliant discussion but flawed by consistent underrating of the emperor's influence. Ritter believes that in fact as well as in theory Constantinople 381 was a "free council of bishops" (p. 235).

47. *Ibid.,* pp. 38–40: preserved lists of participants include almost exclusively adherents of the neo-Nicene bishop Meletius of Antioch (*supra,* n. 41), who was present in Constantinople in early 381 when invitations were issued and presumably helped Theodosius put together a pliant majority.

48. Soc. 5. 8. 12, Soz. 7. 8, Thdt. *HE* 5. 9. 15, Rufin. *HE* 12. 21, Marcell. com. *a.* 381. 1 (*MGH: AA*, XI, 61); cf. Ritter, *Konzil*, pp. 112–15, 234–35, again attempting to deny that the emperor's influence was decisive.

49. *CTh* 16. 5. 6, in which Theodosius declares "haec profecto nobis magis probata, haec veneranda sunt"; also *Conciliorum oecumenicorum decreta*, ed. J. Alberigo et al., 3rd ed. (Bologna, 1972), p. 24, for the text of the confession and Ritter, *Konzil*, pp. 132–95, on its authenticity and genesis.

ranked second only to the bishop of Rome, because Constantinople was "New Rome."[50]

Despite his piety, Theodosius aimed to encompass also the large portion of the eastern *populus romanus,* especially of the aristocracy, that stood apart not only from the dynastic faith but from Christianity itself. Official propaganda addressed pagans in Constantinople when it made the emperor "second Helios," but Theodosius cast his net more widely. In 382 he reversed an earlier constitution (an *oraculum obreptivum,* he declared, "obtained surreptitiously") and reopened a popular temple on the Euphrates frontier, so long as devotees did not actually sacrifice victims to its splendid cult images.[51] As "living law" (*nomos empsychos*) the emperor possessed not only the exclusive right to make new law but also the power to ignore his enactments, revise them, or apply them inconsistently to suit his dynastic advantage.[52]

A few years later (386/87), the praetorian prefect Maternus Cynegius, in apparent conflict with the emperor's line, progressed through the eastern provinces supervising the attacks of monks upon pagan cult centers—including, perhaps, the same popular temple on the Euphrates frontier. Buildings and images were smashed and temple properties broken up, to destroy their social and economic importance.[53] The celebrated sophist Libanius of Antioch reacted with a reasoned and eloquent address, *Pro templis.* Respectfully and with promises of obedience, he urged that such violence was illegal and ought not to go unpunished. The law did not forbid paganism as such, he argued, but only bloody sacrifice, while Theodosius had done much to encourage pagans, promoting them in his service, admitting them to the familiarity of his table, and "even now joining with yourself [as ordinary consul, the greatest honor of all] a man [probably Eutropius cos. 387] who in your very presence swears his oaths by the pagan gods."[54] Whether he read *Pro templis* or not, Theodosius did respond to such pleading. When Cynegius died in 388, traditionalists received Tatianus, a more compatible successor.

50. *Conciliorum oecumenicorum decreta,* pp. 31–32.
51. *CTh* 16. 10. 8.
52. A. Steinwenter, "ΝΟΜΟΣ ΕΜΨΥΧΟΣ," *Anzeiger der Akademie der Wissenschaften in Wien, Philosophisch-historische Klasse* 83 (1946), 250–68; Dagron, "Empire," pp. 127–34.
53. Liban. *Or.* 30. 8–23, 44–49 (III, 91–99, 111–15 Foerster); P. Petit, "Sur la date du «Pro Templis» de Libanius," *Byzantion* 21 (1951), 298–304, for the campaign of Cynegius; J.H.W.G. Liebeschuetz, *Antioch* (Oxford, 1972), pp. 224–42, on the context of religious and social change.
54. Liban. *Or.* 30. 17–19, 50–53 (III, 96–97, 115–17 Foerster); Petit, "Sur la date," p. 305 and *passim*.

There was method in this imperial prevarication, because it trained both sides to place their confidence in Theodosius. But little of it survived the emperor's residence in Italy during several periods between 388 and 391 (after the defeat of Maximus) and his encounter there with the most impressive of his contemporaries, Bishop Ambrose of Milan. Tension between the emperor and this bishop reached a crisis in 390, when the people of Thessalonica assassinated one of the emperor's trusted but unpopular German officers in a brawl. Turned loose, by imperial command, in the hippodrome of the city, the soldiers inflicted punishment with their customary savagery, massacring indiscriminately thousands of spectators. Ambrose properly blamed Theodosius and required penance. At the end of the year, after months of impasse and a reconciliation which the Aquitanian Rufinus seems to have mediated, the congregation of Milan witnessed the incredible contrition of an emperor who laid aside the imperial diadem and purple mantle to stand humiliated with them, awaiting the absolution of Ambrose and admission to the Nativity sacrifice.[55]

It is hazardous to attempt to search the heart of an emperor, but the readiness of Theodosius to embrace public humiliation does indicate a very bad conscience, and suggests that both the bishop who eased his anxiety and the agent of reconciliation acquired a hold over him. This is a reasonable explanation for a new official line on the religious questions that helped fix ideological positions for confrontation on the Frigidus. On February 24 and June 16, 391, within a few months of the Christmas absolution, and on November 8, 392, when Theodosius had taken his court back to Constantinople, he legislated comprehensively against paganism, forbidding attendance in temples and every form of cult from public sacrifice of victims to burning candles or incense for one's household gods.[56] Significantly, the third constitution in the series was addressed to Rufinus, who some months earlier had engineered the fall of Tatianus and his son.

Alienated now from the pagan aristocracy and ready to permit violence against its leaders, Theodosius was to depend more and more upon powerful friends of another kind. In February, 392, he trans-

55. A remarkable confrontation often misunderstood; see J.-R. Palanque, *Saint Ambroise et l'Empire romain* (Paris, 1933), pp. 227–44, 536–39; F. Homes Dudden, *The Life and Times of St. Ambrose* (Oxford, 1935), II, 381–92; Ensslin, *Religionspolitik*, pp. 67–74; Matthews, *Aristocracies*, pp. 234–36. The main sources are Amb. *Ep.* 51 (*PL*, XVI, 1209–14), Rufin. *HE* 11. 18, Soz. 7. 25. 1–7, and Thdt. *HE* 5. 17–18. On chronological uncertainties cf. Lippold, *RE*, suppl. XIII, 888, "Theodosius I."
56. *CTh* 16. 10. 10–12

lated the severed head of John the Baptist in a public procession and
deposited it in a newly constructed chapel at the Hebdomon,[57] the
army parade field seven milestones from Constantinople where emperors were proclaimed and where they addressed the troops before
campaigns. The significant place or *locus* Theodosius selected demonstrates that he considered this head to be an imperial and dynastic
relic, a promise of victory. Two years later, as he broke camp from the
Hebdomon for the war against Arbogast and Eugenius, he entered
the chapel to pray for an outcome favorable to himself, his troops,
and the Roman Empire, and that the Baptist might come forth to
fight at his side.[58]

In the sixteen years since Adrianople, Theodosius had revitalized
the eastern Roman monarchy beyond expectation, rebuilding its shattered armies, advancing a new creed and a new ideological unity,
promoting the metropolis of the East to rank with Rome as a fountain
of imperial legitimacy and social prestige. In each case he had demonstrated the proclivities of a dynast, making his private religion the test
of orthodoxy and his friends the instruments of social order—along
with his troops, of course, and the Roman people which acclaimed
him in the hippodrome of his dynastic city. On the morning of September 6, 394, as Theodosius prepared to attack Eugenius, the future
of these accomplishments still hung in the balance. But in the
anxious world of Late Antiquity, receptive as it was to the breaking in
of transcendence, history could be made by meteorological chance, by
an occurrence so mundane as the sudden blast of a hurricane.[59]

The Domestic Side

About 385 Constantinople had suffered an "earthquake," as St.
Gregory of Nyssa described it, but this time not one of the mundane

57. Soz. 7. 21; cf. *Chron. pasch. a.* 391 (p. 564 Bonn) for the date with the
correction proposed by G. Rauschen, *Jahrbücher der christlichen Kirche unter dem
Kaiser Theodosius dem Grossen* (Freiburg i. B., 1897), p. 356; on the Hebdomon
and its monuments and ceremonial functions R. Demangel, *Contribution à la topographie de l'Hebdomon*, Recherches françaises en Turquie, fasc. 3 (Paris, 1945); R.
Janin, *Constantinople byzantine*, Archives de l'Orient chrétien no. 4a, 2nd ed.
(Paris, 1964), pp. 446–49.
58. Soz. 7. 24. 2.
59. A comment of Norman Baynes is worth recalling apropos of the Frigidus
battle: "If your mind becomes queasy at the very idea of a miracle, the early Middle
Age is not a proper field for your study: That synthesis of political and religious
history which is essential for its understanding will remain for you an impossibility,"
"Rome and the Early Middle Age," *History* 14 (1930), 293.

variety that struck the region periodically with inscrutable destructive-
ness, producing mass outpourings of anxiety and repentance.[60] This
"earthquake" was the death of Pulcheria, the emperor's daughter.
Although she was only a child of seven or eight, "a new-sprung
blossom, with shining petals not yet lifted fully from the bud," her
passing afflicted the city's inhabitants with a kind of seismic hysteria:

They filled the church and its forecourt, the square beyond, the alleyways
and tenements, the *mese* and the cross-streets, the open spaces atop buildings—all one could see was a mass of humanity, as if the whole world had
rushed to a single place in its grief. And there one could view that sacred
blossom brought forth on a golden bier. How dejected were the faces of all
who gazed upon her! How their eyes flowed with tears! They struck their
hands together, and their keening too made known the pain that filled
their hearts.

Gregory drew the parallel in a stylishly baroque *oratio consolatoria*
delivered on the day following the public funeral procession.[61] His
vivid description demonstrates that a lively popular attachment existed even for the least of the emperor's family, and that the dynastic
edifice of Theodosius had an important domestic side.

The girl's mother, Aelia Flavia Flaccilla, was descended from
Spanish aristocracy, as her *nomen* Aelia declared. Passed from Flaccilla to other imperial women of the family's eastern branch, this
nomen was to become in effect a title of female distinction and
dynastic exclusiveness.[62] Theodosius must have married the woman
at the latest during his temporary retirement, 376–78, for when she
arrived with him in the East she had already given birth to two
children, Pulcheria and her first son Arcadius.[63] In the following years
Flaccilla's relatives emerged together with those of Theodosius among

60. Cf., e.g., Philostorg. 12. 9–10 and Nest. *Heracl.*, trans. Nau, pp. 317–18,
for contemporary reaction to earthquakes, and Cosmas Indicopleustes *Topographia
christiana* 1. 21–22 (ed. Wolska-Conus) for a pious monk's rejection of current
"scientific" explanations.

61. *Oratio consolatoria in Pulcheriam*, ed. Spira, pp. 461–63 (vol. IX Jaeger-
Langerbeck).

62. Claud. *Ser.* 50–51, 56: "Quid dignum memorare tuis, Hispania, terris /
vox humana valet? . . . series his fontibus Aelia fluxit." In the coinage, obverse
legends employ this *nomen* for all eastern empresses from Flaccilla through the fifth
century, even after the extinction of the Theodosian dynasty in 453, and for the
western empresses Galla Placidia and Licinia Eudoxia on coins struck for them in the
East; see, e.g., L. Laffranchi, "Nuovo aureo di Licinia Eudossia e il corpus numismatico di questa Augusta," *Rassegna numismatica* 28 (1931), 255–56.

63. O. Seeck, *RE*, VI (1909), 2431–33, "Aelia Flaccilla Augusta 3," and
PLRE, I, 341–42, "Aelia Flavia Flaccilla," on Flaccilla and her children.

the social and political elite of Constantinople, although only Nebridius, in his first marriage the husband of her sister, is attested in high
office, as *comes sacrarum largitionum* (383–84) and as city prefect
(386).[64] At one point Flaccilla dissuaded Theodosius from a colloquy
with the impressive Arian bishop Eunomius of Cyzicus, so fearful was
she that in his efforts toward reconciliation her husband might be
induced to betray the Nicene faith she too had carried with her from
the West.[65] She bore a second male child, Honorius, on September 9,
384, in the imperial palace of Constantinople. About three years later
she died at a place called Skotoume in Thrace, where healing springs
had failed to relieve her illness.[66]

This record would hardly make Flaccilla a figure of unusual
importance, were it not that among her contemporaries a process of
enhancement set in. Called forward to deliver another *oratio consolatoria* on the occasion of her death, Gregory of Nyssa again drew the
analogy with earthquakes, but added wars, floods, and the
appearance of fissures in the earth's crust, declaring that the loss of
Flaccilla surpassed all of these because it struck the whole inhabited
world simultaneously. "As his partner in the *basileía* [imperial do-
minion]," "functioning with him in the same *archē* [office]," she
supported her husband's best qualities and also exhibited virtues of
her own:

This ornament of the Empire has gone from us, this rudder of justice, the
image of *philanthropy* or, rather, its archetype. This model of *wifely love*
has been taken away, this undefiled monument of chastity, dignified but
approachable, clement but not to be despised, *humble but exalted,* modest
but ready to speak boldly—a harmonious mixture of all the virtues. This
zeal for the faith has departed from us, this pillar of the church, decoration
of altars, wealth of the needy, the right hand which satisfied many, the
common haven of those who are heavy laden. Let virgins mourn, widows
grieve, and orphans lament: let them know what they had now that they
have her no more![67]

64. *PLRE,* I, 620, "Nebridius 2"; Matthews, *Aristocracies,* pp. 109–10.
Wrede, "Errichtung," p. 194, identifies the two "princes" who flank Arcadius in
the *kathisma* on the NE and SE reliefs of the Theodosius obelisk base (Bruns,
Obelisk, figs. 45, 78) as two "nephews" of Flaccilla, one of them presumably
"Nebridius 3," *PLRE,* I, 620. If this identification is correct, it provides striking
visual evidence for the ceremonial exaltation of Flaccilla's relatives.
65. Soz. 7. 6. 3.
66. Greg. Nyss. *Oratio funebris in Flacillam Imperatricem,* ed. Spira, p. 481
(vol. IX Jaeger-Langerbeck).
67. *Ibid.,* pp. 478, 480, 488.

Conventional and hackneyed though it may appear,[68] this catalogue includes four virtues to which Gregory attached special significance; he returned to emphasize them at the conclusion of his sermon.[69] The same virtues manifested themselves publicly in Flaccilla's career and received enough approval among contemporaries to suggest deliberate creation of an imperial image for women, an image that Flaccilla would pass, like her *nomen* Aelia, to other empresses of the Theodosian house.

In Gregory's interpretation, "zeal for the faith" or "piety" (*eusebeia*) was Flaccilla's chief virtue and, more than the rest, would assure his congregation that she had exchanged her earthly *basileía* for a heavenly one. It connoted "hatred" of pagan idolatry, of course, but especially "disgust" for Arianism, which, by denying the homoousian divinity of Christ, likewise implicated its followers in idolatrous worship of a created being.[70] Christian *eusebeia* had characterized a number of Flaccilla's predecessors, especially Constantine's mother, Helena. The arduous pilgrimage to the holy places of Jerusalem she had undertaken in 326 had moved Eusebius of Caesarea to include a brief *encomium* of her piety in his work *De vita Constantini*. By the end of the century legend had added to this achievement her discovery of the True Cross.[71] When doctrine was the issue, however, imperial women since Helena had promoted Arianism, using their influence to exile Nicene bishops and restore Arians to their sees, and to provide the latter with a favorable hearing at court.[72] As late as 385–86, Justina, mother of the young western emperor Valentinian

68. To judge from Jul. *Or.* 3. 104b and Claud. *In cons. Olybr. et Prob.* 191–205, litterateurs had a stock of *laudes* for women that paralleled those for men. Traditional *laudes* for imperial women may be found in Julian's panegyric on Eusebia, the wife of Constantius II (*Or. 3*), and in Claudian's verse panegyric *Laus Serenae*. Gregory's *laudes Flaccillae* have little in common with either but much to do with a passage in Eusebius' *Vita Constantini (infra)*.

69. Pp. 487–90. Unless otherwise specified, further references to Gregory will indicate this passage.

70. Cf. Amb. *De ob. Theod.* 40 (*CSEL*, LXXIII, 392): "Flaccilla . . . fidelis anima Deo."

71. Euseb. *VC* 3. 41. 2–47. 4, Amb. *De ob. Theod.* 40–48 (*CSEL*, LXXIII, 392–97); cf. J. Straubinger, *Die Kreuzauffindungslegende*, Forschungen zur christlichen Literatur- und Dogmengeschichte vol. XI, no. 3 (Paderborn, 1912). On the chronology of Helena's pilgrimage I follow H. Chadwick, "The Fall of Eustathios of Antioch," *Journal of Theological Studies* 49 (1948), 32–35 (with thanks to Hal Drake for referring me to this article).

72. Helena herself: Athan. *Hist. Ar.* 4. 1–2 (ed. Opitz, pp. 184–85). Constantia, sister of Constantine: Philostorg. 1. 9, Soz. 3. 19. 3. Eusebia, wife of Constantius II: Soc. 2. 2. 4, 6. Domnica, wife of Valens: Thdt. *HE* 4. 12. 3–4.

II, engaged in a notable struggle with St. Ambrose to secure toleration and use of one of Milan's churches for the embattled Arian
faithful.[73] If knowledge of this conflict had penetrated to Constantinople by the time of Flaccilla's death, it must have given special
point to Gregory's praise of her *eusebeia*, because now a woman of
her prestige had intervened for the new dynastic orthodoxy.

The Gospel admonition to "humble oneself as this little child"
(Matthew 18:4) imposed special burdens on a woman in Flaccilla's
position. Married to an emperor (*basileus*), she entered the imperial
palace (*basileia*) and became, in common parlance, *basilis* or *basilissa*
(Latin *regina*). Without a legal or constitutional significance, this title
derived entirely from a woman's consanguinity or marital association
with a *basileus*.[74] But it did bring with it the sacred, numinous
quality that distinguished the emperor from his subjects, making his
imperial apartments, for example, the *sacrum cubiculum* and his
countenance the *sacer vultus*. As Gregory observed, Flaccilla occupied
the same "secret places of the emperor," and normally her countenance remained hidden from all but a few, in curtained chambers
patrolled by the palace guard (*scholares*).[75] When she did travel
abroad, concealed in an imperial wagon decorated with gold and
purple, the same guard accompanied her, and on her return to Constantinople residents of all ages and 'classes came forth from the city
gates to hail her *adventus,* while men of the highest rank formed an
escort to lead her through the city amid chants of praise from the
people.[76]

Despite this exaltation, Gregory insisted, Flaccilla remembered
her human limitations and preserved her "humility" (*tapeinophrosynē*). Gregory provided no details, but another author described the
type of conduct he had in mind. When Flaccilla visited the sick and

73. Sources in *PLRE,* I, 488–89, "Iustina"; for chronology Palanque, *Ambroise*, pp. 511–14.

74. Julian expresses this neatly in his panegyric on Eusebia (*Or.* 3. 112b):
ἐπειδὴ τῶν βασιλείων εἴσω παρῆλθε καὶ τῆς ἐπωνυμίας ταύτης ἠξιώθη. . . .
Although employed commonly for emperors, the title *basileus* did not enter the
official titulature until the early seventh century: L. Brehier, "L'origine des titres
impériaux à Byzance," *BZ* 15 (1906), 165–73.

75. Pp. 483–84; cf. A. Alföldi, "Die Ausgestaltung des monarchischen Zeremoniells am römischen Kaiserhofe," *Mitteilungen des Deutschen Archäologischen
Instituts, Römische Abteilung* 49 (1934) = *Die monarchische Repräsentation im
römischen Kaiserreiche* (Darmstadt, 1970), pp. 29–38.

76. Gregory *Oratio*, pp. 481–82, contrasting the sad spectacle of Flaccilla's
cortege and arrival with the joy of a normal *adventus* κατὰ τὸν βασίλειον κόσμον.
Jul. *Or.* 3. 129b–c mentions Eusebia's *adventus* in Rome (354?), when the senate

maimed in the hospitals of Constantinople, she "brought the pot, fed them soup, gave them their medicine, broke their bread, served them morsels, and washed the bowl, performing with her own hands all the tasks normally given to servants and handmaids."[77] In a handmaid such conduct would have attracted no attention. In Flaccilla, a figure invested with brilliance and mystery, it became exalted *tapeinophrosynē*, a highly effective virtue which must have humanized the monarchy and brought the dynasty closer to the everyday anxieties of the people.

How might one believe, Gregory inquired, that she had entered the heavenly *basileía* with those on the Lord's right hand? Again a Gospel text set a standard for imperial conduct as it offered consolation for the bereaved: "Inasmuch as you have done it unto one of the least of these, you have done it unto me" (Matthew 25:40). Once an attribute of benevolent deities, *philanthropia*, "love of mankind," had long since counted among the chief imperial virtues.[78] In the fourth century, as the impact of Christian *agapē* and charitable institutions manifested itself, the emperors and their ideologues applied it more insistently to "the least of these," an effort to tap a rich source of popularity in which imperial women assumed a prominent role. Thus Eusebius praised Helena for benefiting the entire East on a scale made possible only by imperial resources. Constantine sup-

and people received her ὑπαντῶντες καὶ δεξιούμενοι καθάπερ νόμος βασιλίδα. On *adventus* in general see now S. MacCormack, *Art and Ceremony in Late Antiquity* (Berkeley-Los Angeles-London, 1981), pp. 17–89. For the wagon and retinue of a *basilis* cf. Jul. *Ep. ad Ath.* 285b, Amm. 29. 6. 7, Soc. 5. 11. 6–9, Thdt. *HE* 5. 19. 2, and R.I. Frank, *Scholae Palatinae,* Papers and Monographs of the American Academy in Rome vol. XXIII (Rome, 1969), p. 100.

77. Thdt. *HE* 5. 18. 2–3. Cf. the contemporary image of Helena—Amb. *De ob. Theod.* 41 (*CSEL,* LXXIII, 393): "bona stabularia, quae maluit aestimari stercora, ut Christum lucrifaceret"; esp. Rufin. *HE* 10. 8: "virgines, quas ibi [Jerusalem] repperit deo sacratas, invitasse ad prandium et tanta eas devotione curasse dicitur, ut indignum crederet, si famulorum uterentur officiis, sed ipsa manibus suis famulae habitu succincta cibum adponeret, poculum porrigeret, aquam manibus infunderet et regina orbis ac mater imperii famularum Christi se famulam deputaret"; also the Greek ecclesiastical histories dependent on Rufinus—Soc. 1. 17. 12: δι' ἑαυτῆς λειτουργοῦσα; Soz. 2. 2. 2: λέγεται . . . ὑπηρέτιν γενέσθαι; Thdt. 1. 18. 8: αὐτὴ θεραπαινίδος ἔργον ἐπλήρου.

78. G. Downey, "*Philanthropia* in Religion and Statecraft in the Fourth Century after Christ," *Historia* 4 (1955), 199–208; J. Kabiersch, *Untersuchungen zum Begriff der Philanthropia bei dem Kaiser Julian,* Klassisch-philologische Studien no. 21 (Wiesbaden, 1960); H. Hunger, "ΦΙΛΑΝΘΡΩΠΙΑ," *Anzeiger der Österreichischen Akademie der Wissenschaften, Philosophisch-historische Klasse,* Jahrgang 1963, pp. 1–20; L.J. Daly, "Themistius' Concept of *Philanthropia*," *Byzantion* 45 (1975), 22–40.

ported her generosity, he claimed, by granting her the authority to draw as she saw fit on the imperial treasuries. Among the recipients of her largesse Eusebius listed the populations of various cities she visited during her pilgrimage, the soldiers, the churches "even in the smallest cities," the "naked and helpless poor," and the most wretched criminals, condemned to chains and servitude in the mines, whom she called back from exile and set free.[79]

Flaccilla undertook no pilgrimage, so far as is known, but if she concentrated her efforts on the dynastic city and its environs their results must have been no less impressive. The sick and maimed received her attention, as did virgins, widows, and orphans, the naked and the hungry. Like Eusebius, however, Gregory stressed philanthropy toward those beyond the resources of ordinary human sympathy. "The proof is before your eyes," he said, "for you saw a wretch at the altar despairing of his salvation. You saw a contemptible woman grieving at her brother's condemnation. You heard the good news announced to the congregation, that in memory of the empress the baneful sentence of death has been commuted and he will live." An act of imperial clemency made public at her funeral[80] revitalized for Gregory's listeners the philanthropy Flaccilla had practiced during her life. "Through her how many have discovered the grace of the resurrection for themselves, who, having died in the laws and received the sentence of death, in her have been recalled to life?" The image was remarkable indeed. Gregory's language evoked the *agapē* which through Christ's death likewise "recalled to life" those who had "died in the laws."[81] Again, only imperial resources permitted philanthropy on this scale, because such philanthropy required inconsistent application of the laws.

Finally, Gregory emphasized Flaccilla's "wifely love" (*philandria*). The dead woman had made a loving division of her wealth, choosing Pulcheria for herself, "since offspring are the chief of blessings," but assigning her male children to their father "to serve as bulwarks of the *basileía*." This definition of *philandria* appears contrived and the praise gratuitous.[82] Flaccilla deserved no credit for the simple accident that her daughter preceded her in death. But

79. Euseb. *VC* 3. 44–45.
80. Cf. p. 479. Them. *Or.* 18. 225b, 19. 231a emphasizes Flaccilla's *justice*, but for Gregory of Nyssa her *philanthropy* went beyond justice.
81. Rom. 7:4, Gal. 2:19, Col. 2:13.
82. Traditionally this virtue consisted of devotion to one's husband and his interests, as with Penelope: Jul. *Or.* 3. 106a, 113c–114a, 127c, Claud. *Ser.* 212–36.

Gregory's words nonetheless had a force which may be appreciated at once from the melancholy example of a woman who was less fortunate. Constantius II (d. 361) married his second wife Eusebia "to procreate children who would inherit his rank and power," but she could not conceive. Eusebia embraced Arianism, it was said, when the intercessions of orthodox priests failed to cure her. Contemporaries also blamed her for the childlessness of Helena, sister of Constantius and wife of his cousin and rival Julian the Apostate. Helena's first child died at birth, but her fertility frightened Eusebia so much that according to rumor she tricked her sister-in-law into accepting a drug that caused her to abort subsequent pregnancies. A few years later Eusebia perished under the ministrations of a female practitioner who claimed the ability to restore her uterus.[83] Childbearing was crucial to the success of these women, and failure to produce might drive one to extremes.

Thus Gregory's interpretation received its force from Flaccilla's success in childbearing. The scale of her success became apparent on January 19, 383. On that day, the fourth anniversary of his own *dies imperii,* Theodosius elevated Flaccilla's elder son Arcadius to the rank of Augustus, the imperial distinction held at the time by Theodosius himself and by his western colleagues Gratian and Valentinian II. To emphasize the theoretical origin of the imperial power in the will of the troops, the court chose to conduct the elevation ceremony at the Hebdomon. Presumably Theodosius himself presented the insignia, draping Arcadius with the imperial *paludamentum* (Greek *chlamys*), a military cloak of purple fastened on the right shoulder with a jeweled imperial *fibula,* and binding on his head the diadem of an emperor. (These insignia can be readily examined on contemporary coins, fig. 5, and on the Missorium of Theodosius, fig. 8, an object created in 388.) Presumably also, an assembly of troops responded with acclamations signifying approval of the new monarch and willingness to obey his orders.[84] With the imperial distinction, Arcadius

83. Jul. *Or.* 3. 109b, *Ep. ad Ath.* 271a, Philostorg. 4. 7, Amm. 16. 10. 18–19, Joh. Chrys. *In Ep. ad Philipp.* 5 (*PG,* LXII, 295); cf. O. Seeck, *RE,* VI (1909), 1365–66, "Eusebia 1."

84. *Chron. pasch. a.* 385 (pp. 562–63 Bonn), Marcell. com. *a.* 383. 2 (*MGH: AA,* XI, 61), *Cons. Const. a.* 383. 1 (*MGH: AA,* IX, 244), Soc. 5. 10. 25; cf. Rauschen, *Jahrbücher,* p. 146, for the date. H.-G. Beck, *Senat und Volk von Konstantinopel,* Sitzungsberichte der Bayerischen Akademie der Wissenschaften, Philosophisch-historische Klasse, Jahrgang 1966, Heft 6 (Munich, 1966), pp. 4–10, correctly stresses the military origins of the *basileía* in this period. For the contemporary ceremonial of

received the supreme magisterial powers of legislation, jurisdiction, and military command. Obviously, these powers meant little vested in a child under the thumb of his father, but even so they made Arcadius a "bulwark of the *basileía*," as Gregory insisted, for the elevation of Arcadius implied the survival of the dynasty into the next generation and secured the futures of ambitious men who attached themselves to it.

At the same time or shortly thereafter,[85] the child's mother received the rank Augusta, the imperial distinction held by the Augusti. Gregory must have had this rank in mind when he said that Flaccilla shared *basileía* and *archē* with her husband. His words seem precise enough but require qualification, because the author did not mean that with her new rank Flaccilla acquired the magisterial powers of an Augustus. The Romans had never admitted women to the magistracies or to the senate, and when on rare occasions they enter-

---

imperial elevations see in general MacCormack, *Art and Ceremony*, pp. 161–266; and esp. Claud. *De IV cons. Hon.* 170–211 on the elevation of Honorius, January 10, 393, with W. Ensslin, "Zur Torqueskrönung und Schilderhebung bei der Kaiserwahl," *Klio* 35 (1942), 297 and *passim*, and A. Christophilopoulou, *Eklogē, anagoreusis kai stepsis tou Byzantinou autokratoros*, Pragmateiai tēs Akadēmias Athēnōn, vol. XXII, no. 2 (Athens, 1956), p. 10; also V. Tiftixoglu, "Die Helenianai nebst einigen anderen Besitzungen im Vorfeld des frühen Konstantinopel," *Studien zur Frühgeschichte Konstantinopels*, ed. H.-G. Beck, Miscellanea byzantina monacensia vol. XIV (Munich, 1973), pp. 79–83, associating the protocol contained in Const. Porph. *De cer.* 1. 91 (I, 412–17 Bonn) with the elevation of Honorius. Averil Cameron in Flavius Cresconius Corippus, *In laudem Iustini Augusti minoris*, ed. and trans. with commentary by Averil Cameron (London, 1976), p. 176, states that "it is not until the 6th [century] that the crowning with the diadem comes to assume the major importance in inaugurations," but *stellati . . . crines* in Claud. *loc. cit.* line 209 must mean the diadem, while Philostorg. 11. 2 reports that Theodosius Ὀνωρίῳ τὸν βασίλειον παρατίθησι στέφανον (cf. *infra*, n. 90); similarly, the use of ἀναδεῖν in the general sense, "to create an emperor," implies that the constitutive act was a "binding up" (i.e., with the diadem), e.g., Them. *Or.* 14. 182d: βασιλέα βασιλεὺς ἀναδεῖ καὶ οὐκ ἐλαττοῦται διδούς.

85. No literary source mentions the coronation of Flaccilla, but numismatic evidence proves that it occurred before eastern mints ceased issuing coins for Gratian, after his assassination on August 25, 383. Mint-marks show that at least Heraclea, Constantinople, Nicomedia, and Antioch struck Aes II (large bronze) pieces of Flaccilla (obverse legend AEL FLAC—CILLA AVG, *infra*, p. 32) concurrently with the Aes II GLORIA RO—MANORVM coins of Gratian: *RIC*, IX, 195.13/194.11, 226.55/225.52, 257.28/256.25, 284.43/283.40. The same Flaccilla Aes II pieces also parallel the first Arcadius Aes II GLORIA RO—MANORVM coins with the divine hand crowning the emperor on the obverse: *RIC*, IX, 195.12, 226.53, 257.26, 283–84.41; cf. *infra*, p. 66. Thus the elevation of Arcadius provides a *terminus a quo* for Flaccilla's coronation, as J.W.E. Pearce assumed: *RIC*, IX, 194, 222, 256, 282.

tained the possibility, the notion struck them as illegal and positively revolting.[86] Gregory himself adduced only ceremonial exaltation of Flaccilla and laudable wifely admonitions that encouraged Theodosius to exercise his powers virtuously.[87] It was influence, not power, that permitted her to demonstrate imperial *philanthropia.*

The circumstances of Flaccilla's coronation suggest that the distinction Augusta had a more specific meaning. Like Arcadius, Flaccilla presumably received it from Theodosius himself. Since she would not be giving orders, Theodosius probably conferred it not at the Hebdomon but in a court setting, perhaps in the confines of the imperial palace of Constantinople.[88] Most important, chronological proximity to the elevation of Arcadius indicates that Theodosius made Flaccilla an Augusta to draw attention to her childbearing, the implications of which became abundantly clear in the figure of her son. For Theodosius and his friends, the great men of the *comitatus* who

---

86. Some notable examples: Tac. *Ann.* 13. 5 reports that in A.D. 54 Agrippina approached the *suggestus imperii* to preside with Nero over the senate, but "though the rest were numb with fear" Seneca warned Nero and intercepted his mother to prevent "disgrace"—"ita specie pietatis obviam itum dedecori." According to the *SHA Elag.* 4. 1–2, the emperor's mother, Soaemias, was the only woman who ever entered the senate chamber, sat on the consuls' bench, and participated in the proceedings—"solusque omnium imperatorum fuit, sub quo mulier quasi clarissima loco viri senatum ingressa est." *CTh* 6. 4. 17 (370) required heiresses to assume senatorial and praetorian financial obligations incurred by their fathers, "although it appears to be unlawful and disgraceful for women to advance to the Senatorial garb and insignia" (trans. Pharr). Claud. *In Eutrop.* 1. 319–21 declares that Janus forbids a eunuch to enter the *fasti,* that it would be less "disgusting" if a woman held the consulship illegally—"sumeret inlicitos etenim si femina fasces, / esset turpe minus. . . ." Such passages make it impossible to accept without qualification the view of St. Maslev (following Mommsen) that "in der römischen Zeit gab es keine Rechtshindernisse, welche den Frauen den Weg zum Prinzipat versperrt hätten," "Die staatsrechtliche Stellung der byzantinischen Kaiserrinnen," *Byzantino-slavica* 27 (1966), 308. See also R. MacMullen, "Women in Public in the Roman Empire," *Historia* 29 (1980), 207–18, and *infra*, pp. 97, 213.

87. Contemporary panegyric did not hesitate to praise such interventions: Jul. *Or.* 3. 114a–115a, stressing that Eusebia did not "constrain" Constantius; also Claud. *Ser.* 134–39, for Theodosius unburdening himself to Serena.

88. Constantine conferred the distinction on Helena (Euseb. *VC* 3. 47. 2) and supposedly on his daughter Constantina (*infra,* n. 90), while in 421 Galla Placidia received it from Honorius and Constantius III: τοῦ τε ἰδίου ἀδελφοῦ καὶ τοῦ ἰδίου ἀνδρὸς χειροτονησάντων—Olymp. frg. 34 (*FHG*, IV, 65). The language employed for elevations is conventional (e.g., ἀναγορεύεσθαι, χειροτονεῖν, ἐπαίρειν) and permits no conclusions as to the nature of the ceremonial; cf. Ensslin, "Torqueskrönung," p. 295, and W. Sickel, "Das byzantinische Krönungsrecht bis zum 10. Jahrhundert," *BZ* 7 (1898), 520–21, esp. 544 n. 68 on the *loci* of later Augusta coronations.

depended upon continuation of the dynasty, the woman's function paralleled in importance the magisterial function of her consort and might be thought to merit the same distinction.

An Augusta was not an unprecedented phenomenon. The first emperor Augustus had invented the rank for his wife, Livia, and his successors had employed it often for mothers, wives, and sisters.[89] Constantine the Great had conferred it in 324 on his mother, Helena, and on his wife, Fausta, in a flourish of dynastic confidence that accompanied the promotion of his son Constantius II to the rank Caesar.[90] With Constantine's death in 337 the practice fell into abeyance. His sons remained without heirs, as did their cousin Julian, and consequently had no occasion to emulate him. But this was not the case with Valentinian I (d. 375), founder of the next dynasty. Valentinian I elevated neither his first wife, Marina, nor his second, Justina, although each produced a son (Gratian and Valentinian II) who was made Augustus in the lifetime of his mother.[91] Flaccilla's new rank must have impressed contemporaries as a dramatic innovation and as reversion to prestigious Constantinian practice. Despite the youth of her son, Flaccilla, like Helena, was celebrated ''for her pious deeds and for the towering and wonderful plant that sprang from her.''[92]

89. K. Neumann, *RE,* II (1896), 2371–72, ''Augustus,'' and for analysis esp. E. Kornemann, *Doppelprinzipat und Reichsteilung im Imperium Romanum* (Leipzig and Berlin, 1930), pp. 35–40, 51, 67–68, 71–72, 92–95.

90. Again the only evidence is numismatic: P. Bruun, *RIC,* IX, 45, 53. The famous *Ep. Eusebii ad Constantiam Augustam,* Mansi, XIII, 313, has been taken as evidence that Constantine also conferred the rank on his sister Constantia (e.g., O. Seeck, *RE,* IV [1901], 958, ''Constantia 13''), but see now C. Murray, ''Art and the Early Church,'' *JThS* n.s. 28 (1977), 326–36, casting grave doubts on the document's authenticity. Similarly, Philostorg. 3. 22 (cf. 28) reports that Constantine had made his daughter Constantia (Constantina) an Augusta—διαδήματί τε αὐτὴν ἐταινίωσεν καὶ Αὐγοῦσταν ἐπωνόμασεν—and that she thus had the power to appoint Vetranio Caesar in 350 to resist the usurper Magnentius. The episode is revealing (cf. *infra,* n. 102), but if Constantine had elevated his daughter (or his sister, for that matter) one would expect to find coins confirming the rank Augusta. More likely, the rank of Constantina was a convenient fiction that lent weight to the temporary promotion of Vetranio (cf. Stein, *Histoire,* I, 319, for the context).

91. Joh. Mal. 13 (Bonn, p. 341) makes Marina an Augusta, and Jord. *Rom.* 314 (*MGH: AA,* V: 1, 40) gives the same rank to Domnica, the wife of Valens. Both authors wrote, however, in the sixth century, when this distinction had become normal for imperial consorts. Again, neither empress appears in the coinage. The Jordanes passage depends on Soc. 5. 1. 3, where Domnica is styled simply ἡ τοῦ βασιλέως γυνή.

92. Euseb. *VC* 3. 47. 1.

Even more impressive was the appearance of Flaccilla in the coinage, a ubiquitous and at least in some cases an effective medium of imperial propaganda.[93] From her elevation in 383 until her death in 387, Constantinople and other eastern mints struck coins with her image in gold, silver, and bronze.[94] Figure 6 presents a beautiful specimen, a solidus minted at Constantinople (mint-mark CONOB) and preserved in the collection of the Staatliche Museen, Berlin. The concise idiom of numismatists permits a neutral description:

Obverse. AEL(IA) FLAC—CILLA AVG(VSTA) Bust right, mantled, with necklace and elaborate headdress.

Reverse. SALVS REI—PVBLICAE Victory enthroned right, writing chi-rho on shield resting on small column. CONOB in the exergue.

The reverse will not bear much interpretation. The designer employed the commonplace legend SALVS REI—PVBLICAE ("well-being of the state") with the throned goddess Victory from contemporary VOTA issues of the Augusti, replacing the VOTA numbers of the latter with the chi-rho to create a distinct but trivial reverse type for an empress.[95]

The obverse is a different matter entirely. The legend specifies Flaccilla's *nomen*, Aelia, and her rank, Augusta. The mantle is clearly a *paludamentum* of the imperial type, and the *fibula* securing it on Flaccilla's right shoulder has the same triple pendants or chains that characterize the emperors' *fibulae* on the coins and the Missorium of Theodosius. The style of Flaccilla's headdress, as she wore it when she appeared before the court or people on ceremonial occasions, can readily be imagined. Those who constructed it began with the so-called *Scheitelzopf-Frisur,* familiar also from the coins of Helena and other portraits of empresses of the period (cf. figs. 3, 11). They divided the hair at the crown of the head and formed it into plaits or braids, which they then brought forward over the crown to the forehead. Strands of pearls were laid in sharp vertical waves along the

93. C.H.V. Sutherland, "The Intelligibility of Roman Imperial Coin Types," *JRS* 49 (1959), 46–55, responding to A.H.M. Jones, "Numismatics and History," *Essays in Roman Coinage Presented to Harold Mattingly,* ed. R.A.G. Carson and C.H.V. Sutherland (Oxford, 1956), pp. 13–33. For a case in point from the early fifth century cf. *infra,* pp. 109–10.

94. *RIC,* IX, 305 (Index I), "Flaccilla, Aelia."

95. *Ibid.,* pp. 316 (Index IV), "VICTORY," 320–21 (Index V), "SALVS REIPVBLICAE." A secondary Flaccilla reverse is equally distinct but trivial: "SALVS REI—PVBLICAE Empress standing facing, head right, with arms crossed on breast," *ibid.,* p. 313 (Index IV), "EMPRESS."

temples, and pearl-headed pins were inserted to enrich the hairdo beneath the braids.[96] Before completing their work, the stylists bound an imperial diadem around Flaccilla's head, a band of cloth or other pliable material decorated, in this case, with precious stones in rosette settings. The Berlin solidus also shows clearly the forehead jewel which characterized the diadem and the lively ties or ribbons that secured it at the back, visible here as they emerge from the plaits of Flaccilla's hair.[97]

Although the images of Augustae had appeared in the coinage ever since the Julio-Claudian period,[98] the women's headgear was most often the *stephanē* of a goddess, not the laurel crown or other insignia of the Augusti, from whom the females were systematically distinguished.[99] Constantine's mints observed the rule in coins struck for Helena and Fausta as Augustae from the time of their coronation in 324. Reverses of Fausta explicitly associate her rank with child-bearing, embodied in her sons Constantius II and Constans, the "hope of the state" (fig. 4):

SPEISREIP—VBLICAE Empress standing left, draped and veiled, holding two infants and leaning on column.

On the obverses Fausta usually appears bareheaded, while the decorated headband of Helena's coin portraits lacks the forehead jewel and especially the ties or ribbons, and therefore cannot represent the diadem, which Constantine first introduced for his *Vicennalia* celebration in 325 (figs. 2, 5).[100] Nor does Helena's mantle include any

96. K. Wessel, "Römische Frauenfrisuren von der severischen bis zur konstantinischen Zeit," *Archäologischer Anzeiger* (1946–47), 66–70 (with useful drawings); R. Delbrueck, *Spätantike Kaiserporträts von Konstantinus Magnus bis zum Ende des Westreichs* (Berlin and Leipzig, 1933), pp. 51–52, 66. As Delbrueck points out (p. 35), the "Staatsfrisuren" formed "einen Teil des säkularen Ornats," an observation true, naturally, of female as well as of male hairstyles. Cf. Amm. 22. 4. 9–10 for Julian's reaction when a lavishly paid and richly adorned imperial *tonsor* appeared to trim his hair.

97. Delbrueck, *Kaiserporträts,* pp. 58–66, for diadem typology; M.R. Alföldi, *Die constantinische Goldprägung* (Mainz, 1963), pp. 139–41, on the significance of the forehead jewel.

98. U. Kahrstedt, "Frauen auf antiken Münzen," *Klio* 10 (1910), 291–99, 304–10.

99. A. Alföldi, "Insignien," pp. 123–24 (= *Repräsentation,* pp. 241–42); also p. 21 (= p. 139), referring to the "Göttinkränze" of empresses as "Versuche, den Augustae eine, der der Augusti entsprechende, rangbezeichnende Kranztracht zu erfinden."

100. M.R. Alföldi, *Goldprägung,* p. 93, for introduction of the diadem; cf., however, Bruun, *RIC,* IX, 44, 53, 465, 476. 56. 489, 514. 131, dating the earliest

distinctive feature that might have permitted those who handled her coins to recognize in it the *paludamentum* or other male costume.[101]

Thus the coin portraits of Flaccilla reveal another dramatic break with tradition, for on them she wears precisely the insignia—diadem, *paludamentum* with imperial *fibula*—that identified an Augustus. With Flaccilla the practice of distinguishing females from males in coin iconography gave way to iconographic assimilation. It is likely, moreover, that this change in iconography reflected parallel changes in ceremonial and imperial ideology. Theodosius may well have presented these insignia when he elevated Flaccilla in 383.[102] If this interpretation is correct, he presented them both to draw attention to Flaccilla's childbearing and to assimilate this essential function of women to the magisterial functions of an emperor.

The court of Theodosius also ordered or encouraged adoption of this new official line in other media of propaganda. Imperial officials and local authorities raised portrait statues of Flaccilla Augusta, just as the praetorian prefect Tatianus dedicated statues of Theodosius and his colleagues, in order to emphasize her legitimacy and represent her *basileía* in various cities of the East.[103] A well-known dedicatory inscription found in Aphrodisias provides one example, [104] while dedications published more recently have added two from Ephesus.[105] That from Aphrodisias records the fullest style of Flaccilla's imperial titulature:

---

solidi with the plain band diadem to 324, thus perhaps contemporaneous with the elevation of Fausta and Helena to the rank Augusta. In my opinion Alföldi (pp. 144–45) has proved (*contra* Delbrueck et al.) that Helena's headband represents not an *insigne* of rank but "ein integrierender Bestandteil der Haartracht."

101. A. Alföldi, "Insignien," pp. 26–28 (= *Repräsentation*, pp. 144–46), calls this mantle "das der Toga entsprechende Kleidungsstück der Kaiserinnen."

102. Writing early in the fifth century, Philostorg. 3. 22 (quoted *supra*, n. 90) assumed that elevation of an Augusta included coronation with the diadem. Gregory, pp. 486–87, states that when Flaccilla died she "laid down her crown of precious stones" and "removed her mantle of purple," implying that these were the primary insignia of an Augusta, presumably received at her elevation.

103. In general H. Kruse, *Studien zur offiziellen Geltung des Kaiserbildes im römischen Reiche* (Paderborn, 1934), esp. pp. 31–32, and *infra*, pp. 66–67, on the official treatment of Eudoxia Augusta's *imago muliebris*.

104. H. Grégoire, *Recueil des inscriptions grecques-chrétiennes d'Asie Mineure* (Paris, 1922), no. 280.

105. J. Keil and G. Maresch, "Epigraphische Nachlese zu Miltners Ausgrabungsberichten aus Ephesos," *Jahreshefte des Österreichischen Archäologischen Instituts in Wien* 45 (1960), Beiblatt, 85–86, nos. 11–12; *L'année épigraphique* (1966), no 434.

Figure 2
Solidus of Constantine,
minted Constantinople 326 (2X),
Dumbarton Oaks

Figure 3
Double solidus of Helena
minted Ticinum 324–25 (1.5X),
Paris, Bibliothèque Nationale, Cabinet des Médailles

Figure 4
Solidus of Fausta,
minted Thessalonica 324 (2X),
Dumbarton Oaks

Figure 5
Solidus of Theodosius I,
minted Constantinople 383–88 (2X),
Dumbarton Oaks

Figure 6
Solidus of Flaccilla,
minted Constantinople 383–87 (2X),
Berlin, Staatliche Museen, Münzkabinett

Figure 7
Solidus of Eudoxia,
minted Constantinople 400–404 (2X),
Dumbarton Oaks

Figure 8
Missorium of Theodosius, 388 (detail),
Madrid, Real Accademia de Historia

Figure 9
Head of an Augusta, wearing diadem,
about life-size, *ca.* 440,
Rome, Private Collection

Figure 10
Statue of an Augusta,
wearing *paludamentum*,
about life-size, *ca.* 400, Rome,
Norwegian Archaeological Institute

Figure 11
Statuette of an Augusta,
height 78 cm, *ca.* 400,
Paris, Bibliothèque Nationale,
Cabinet des Médailles

[τ]ὴν αἰωνίαν καὶ θεοφιλε-	This eternal and God-loving
[σ]τάτην Αὐγοῦσταν Αἰλίαν	Augusta Aelia
Φλαβίαν Φλακκίλλαν	Flavia Flaccilla
τὴν δέσποιναν τῆς οἰκουμένης	mistress of the inhabited world
Κᾶρες ἵδρυσαν ἐν τῇ ἑαυτῶν	the Carians set up in their
μητροπόλει	metropolis

Literary sources report another portrait, or several portraits, of Flaccilla at Antioch, associated with those of Theodosius and his sons. A mob attacked all of them indiscriminately during a tax riot early in 387, an act of sedition against imperial images that provoked the emperor's special fury, because it was directed in part against his recently deceased spouse.[106]

The fact that Theodosius, like the Antiochene mob, equated the portrait statues of Flaccilla Augusta with those of the reigning Augusti was shown even more clearly in still another example, this one dedicated by Theodosius himself in a significant *locus*. In his oration *On the Philanthropy of Theodosius* (*ca.* early 384), Themistius invoked the Muses, bidding them join in hymning the emperor's praises. Theodosius had recently decorated their "sanctuary," the senate house of Constantinople, with an image *(agalma)* of the empress, "where there is also one of the emperor, and one of the emperor's son, and thus will the majesty of their dances be increased by the partnership."[107] Themistius adopted here the same word for "partnership" *(koinonia)* that Gregory was to use a few years later to describe Flaccilla's participation in the imperial power. But in the Themistius text the word refers specifically to imperial images, confirming the importance of iconographic assimilation in the thinking of contemporary ideologues.

Some full-plastic portraits of high-ranking women survive from Late Antiquity. Not one has been identified positively, either from

106. Liban. *Or.* 20. 4, 10, 22. 8 (II, 423, 425, 475 Foerster); Thdt. *HE* 5. 20. 1; for the context, R. Browning, "The Riot of A.D. 387 in Antioch," *JRS* 42 (1952), 13–20.

107. *Or.* 19. 228b; cf. Dagron, "Empire," p. 24, for the date, and Them. *Or.* 14. 182d for κοινωνία meaning "partnership" in imperial rule. The "Senate of the Augusteion" housed an art collection, assembled by Constantine I, which included images of the Heliconian Muses: Zos. 5. 24. 6. Cf. C. Mango, "Antique Statuary and the Byzantine Beholder," *DOP* 17 (1963), 56–57; esp. Dagron, *Naissance*, pp. 139–41, interpreting this "Senate" as a museum that served to "préserver les liens qui relient la ville à son histoire . . . , de transformer ainsi le présent en continuité historique, de supprimer la peur de l'avenir." To judge from the present dedication (and another in 414, *infra*, p. 97) it also served as a *locus* for the visual display of imperial legitimacy and social prestige.

distinctive physiognomy or from an inscription, with Flaccilla or any other empress.[108] Since the eastern court introduced iconographic assimilation in 383, however, those that feature the diadem or *paludamentum* to mark their subject as an Augusta must date from the decades after Flaccilla's coronation. Moreover, if court artists established a style and an iconography that influenced even provincial workshops,[109] these Augusta portraits, whatever their provenance or the circumstances of their creation, reflected the Theodosian line on imperial women.

Recently H.P. L'Orange published an interesting example,[110] a head from the collection of Count Siciliano di Gentili in Rome (fig. 9) which displays a carefully articulated diadem of the Theodosian period. Rectangular gems in metal frames decorate the band, while the tie at the back and the forehead jewel confirm that this is the same *insigne* as that visible on the coins. L'Orange has also drawn attention to a headless statue (fig. 10) that came in 1962 from a private collection to the Norwegian Archaeological Institute in Rome.[111] He discerns an elaborate female outergarment that has an

108. For more or less hypothetical datings and attributions see Delbrueck, *Kaiserporträts*, pp. 163–75, 192–93, 202–3, 234–36; B. Felletti Maj, "Contributo alla iconografia del IV secolo d.C.," *Critica d'arte* 6 (n.s. 1) (1941), 74–90; esp. H. von Heintze, "Ein spätantikes Mädchenporträt in Bonn," *JfAC* 14 (1971), 61–91, and cf. the generally critical reaction of E. Alföldi-Rosenbaum, "Bemerkungen zur Porträtbüste einer jungen Dame justinianischer Zeit im Metropolitan Museum," *JfAC* 15 (1972), 174–78.

109. See, most recently, P. Bruun, "Notes on the Transmission of Imperial Images in Late Antiquity," *Studia romana in honorem Petri Krarup septuagenarii* (Odense, 1976), pp. 122–31; also W. von Sydow, *Zur Kunstgeschichte des spätantiken Porträts im 4. Jahrhundert n. Chr.*, Antiquitas ser. 3, no. 8 (Bonn, 1969), pp. 58–62, observing that in the fourth century the official iconography known from the coinage lost some of its influence over portraits in other media. The few examples to be discussed here confirm this observation.

110. H.P. L'Orange, "Ein unbekanntes Porträt einer spätantiken Kaiserin," *Acta ad archaeologiam et artium historiam pertinentia* 1 (1962), 49–52, identifying the empress as Galla Placidia. Without argument H. von Heintze, "Ein spätantikes Frauenbüstchen aus Elfenbein," *Berliner Museen* 20 (1970), 55 n. 24, rejects the head as "eine typische antikisierende Gartenplastik." R. Calza, *Iconografia romana imperiale da Carausio a Giuliano (287–363 d.C.)*, Quaderni e guide di archeologia, vol. III (Rome, 1972), pp. 336–38, proposes a date *ca.* 350 and favors Constantina, sister of Constantius II, an identification which is of course impossible if the diadem was not introduced for imperial women until 383.

111. H.P. L'Orange, "Statua tardo-antica di un'imperatrice," *Acta ad archaeologiam et artium historiam pertinentia* 4 (1969), 95–99; also the same author's "Nochmals die spätantike Kaiserin im Norwegischen Institut in Rom," *ibid.* 6 (1975), 57, suggesting that this piece repeated a silver statue of Eudoxia dedicated in Constantinople in 403 (*infra*, p. 76), because both wore the *paludamentum*.

overfold with cincture beneath the bosom not unlike that of the classical *peplos,* but apparently also has the short, full sleeves of the normal long tunic of Late Antiquity, the *dalmatica.* Above this outergarment, the figure wears a mantle, draped over the left shoulder and secured on the right, which must be identified as the *paludamentum* even though the characteristic *fibula* has not been preserved (cf. fig. 8). Figure 11 presents yet another example, a statuette found on Cyprus and preserved in the Cabinet des Médailles, Paris, which a number of scholars over the years have identified as Flaccilla.[112] Around the head is bound a pearl-bordered diadem with the characteristic front jewel. A strut at the back precluded working in the ties. The outergarment, a *dalmatica* of the usual type, was originally richly decorated with broad stripes (*clavi*) inlaid in another material. Over it this Augusta wears not the *paludamentum* but the normal mantle of a woman (the *palla*).[113]

To judge from these plastic portraits, imperial officials and local authorities assimilated an Augusta to her male counterparts when they dedicated her image in the cities of the Empire. But the sculptural evidence also emphasizes that assimilation had its natural limits. In the coin portraits physiognomy, jewelry, and especially the hairdo distinguished an Augusta from her male counterparts, while other media presented Augustae in luxury dress appropriate only for females, in some cases without the *paludamentum.* The full-length portraits also lack the *cingulum* or magistrate's belt. This belt did belong to the costume of an Augustus, but it symbolized magisterial power rather than imperial rank,[114] and would have implied a confusion of female with male functions if used in Augusta iconography. Purveyors of imperial ideology chose their symbols carefully and deliberately to express the nuances of the official line.

The same is true of Gregory's *oratio consolatoria* as a whole. Although he composed it in the tradition of classical consolation rhetoric,[115] the work must also be read as imperial oratory. Its treat-

112. Delbrueck, *Kaiserporträts,* p. 165, makes it "bestimmt" Helena *ca.* 325, again impossible because of the diadem; von Heintze, "Mädchenporträt," p. 83, adopts the *communis opinio.*

113. Delbrueck, *Kaiserporträts,* pp. 163–65.

114. R. Delbrueck, *Die Konsulardiptychen und verwandte Denkmäler* (Berlin and Leipzig, 1929), pp. 36–37, 40; A. Alföldi, "Insignien," pp. 64–65 (= *Repräsentation,* pp. 182–83).

115. J. Soffel, *Die Regeln Menanders für die Leichenrede in ihrer Tradition dargestellt, herausgegeben, übersetzt und kommentiert,* Beiträge zur klassischen

ment of Flaccilla's virtues owes much to a public image of Augustae that had existed since Eusebius praised Helena, but the imperial virtues of women acquired nuances in Gregory's thinking which must have been deliberate. He stressed that Flaccilla's *eusebeia* had done its work for the homoousian creed of 381. Establishment of a sedentary court had permitted her *philanthropia* and her exalted *tapeinophrosynē* to tighten the bonds between the new imperial family and the Roman people of Constantinople, in whose lives her death must indeed have struck like an earthquake. Flaccilla's *philandria,* in Gregory's contrived interpretation, meant that the relatives, westerners, and other ambitious men who emerged in power with Theodosius no longer had to depend on the precarious safety of one Augustus. Gregory declared that Flaccilla participated with her husband in the *basileía,* a propaganda line also adopted by the court when it assimilated her portrait to that of the Augusti. It thus appears that in his *oratio* Gregory articulated a new official ideology for imperial women. It is also likely that this new ideology, as much as the Gothic treaty of 382, for example, or the advancement of Constantinople to rank with Rome, owed its originality to the proclivities of the dynasty's founder.

After Flaccilla's death in 387, Theodosius married again. His second marriage created an entanglement which will likewise help to explain the importance of women in the Theodosian house.

Magnus Maximus, the usurper who had overthrown Gratian in 383, had strong claims on Theodosius. The man was a Spaniard of impeccable Nicene orthodoxy, had risen in military service under the father of Theodosius, and even boasted of being a relative of the family.[116] He had been acclaimed Augustus in an acceptable manner by the troops of Britain and Gaul, and could deny responsibility for the ensuing murder of Gratian as the unauthorized work of a subordinate. Preoccupied with labors in the East, Theodosius had felt no compulsion to move against him, and by 386 even demonstrated

Philologie, no. 57 (Meisenheim am Glan, 1974), pp. 82–89; also A. Spira, "Rhetorik und Theologie in den Grabreden Gregors von Nyssa," *Studia Patristica* 9 (1966) (= *TU,* XCIV) 106–14, stressing the "theologischer Hintergrund." Neither author recognizes the imperial ideology contained in the *oratio* on Flaccilla.

116. In general J.-R. Palanque, "L'empereur Maxime," *Les empereurs romains d'Espagne,* Colloques internationaux du Centre National de la Recherche Scientifique, Sciences Humaines, Madrid-Italica, 31 March–6 April 1974 (Paris, 1965), pp. 255–63 (also discussion, pp. 263–67); Matthews, *Aristocracies,* pp. 173–82, 223–25.

readiness to accept the legitimacy of his elevation.[117] In the next year, however, Maximus crossed the Alps and occupied Italy, forcing Gratian's youthful half-brother Valentinian II, who reigned in Milan at the time, to take refuge at Thessalonica with his Arian mother, Justina. The advance of Maximus also persuaded Theodosius to throw in with the house of Valentinian. With much of the western Empire at his back, Maximus now had the power to threaten Theodosius himself, or at least to limit his freedom of action.[118] Conveniently, the house of Valentinian also included Justina's daughter Galla, and just as conveniently the eastern emperor had lost Flaccilla a year or so earlier. To cement a bond between the two imperial houses, Theodosius married Galla at Thessalonica late in 387.

From these events contemporary invective constructed an unflattering portrait of Theodosius. Maximus "had murdered Gratian, appropriated his imperial power, and, having succeeded in this, had moved forward to seize what remained to Gratian's brother." Despite the enormity of these crimes, Theodosius abandoned his usual lethargy only when Justina, who knew that he was susceptible to sexual advances, displayed Galla's beauty in his presence and then refused to let him marry her unless he took up Valentinian's cause.[119]

It is not unlikely that the middle-aged widower found the young woman attractive. But whether he inclined to sensuality or not, Theodosius certainly was a dynast and must have expected weightier advantages from the transaction. In the next years Galla (who died in 394) was to emulate Flaccilla's *philandria*, although from at least three pregnancies only one child survived infancy, the famous Galla Placidia.[120] More immediately, Theodosius welcomed the opportunity to replace a formidable western Augustus with one he could readily

---

117. Matthews, *Aristocracies*, p. 179: in 386 Theodosius recognized the consulship of Evodius, praetorian prefect of Maximus; about the same time (*supra*, p. 19), Cynegius set up the official portraits of Maximus in Egypt, Zos. 4. 37. 3. Equally important is the numismatic evidence (not adduced by Matthews). When striking the Aes II VIRTVS E—XERCITI series initiated perhaps midway through the period 383–88, the Constantinople mint reserved one of its sections, *officina* Δ, for Maximus, just as A struck for Theodosius, B for Valentinian II, and Γ for Arcadius; Pearce, *RIC*, IX, xxii–xxiii, 205, 233. 83a–d. Maximus types are extremely rare, however, and Pearce believes they must soon have been withdrawn from circulation.

118. Cf. Oost, *Placidia*, p. 47.

119. Zos. 4. 43, drawing on Eunapius of Sardes, who composed his history in the first decades of the fifth century; *infra*, pp. 100–101; and F. Paschoud, *RE*, XA (1972), 822, "Zosimus 8."

120. Oost, *Placidia*, pp. 56–57.

dominate. Above all, the marriage justified an embarrassing change in policy and a necessary but dirty war. By 387 the claims of Maximus must have seemed genuine, and some powerful men on whom Theodosius depended would not understand how he could support Valentinian II and his Arian mother against a thoroughly Nicene Augustus, or why he proclaimed himself to be the avenger of Gratian when the house of Valentinian bore responsibility for the execution of his own father.[121]

The marriage of 387 counteracted these objections and invested Theodosius' undertaking with moral purpose. In Late Antiquity powerful men recognized no greater imperatives in their relations with one another than those of *ankisteia* or *kedeia* (Latin *adfinitas*), the most intimate bond of family and blood. It might seem odd, for example, that Themistius could praise Theodosius for ranking merit (*aretē*) second to kinship (*ankisteia*) when he selected men for the consulship,[122] but in this period favoritism toward relatives was expected. Conversely, Eusebius assailed Licinius, who waged an "impious and monstrous war" against Constantine the Great in 321–24, "violating nature's laws, forgetful of oaths, the blood bond, and treaties," when Constantine had condescended to share power with him as imperial colleague and "intimate kinsman" (*kedestes*).[123] Theodosius hesitated to provoke similar revulsion by attacking a man who boasted of his "favor and kinship" (*adfinitas*),[124] until with his marriage to Galla the claims of Maximus evaporated. In contemporary thinking, the *kedeia* that emerged from the marriage created obligations more binding than those to an imperial colleague or to less immediate kin.[125]

For Theodosius, therefore, a tight bond of *kedeia* was Galla's weightiest attraction and the main convenience of his entanglement

121. *Supra*, n. 6.
122. *Or.* 16. 203d; cf. J.R. Martindale, "Note on the Consuls of 381 and 382," *Historia* 16 (1967), 254–56, identifying the relatives to whom Themistius refers as Fl. Eucherius and Cl. Antonius.
123. Euseb. *HE* 10. 8. 3–4, *VC* 1. 50. 1. Conversely again, Eutr. *Brev.* 10. 5–6 attacks *Constantine* for waging the same war against *Licinius,* "quamquam necessitudo et adfinitas cum eo esset."
124. Pacat. *Pan.* 24. 1: "et adfinitate et favore iactanti. . . ." The claim carried so much charge that the orator could not ignore it.
125. See esp. Them. *Or.* 4. 59a: . . . καὶ αἵματι πάνυ ἀγχοῦ προσεχόμενον [Julian] ἔτι προσηγάγετο [Constantius II] ἐγγυτέρω τῇ ἐκ τοῦ γάμου κηδείᾳ [through Julian's marriage with Constantina] καὶ συνεδήσατο πρὸς τὴν πόλιν δεσμῷ ἀναγκαίῳ, μείζω ποιήσας τὴν πρὸς τὸν οἰκιστὴν ἀγχιστείαν.

with the house of Valentinian. The obligation of *kedeia* likewise accounts for the promotion of men like Flaccilla's relatives and the Vandal Stilicho, the husband of his niece. In the sixteen years since Adrianople, Theodosius had created a vast network of such obligations, which bound him to his relatives and them to him.[126] This network was also a result of his dynastic impetus, and was part of the edifice that received its divine capstone on the river Frigidus.

126. *Supra*, pp. 9–10, 15, 22–23.

CHAPTER TWO

Aelia Eudoxia Augusta

There was in her no little insolence . . .

The obligation of *kedeia*, which Theodosius the Great employed effectively in his dynastic policy, operated in the next generation when his son Arcadius married Eudoxia. During a brief career (395–404), Aelia Eudoxia embraced the image of womanhood that Gregory of Nyssa had articulated for Flaccilla, and like Flaccilla she received the distinction Augusta. In contrast with her model, however, Eudoxia parlayed the image and the distinction into power she could use. Her ability to do so depended in part on her husband's dismal character, but also, again, on the miracle of the Frigidus.

Victory on the Frigidus had left Theodosius with a troubled conscience. St. Ambrose journeyed to join him at Aquileia, expecting that pleading would be necessary to save the surviving rebels, but instead met a penitent emperor who credited his success to the prayers and merit of the bishop and readily granted clemency. Evidently the exertions of the campaign had brought on an edemic condition, and as it became acute Theodosius thought himself condemned for taking the lives of his enemies. He refused to accept the sacraments until the arrival of his children from Constantinople could prove that he remained in God's favor. Honorius did come to his father in Milan, and with him his younger half-sister Galla Placidia. Not long after, on January 17, 395, Theodosius succumbed to his illness.[1] Valentinian II had died conveniently nearly three years ear-

---

1. Soc. 5. 26, Philostorg. 11. 2, Hydat. *a.* 395 (*MGH: AA,* XI, 16), Amb. *De ob. Theod.* 4, 34 (*CSEL,* LXXIII, 373, 388–89), Paulin. *V. Amb.* 31 (ed. Kaniecka). Alan Cameron, "Theodosius the Great and the Regency of Stilico," *HSCP* 73 (1969), 247–80, defends the account of Zos. 4. 59 that Theodosius visited Rome late in 394 and addressed the senate there, but see now F. Paschoud, *Cinq études sur Zosime* (Paris, 1975), pp. 100–124, pointing out that the emperor's illness would have made such a journey impossible: "et cette maladie n'était pas venielle, puisqu'il en mourut" (p. 124).

lier, probably driven to suicide,[2] so this left Honorius (elevated in 383) Augustus in the West, as Theodosius had long since planned,[3] and Arcadius in the East.

In his oration *On the Fourth Consulship of Honorius*, delivered in 398, the court poet Claudius Claudianus recalled Theodosius, before the war against Eugenius, instructing a bellicose Honorius on the advantages of personal command:

> Mounted thyself, ride amid thy squadrons of horse or again stand foot to foot with the infantry. They will advance the bolder for thy presence, and with thee to witness glorious and glad shall be the fulfillment of their task.[4]

Surely Claudian's audience knew better. Raised in the effete atmosphere of the eastern court, sheltered, after Flaccilla's death, in the lap of their cousin Serena,[5] neither son would ever emulate their father's military capacities. In the last months of his life Theodosius had entrusted command in the West to Stilicho, Serena's husband, appointing him generalissimo (*magister militum praesentalis*) and adding a deathbed charge—so Stilicho claimed—to watch over both sons with the moral authority of a senior kinsman (*parentela*).[6] Stilicho employed his moral authority in the next years to place his western protégé at stud with Maria and later Thermantia, his two daughters by Serena,[7] but Honorius failed even in this function. Although Silicho could boast of *adfinitas regia* from his daughters' marriages, he never bounced on his knee in potent intimacy a grandson, born to the purple, heir to imperial dominion.[8]

2. B. Croke, "Arbogast and the Death of Valentinian II," *Historia* 25 (1976), 235–44.

3. O. Seeck, *Geschichte des Untergangs der Antiken Welt*, V (Stuttgart, 1920), pp. 227–28; Alan Cameron, "Theodosius and the Regency," p. 266.

4. 350–53 (trans. Platnauer).

5. Claud. *Epith.* 341–43.

6. W. Ensslin, "Zum Heermeisteramt des spätrömischen Reiches, III," *Klio* 24 (1931), 467–70; J. Straub, "Parens Principum," *Nouvelle Clio* 4 (1952), 94–115; Alan Cameron, "Theodosius and the Regency," pp. 274–80; *idem, Claudian* (Oxford, 1970), pp. 38–40, 42–44, 49–50.

7. Demougeot, *Division*, pp. 82–83, 373.

8. *CIL*, VI, 1730, emphasizes Stilicho's *adfinitas* with Theodosius I and the marriage of Honorius with his daughter, Claud. *Epith.* 341–42 his hopes from that marriage: "sic natus in ostro/parvus Honoriades genibus considat avitis." A number of sources comment on Honorius' childlessness, attributing it to impotence (Philostorg. 12. 2, Zos. 5. 28. 2–3) or to voluntary chastity (Oros. 7. 37. 11, Thdt. *HE* 5. 25. 2), or remaining undecided (Marcell. com. *a.* 408. 1 [*MGH: AA*, XI, 69]). Cf. Alan Cameron, *Claudian*, p. 153 n. 1.

In the East, meanwhile, Arcadius attracted sarcasm for permitting ministers to lead him "like an ox" and for a generally lethargic temperament: "his halting speech betrayed a sluggish spirit, like the torpid glance of his drooping eyes."[9] In 399 Synesius of Cyrene even leveled jibes of this sort at Arcadius in person, if indeed he delivered his address *De regno* before the emperor and his courtiers:

You take pleasure only in corporal enjoyments of the most sensual kind which touch and taste provide, living the life of a jelly-fish. . . . And because their access to the palace is less dangerous to you than that of generals and captains, you select men to share your existence and otherwise to approach you who are to your liking, men of small heads and petty minds, . . . who join you in wasting time and by their encouragement contribute to the evil—that foggy mind of yours which comes from unnatural living.[10]

Unlike Claudian, Synesius spoke the unvarnished truth: Arcadius was woefully unfitted to be master of victory in the traditional sense. "The emperor is a craftsman of war," he declared; "how will he understand the use of his tools if he does not acquaint himself with his soldiers?"[11] The question had no answer, and the truth Synesius spoke threatened the continuation of the dynasty.

Yet, paradoxically, the effete Honorius and Arcadius (unlike their pre-Frigidus exemplars Gratian and Valentinian II) survived to die natural deaths. Their survival was connected with a new direction in imperial ideology that emerged after the battle of the Frigidus. In that battle, contemporary authors stressed, the soldiers' weapons had accomplished nothing at all. Theodosius had mastered Eugenius through piety alone, through his tears and prayers. Thus God had allied himself with Theodosius. Honorius and Arcadius were not left destitute after their father's death, because Theodosius had won for them Christ's favor and also "the loyalty of the troops, in whose eyes he was proof that God rewards piety and avenges perfidy." Victories, peace, and the well-being of the state would always be secured by the piety of the ruler.[12] On the Frigidus Theodosius had shown himself

9. Zos. 5. 12. 1, Philostorg. 11. 3.

10. 14 (pp. 30–31 Terzaghi). Synesius confirms elsewhere that he addressed Arcadius with unparalleled courage: *De insomniis* 14 (p. 176 Terzaghi).

11. *De regno* 13 (pp. 28–29 Terzaghi).

12. Amb. *De ob. Theod.* 2, 7–8, 10, 52 (*CSEL*, LXXIII, 372, 375–76, 388–89); Joh. Chrys. *Hom. VI in eccl. apost.*, *PG*, LXIII, 491–92; Paulin. Nol. in Gennad. *De script. eccl.* 49 (ed. Herding); Aug. *De civ. Dei* 5. 26; Oros. 7. 35. 14, 20–22; Severian of Gabala in A. Wenger, "Notes inédites sur les empereurs Théodose I, Arcadius, Théodose II, Léon I," *REB* 10 (1952), 48. The theme gets special treatment in the ecclesiastical historians of the reign of Theodosius II: Soc. 5. 25. 12, Soz.

once again to be master of victory. The new ideology owed much to the old, but the personal qualities on which victory depended had been transformed, from strategic ability and brute military strength to the emperor's Christian *eusebeia*.

Such interpretations of the Frigidus miracle came easily to Christian apologists, but soon even the more conservative visual media of official propaganda[13] took up the theme. After another imperial victory in 400, the eastern court ordered the erection of a column of Arcadius in the dynastic city that was similar to the victory column of Theodosius (see fig. 1). On the west side of its base, two flying Victories bore a victory wreath surrounding a Christian cross, symbolizing Christ's victory on Golgotha and the promise that the victory of Christ would be repeated in victories of a pious emperor.[14] In close chronological proximity with the design of this base, a city prefect set up images of imperial victory in the hippodrome of Constantinople, the primary *locus* of victory propaganda. Reaching forth from a cloud, the divine hand intervened for Arcadius, according to subjoined inscriptions "driving off the barbarians" who "took flight before God."[15] As the reactionary pagan Eunapius of Sardes recognized, this new line belittled "the emperor's courage, the strength of his troops, and the conditions of real battle,"[16] the very factors on which Claudian and Synesius insisted in their portraits of the ideal ruler. The new line had potent advantages, however. Even an Arcadius could demonstrate piety and claim legitimacy as master of victory, and, despite her sex, so could a woman.

The advertised lethargy of Arcadius, which thus presented no insuperable barrier to the continuation of the dynasty in the East, also

7. 24. 4–6, Thdt. *HE* 5. 24. 3–4, 8–9, 17, 25. 1–2. If he was indeed "paganus pervicacissimus" (Oros. 7. 35. 21) Claudian may have had more difficulty with the Frigidus miracle, but he mentions it nonetheless: *De III cons. Hon.* 96–98; cf. Alan Cameron, *Claudian*, p. 191.

13. The coinage reveals no departure from traditional victory ideology after the Frigidus: e.g., *RIC*, IX, 83–84. 35a–c; O. Ulrich-Bansa, *Moneta Mediolanensis* (Venice, 1949), pp. 159–61, 177–80.

14. Kollwitz, *Plastik*, pp. 17–62; Becatti, *Colonna*, pp. 151–264; esp. Kollwitz, *Plastik*, pp. 47–50, for interpretation of the cross motif on the west side of the base; also *infra*, pp. 108–109.

15. Eunap. frg. 78 (*FHG*, IV, 49); cf. B. Baldwin, "'Perses,'" *Byzantion* 46 (1976), 5–8, on the circumstances alluded to in the passage, and Becatti, *Colonna*, pp. 218–20, for association with the ideological program of the column of Arcadius. Becatti fails to recognize, however, that location of the images in the hippodrome made them instruments of imperial propaganda.

16. Eunap. *loc. cit.*

made possible the remarkable career of his consort Eudoxia.[17] Daughter of a Roman mother and of Bauto (cos. 385), a Frankish general prominent in the West under Valentinian II, this *semibarbara* had come somehow to Constantinople after her father's death in 388. She grew to young womanhood there in the care of the wealthy and powerful family of Promotus,[18] a *magister militum* of Theodosius whose fall in 391/92 contemporaries attributed, like that of Proculus and Tatianus, to the machinations of Flavius Rufinus.[19]

The death of Theodosius left Rufinus in the praetorian prefecture of the East, a position of real power but suddenly precarious because the enemies he had assembled would naturally attempt to turn the pliant Arcadius against him. Happily, a marriageable daughter offered a quick route to comparative invulnerability, through the same *adfinitas regia*[20] Stilicho exploited and the same prospect of holding on his knee a grandson born to the purple. But an emergency intervened. In the first months of 395 Rufinus had to visit Antioch to punish a protégé who had angered Arcadius' great-uncle, and while he was absent [21] a palace eunuch named Eutropius crossed his plans. This person held the position of *praepositus sacri cubiculi*, "chief of the sacred household." During years of intimate association with the imperial family he had acquired a hold over Arcadius which could now be put to use.[22]

A fanciful story related that Eutropius brought a portrait of Eudoxia before Arcadius and enlarged so effectively on her charms that the emperor conceived a passion for her. In reality, Arcadius must have already known of Eudoxia, and their union was less the

17. In general O. Seeck, *RE*, VI (1909), 917–25, "Eudoxia 1."

18. Zos. 5. 3. 2 reports somewhat puzzlingly that after Promotus' death (392) his two sons "associated with" or "lived with" the sons of the emperor (τοῖς αὐτοῦ παισὶν συναναστρεφόμενοι) and that one of them, presumably an age-mate of Arcadius, had Eudoxia with him (ἄτερος εἶχε παρ'ἑαυτῷ παρθένον). Clearly, the family of Promotus remained prominent, and Eudoxia too belonged to the imperial orbit. For family properties in Constantinople and on the Bosporus see Janin, *Constantinople*,[2] p. 417, and Auson. *Ep.*9. 38–40 (*MGH: AA*, V: 2, 167); in general *PLRE*, I, 750–51, "Flavius Promotus."

19. Zos. 4. 51, Claud. *In Ruf.* A. 308–22, *De cons. Stil.* 1. 95–96, 102–4, 112–15.

20. Zos. 5. 1. 4, 3. 1(following Eunapius): τὰ περὶ τὴν βασιλέως κηδείαν ἐπραγματεύετο.

21. Zos. 5. 2; Alan Cameron, *Claudian*, p. 64; for chronology J.B. Bury, *History of the Later Roman Empire* (London, 1923), I, 109 n. 2.

22. *Infra*, n. 51.

fruit of passion than of political infighting, with the house of Promotus prominent in the tangle as well as Eutropius.[23]

The story also related the humiliation of Rufinus. Eutropius ordered the people of Constantinople to deck themselves with wreaths for an imperial wedding and dispatched palace guards with vestments and jewelry "fit for an emperor." Only when the procession halted before the house of Promotus, and Eudoxia instead of Rufinus' daughter received the wedding gifts, did the throngs of people learn that the prefect's hopes had been demolished. Whatever the truth of this story,[24] chronology alone suggests urgency and the weightiest political implications. Even the impending public funeral of the dynasty's founder did not postpone the celebration. Arcadius married Eudoxia on April 27, 395, more than seven months before the corpse of Theodosius had reached its place of rest in the Apostles Church of Constantinople.[25]

Admitted now to the palace as *basilis*, Eudoxia embraced the image of imperial womanhood proclaimed by Gregory of Nyssa.[26] No one could deny her commitment to childbearing, to Gregory's version of *philandria*. The first child appeared on June 17, 397, and was named Flaccilla, to stress the continuity of generations, no doubt, and enliven remembrance of her paternal grandmother.[27] Similarly, Pulcheria, born January 19, 399, would reincarnate the emperor's dead sister. In rapid succession came Arcadia, on April 3, 400, and on April 10, 401, after an even shorter interval, the expected heir, Theodosius II. Eudoxia bore her last child, Marina, on February 10, 403, but managed still another pregnancy. On October 6, 404, she died of a miscarriage perhaps brought on by the terror occasioned by a hailstorm. The woman had shared the bed of Arcadius for nine years and

---

23. *Supra,* n. 18.

24. Zos. 5. 3; cf. Claud. *Epith.* 23–27 for confirmation that the story circulated by 398. Alan Cameron, *Claudian,* p. 65, rightly finds it "a little too dramatic" but fails to exploit the Promotus connection (*supra,* n. 18).

25. *Chron. pasch. a.* 395 (pp. 565–66 Bonn), Soc. 6. 1. 4.

26. *Philanthropia* "for the least of these" may safely be assumed, though the only evidence I have found is Marc. Diac. *V. Porph.* 53 (ed. Grégoire-Kugener) reporting construction of a hospice for the homeless (ξενών) in Gaza and Joh. Chrys. *Hom. post redit.* 4 (*PG*, LII, 446) praising Eudoxia as "the beggars' staff and support" (τῶν πτωχῶν τὴν βακτηρίαν).

27. Thus Theodosius named his son Honorius for a dead brother: "addidit et proprio germana vocabula nato / quaque datur fratris speciem sibi reddit adempti": Claud. *Laus Ser.* 109–10.

five months, during at least six years of which she had carried the emperor's children.[28] A fecundity straining physiological limits accounted in part for Eudoxia's exceptional authority and for the stability of the dynasty.

Eudoxia likewise demonstrated *eusebeia* in the manner of Flaccilla, devoting her imperial resources to the victory of the dynastic faith. Although restricted now to churches in the suburbs, the Arians still attracted adherents with impressive antiphonal choruses and dawn processions through Constantinople on Saturdays, Sundays, and major festivals. The orthodox responded with similar display,[29] and attracted even greater numbers because the empress provided silver candlesticks in the shape of crosses, to make their processions more spectacular. One of her eunuchs organized the singing.

In his *Life of Porphyry*, the bishop of Gaza, Mark the Deacon, included a narrative which, if the truth can be extracted from it, casts further light on Eudoxia's dynastic brand of *eusebeia*. Porphyry traveled to Constantinople late in 400 with Mark himself and other holy men, to request that the government take action against paganism in Gaza and in particular that Arcadius order that the temple of Zeus Marnas there be destroyed. Porphyry and his colleagues gained an audience with the empress through Amantius, her chief eunuch (*castrensis*) and a "servant of God." Eudoxia agreed immediately, because these were holy men—and because they recognized the importance of imperial childbearing. As usual, she was pregnant. Giving her their blessing for the approaching birth, the holy men even promised a male child if Eudoxia would exert herself in their interest. According to Mark, "at these words the empress blushed with happiness, and her face took on more than its natural beauty." But Arcadius (or, rather, his advisers) remained adamant. The people of Gaza paid their taxes, so the government refused to take any action that might cause them to avoid their obligations.

Apparently, Bishop Porphyry was determined enough to cool his heels in Constantinople through all of 401, until the predicted birth of a son had strengthened his hold over Eudoxia and Eudoxia's over her husband. On the Epiphany feast, January 6, 402, the child

---

28. Seeck, *RE*, VI, 917 (sources); H. Grégoire and M.-A. Kugener, "Quand est né l'empereur Théodose II?" *Byzantion* 4 (1927–28), 337–48, on chronological problems raised by Marc. Diac. *V. Porph.* (*infra*, n. 31).

29. Soc. 6. 8. 1–9, Soz. 8. 8 adding that the orthodox continued the practice in his own day.

was baptized and Eudoxia contrived to get her way at last. As the imperial cortege left the church, Porphyry and his associates, instructed by the empress, brought a petition to the infant Theodosius and the man who bore him. Demanding silence, the bearer, who was in on the charade, glanced at the petition, raised the child's head with his hand, and proclaimed: "His majesty ordains that whatever is in this petition shall be granted." Those who observed prostrated themselves in wonder and congratulated Arcadius for his son's precocity—a welcome manifestation, since the infant was to receive the imperial distinction only four days later, on January 10, 402.[30] Arcadius soon discovered that his son had granted Porphyry's requests, but acquiesced because "the lady empress nagged him incessantly." Eudoxia herself then arranged for the holy men to consult with the *quaestor sacri palatii* and assist him in drafting appropriate legislation.[31]

Eudoxia next directed Amantius to find among the great men of Constantinople a "zealous Christian" to execute the law. Amantius selected Cynegius, a *clarissimus* and member of the *consistorium* (imperial advisory council). Plausibly identified as a son or close relative of Maternus Cynegius,[32] he certainly lived up to his namesake's reputation. Eudoxia herself commissioned him to "demolish to their foundations all temples of idols," so Cynegius brought to Gaza troops which he employed to intimidate the pagan populace, to keep

30. Marcell. com. *a.* 402. 2 (*MGH: AA*, XI, 67), *Chron. pasch. a.* 402 (p. 568 Bonn), specifying the Hebdomon tribunal as the place of elevation and that Theodosius II received the distinction from his father.

31. Marc. Diac. *V. Porph.* 33–50 (ed. Grégoire-Kugener). This narrative contains embarrassing inaccuracies. Mark (c. 46) dates the baptism within days of Theodosius' birth on April 10, 401, but Grégoire and Kugener, "Quand est né," p. 348, argue for January 6, 402, and a new text published by Wenger, "Notes inédites," pp. 51–54, proves their thesis. On the other hand, the narrative contains enough circumstantial detail and contemporary language to permit confidence in its basic authenticity, e.g., that the "command" of the infant Theodosius, four days before his elevation, lacked the force of law and needed to be incorporated into an imperial constitution (θεῖον γράμμα) issued in the name of Arcadius and Honorius (ἐξ ὀνομάτων τῶν δύο βασιλέων, c. 50). I accept in general the conclusions Grégoire and Kugener reach in their edition (Paris, 1930), introduction, pp. vii–lxxxix—that Mark, a contemporary, composed an account from his own eyewitness which a later "remanieur" expanded somewhat and dramatized, introducing chronological inaccuracies. The identity of the "great man" (εἷς τῶν μεγιστάνων) who carried Theodosius II in the baptismal procession is a mystery, but the enigmatic Count John is a good guess (*infra*, p. 64 with n. 68).

32. Marc. Diac. *V. Porph.* 51, 54; J. F.-M. Marique, "A Spanish Favorite of Theodosius the Great," *Classical Folia* 17 (1963), 60–61; Matthews, *Aristocracies*, pp. 142–43, calling the identification "inevitable"; *PLRE*, II, 331, "Cynegius 2."

a modicum of order, and to join Porphyry and his followers in destroying the temple of Marnas.[33] On its ruins Porphyry built a great Christian basilica, in fulfillment of a vow Eudoxia had made during her pregnancy in order to give substance to her prayers for a male child. The empress funded this project generously and dispatched an imperial messenger from Constantinople with a ground-plan for the church's construction. As work progressed she also provided thirty-two monolithic columns of Carystian marble; the entire Christian community of Gaza, men and women, young and old, joined enthusiastically in transporting them from the port to the site. When the church was completed, two years after Eudoxia's death, Porphyry dedicated it *Eudoxianē* in her memory.[34] The episode demonstrates that an empress could rally support even in distant provinces for herself and for the dynastic faith.

Between 400 and early 402,[35] presumably during one of the intervals when Eudoxia was not pregnant, the people of Constantinople participated with her in an equally intense demonstration of enthusiasm for the holy bones of martyrs:

For as the swelling waters are not contained within their own spaces but burst forth and flow freely, so does the grace of the Spirit which rests in the bones and inhabits the saints go forth into those who pursue it with faith.[36]

Like the exact date of the demonstration, the identity of the martyrs is unknown. From a temporary deposit in the Great Church of Constantinople their bones were brought to the martyr chapel of St. Thomas at Drypia—a suburb nine miles from the city[37]—translated in a nocturnal procession of the faithful carrying candles and torches so numerous that they evoked for St. John Chrysostom a sea of fire.

33. Marc. Diac. *V. Porph.* 63, 65, 69–70. Jerome *Comm. in Isaiam* 7. 17 (*PL*, XXIV, 241) confirms the destruction and the building of a church on the ruins. Cf. G. Armstrong, "Fifth and Sixth Century Church Building in the Holy Land," *Greek Orthodox Theological Review* 14 (1969), 17–18.

34. Marc. Diac. *V. Porph.* 43, 53, 75, 78, 84, 92.

35. Limits provided by the elevations of Eudoxia on January 9, 400 (*infra*, p. 65) and of Theodosius II on January 10, 402. In the sermon to be discussed, John Chrysostom evokes Eudoxia wearing the diadem, an indication that she was Augusta at the time, but does not mention Theodosius, who as Augustus would have figured somehow in the episode.

36. Joh. Chrys. *Hom. 2 cum imperatrix media nocte in magnam ecclesiam venisset . . .* , *PG*, LXIII, 469.

37. Janin, *Constantinople²*, p. 445; *idem, La géographie ecclésiastique de l'Empire byzantin*, pt. I, vol. III: *Les églises et les monastères*, 2nd ed. (Paris, 1969), pp. 251–52.

Enthroned as bishop of Constantinople a few years earlier (February 26, 398), John had already acquired a following through eloquent preaching (thus his name "with mouth of gold").[38] On the day following the procession, when the relics had reached their destination, in St. Thomas' *martyrium* he spoke with characteristic verve of communal piety and Eudoxia's part in generating it.[39]

The road was long, Chrysostom said, and the exertion considerable, yet the people of Constantinople turned out with one purpose —monks, nuns, and priests, ordinary laboring men both slave and free, rulers and ruled, rich and poor, citizens and homeless strangers. Women "softer than wax" emerged from their usual seclusion, and high officials abandoned their carriages and bodyguards to mix with the ordinary folk.

But why speak of women or magistrates when she who wears the diadem and purple mantle would not abide the slightest separation from the relics through the whole distance but attended the saints like a handmaid (*therapainis*), clinging to the relic box and to the linen that covered it? . . . Through the whole distance they saw her, holding tightly to the bones, not flagging or giving in to her weariness.

"Although even eunuchs who haunt the palace courts may not always catch sight of this woman," unexpectedly the entire city saw her now shining amid the throngs like the moon amid the stars. Unexpectedly also, her brilliance was not that of human vanity, for she had cast off emperorship and diadem and exchanged the purple for the mantle of humility (*tapeinophrosynē*).

But does the moon really shine with such brilliance as one so exalted but who yet possesses the ornament of such faith? Which should one rather admire? Her zeal hotter than fire? Her faith tougher than steel? The contrition of her spirit? This humility, which has obscured that of the rest?

For John Chrysostom the figure of Eudoxia displayed the manner in which the community as a whole should respond to the translation of relics. "Schoolmistress [*didaskalos*] for the employment of fair and spiritual merchandise, she teaches all to draw from a well that is always brimming and never runs dry." His imagery acquired its force from the radical nature of Eudoxia's humility, from the same exalted

---

38. In general, P. Chrysostomus Baur, *Der heilige Johannes Chrysostomus und seine Zeit*, 2 vols. (Munich, 1929–30), esp. I, 166–212, II, 72–83, on his preaching. Soc. 6. 2. 11 gives the date of his enthronement; cf. *infra*, pp. 69–78.
39. Joh. Chrys. *op. cit.*, *PG*, LXIII, 467–72.

tapeinophrosynē included by Gregory of Nyssa among Flaccilla's imperial virtues.

Of course, John Chrysostom's interpretation of Eudoxia's conduct need not have corresponded exactly with that of the court. As in the Porphyry episode, she exerted herself not only for the faith but for the dynasty identified with it. Mass participation publicized Eudoxia's physical association with potent relics, and like the outpouring of grief at the funeral of an imperial child riveted attention on the domestic side of the *basileía*. Near the conclusion of his sermon Chrysostom added details that lend color to these observations.[40] Arcadius attended neither the procession nor the gathering at St. Thomas' in Drypia, because the horses and armed men which always accompanied him might have "caused injury to the maidens and to the older men and women, and would have brought the festival into confusion." Surrounded by the accouterments of magisterial power, the emperor would have introduced an ambivalence into the desired bond between dynasty and city. "Thus today we see the Christ-loving empress with the *polis*," Chrysostom explains, "tomorrow the God-loving emperor in presence with his army." Chrysostom also admitted that Eudoxia had planned it this way. "With characteristic sagacity" she orchestrated her own appearance while instructing her husband to stay home.[41]

Eudoxia's "sagacity" and the determination she used to get her way for Porphyry indicate that she was an astute politician and an imperious woman. These qualities did not enter the traditional portrait of Flaccilla, presumably because the imperiousness of Theodosius left little room for them, perhaps also because court image-makers did not choose them for exhibition. Contemporaries did recognize imperiousness in Eudoxia, however, and at least one of them found it reprehensible, an un-Roman "insolence" less suited to a *basilis* than to a barbarian queen.[42] During the troubled years of Eudoxia's career,

40. *Ibid.*, col. 472.
41. ἀλλὰ καὶ τοῦτο τῆς σῆς ἐγένετο συνέσεως, τὸ κατασχεῖν αὐτὸν σήμερον οἴκοι, καὶ εἰς τὴν αὔριον ὑποσχέσθαι τὴν παρουσίαν. . . . ἄξια τῆς ἑαυτῆς συνέσεως ποιοῦσα διενείματο τὴν πανήγυριν. Arcadius did appear the next day with his guard to attend a service but did not stay for Chrysostom's sermon: *Hom. 3 insequenti die adveniente imperatore in martyrium*, PG, LXIII, 473.
42. Philostorg. 11. 6: τὸ δὲ γύναιον οὐ κατὰ τὴν τοῦ ἀνδρὸς διέκειτο νωθείαν, ἀλλ'ἐνῆν αὐτῇ τοῦ βαρβαρικοῦ θράσους οὐκ ὀλίγον.

success in court politics depended to a remarkable extent upon one's reaction to her imperiousness and ability to cope with it.

These years were troubled indeed. In 395 Huns from north of the Black Sea transversed the Caucasus and devastated the Roman Orient, terrifying even St. Jerome in Bethlehem.[43] Rumors surfaced of impending hostilities with Persia, Rome's powerful antagonist to the east. Of greater weight for the eastern *basileía*, the risky side of Theodosius' Gothic policy became evident shortly after his death, when the *foederati* he had employed at the Frigidus revolted under the Visigothic chief Alaric and began destructive wanderings in both East and West which were to culminate in the sack of Rome in 410. Weightier still, Stilicho exploited these crises to exert his claim of *parentela* over Arcadius as well as Honorius, interference which the equally ambitious Rufinus and his successors in the East naturally could not tolerate. Whatever the motives,[44] Stilicho's policy led to the divergence between East and West which Emilienne Demougeot recognized as the major historical trend of the period.[45]

The first victim was Rufinus. Stilicho had marched eastward and surrounded Alaric's camp in the plain of Thessaly. A dispatch arrived from the court of Arcadius ordering him to give up eastern troops still included in his army from the Frigidus campaign and to abandon Thessaly and the strategic prefecture of Illyricum, which belonged to the eastern government.[46] Stilicho obeyed, implicitly accepting a

43. See now Maenchen-Helfen, *Huns*, pp. 51–59; Jerome *Epp*. 60. 16. 5, 77. 8 (III, 106–7, IV, 48–49 Labourt).

44. I find most attractive the thesis of S. Mazzarino, *Stilicone* (Rome, 1942), that Stilicho worked against *eastern* separatism to uphold the Theodosian notion of imperial unity: "Egli è, appunto, l'ultimo uomo di questo mondo *imperiale ed universalistico*. . . . Stilicone sostiene, in questa lotta di due mondi che solo ora si riconoscono antitetici, la continuazione di una politica unitaria e tradizionalistica. . . . Nella grande trasformazione, Stilicone volle restare fermo alle formule teodosiane . . ." (pp. 317, 322–23). His policy had the opposite of its desired effect.

45. Demougeot, *Division*, esp. her conclusions, pp. 487–570.

46. Claud. *In Ruf*. 2. 161–63, 169–70, 195–96, identifying Rufinus as author of the dispatch. A number of scholars—e.g., E. Stein, "Untersuchungen zur spätrömischen Verwaltungsgeschichte," *Rh. Mus*. 74 (1925), 347–54; *idem, Histoire*, I, 229; J. W. E. Pearce, "Gold Coinage of the Reign of Theodosius I," *Num. Chron*. ser. 5, 18 (1938), 229–42; Demougeot, *Division*, pp. 144–45, 149; and Lippold, *RE*, suppl. XII (1973), 913, "Theodosius I"—have argued that when Theodosius I died the entire prefecture belonged to the West, but a perceptive reading of Claudian has proved otherwise; see R.P.V. Grumel, "L'Illyricum de la mort de Valentinien Ier (375) à la mort de Stilicon (408)," *REB* 9 (1951), 23–34, effectively supported by Alan Cameron, *Claudian*, pp. 59–62.

territorial division between the two *partes imperii* which, with one significant modification, was to endure.[47] But to command the troops recalled by Arcadius he sent Gaïnas, a trusted subordinate of Gothic race. On November 27, 395, Rufinus appeared with Arcadius at the Hebdomon to receive the returning army. As Rufinus passed among the troops, they cut him to pieces before the eyes of the emperor.[48]

Incredibly, the government of the East now fell to Eutropius, the elderly palace eunuch who had helped to contrive Eudoxia's marriage. His origins were base, probably servile and "barbarian" (Persian or Armenian) rather than Roman. The trauma of castration and a lifetime of hormonal imbalance and social abuse must have affected his character as well as his body.[49] Indeed, his qualifications for office were precisely the opposite of those traditionally expected. As M.K. Hopkins put it, to grasp the anomalous potency of such political eunuchs one need only "imagine the horror with which a blue-blooded aristocrat must have approached such tainted upstarts to beg for favours."[50]

A eunuch drew his potency from the emperor alone, and it always remained contingent upon the emperor who placed him in office. The repulsive deformity of eunuchs discouraged great men from cooperating with them to control the monarchy, just as it prevented eunuchs (unlike Stilicho and Rufinus, for example) from seeking independent stature through *kedeia*, an imperial marriage connection. Yet as *praepositus sacri cubiculi* a eunuch not only

47. In 396 the East gave western Illyricum to Stilicho, but retained the dioceses of Macedonia and Dacia as its Illyrian prefecture; see Claud. *De cons. Mall. Theod.* 200–206; Grumel, "Illyricum," pp. 32–34; Alan Cameron, *Claudian*, p. 61; and cf. Dagron, *Naissance*, p. 72, on the importance of the division.

48. Claud. *In Ruf.* 2. 278–439 ("a dramatic masterpiece": Alan Cameron, *Claudian*, p. 89); Soc. 6. 1. 4–5 for the date; and the other sources cited by Demougeot, *Division*, pp. 155–56. Following the principle *cui bono*, Cameron (pp. 90–92) makes Eutropius responsible, not Stilicho.

49. Claud. *In Eutr.* 1. 24–109 on Eutropius' origins, 110–37 on his physical deformity, no doubt exaggerating freely. Without much danger of hyperbole Alan Cameron, *Claudian*, p. 126, calls *In Eutropium* "the cruellest invective in all ancient literature," but Claudian's invective does reveal the reasons for the common prejudice; see esp. M.K. Hopkins, "Eunuchs in Politics in the Later Roman Empire," *Proceedings of the Cambridge Philological Society* n.s., 9 (1963), 62–80, and *idem*, *Conquerors and Slaves* (Cambridge, 1978), pp. 172–96, on whom my interpretation depends; also J.E. Dunlap, *The Office of the Grand Chamberlain in the Later Roman and Byzantine Empires*, University of Michigan Studies in the Humanities, vol. XIV (New York and London, 1924), pp. 178–223; and W. Ensslin, *RE*, suppl. VIII (1956), 556–67, "Praepositus sacri cubiculi."

50. "Eunuchs," p. 79.

profited personally from continuous access to the emperor's person but regulated the access of others. When great men kowtowed to a eunuch to gain access, they also learned something of the distance that separated them from the eunuch's master. Even if a great man had advanced from the ordinary senatorial rank of *clarissimus* to the brilliant eminence of the *illustris*—a title reserved for a select inner circle of high officeholders and counts—he could still claim no more than this creature of the emperor, who by the end of the fourth century likewise ranked as *illustris*. Thus, if a eunuch operated skillfully and retained the emperor's confidence, he could exercise real power.

In the years that followed the Hebdomon murder, Eutropius did enjoy the confidence of Arcadius[51] and used it to master the eastern court.[52] Under his influence the emperor dismissed and exiled Timasius and Abundantius, the last Roman *magistri militum* from the previous reign surviving in the East. Eutropius probably replaced one of them with the Goth Gaïnas, whose emergence thus hints at collusion between the eunuch and Stilicho in the death of Rufinus.[53] But the western generalissimo soon found Eutropius no less determined than his predecessor to remain independent. When Stilicho appeared a second time in the Balkans to defend the Empire against Alaric (early 397), the eastern government not only ordered him to withdraw but declared him a public enemy. In the summer of 398 Eutropius himself took the field in the Empire's defense and managed a significant victory in Armenia over Huns and other marauders. When he returned, Constantinople saluted him with a victory celebration. Statues in his image went up before the senate house, along the thoroughfares, and throughout the East,[54] and Arcadius decorated

51. In general, Eunap. frgg. 69, 74 (*FHG*, IV, 44, 46–47); Zos. 5. 8. 1, 11. 1, 14. 1; Pall. *Dial.* 5 (pp. 29–30 Coleman-Norton); Claud. *In Eutr.* 1. 170–81, 2. 58–83, 549–50. In 399 Arcadius wept when the soldiers attempted to seize Eutropius: Joh. Chrys. *De capt. Eutr.* 1 (*PG*, LII, 397).

52. For detailed discussion (with sources) see *PLRE*, II, 440–41, "Eutropius 1," and esp. Mazzarino, *Stilicone*, pp. 196–217, and Demougeot, *Division*, pp. 158–94, 220–32; also Alan Cameron, *Claudian*, pp. 124–49, on the poem *In Eutropium*.

53. *Supra*, n. 48. Demandt, *RE*, suppl. XII (1970), 732–34, "Magister Militum," and *PLRE*, I, 379, "Gaïnas," make Gaïnas only *comes rei militaris* from 385 to 399. I take Zos. 5. 13. 1, οὔτε τῆς πρεπούσης στρατηγῷ τιμῆς ἀξιούμενος, to mean that Gaïnas broke with Eutropius in 399 because he did not enjoy the prerogatives and influence on policy that a *magister militum* expected.

54. Claud. *In Eutr.* 1. 254–58, 2. 70–83; *CTh* 9. 40. 14; on statuary and the senate house *supra*, p. 41 and *infra*, p. 97.

him with the highest honors—the distinction *patricius*[55] and the consulship for 399.

Then the troubles mounted. The western government naturally would not accept the prodigy of a eunuch consul—"omnia cesserunt eunucho consule monstra"[56]—but the resistance of great men in the East was of more consequence. Eutropius had taken a hard line in enforcing the court's authority over them, while his efforts to finance strong government through confiscations and "sale of offices"[57] confirmed the impression of eunuch rapacity. Thus "the senatorial class unanimously loathed this wretched state of affairs."[58] Nature conspired also, it appears, to protect 399 from the disgrace of an eponymous eunuch. As the consulship approached, an earthquake struck Constantinople causing flooding and fires, rumors of plague, showers of stones and blood, and heavenly conflagrations which drove the people from the city in another furor of penitence.[59] This must have unnerved Arcadius and especially Eudoxia, who was late in her second pregnancy and faced childbirth under such ominous circumstances. Then in the spring of the fateful year more Gothic *foederati* revolted in Phrygia, and when Gaïnas was ordered out to pacify them he supported the demand of their chief Tribigild that Eutropius be removed.

Even so, the decisive stroke came from the empress. In July, 399, Eudoxia approached Arcadius with her daughers Flaccilla and Pulcheria, now six months old, in her arms. The eunuch had threatened to send her away, she claimed, "lamenting like a woman and holding her babies out to her husband." Arcadius dismissed Eutropius at once. "Compassion entered him for his children, as they cried

55. The distinction evoked kinship and paternalism toward the emperor and court, as Claudian ironically suggests, *In Eutr.* 2. 68–69: ". . . genitorque vocatur/ principis et famulum dignatur regina patrem." Cf. Jones, *Later Roman Empire*, I, 106, III, 155 n. 28 (omitting Eutropius); and T.D. Barnes, "*Patricii* under Valentinian III," *Phoenix* 29 (1975), 169 (including him among only six *patricii* "indubitably attested before 400").

56. Claud. *In Eutr.* 1. 8.

57. On "venal *suffragium*" see *infra*, p. 100 with n. 97.

58. Zos. 5. 13. 1, also Joh. Ant. frg. 189 (*FHG*, IV, 610), both reflecting Eunapius.

59. Claud. *In Eutr.* 1. 1–7, 2. 24–46, Philostorg. 11. 7 linked by Seeck, *Geschichte*, V, 305–6, 563 *ad* 305. 17, with Marcell. com. *a*. 396. 3 (*MGH: AA*, XI, 64), *Chron. gall. a*. 452 33 (*ibid*., IX, 650), and Aug. *De excidio urbis Romae sermo* 7–8 (ed. O'Reilly). Cf. J. Hubaux, "La crise de la trois cent soixante cinquième année," *Antiquité classique* 17 (1948), 343–54.

loudly with concern for their mother.''⁶⁰ The moral requirements of *kedeia* and hopes for the dynasty's future weighed far more heavily than the services of a talented official, and Eudoxia understood how to impress the importance of these matters upon her husband, as in the Porphyry episode. Asylum in the church of John Chrysostom rescued Eutropius from the aroused people and troops, but he was later recalled from exile on Cyprus, tried on a specious charge, and beheaded.

In *De providentia* or the *Egyptian Tale*, written in 400, about a year after the fall of Eutropius, Synesius of Cyrene described allegorically the conflict that raged in the intervening period between virtue and evil, embodied in Osiris and Typho, two brothers who competed for rule of Thebes and the Egyptians. Properly interpreted, Egypt was the eastern Roman Empire, and the "brothers" must have been Aurelian and Eutychian.⁶¹ Already powerful in the previous reign, the latter had advanced to the praetorian prefecture of the East under Eutropius, but lost that office with the eunuch's fall.⁶² City prefect of Constantinople, 393–94,⁶³ Aurelian's next political exploits were acquisition of the prized eastern prefecture in succession to Eutychian (summer of 399) and presidency of the tribunal that condemned Eutropius.⁶⁴ In the autumn (September or so) Arcadius designated him consul for 400.

60. Philostorg. 11. 6, also Soc. 6. 2. 7 reporting that Arcadius condemned Eutropius διά τινα πταίσματα and Soz. 8. 7. 3 that he fell to an aulic conspiracy, ὡς εἰς τὴν βασιλέως γαμετὴν ὑβρίσας ἐπιβουλευθείς; Demougeot, *Division*, p. 229.

61. O. Seeck, "Studien zu Synesius," *Philologus* 52 (1894), 450–54, identifies Typho with Caesarius, PPO *Or.* 395–97, 400–403 (*PLRE*, I, 171, "Fl. Caesarius 6''), and most scholars have followed him in reconstructing the Gothic crisis of 399–400, e.g., Mazzarino, *Stilicone*, pp. 206–26, and Demougeot, *Division*, pp. 236–66 (the fullest discussion, with sources). A. H. M. Jones, "Collegiate Prefectures," *JRS* 54 (1964), 78–89, not only demolishes the theory of collegiate prefectures, which "reached their zenith under Seeck," but demonstrates (pp. 79–81) that the succession of prefects known from dated laws in the codes can be fitted most readily into the *De providentia* if Typho is equated with Eutychian, PPO *Or.* 397–99, 399–400, 404–5 (*PLRE*, I, 319–21, "Flavius Eutychianus 5''). My reconstruction rests on Jones and his chronology.

62. *PLRE*, I, 319–21, for Eutychian's career, including the identification with Typho (accepted also by Dagron, *Naissance*, p. 204 n. 4). His consanguinity with Aurelian / Osiris, known only from the *De providentia*, may well have been part of the allegory. The imperatives of *kedeia* would have inhibited such a tangle between blood brothers. *PLRE*, I, 1146, stemma 28 requires modification.

63. *PLRE*, I, 128–29, "Aurelianus 3," for his career.

64. Philostorg. 11. 6.

Thus far Synesius' conflict between virtue and evil looks suspiciously like normal maneuvering for advancement among ambitious men. Aurelian temporarily had the upper hand, but his rival could muster formidable allies. No less disenchanted with the new government than with its predecessor, Gaïnas threw in with Tribigild's revolt and marched toward Constantinople. When he reached Chalcedon (about November) Eutychian slipped across the Propontis to join him.[65] Together they required Arcadius to parley in the church of St. Euphemia near Chalcedon and to cooperate with them in overthrowing Aurelian. The prefect himself was handed over, threatened with execution, then exiled, as were his associates Count John and Saturninus.[66] Once again praetorian prefect of the East, Eutychian established a military regime backed by Gaïnas, who now entered Constantinople with his largely Gothic army.

Aurelian also had formidable backing. His presidency of the Eutropius tribunal and succession to the prefecture already hint at collusion with the empress, but the suspicions are more solidly founded. Among those with a hold over Eudoxia were two distinguished matrons of Constantinople, Marsa, the widow of Promotus, who had presumably mothered the empress, and her friend Castricia, the wife of Saturninus.[67] The enigmatic Count John frequented the palace with such incautious intimacy that gossip made him the father of Eudoxia's child.[68] Acquainted with his opposition, Eutychian had known where to strike. With Count John, Saturninus, and Aurelian under their

65. Syn. *De prov.* 1. 15 (p. 101 Terzaghi).
66. Zos. 5. 18. 6–8 (Eunapius); Soc. 6. 6. 8–12; Soz. 8. 4. 4–5; Joh. Chrys. *Hom cum Sat. et Aur. acti ess. in exil.*, title, *PG*, LII, 413. Only Zosimus mentions Count John, perhaps because it was his influence with the empress (*infra*) that prompted Eutychian and Gaïnas to demand his extradition. The fact offered an embarrassing glimpse into contemporary *arcana imperii* which Chrysostom and the ecclesiastical historians would have suppressed (Demougeot, *Division*, p. 251 n. 86).
67. Pall. *Dial.* 4 (p. 25 Coleman-Norton), also 8 (p. 45), for Chrysostom's censure of Eugraphia and other women of the group who did not conduct themselves as proper widows but primped excessively and affected elaborate hairdos. This censure was part of a sermon Chrysostom delivered against Eudoxia's circle in 403: *infra*, p. 73 with n. 102.
68. Zos. 5. 18. 8. On the dangers of such intimacy and the inevitable rumors cf. the Honoria episode of 434 and the fate of Paulinus in 443/44 (*infra*, pp. 193–94). The synod of The Oak in 403 (*infra*, p. 74) accused John Chrysostom of denouncing John during the revolt of the soldiers, i.e., to Gaïnas in 399–400: Phot. *Bibl.* cod. 59 (I, 53 Henry). He retained his influence even after Eudoxia's death, if he was the man "to whom the emperor's ears are open, who moreover can employ the [emperor's] will however he wishes" mentioned Syn. *Ep.* 110 (dated summer, 405: Seeck, "Studien," pp. 473, 483). Cf. *PLRE*, II, 593–94, "Ioannes 1."

control and the threat of death, Eutychian and Gaïnas would not expect Eudoxia to exert her power against them.

On January 9, 400, a month or two after Gaïnas had seized control of Constantinople, Eudoxia received the rank Augusta.[69] The sources give no details, but her elevation, like that of Flaccilla, was probably conducted in a court setting, with the Augustus himself presenting the *paludamentum* of purple and the imperial diadem. Like Gregory of Nyssa, John Chrysostom considered these to be the primary insignia of an Augusta, declaring (as was observed earlier) that Eudoxia cast them off to display her humility when she followed the bones of saints. From her elevation in 400 until her death in 404, again as in the case of Flaccilla, Constantinople and other eastern mints struck coins of Eudoxia in gold, silver, and bronze.[70] Figure 7 presents a beautiful specimen, a solidus from Constantinople now in the collection of Dumbarton Oaks. Obverse and reverse repeat the main type of Flaccilla (fig. 6), including on the obverse the same costume of an Augusta—here with a pearl-bordered diadem—and the characteristic legend AELIA EVDO—XIA AVG(VSTA). Since the *nomen* Aelia probably did not come to Eudoxia from a family connection with Flaccilla or from aristocratic Spanish extraction, it must have been regarded by contemporaries as a dynastic title of female distinction. Ceremonial and costume, coin legends and iconography thus suggest continuity with Theodosian precedent, and that the eastern court purposely evoked an established image of female rule when it advertised the elevation of Eudoxia.

There were also important elements of innovation. On the obverses of Eudoxia's coins, a disembodied hand reaches down from above to crown her head with a wreath. This hand is readily identifiable as the *dextera Dei*, the right hand of God known in Jewish iconography as early as the third century and in the fourth and early fifth from a few representations in Christian art.[71] The motif also

---

69. *Chron. pasch. a.* 400 (p. 567 Bonn): ἡ ἐπιφανεστάτη Εὐδοξία ἐπήρθη Αὔγουστα.

70. I.I. Tolstoi, *Monnaies byzantines,* I (St. Petersburg, 1912), pp. 46–51, nos. 136–40, 142–53 (nos. 135 and 141 belong to Licinia Eudoxia, *infra,* pp. 129, 183); J.P.C. Kent and R.A.G. Carson, *Late Roman Bronze Coinage* (London, 1960), nos. 2217–20, 2442–45, 2586–89, 2797–2800, 2919.

71. A. Alföldi, "Insignien," pp. 55–56 (= *Repräsentation,* pp. 173–74), suggests a pagan origin for the iconography; J.D. MacIsaac, "'The Hand of God,'" *Traditio* 31 (1975), 322–28, stresses Jewish and Christian parallels. The evidence is too slight to permit a decision.

belonged to the repertoire of coin designers as early as 333. A well-known medallion of Constantius II shows, on its reverse, his father Constantine crowned by a hand which emerges from a cloud above.[72] In the fourth century, however, the *dextera Dei* was conspicuously infrequent in numismatic art. Its blatant monotheism offended conservative opinion, no doubt, but it also detracted from the main official line—that an Augustus received his power directly from the troops. For this reason imperial image-makers had found it appropriate for the earliest obverses of Arcadius, struck following his elevation at the unwarlike age of seven, when it must have seemed wise to emphasize the alternative theory that his *basileía* was of divine origin,[73] and thus the image-makers adopted it for Eudoxia's obverses as well. A woman's *basileía* could have nothing to do with the troops and might best receive sanction and permanence from the ideology of divine kingship. Comparison with the earliest Arcadius obverses also suggests that the *dextera Dei* on Eudoxia's coins should be interpreted specifically as commentary on her elevation. Arcadius conferred the *paludamentum* and diadem, but those who handled Eudoxia's coins were to recognize her coronation as an act of transcendence. Eudoxia, therefore, was *a Deo coronata*.[74] The coins prove that on this occasion ideologues of the eastern court conceived the sacral *basileía* of empresses.

A few years later the western court, still under the influence of Stilicho and still at odds with the East, directed a peevish letter to Arcadius.[75] In it Honorius scolded his brother for another "innovation," the transmission of Eudoxia's official images (*laureatae*) throughout the provinces, where, like those of an Augustus, they were to be received joyously by the people in response to her elevation and as a celebration of her new *basileía*.[76] With verbosity typical of the court style, Honorius spoke of "voices raised in objection around the world" and admonished his brother to stop the practice, "allowing zealous gossip to die away and giving the public tongue

---

72. F. Gnecchi, *I medaglioni romani*, I (Milan, 1912), pl. 12; J.M.C. Toynbee, *Roman Medallions*, American Numismatic Society: Numismatic Studies no. 5 (New York, 1944), p. 198.

73. *RIC*, IX, 153. 33, 183. 45a–b, 195. 12, 197. 22, 226. 53a–b, 233. 80, 257. 26, 260. 41, 281. 41b, 291. 60, 300. 7, 302. 16; *supra*, p. 29, n. 85.

74. Ensslin, *Gottkaiser*, p. 55, comments on the Constantius medallion: "Das ist der Sinnfällige Ausdruck dafür, dass die Kaisergewalt von Gott verliehen und der Kaiser *a deo coronatus* ist. . . ."

75. *Coll. Avell.* 38. 1 (*CSEL*, XXXV: 1, 85); Kruse, *Geltung des Kaiserbildes*, pp. 31–32.

76. Kruse, *Geltung des Kaiserbildes*, pp. 23–50.

nothing to complain of in the customs of our time." Apparently *laureatae* of Eudoxia had reached Italy and the western court, where this manifestation of her power did not sit well with the ruling circles. The letter reveals also that assimilation of an Augusta with her male counterparts had advanced in the East, where court ideologues not only conceived the sacral *basileía* of empresses but meant that it be taken seriously.

The coronation of Eudoxia on January 9, 400, and associated ideological innovations may strike modern observers as puzzling. At the time she had produced two daughters and carried a third child of unknown sex, but unlike Flaccilla's at the time of her coronation, Eudoxia's childbearing had not yet provided an heir, much less one raised to imperial distinction. Previous scholarship has linked Eudoxia's coronation with Aurelian and his associates, but chronology forbids a direct connection.[77] Her friends were in exile, while Gaïnas occupied Constantinople and Eutychian headed a government whose views on female *basileía*, if anything, agreed with those of the western court. Initiative for the coronation may therefore have come from Eudoxia herself and her familiar imperiousness. She may have arranged her own promotion in order that she might resist more effectively the revolt of Gaïnas and Eutychian.

A glance at the revolt's denouement and the reaction to it reinforces this supposition. Gaïnas held the dynastic city with his mainly Gothic army for more than six months, until a popular uprising put an end to his occupation. The Goths' Arian heresy and their habitual looting irritated the people of Constantinople and eventually induced them to arm themselves. On the night of June 11, 400, Gaïnas left the city, ostensibly to escape the tension and calm his nerves. His men naturally assumed that he was abandoning them, and as they crowded through the gates in pursuit, the aroused population slaughtered many. After another defeat at the Hellespont, Gaïnas escaped across the Danube, where a Hun chief named Uldin struck off his head.[78]

In his allegorical *De providentia*, Synesius of Cyrene interpreted these dramatic events as that final destruction of evil which enabled Osiris/Aurelian to return and institute praiseworthy reforms. De-

---

77. Jones' chronology (*supra*, n. 61) refutes, e.g., Seeck, *Geschichte*, V, 317–18; Mazzarino, *Stilicone*, p. 216; Demougeot, *Division*, p. 245.

78. See Demougeot, *Division*, pp. 252–62, for a detailed account (with sources).

pendence on barbarians ended, Synesius maintained, and Aurelian began recruiting Roman troops to replace them.[79] Convinced by Synesius, and reading into his allegory more recent modes of political action, scholars have interpreted Aurelian's return as the triumph of a nationalist, anti-barbarian "party" whose adherents may be easily recognized among the correspondents of Synesius.[80] But it is doubtful whether such a coalition existed, or that the word "party" should be applied to fashionable literary and philosophical interchange among like-minded men. In Constantinople, politics centered on the court. As the conflict between Aurelian and his rival made abundantly clear, political ends could be achieved only by controlling the emperor.

No convincing evidence exists that the sentiments of Synesius motivated either Arcadius or Eudoxia (or, for that matter, Aurelian and his friends). Following Theodosian precedent, the eastern court relied in the crisis on trustworthy soldiers of whatever nationality.[81] For the emperor and his consort the real issue was dynastic security and independence. Gaïnas and Eutychian had humiliated Arcadius, and they had offended Eudoxia gravely when they forced the emperor to hand over her friends. For more than six months the revolt of Gaïnas inhibited the two rulers, until it succumbed to a popular uprising. Perhaps that uprising was connected not only with popular irritation but also with the desperate situation of the eastern court.

79. Syn. *De prov.* 1. 15 (p. 98 Terzaghi). O. Seeck, *RE,* II (1896), 1151, "Arkadios 2," observed an absence of German names among officers attested later in the reign of Arcadius. This may indicate an antibarbarian reaction *after* the Gaïnas rebellion, as might well be expected, but proves nothing regarding Aurelian's motives in 399.

80. C. Zakrzewski, *Le parti théodosien et son antithèse,* Eus supplementa vol. XVIII (Lvov, 1931), pp. 56–131, presents an extravagant version, but the view has long been *communis opinio* (e.g., Seeck, Stein, Mazzarino, Demougeot). For Aurelian's supposed "partisans" see esp. C. Lacombrade, *Synésios de Cyrène, hellène et chrétien* (Paris, 1951), pp. 84–130; and Demougeot, *Division,* p. 237. Saturninus, necessarily a major antibarbarian "partisan," had earlier been an architect of the Theodosian Gothic settlement in 382, whence the barbarian "problem" took its roots (Them. *Or.* 16. 208b–209d, 210d), while both Eutychian and Caesarius held the praetorian prefecture during the period 400–405, when the supposed "antibarbarian party" was in power (*PLRE,* I, 171, 320). Neither, therefore, would be a good candidate for chief of an opposing "party" if the term is to have any sense at all. Dagron, *Naissance,* pp. 204–6, expresses justified suspicions, but his theory of a "«parti» sénatorial" is likewise misleading. As Dagron himself admits, "le débat devise aussi bien le sénat lui-même."

81. Thus Fravitta *magister militum* defeated Gaïnas on the Hellespont in late 400 and was rewarded with the consulship for 401: *PLRE,* I, 372–73, "Flavius Fravitta."

The coronation of Eudoxia, January 9, 400, may best be interpreted as the court's response to the Gothic occupation of Constantinople. As an Augusta, Eudoxia would bring new resources to the
struggle from the domestic side of the *basileía,* and she could therefore
rouse the people of Constantinople more effectively against her
enemies. To buttress Eudoxia's authority, imperial mints evoked a
transcendent source. When the victory had been won, official propaganda did not attribute it to the popular disturbances that had plagued
Gaïnas or to a "party" among the great men, but to the same *dextera
Dei* that crowns Eudoxia on her coins, this time, however, seen
emerging from a cloud to "drive off the barbarians," who "fled
before God." This was the occasion on which a city prefect set up
images of imperial victory in the hippodrome of Constantinople, with
innovative iconography that confirms a link between Eudoxia's coronation and the crisis of 399/400. That coronation was clearly a political
event of first magnitude. Like Eutropius before them, Gaïnas and
Eutychian failed partly because they collided with Eudoxia.

Finally, Eudoxia's "imperiousness" accounts for her conflict
with the bishop John Chrysostom, a collision of such proportions that
it shattered for a time the crucial bond between the people of Constantinople and the Theodosian house. A priest of Antioch, John had
been selected for the episcopacy "by the unanimous vote of all, the
clergy and the people," but also, apparently, because the court
expected his "learning and eloquence" to deepen popular attachment to the dynastic faith.[82] Thus the emperor dispatched Eutropius
to fetch him from Antioch, and when Chrysostom arrived in Constantinople, escorted by a contingent of the palace guard, a synod of
eastern bishops assembled there by imperial command to carry out
the enthronement.[83]

The choice was not unsuccessful. When Eudoxia followed the
relics of saints, Chrysostom drew out forcefully the image of her
imperial virtues expected by the court. But the new bishop directed
most of his energies to the advancement of his see.[84] He intervened
in the affairs of other bishops, for example, in line with the conciliar
decision of 381 that "New Rome" possessed special authority among

82. Soc. 6. 2. 2–3.
83. Pall. *Dial.* 5 (p. 30 Coleman-Norton); Soc. 6. 2. 4; Dagron, *Naissance,*
pp. 463–65.
84. Dagron, *Naissance,* pp. 465–69; more generally, Baur, *Chrysostomus,* II,
20–166.

the churches. He enforced strict discipline over his local clergy as well. He evangelized the Goths of Constantinople and the vicinity, most of them from among the emperor's troops, and attracted some into his own orthodox communion. He labored also to counteract the threat of nascent monasticism. Tainted in the vicinity of Constantinople by Macedonian (semi-Arian) origins, the ascetic movement had recently become an urban phenomenon and a threat to ecclesiastical order. When monks abandoned isolation in the countryside for service among the sick and homeless of Constantinople, they acquired enough public sympathy to make their archimandrite Isaac a contender for spiritual leadership. Chrysostom attempted to depose Isaac,[85] but his response included devoting the growing financial resources of the episcopacy to his own charitable institutions of less revolutionary character.[86] The court supported these efforts, by and large,[87] but before long even the great city of Constantine and Theodosius would not have the space for both John Chrysostom and Eudoxia's *basileía*.

When Chrysostom expressed himself on the subject of women he adopted conventional sarcasm colored by the usual suspicions of a Christian ascetic. For him, females bore the mark of Eve. By nature vain, disobedient, and malicious, they were useful for procreation and household management but positively dangerous for anyone wishing to advance morally. Deprived by God of the right to spiritual leadership, they would nonetheless insinuate themselves when possible into positions of authority.[88]

Eudoxia fitted this image nicely. In 401 Chrysostom expelled from Constantinople a prominent ecclesiastic named Severian. The man was a troublemaker. On vacation from his responsibilities as bishop of Gabala in Syria, he had come to Constantinople to seek his fortune (in the crassest sense, the source claims), and in a short time had won a following in the city and the court and a dangerous hold

85. G. Dagron, "Les moines et la ville: le monachisme à Constantinople jusqu'au concile de Chalcédoine (451)," *Travaux et mémoires* 4 (1970), 262–65.

86. Pall. *Dial.* 5 (p. 32 Coleman-Norton); D.J. Constantelos, *Byzantine Philanthropy and Social Welfare* (New Brunswick, N.J., 1968), pp. 155–56.

87. According to Thdt. *HE* 5. 31. 3, Chrysostom wrote to a bishop near Antioch offering to secure legislation against the heresy of Marcion, ἀπὸ τῶν βασιλικῶν νόμων ἐπικουρίαν ὀρέγων. This implies the cooperation of the court. In 404 some of his Gothic following occupied a convent ἐν τοῖς Πρωμότου: *Ep.* 207 (*PG*, LII, 726). Promotus' family probably offered the space before *ca.* 403, when the court and with it his widow Marsa (*supra*, p. 64) began tangling with Chrysostom. Eudoxia may well have arranged or approved the foundation, a part of Chrysostom's evangelizing efforts.

88. Joh. Chrys. *De virg.* 46–47 (ed. Musurillo), *Comm. in Isaiam* 3. 8 (*PG*, LVI, 50–51), *De sacerd.* 3. 9 (ed. Nairn).

over Eudoxia. Thus his expulsion supported discipline and the bishop's authority. When the empress heard of it, however, she ordered that Severian return immediately and employed a familiar technique to compel Chrysostom's acquiescence. Approaching the surprised bishop in the Apostles Church, she deposited an infant on his knees, imploring that if he cared for the child's well-being, he abjure further dissension with Severian. The infant, of course, was Theodosius II, born only a few months earlier, so Chrysostom could hardly refuse.[89] But the incident confirmed private suspicions and led to resentful outbursts.

John Chrysostom did approve of some women, those who conducted themselves with modesty in dress, habits, and speech in obedience to their priests and bishop. Among the obedient were his "battalion of widows," rich and aristocratic ladies like Pentadia, Procle, and Silvine, and especially Olympias, "who refused to be budged from his church."[90] A descendant of Flavius Ablabius, praetorian prefect in the time of Constantine, and heiress to an immense fortune with properties in Constantinople, its suburbs, and the neighboring provinces, Olympias had seemed a proper match for Nebridius, prefect of Constantinople in 386 and brother-in-law of Flaccilla Augusta. When her husband died shortly after the marriage, she "leaped like a gazelle over the snare of a second union" despite the insistence of the emperor himself, who had selected another kinsman to succeed Nebridius.[91]

The designs of Theodosius reveal another side of founding a dynasty, the amassing, through *kedeia,* bequest, and less acceptable methods, of the property required to finance imperial magnificence. The estates of Olympias, however, escaped at least temporarily from the Theodosian net.[92] Nectarius ordained her a deaconess of the Great Church of Constantinople, a dignity which would protect her from similar secular attempts at manipulation.[93] And when Chrysostom became bishop in 398 he volunteered to advise her on the proper

89. Soc. 6. 11. 1–7, 11–21.

90. Pall. *Dial.* 5, 10, 16–17 (pp. 32, 60–61, 98–102, 107–10 Coleman-Norton). On Olympias see also *PLRE,* I, 642–43, "Olympias 2," and esp. Jean Chrysostome, *Lettres à Olympias,* ed. with introduction, translation, and notes by A.-M. Malingrey (Paris, 1968), including the anonymous *vita,* pp. 406–49. Further *infra,* pp. 143–44.

91. Pall. *Dial.* 16 (pp. 108–9 Coleman-Norton); *V. Olymp.* 3 (ed. Malingrey); Matthews, *Aristocracies,* pp. 109–10.

92. The loss was considerable. See *V. Olymp.* 5, 7 (ed. Malingrey) with Dagron's discussion, *Naissance,* pp. 503–4.

93. Soz. 8. 9. 1; on deaconesses *infra,* pp. 140, 144.

distribution of her assets: "Thus will your generosity benefit the needy, and God will grant you the reward of your earnest and merciful caring."[94] There was another side to a strong bishop as well, and Chrysostom's efforts to finance his operations would inevitably bring difficulties with the court.

When Porphyry of Gaza reached Constantinople late in 400, he and his companions naturally took their concern first to the bishop. Chrysostom could not help, however, because the empress had poisoned his relations with the emperor; "for I reproached her," he explained, "on account of a property which she coveted and finally seized."[95] Late biographers of Chrysostom elaborated the story, which recalled for them the biblical account of Naboth's vineyard. Like Naboth, a poor widow owned a vineyard which the empress, like King Ahab, coveted for her own. Unlike Ahab's queen Jezebel, Eudoxia did not need to resort to murder, for she had gathered grapes in the vineyard and could therefore claim it by an imperial law.[96] (In reality no such law ever existed, but apocryphal features need not cast doubt on the story's basic veracity.) The perils of Olympias' properties suggest Eudoxia's genuine motives, as Gilbert Dagron has pointed out,[97] and offer a reason why the bishop stepped forth to protest like the prophet Elijah when the court seized the "vineyards" of widows. Moreover, it was Chrysostom himself, not later authors, who invented the biblical parallel. He employed it on this or a later occasion to attack the empress, with familiar verve but an amazing lack of tact. Eudoxia was Jezebel, he declared,[98] the embodiment of queenly evil. One wonders whether like the prophet he predicted also that dogs would lick her blood.

94. Soz. 8. 9. 2–3. I detect a touch of sarcasm (ἦν οὖν ἐμοὶ πείθη . . .). Sozomen also tells of one such woman who escaped Chrysostom's net. Nicarete, daughter of an aristocratic Bithynian family, refused with admirable modesty to accept the dignity of deaconess, "although John urged her repeatedly to head the community of virgins at his church" (8. 23. 4–7).

95. Marc. Diac. *V. Porph.* 37 (ed. Grégoire-Kugener).

96. The full version appeared earliest in the Chrysostom *vitae* of Theodore of Trimithus (c. 15) and Pseudo-George of Alexandria (c. 41), both about 700. See now F. Halkin, *Douze récits byzantins sur saint Jean Chrysostome*, Subsidia hagiographica no. 60 (Brussels, 1977). Theodore and Pseudo-George say that the property of the widow's late husband had been confiscated. Thus the operative law may in reality have been *CTh* 9. 14. 3 (dated 397) prescribing confiscation for men convicted of treason and including in the property implicated the dowries of their wives.

97. *Naissance*, pp. 498–505.

98. Pall. *Dial.* 8 (p. 51 Coleman-Norton) (*infra*, n. 105). As Baur observed (*Chrysostomus*, II, 144), Chrysostom's choice of Jezebel indicates a scenario like that in Theodore and Pseudo-George.

When Theodosius II was baptized, on the feast of the Epiphany, January 6, 402, relations between episcopacy and *basileía* remained correct enough for John Chrysostom to officiate while Severian of Gabala, Eudoxia's favorite, took the part of godparent.[99] But the next two years were to prove that Chrysostom's resentment of an imperious female worked more strongly in the opposite direction. In 402–3 he became embroiled with Theophilus, bishop of Alexandria. The latter, an almost brutal man, had excommunicated and hounded from Egypt and Palestine the Tall Brothers, four monks of exemplary piety, for espousing the teaching of Origen (third century) that God the Father did not exist in human form.[100] When the Tall Brothers took refuge in Constantinople, Chrysostom received them warmly and wrote to Theophilus inviting him to explain himself and lift the ban. This demarche proved ineffective, however, so the monks turned to Eudoxia, in the manner of Porphyry. Having access neither through Chrysostom nor through the palace eunuchs, they accosted her as she progressed through the city in her imperial wagon. She greeted them approvingly, and with a prayer for "the emperor and herself, for their children and the Empire" promised a synod at which Theophilus would answer for his action.[101]

Instructed by his wife, Arcadius did order Theophilus to appear at a synod. But by the time it took place the Tall Brothers had been forgotten and Chrysostom was the accused. In the interim he had pronounced a sermon against females in general which the multitudes interpreted (and he probably intended) as a veiled attack on the empress.[102] Reports quickly reached Eudoxia, exaggerated, perhaps, by Chrysostom's enemies. She complained to the emperor, insisting that insults against herself struck her consort as well.[103] It was arranged

99. Gennad. *De vir. illus.* 21 (ed. Herding); Wenger, "Notes inédites," p. 54.

100. On Theophilus, the Tall Brothers, and the Origenist controversy see most recently E. D. Hunt, "Palladius of Helenopolis," *JThS* n.s. 24 (1973), 456–80; and J. N. D. Kelly, *Jerome, His Life, Writings, and Controversies* (New York-London, 1975), pp. 243–46, 259–63.

101. Soz. 8. 13. 5. Pall. *Dial.* 8 (p. 43 Coleman-Norton) reports another (later?) encounter in the *martyrium* of St. John, at which the Tall Brothers handed Eudoxia a formal petition (δέησις).

102. Soc. 6. 15. 1–3, Soz. 8. 16. 1–2; cf. Pall. *Dial.* 8 (p. 45 Coleman-Norton) (*supra*, n. 67) and Zos. 5. 23. 2 for additional reflections of this sermon which, to judge from Palladius, was directed mainly against Eudoxia's group of friends. Socrates says that Chrysostom lost his temper because Eudoxia had turned the famous heresy-hunter Epiphanius of Salamis against him. Sozomen suspects that he did it from personal inclination.

103. Soc. 6. 15. 4: αὐτοῦ ὕβριν εἶναι λέγουσα τὴν ἑαυτῆς.

that not Theophilus but Chrysostom would answer to the synod, and when it convened, in the autumn of 403 at a palace called The Oak (near Chalcedon), the bishop of Constantinople was deposed. The charges against him were ecclesiastical in character and relatively minor, reflecting the enmity a strong prelate was bound to provoke among his own clergy and flock.[104] The fathers of The Oak found themselves incompetent to examine Chrysostom's habitual insults, but in their formal response to the emperor, in which they also announced his deposition and requested a forceable ejection, they recommended that he be tried by a civil court as well, on a charge of lèse-majesté (καθοσίωσις) for reviling the sacred person of the empress.[105]

Report of the deposition quickly reached the city. The people of Constantinople massed in revolt before the Great Church, and when palace guards appeared to take away their bishop they could not bear to let him go.[106] Chrysostom welcomed and encouraged the intimacy of their attachment:

What God has joined, man cannot put asunder. . . . Wherever you go, there I go also. We are one body. The body may not be separated from the head, nor the head from the body. . . . You are my limbs, my body, my light, even sweeter to me than this light of day.

In the same sermon he spoke of the source of his troubles, but compounded the usual insults by evoking Herodias, persecutor of John the Baptist:

104. Phot. *Bibl.* cod. 59 (I, 53–57 Henry) gives the accusations excerpted from recorded *acta*.

105. Pall. *Dial.* 8 (pp. 50–51 Coleman-Norton) quotes from the response (ἀναφορά), which mentions briefs (λίβελλοι) containing a formal charge of καθοσίωσις. As quoted, the response appears to be authentic. Palladius adds that the response (ἀνήνεγκαν) specified the nature of the charge: ἦν δὲ ἡ καθοσίωσις ἡ εἰς τὴν βασίλισσαν λοιδορίαν, ὡς ἐκεῖνοι ἀνήνεγκαν, ὅτι εἶπεν αὐτὴν Ἰεζάβελ. As I read it, this passage expresses indignation that the fathers of The Oak considered John's diatribes against Eudoxia to be καθοσίωσις meriting capital punishment. F. van Ommeslaeghe, "Jean Chrysostome en conflit avec l'impératrice Eudoxie," *An. Boll.* 97 (1979), 132–33, takes the same words to mean that Palladius did not believe John had called Eudoxia Jezebel, "même s'il ne le dit pas expressément." On the contrary, the passage suggests that Chrysostom did employ provocative language against the empress, for Palladius would have expressed himself directly had he been able to do so. The text van Ommeslaeghe employs in his effort to clear Chrysostom (*infra*, n. 117) itself implies that the bishop had used unflattering comparisons with both Eve and Jezebel when he spoke of the empress (van Ommeslaeghe, "Chrysostome en conflit," pp. 153, 155).

106. Soc. 6. 15. 18–20, Soz. 8. 18. 1–2.

The seed of Jezebel is still with us. . . . But bring on the wondrous, resourceful herald of life, John the poor man who owned not even a candle but possessed the lamp of Christ. Eve's helpmate wanted his head![107]

John Chrysostom abandoned his resistance far sooner than his namesake had. He knew that to compete with the dynasty for popular attachment was an exceptionally dangerous business.[108] On the third day, when the crowds had dispersed at midday to pursue their normal occupations, the bishop slipped quietly from his church and accepted exile.

Then Eudoxia changed her mind. A misfortune struck her, very likely the fatal illness or accident that killed her daughter Flaccilla, and she feared terribly for the other children.[109] In addition, "the people raised an intolerable tumult." The bishop's departure so enraged his followers that their demonstrations spilled forth from the Great Church, filled the markets, and reached the gates of the palace.[110] Eudoxia took these occurrences to be God's judgment for her treatment of Chrysostom. The words she wrote begging him to return hint at her superstitious panic:

Let your Holiness not think that this was my doing! I am guiltless of your blood. Base and depraved persons have contrived this against you. God is witness of my tears, for to Him I offer them as sacrifice. . . . I remember that by your hands my children were baptized.

But Chrysostom could not be found.

Then a marvelous thing happened! Like a woman possessed by fear for her lost child, she searched everywhere, not in her own body but by dispatching

107. Joh. Chrys. *Hom. ante exil.*, *PG*, LII, 431. Doubts as to the authenticity of Chrysostom's words here and in the *Hom. cum ir. in exil.*, *ibid.*, cols. 435–38, are unfounded. These "sermons," which repeat one another and occasionally lack coherence, seem to have been patched together from the same address, based on listeners' notes; Baur, *Chrysostomus*, I, 181. Cf., however, J. A. de Aldama, *Repertorium pseudochrysostomicum* (Paris, 1965), pp. 155 no. 422, 198 no. 528.

108. Soc. *loc. cit.*: ἐφυλάττετο γὰρ μή τις ταραχὴ γένηται δι᾽ αὐτόν; Soz. *loc. cit.*: δείσας, μή τι ἕτερον αὐτῷ ἔγκλημα πλακείη ὡς . . . τὸν δῆμον ταράττοντι.

109. Pall. *Dial.* 9 (p. 51 Coleman-Norton): θραῦσίν τινα γενέσθαι ἐν τῷ κοιτῶνι; cf. Seeck, *Geschichte*, V, 362, 582 *ad* 362. 18. Baur, *Chrysostomus*, II, 227, suggests a miscarriage, but the chronology of Eudoxia's pregnancies (*supra*, p. 53) makes this unlikely. Pall. *Dial.* 9 (p. 56 Coleman-Norton) confirms fears for the imperial children: Εὐδοξία, φοβήθητι τὸν Θεόν, ἐλεήσασά σου τὰ τέκνα.

110. Soc. 6. 16. 1–5, Soz. 8. 18. 1–4. Note that Chrysostom attributed his "victory" to "the people of Constantinople" and insisted that their conduct showed zeal rather than *stasis*: *Hom. post redit.* 2, 5 (*PG*, LII, 444, 446; cf. next note).

soldiers from her pesonal guard. . . . She sent everywhere in desperation that the quarry might be surrounded by cunning enemies, killed, and lost. . . . Then she called her husband, clasped his imperial knees, made him a partner in the hunt as Sarah did with Abraham. "We have lost our priest," she said, "so let us bring him back. There is no hope for our *basileía* if we do not."[111]

It was Eudoxia's eunuch Briso who turned up Chrysostom, in hiding at a market-town in Bithynia. He returned with an imperial escort but could not reoccupy his see canonically until the decision of The Oak was overturned by another, more authoritative synod. In the meantime Eudoxia provided a suitable resort, one of her suburban palaces called Marianai.[112] Continuing popular disturbances, however, forced Chrysostom to accede to imperial persuasion and reenter Constantinople. "I will work henceforth in concert with you," he declared to the delighted people, "and with the God-loving Augusta." She too had pledged her efforts to maintain the fragile peace.[113]

Within a few months Eudoxia again changed her mind. A city prefect erected a silver statue of the empress wearing the *paludamentum,* locating it to the south of the Great Church before the senate house and providing public shows of dancers and mimes to celebrate, "as is the custom when imperial images are dedicated."[114] Chrysostom should have known by this time not to challenge the ceremonial exaltation of Eudoxia's *basileía,* but he could not abide the shows or the noise so close to his church. He complained in a sermon. She responded with the threat of another synod. He returned to the familiar insults: "Again Herodias rages, again she storms, again she aims to have the head of John on a platter."[115]

Hostile bishops assembled in Constantinople to consider new charges—that Chrysostom had reoccupied his see without proper conciliar authority. Arcadius broke off relations and, in the spring of 404, confined the bishop to his episcopal palace. On Easter morning,

111. Joh. Chrys. *op. cit.* 4 (cols. 445–46). The sermon is authentic Chrysostom, certainly known to Sozomen (8. 18. 5).
112. Soc. 6. 16. 6–8, Soz. 8. 18. 5–6; cf. Janin, *Constantinople*², p. 515, on the Marianai.
113. Joh. Chrys. *op. cit.* 5 (col. 447).
114. Soc. 6. 18. 1–5, Soz. 8. 20. 1–3, Marcell. com. *a.* 403. 2 (*MGH: AA,* XI, 67), Theoph., p. 79 de Boor. An inscription still exists on the statue's base, *CIL,* III, 736; cf. C. Mango, "The Byzantine Inscriptions of Constantinople: A Bibliographical Survey," *AJA* 55 (1951), 63.
115. Soc., Soz. *locc. citt.* The associated Chrysostom sermon in *PG,* LIX, 485–90, is unfortunately not authentic: Baur, *Chrysostomus,* II, 237 n. 8; Aldama, *Repertorium,* pp. 138–39 no. 381.

April 17, 404, and again the next day, government troops attacked white-clad catechumens who awaited baptism, leaving many dead. Although he had written to Innocent I, bishop of Rome (401–17), calling for an ecumenical council to hear his case, early in June, 404, Chrysostom was permanently exiled to Roman Armenia. His enraged followers (or perhaps their opponents) set fire to the Great Church of Constantinople, and the flames spread to the senate house and parts of the palace. Arsacius, the elderly brother of Nectarius, was ordained in John's place, but many refused to accept him. The popular revolt spread also to other cities, taking on alarming proportions.

On October 6, 404, Chrysostom's antagonist Eudoxia, exhausted by the ordeal, suffered a fatal miscarriage. It may have been induced by a savage hailstorm four days earlier, which she took to be a sign of divine anger at her treatment of the bishop.[116] In antiquity pregnancy and childbearing always threatened a woman's life, and to oppose a holy man like Chrysostom was no less risky, subjecting one to the terror of heaven's wrath at any moment. Eudoxia accepted the risks. Like most women she gloried in children; her pride had a special depth, however, because her offspring meant public order and dynastic security. Chrysostom's insults not only belittled a woman but challenged the authenticity of an empress' sacral *basileía*.[117]

John Chrysostom's words and conduct prove that there was another view. He thought himself beset by the archetypal female, controlled by sensuality, by nature fickle, and therefore to be pitied:

You who are in the flesh make war against the incorporeal one. You who enjoy baths and perfumes and sex with a male do battle with the pure and untouched church. But you too will find yourself a widow, although your man still lives. For you are a woman, and you wish to make the church a widow. Last evening you addressed me as the thirteenth apostle, and today you call me Judas. Yesterday you sat with me as a friend, but now you spring on me like a wild animal.[118]

116. Soc. 6. 19. 4–6; Soz. 8. 27. 1–2; Phot. *Bibl.* cod. 77 (I, 158 Henry); *Chron. pasch. a.* 404 (p. 569 Bonn); Seeck, *Geschichte*, V, 370; Baur, *Chrysostomus*, II, 300–305.

117. For discussion of Chrysostom's conflict with Eudoxia see Baur, *Chrysostomus*, II, 119–289, and Demougeot, *Division*, pp. 296–337; for examination of the main sources T. Gregory, "Zosimus 5. 23 and the People of Constantinople," *Byzantion* 43 (1973), 61–83; and F. van Ommeslaeghe, "Que vaut le témoinage de Pallade sur le procès de Saint Jean Chrysostome?" *An. Boll.* 95 (1977), 389–414, and "Chrysostome en conflit," pp. 132–59, drawing attention to the important *vita* or funeral oration by Pseudo-Martyrius of Antioch, soon to be published.

118. Joh. Chrys. *Hom. cum ir. in exil.*, PG, LII, 437 (*supra*, n. 107).

This apprehension of Eudoxia's motivation was tragically wrong-headed. It resulted from prejudices against women which, where an empress was concerned, were now dangerously out of date. Eventually the court lost patience, when Chrysostom's challenge to Eudoxia's *basileía* provoked the people of Constantinople into sedition against the domestic side of the monarchy. In the reign of Arcadius, sedition against the domestic side struck all too close to the heart.

CHAPTER THREE

Aelia Pulcheria Augusta

She conceived a godly resolve . . .

Eudoxia Augusta died in 404, leaving a worthy successor. During a long career (413–53), her daughter Pulcheria brought female *basileía* to full fruition and employed it to change the course of history. Her ability to do so depended in part on inherited factors—on the Theodosian dynastic impetus, its enhancement of women, and the demilitarization of imperial ideology. But Pulcheria addressed her tasks with a unique and forceful personality, shaped during her childhood in the impressive environment of the eastern court.

In July or August of less troubled years, the imperial family and the court habitually made their encumbered way to Ancyra in the highlands of Galatia, to give Arcadius a change of scenery, Claudian asserted, and to escape the full warmth of summer.[1] Apart from this the emperor and his family occupied more or less continuously the great palace of Constantinople, a labyrinthine array of structures extending from the hippodrome southeastward on terraces overlooking the sea (fig. 1). In most of its quarters exterior walls established the proper distance between encroaching private structures and the haunts of *basileía*.[2] These walls enclosed gardens, galleries and walkways, private apartments, the barracks of the guard, and, importantly, a venerable complex known as Daphne that included the grand audience hall of Constantine, now the ceremonial focus of the palace.[3] This architectural setting repelled Synesius, who

1. Claud. *In Eutr.* 2. 97–102, 416; O. Seeck, *Regesten der Kaiser und Päpste* (Stuttgart, 1919), pp. 291, 293, 295, 309.
2. *CTh* 15. 1. 47 (February 21, 409) orders removal of private structures from the palace vicinity, "nam imperio magna ab universis secreta debentur."
3. For the palace in general see Janin, *Constantinople*², pp. 106–22, and W. Mueller-Wiener, *Bildlexikon zur Topographie Istanbuls* (Tübingen, 1977), pp. 229–37, citing further literature; on its development in the fourth and fifth centuries esp. Dagron, *Naissance*, pp. 92–97, and C. Mango, "Autour du Grand Palais de Constantinople," *Cahiers archéologiques* 5 (1951), 179–86; on the Daphne see

attributed to it and its inhabitants the lethargy of Arcadius and his unwarlike temperament. But for John Chrysostom it provided an image of heaven, of God enthroned in majesty, flanked not by eunuchs and dissipated courtiers but by angels, archangels, and the host of saints.[4] As if approaching divine majesty in silence and trembling, great men entered the palace from the *mesē* through the fortified and heavily guarded Chalke gate, the antechamber of earthly *basileía*.[5] Less exalted folk confronted such majesty in contiguous exterior space, in the hippodrome or when they filled the nearby Augusteon square, to the left of the *mesē* as it led toward the Chalke. The people massed on this square to mourn the death of the emperor's child or to express revolutionary outrage when the emperor exiled their bishop. Thus the sedentary habits of Arcadius had a function. When he resided at home, a potent setting emphasized his numinous quality and at the same time brought him into necessary intimacy with the dynastic city.

Into this setting the children of Arcadius and Eudoxia were born, and here they flourished during their early years. Architecture imposed on them a notion of *basileía*, as well as a consciousness of the dynasty's purpose. Parental influence may also be suspected, primarily that of the mother on her oldest surviving daughter.[6] Eudoxia's forceful character, the superstitious piety and imperiousness apparent in her conflict with John Chrysostom, might have molded all of her children in its own image, but by the time of her death only Pulcheria and perhaps Arcadia were old enough to be affected. Supervision of the imperial household then fell to the eunuch Antiochus, a young but "paunchy" individual of Armenian or Persian origin. Like Eutro-

---

Janin, pp. 108, 112–13, and for early mention of it under that name Proclus of Constantinople in *PG*, L, 715, cf. F. Leroy, *L'homilétique de Proclus de Constantinople*, Studi e testi no. 247 (Vatican City, 1967), p. 158.

4. Joh. Chrys. *In Matth. hom.* 2. 1. (*PG*, LVII, 23).

5. C. Mango, *The Brazen House*, Det Kongelige Danske Videnskabernes Selskab: Arkaeologisk-kunsthistoriske Meddelelser vol. IV, no. 4 (Copenhagen, 1959), discusses the Chalke and surrounding monuments.

6. The mother's influence goes without saying for the girls. That boys were also raised by their mothers in aristocratic families during this period may be gathered from several passages of Chrysostom's *De inani gloria*. He condemns the ornamentation of male children with gold, fine fabrics, necklaces, and even perfumes (16, 54), all presumably signs of female influence. He speaks of the mother, pedagogue, and body servant as the important influences on a boy's developing speech habits (31–32), and condemns the practice of allowing growing boys to bathe with the women of the family (60).

pius earlier in the reign, he had gained the confidence of the imperial family and headed the corps of eunuchs as *praepositus sacri cubiculi.* In a letter to his brother, probably from the year following Eudoxia's death, Synesius of Cyrene reported that Antiochus was so powerful at court that he could accomplish "whatever he wishes."[7] The death of Arcadius (in 408) apparently changed little. Probably sometime between 408 and 412 St. Isidore of Pelusium wrote to the eunuch urging him to avoid the temptations resulting from his good fortune and to enforce justice, tottering and nearly extinguished as it was, "for you are not only a minister of the *basileía* but are able to direct it however you please."[8]

Antiochus, however, did not match the ascendancy of Eutropius. The government remained in other hands, while the chief eunuch managed only the imperial household, including the "most noble princesses" (*nobilissimae*)[9] and the person of the orphaned Augustus Theodosius. Antiochus, for example, arranged for the earliest education of the young emperor and his sisters, the traditional instruction in Greek and Latin reading and composition. Presumably a professional tutor was employed, as was the normal practice in wealthy Roman houses.[10] To provide healthy competition and to assimilate the education of Theodosius to that of any other aristocratic youth,[11] at least two companions, Paulinus and Placitus, were brought in to share his lessons,[12] and a similar procedure may have been followed for his sisters. Pulcheria, at least, excelled. In later years she would

7. *Ep.* 110; for the date *supra,* Chap. 2, n. 68. On Antiochus in general see *PLRE,* II, 101–2, "Antiochus 5," and R. Naumann and H. Belting, *Die Euphemia-Kirche am Hippodrom zu Istanbul und ihre Fresken* (Berlin, 1966), pp. 15–21. A statue base found during excavation of the Euphemia church confirms him as ANTIOXOY ΠΡΕΠΟ [σίτου].

8. *Ep.* 1. 36 (*PG,* LXXVIII, 204); cf. M. Smith, "The Manuscript Tradition of Isidore of Pelusium," *HThR* 47 (1954), 205–10, on the nature of the letters. The one in question must date from before Antiochus' fall from power in 412. That it was written after the death of Arcadius is less certain, but Isidore's words would be particularly fitting for the de facto guardian of the child emperor.

9. For the title *Chron. pasch. a.* 414 (p. 571 Bonn) and *CTh* 13. 1. 21; for its significance Grégoire and Kugener, "Quand est né," pp. 341–44.

10. H.-I. Marrou, *Histoire de l'éducation dans l'antiquité,* 7th ed. (Paris, 1965), p. 390. For this practice in the reign of Arcadius see Jerome *Ep.* 107. 4 (V, 148 Labourt) and Joh. Chrys. *De inani gloria* 38.

11. Jerome *Ep.* 107. 9 (V, 153–54 Labourt); Joh. Chrys. *De inani gloria* 67, 77; cf. Marrou, *Education,* p. 398.

12. Paulinus at least was from a powerful family, being the son of a *comes domesticorum.* See Joh. Ant. frg. 192 (*FHG,* IV, 612) and Joh. Mal. 14 (p. 352 Bonn), also *PLRE,* II, 846, "Paulinus 8," 891, "Placitus."

receive praise for her unusual skill in speaking and writing both languages of the Empire.[13]

St. Isidore's letter implies that Antiochus had enemies, aristocrats like those who had found the power of Eutropius so distasteful some years earlier. As long as he profited from the affection of the imperial children, the eunuch could feel secure. But the house of Theodosius might itself be overthrown, a possibility so real that some contemporaries were astonished it did not happen.[14] There may in fact have been one attempt to remove the dynasty by force in this period. In his *Life of Isidore* the Neoplatonist Damascius (sixth century) told the story of Lucius, a pagan who held the office of *magister militum* in the time of Theodosius. Lucius penetrated into the imperial apartments one day with the intention of killing the emperor. But when he had tried vainly three times to draw his sword from its scabbard he gave up and withdrew in terror, for he had seen "a giant and burly woman" standing behind the emperor and folding him in her protecting arms.[15] It seems that pagan speculation on the emperor's divine protectors crept into this account. The "woman" in question may have been the hypostasized Fortune or Tyche of the emperor, the rough equivalent of the *genius publicus* which, according to the historian Ammianus, had accompanied Julian during his reign.[16] Presumably some more concrete defense turned aside the sword of Lucius. But the attempt itself was genuine, and it probably occurred during the vulnerable early years of Theodosius II.[17]

Thus Antiochus had reason to undertake a diplomatic campaign to protect both the child emperor and himself. A number of later

13. Soz. 9. 1. 5.

14. Soz. 9. 6. 1, Thdt. *HE* 5. 36. 3.

15. Damasc. *V. Isid.* frg. 303 Zintzen.

16. Amm. 20. 5. 10, 25. 2. 3–4; cf. S. MacCormack, "Roma, Constantinopolis, the Emperor, and His Genius," *CQ* n.s. 25 (1975), 144–45.

17. Demandt, *RE*, suppl. XII (1970), 747, "Magister Militum," makes Lucius *magister militum praesentalis* and places him early in the reign of Theodosius II. He may well have been the Lucius whom Anthemius ordered to drive Chrysostom's followers from the Baths of Constantine on Easter morning, 404: Pall. *Dial.* 9–10 (pp. 57, 60 Coleman-Norton). That Lucius was also a military man, a pagan, and, to judge from his name, a Roman. He was precisely the kind of man Anthemius would have promoted to the upper ranks of the army. Note also that an otherwise unknown Lucius served as eastern consul in 413, an honor that often went to *magistri militum* and others of the highest rank in the year of their promotion, for example, Plinta in 419, Asclepiodotus in 423, and Zeno in 448. Demandt, col. 755, observes the relative frequency with which the consulship was conferred upon *magistri militum* during this reign. *PLRE*, II, 691–92, recognizes three separate Lucii.

authors, the earliest writing well over a century later than the events, reported that as Arcadius lay dying he foresaw the precarious situation of his son. Worried about possible usurpers, but not wishing to set up a co-emperor who would surely replace his own dynasty, Arcadius made the Persian king Yazdgard I (399–420) the boy's "guardian" (ἐπίτροπος), including a provision to this effect in his will and writing personally to the Persian to request his protection. The latter did not refuse. He dispatched a letter to the senate of Constantinople threatening war on any who might conspire against Theodosius II.[18] Despite the skepticism of both ancient and modern authors,[19] there is no reason to reject this much of the story. Cooperation of this type between the two great monarchies was not impossible. In the next century the Persian king Kavadh (d. 531) was to propose the converse arrangement, that the Roman emperor adopt his son and successor and protect him against a rebellious nobility.[20] Moreover, excellent relations with Yazdgard made the project feasible, and it would have been effective. Prospective challengers for the *basileía* would face the likelihood of an immediate Persian attack. But the ancient sources are probably wrong in their assertion that Yazdgard sent one of his eunuchs to exercise his guardianship. The eunuch mentioned is Antiochus, and he had been powerful in the Roman court some years before the death of Arcadius. More likely Antiochus sponsored the idea. His initiative and his own Oriental origins reinforced the notion that he acted as agent of the Persian king.

18. The Greek sources are Procop. *B. Pers.* 1. 2. 1–10; Agath. 4. 26; Theoph. *a.m.* 5900 (p. 80 de Boor); Cedren. 334c (p. 586 Bonn); Zon. 13. 22. The episode also appears in a number of Oriental sources, some of which may represent independent tradition. See Mich. Syr. 8. 1. (II, 2 Chabot); Bar Hebr., I, 66 Wallis-Budge; *Chron. ad a. 1234* 28 (*CSCO: SS*, CIX, 136–37); and esp. the odd account in U. M. Daudpota, "The Annals of Hamzah al-Ishfahani," *Journal of the K. R. Camal Oriental Institute* 22 (1932), 71–72.

19. In antiquity Agath. 4. 26 expressed skepticism. Among modern scholars P. Sauerbrei, "König Jazdegerd der Sünder, der Vormund des byzantinischen Kaisers Theodosius des Kleinen," *Festchrift Albert von Bamberg* (Gotha, 1905), pp. 90–108, rejected the story as fabulous; Averil Cameron, "Agathias on the Sassanians," *DOP* 23–24 (1969/70), 149, believes it was a diplomatic gesture on the part of Anthemius (or someone else) to secure peace; and P. Pieler, "L'aspect politique et juridique de l'adoption de Chosroès proposée par les Perses à Justin," *Revue internationale des droits de l'antiquité* ser. 3, 19 (1972), 408–20, takes it as a serious attempt on the part of Arcadius to secure the succession. All three positions have numerous adherents.

20. Procop. *B. Pers.* 1. 11. 1–30; A. A. Vasiliev, *Justin the First* (Cambridge, Mass., 1950), pp. 265–68; B. Rubin, *Das Zeitalter Justinians*, I (Berlin, 1960), pp. 259–60; Pieler, "L'aspect politique," pp. 399–407, 421–33.

Like the attack of Lucius, the intervention of the Persian king on behalf of young Theodosius II demonstrates that the dynasty was indeed in trouble. The historian Socrates, a later contemporary who must have known the truth, included in his work a passage that reveals more clearly the nature of the danger. Socrates did not credit the stability of the monarchy to the emperor's Tyche or the diplomacy of Antiochus but to Anthemius "the Great," praetorian prefect of the East:[21]

When Arcadius died, the East came under his son Theodosius the Younger, who was only seven years old, but Anthemius the prefect had complete charge of the administration. . . . This man won the reputation of being the most intelligent of his time, and in fact he was. He did nothing without counsel, sharing with eminent men his deliberations on the proper course of action. In particular he consulted Troïlus the sophist, who, in addition to his own specialty, was no less an expert at politics than Anthemius. Thus Anthemius nearly always acted on the advice of Troïlus.[22]

The passage diverts attention from *basileía* and the palace to the salutary operations of political genius. It strikingly equates the genius of Anthemius with his accessibility to men of ambition, suggesting as well their identities and the nature of their claims. The historian himself provided one name. Lavish in his praise of Troïlus,[23] Socrates seems to have encountered him during school years in Constantinople and very likely formed ties with others like him who responded favorably to the regime of Anthemius.

Such men may be discovered in greater numbers among the correspondents of Synesius. A prominent Neoplatonist and distinguished native of Cyrene, a city of the Libyan Pentapolis, Synesius had traveled to Constantinople in 399 to advance the interests of his provincial community. While there he delivered *De regno* before Arcadius, interpreted the revolt of Gaïnas in *De providentia,* and acquired many friends, contacts he was able to exploit when he returned to Cyrene in 402.[24] Success depended on the favor of men like the revered Marcion, former governor of Paphlagonia and now

21. For the epithet "great" see *CIL,* III, 739, and Syn. *Epp.* 47, 73.
22. Soc. 7. 1. 1, 3.
23. Cf. 6. 6. 36, 7. 12. 10, 27. 1, 37. 1 with the excellent observation of Henri de Valois (printed in *PG,* LXVII, 18): "toties enim, tamque honorifice eius mentionem facit, ut magistro Minerval solvere videatur."
24. Lacombrade, *Synésios,* pp. 84–130; in general now J. Bregman, *Synesius of Cyrene* (Berkeley-Los Angeles-London, 1982).

head of a literary circle called the Panhellenion.[25] Simplicius, Trypho, and Count Paeonius, men who had served in the Pentapolis as governors or military commanders, would help because of the friendships and common interests they had formed there. Paeonius was also approachable through philosophy, so Synesius presented him with a type of star chart of his own design, constructed in silver.[26] Indeed, learning proved to be Synesius' greatest asset. To Nicander he sent his *Eulogy of Baldness,* asking him to show it to his "Hellenic" friends (τοῖς Ἕλλησιν). The most inspired poet of the time was Theotimus, whom Synesius expected to intervene in favor of the Pentapolis. The sophist Troïlus, whom Socrates admired, was close enough to Synesius to be asked for books, and Synesius confirmed that Troïlus, and Nicander and Theotimus besides, were intimates of the great Anthemius.[27] Count John, on the other hand, had influence at court, as did John's associate Aurelian, a "friend," as Synesius called him, and Osiris in *De providentia.*[28]

Because Synesius wrote for practical reasons, his correspondence illustrates how a man could acquire and use influence in the early years of Theodosius II. A decade or so after his grandfather had closed the temples and outlawed sacrifice, within a few years of the Frigidus miracle and despite the advertised piety of the court, adherence to the dynastic faith had not yet entirely displaced the traditional criteria for political success. Synesius and his correspondents would have felt more comfortable with a Tatianus as the emperor's prime minister than with a Maternus Cynegius or a Rufinus. It was not primarily a matter of religion. For contemporaries the word "Hellene" did evoke paganism,[29] and since Synesius employed it freely in letters that circulated and could have come into the wrong hands, presumably some of his friends did not object to being tagged as such. But Socrates likewise admired Troïlus and Anthemius, and to judge from his *History* he was thoroughly Christian. Count John's name is enough to imply a Christian background, but in any case no self-confessed pagan could have enjoyed such intimacy with Eudoxia. The

25. Syn. *Epp.* 101, 119.

26. *Ibid.* 24, 28, 129–30, 134, 142, 154; also *Ad Paeonium* (ed. Terzaghi).

27. *Epp.* 1, 26, 47, 49, 73, 75, 91, 99, 111, 118, 129. On Theotimus cf. D. Runia, "Another Wandering Poet," *Historia* 28 (1979), 254–56.

28. 22, 31, 34, 38, 43, 46, 79, 100, 110.

29. K. Lechner, *Hellenen und Barbaren im Weltbild der Byzantiner* (Munich, 1954), pp. 16–37.

latter consideration applies to Aurelian as well, and Synesius attested
to his orthodox piety, as did his patronage of St. Stephen Protomartyr, for whom Aurelian constructed a memorial chapel earlier in his
career.[30] The bond that united these men—Socrates, John, Aurelian,
and the rest—was not religion but a shared commitment to Greek
culture and the traditional qualifications for public careers. Their
prospects had risen dramatically since 395, because the fall of Rufinus
and the ensuing division of East from West meant the disappearance
of Theodosian westerners from high office or their amalgamation into
the eastern cultural sphere.[31] As Themistius had recommended long
before, Arcadius and Theodosius II finally did draw from the senate
of Constantinople the men they needed to govern the Empire.[32]

Anthemius was just such a man.[33] Apparently of Egyptian origin,
his family had emerged from obscurity only two generations earlier,
in the time of Constantius II, when his grandfather Philippus, who
was the son of a sausage-seller, learned stenography, entered the
imperial service, and advanced to the praetorian prefecture of the
East.[34] Anthemius himself first appeared in high office as *comes
sacrarum largitionum* in 400, in the wake of the Gaïnas revolt. As
magister officiorum in 404 he dispatched the troops who slaughtered
catechumens in Constantinople on Easter morning, and by November, 405, he was praetorian prefect of the East.[35] No evidence exists

30. On names as an indication of religious adherence see recently R. von
Haehling, *Die Religionszugehörigkeit der hohen Amtsträger des römischen Reiches
seit Constantins I. Alleinherrschaft bis zum Ende der theodosianischen Dynastie*,
Antiquitas ser. 3, vol. XXIII (Bonn, 1978), pp. 25–28; on Aurelian's religion Syn. *De
prov.* 1. 18 (pp. 108–9 Terzaghi), and for his church *V. S. Isaaci* (*AASS*, May, VII,
253), Theod. Anag. *HE* frg. 52, *Epit.* 467 (ed. Hansen). Troïlus himself was most
likely a Christian; see Alan Cameron, "The Empress and the Poet," *Yale Classical
Studies* 27 (1981), 272. In this important study (pp. 271–79 and *passim*) Cameron
rejects the view I expressed in my paper "Pulcheria's Crusade," that political clashes
in this period reflected ideological and cultural differences as well as personal ones, a
view I find amply attested in the sources and more plausible than that of Cameron.

31. The Cynegius attested 402 as *comes consistorianus* (*supra,* Chap. 2, n. 32)
may have been an exception, but his office, if any, is unknown.

32. This was a principal aspect of the division of East from West that escaped
the searching analysis of Demougeot, *Division.*

33. In general Zakrzewski, *Parti,* pp. 156–77; Demougeot, *Division,* pp.
338–51, 499–519 (neither, however, satisfactory); Stein, *Histoire,* I, 245–47; *PLRE,*
II, 93–95, "Anthemius 1"; on the family esp. J. Keil, "Die Familie des Prätorianerpräfekten Anthemius," *Anzeiger der Akademie der Wissenschaften in Wien, Philosophisch-historische Klasse* 79 (1942), 185–203.

34. *PLRE,* I, 696–97, "Flavius Philippus"; A. H. M. Jones, "The Career of
Flavius Philippus," *Historia* 4 (1955), 229–33.

35. *CTh* 7. 10. 1 (July 10, 405) gives the correct *terminus a quo* for his
prefecture; cf. Jones, "Collegiate Prefectures," p. 81.

on the man's religious stance. Like John and Aurelian he must have professed Christianity, while his association with Troïlus confirms receptiveness to the claims of the Hellenes.

In the first years of the new prefecture deaths of several trouble-makers eased the turmoil in the East. With Eudoxia dead, persecution of the "Johnites," as the schismatic followers of Chrysostom were now known, could safely be suspended.[36] But their dissension would have lost its thrust in any case, because in 407 the exiled bishop also died. Stilicho reclaimed all Illyricum for the West in 406, and in 408 prepared to march to Constantinople and impose himself as protector of the orphaned Theodosius II. But in August of that year a clique of enemies persuaded Honorius to execute the western generalissimo, and with his death the Theodosian policy of imperial unity lost its aggressiveness.[37] Simultaneously, old antagonisms subsided on the East's opposite frontier. Earlier in his career Anthemius had taken part in an embassy to the court of Sassanian Persia, an embassy which had established such good relations with King Yazdgard I that John Chrysostom was able to envision the evangelization of his subjects.[38] About 409 a second mission departed with instructions to enlist Yazdgard's assistance in settling quarrels among the Christian bishops of his territory. The effort succeeded beyond expectation. At a synod in 410 the king recognized the Christians of Persia as a lawful entity under the bishop (*katholikos*) of his capital Seleucia-Ctesiphon, and they began to enjoy official toleration.[39]

Anthemius reaped credit on all sides for eastern prosperity. The enthusiasm of Socrates implied more, of course, than attachment from a school connection. Like Socrates John Chrysostom stressed Anthemius' copious sagacity, writing from exile to "Anthemius my most gentle master." Verse panegyrics from the pen of Theotimus

36. Syn. *Ep.* 66 confirms the conclusion of "peace," while Chrysostom him-self congratulated Anthemius from exile for his consulship and the prefecture: *Ep.* 147 (*PG*, LII, 699).

37. Of course the East continued to act as if the Empire were still one; see W. Kaegi, *Byzantium and the Decline of Rome* (Princeton, 1968), pp. 15–29.

38. *Ep.* 14 (*PG*, LII, 618), and cf. Soc. 7. 8. 5, 18, Theoph. *a.m.* 5906 (p. 82 de Boor). For Yazdgard's benevolence toward Christians see J. Labourt, *Le christianisme dans l'Empire perse sous la dynastie Sassanide (224–632),* 2nd ed. (Paris, 1904), pp. 87–103, and A. Christensen, *L'Iran sous les Sassanides,* 2nd ed. (Copenhagen, 1944), pp. 269–72. The embassy of Anthemius, known only from Thdt. *Hist. rel.* 8 (*PG*, LXXXII, 1369), took place before he received the prefecture but cannot be dated precisely.

39. *Synodicon orientale ou recueil de synodes nestoriens,* ed. and trans. J.-B. Chabot (Paris, 1902), pp. 254–75; cf. Labourt, *Christianisme,* pp. 93–99.

were expected to immortalize his accomplishments among Greek litterateurs. As Synesius put it succinctly, "the times belong to Anthemius."[40]

The emperor was equally lavish. Already consul in 405, by the next year the great prefect had received the distinction *patricius*,[41] and, more significantly, his office was extended far beyond the normal four- or five-year maximum. Apparently the court found his services indispensable. He employed his position, as Socrates observed, to cement an unprecedented grip on the government. Within a few months of his father's death, Theodosius II ordered Anthemius

to have the instructions of all provincial delegations read officially and weighed before your sublimity, so that your sublimity might choose out whatever you approve as worthy of our decision and the indulgence of our clemency and bring it without hesitation before us.[42]

This constitution illustrates well the workings of government in the emperor's eighth year. In effect Anthemius received complete authority to formulate a response as he saw fit, and access to the palace to secure the necessary imperial signature. Petitioners such as Synesius must have appreciated some of the Anthemian legislation, for example, the constitutions to hinder military exactions from the provincials[43] and a general remission of taxes in the eastern prefecture that affected all amounts overdue from the past forty years.[44]

The profound objectives of Anthemian statecraft may best be appreciated from another project, one which, like his lengthy tenure of office, extended beyond the normal prerogatives of his prefecture. In the summer of 408 the Hun chief Uldin, who had killed Gaïnas eight years before, led a large host of his warriors and allies across the Danube. Seizing the fortified town of Castra Martis in Dacia, he advanced eastward, pillaging into Thrace. When a Roman prefect of soldiers attempted to negotiate, the Hun demanded an exorbitant tribute, pointing to the morning sun and boasting of the power to conquer "all the lands Helios sees in his rising." To judge from the

40. Joh. Chrys. *Ep.* 147 (*PG*, LII, 699), Syn. *Epp.* 47, 73.
41. *CTh* 9. 34. 10.
42. *CTh* 12. 12. 14; cf. the procedure adopted for similar business in *CTh* 12. 12. 4 (364) and 10 (385).
43. *CTh* 7. 4. 28, 31–32, 11. 1, 8. 5. 66; cf. Zakrzewski, *Parti*, p. 169. Synesius had complained of such abuses in *De regno* 24 (pp. 53–54 Terzaghi).
44. *CTh* 11. 28. 9; cf. Syn. *De regno* 25 (pp. 54–55 Terzaghi).

geographical position, this threat evoked a march on Constantinople. Fortunately, enough of Uldin's allies deserted to force him into retreat and a narrow escape beyond the Danube with heavy losses.[45] But reports of his threat reached Constantinople,[46] and the prospect of similar attacks in the future with similar attempts to intimidate the government induced Anthemius to undertake the most extensive building project of his time and the greatest monument of his prefecture. A new defensive wall went up on the landward side of Constantinople to protect the expanding Theodosian city. Laid out roughly 1,500 meters west of the Constantinian wall, it curved from the Propontis northward to existing fortifications of the Blachernai region overlooking the Golden Horn (fig. 1).[47] Construction of the wall and its towers already approached completion by the summer of 413, when Theodosius issued a constitution attributing these works to the "zeal and foresight" of Anthemius.[48] The chronology is enough to suggest that the prefect refortified Constantinople in reaction to the alarming summer of 408.

A related factor must also have weighed heavily in Anthemius' thinking. Behind Uldin's raid loomed the memory of Gaïnas' revolt in 399–400, when one of the emperor's own generals had seized Constantinople and forced the emperor to do his bidding. That event must have terrified a whole generation of eastern politicians.[49] Anthemius strengthened Constantinople in part to defend civilian government from intimidation and attacks by the field army. His wall defended a new system of government, in which politicians could control a weak emperor in full security.

45. Soz. 9. 5, *CTh* 5. 6. 2–3 (409), Jerome *In Isaiam* 7. 20 (*PL*, XXIV, 113); cf. Maenchen-Helfen, *Huns*, pp. 63–67.

46. Sozomen's account seems to reflect the impression Uldin's boast made on his Constantinopolitan informants.

47. B. Meyer-Plath and A.M. Schneider, *Die Landmauern von Konstantinopel*, II (Berlin, 1943); for a more concise description Janin, *Constantinople²*, pp. 265–83.

48. *CTh* 15. 1. 51. Meyer-Plath and Schneider, *Landmauern*, II, 2–3, 16–17, extend the Anthemian phase of construction to 422 and beyond, but if the bulk of the work had not been completed by 414 when Anthemius fell or died (see *infra*, p. 96) Socrates would not have credited the walls to him (7. 1. 3) nor would an official who undertook repairs later in the fifth century have compared himself with the great prefect: "portarvm valido firmavit limine mvros / Pvsaevs magno non minor Anthemio" (*CIL*, III, 739).

49. Cf. Dagron, *Naissance*, pp. 110–11.

On May 19, 406, Constantinople again celebrated the *adventus* of holy bones, this time those of the prophet Samuel.[50] The emperor himself had commanded that they be brought from the Holy Land. These "merest pieces of ash," as St. Jerome described them, came to Chalcedon under the reverent care of bishops, in a golden box shrouded with silk. Ferried across the Propontis, they arrived on the urban shore, where great men assembled to escort them into the city. The entire senate marched in the cortege, and at its head walked the emperor, flanked by Aemilian, ex-consul and prefect of the city, and by Anthemius, who had received the praetorian prefecture in the previous year. Crowds of the faithful who thronged joyfully to catch sight of the prophet "as if living and present" were treated to an impressive display of social order. Anthemius and Aemilian acquired prestige from physical association with the emperor's sacred person and with the holy dead, but, like the great men of the senate, they also served to add brilliance and authority to the occasion.[51] It was Arcadius who led the procession, issuing forth from the palace to make himself conspicuous in the dynastic city. As in the time of Eudoxia, the court exploited the mass appeal of the cult of relics to solidify popular and religious foundations for Theodosian *basileía*.

Anthemius thus appeared at the beginning of his prefecture as a dutiful minister of the dynasty's interests. No trace has survived of his personal views of *basileía*, but it is unlikely that he favored Synesius' argument that a proper emperor should know his soldiers and share the life of the camp. The existing system admirably suited his interests and those of his friends, and he served it faithfully through the early years of Theodosius II. Then restiveness surfaced in the palace. Pulcheria revealed dangerous signs of precocity, an echo, perhaps, of her mother's imperious character, but also the imprint of formative years in a palace society that imposed a strong sense of dynastic prerogatives. Reconstructing family dynamics among Theodosius and his sisters is a hazardous business, but it may be assumed that the eldest among the orphaned siblings took the role of arbiter among them and that this brought out a domineering side in her personality. The result was public enough to find its way into the chronicles. In 412

50. *Chron. pasch. a.* 406 (p. 569 Bonn), Jerome *Contra Vigil.* 5 (*PL*, XXIII, 358).
51. Cf. the "senate" that presided over the Council of Chalcedon for a similar display of brilliance and authority: *infra*, p. 214.

Pulcheria quarreled with Antiochus, who like Anthemius had served the dynasty faithfully for a number of years, and induced her brother to dismiss him from the duties of *praepositus*. She then took personal charge of the imperial family, directing its affairs with such authority that she became known in society at large as the emperor's "guardian" (ἐπίτροπος).[52]

Elements of family tradition quickly manifested themselves. Pulcheria embraced the image of Flaccilla's piety and exalted humility and imposed it on her sisters and Theodosius as well. As Socrates described it, the imperial palace, in Eudoxia's time the focus of grand society where women like Marsa and Castricia gathered to discuss affairs of state, now took on a decidedly monastic tone. At canonical hours day and night the emperor and his sisters came together to chant antiphons and to recite passages of Scripture learned by heart. They fasted on Wednesdays and Fridays, and the young women, following the precepts of church fathers,[53] gave up such vanities as cosmetics, luxurious apparel, and the usual idleness of aristocratic females, to devote themselves to the loom and other household occupations suitable for "admirable" women. At an early age Pulcheria likewise embraced her family's tradition of philanthropy "for the least of these," founding houses of prayer, refuges for beggars and the homeless, and monastic communities, and providing generously for their support from her personal income.[54] The historian Sozomen, who like Socrates contributed much to this flattering picture of life in Pulcheria's court, invited skeptical readers to look into existing records of her stewards.[55] Also a later contemporary, Sozomen presumably spoke with these stewards and examined their records, so his account has the authority of personal eyewitness.

Meanwhile Theodosius advanced from the grammar lessons of childhood to the study of rhetoric under the respectful guidance of professional teachers.[56] The young emperor devoted himself to the formal aspects of classical education. As he matured he acquired the

52. Theoph. *a.m.* 5905 (p. 82 de Boor), Soz. 9. 1. 2–3. Sozomen's term ἐπίτροπος implied moral authority only and not *tutela* or *curatela* over the emperor, which the Roman civil law did not permit; see Pieler, "Aspect politique," pp. 415–20.
53. For near-contemporary examples see Joh. Chrys. *Laus Max.* 9 (*PG*, LI, 240), *De inani gloria* 17, 90; Jerome *Ep.* 107. 5–6, 10 (V, 150–51, 154–55 Labourt).
54. Soc. 7. 22. 4–6, Soz. 9. 1. 10–11, 3. 1–2, Thdt. *HE* 5. 36. 4.
55. 9. 1. 11.
56. Soz. 9. 1. 6.

reputation of a knowledgeable critic of discourses and an avid corrector of manuscripts who often worked far into the night with his pen and his lamp.[57] According to Sozomen, Pulcheria also provided him with the external qualities of a ruler, with what M.P. Charlesworth fittingly labeled "imperial deportment."[58] Riding masters and instructors in swordsmanship came to the palace, while Pulcheria herself taught her brother how to sit and walk in a grand manner, how to manage the complexities of his official costume, how to keep his laughter in check, to show gentleness and anger appropriately, and to appear knowledgeable when inquiring about matters of state.[59] Thus Theodosius could perform effectively on ceremonial occasions. Ministers such as Anthemius entered the palace regularly to present documents for signature or to participate in sessions of the imperial advisory council. They needed to be impressed,[60] as did the people of Constantinople when the youthful emperor emerged from his mysterious isolation to celebrate in their midst.[61] Significantly, Sozomen said little of statecraft and omitted generalship altogether, areas of little practical value in current imperial practice.

Above all, Pulcheria saw to her brother's religious training, the primary concern of Christian educational theorists.[62] Theodosius learned the importance of worship, ascetic discipline, and works of philanthropy, and of regular intercourse with outstanding holy men, some of whom probably visited the palace to provide the correct examples of virtue.[63] In his rhetorical studies, biblical and patristic texts rich in lessons for Christian conduct would have replaced some of the traditional readings in classical authors.[64] And Pulcheria most likely insulated her brother from the attraction of women, according

57. Soz. praef. 4, 7–8, 10–12, 18, Soc. 7. 22. 6. Because of his interest in manuscripts Theodosius received the appellation "calligrapher," perhaps even among his contemporaries. See George the Monk (p. 604 de Boor), and A. Lippold, *RE*, suppl. XIII (1973), 967, "Theodosius II."

58. M.P. Charlesworth, "Imperial Deportment: Two Texts and Some Questions," *JRS* 37 (1947), 34–38, discussing Amm. 16. 10. 9–11 on the conduct of Constantius II when he visited Rome in 357.

59. Soz. 9. 1. 6–7. Chrysostom *De inani gloria* 74, 84, 89 recommends similar training for young men destined for military or political careers.

60. As they were at a meeting of the consistory, 431, when one participant reacted to Theodosius like "a lion among his thousand whelps": *infra*, p. 169.

61. E.g., 411, when Theodosius presided over the celebration of his decennalia: Marcell. com. *a.* 411. 1 (*MGH: AA*, XI, 70).

62. Joh. Chrys. *De inani gloria* 18; cf. Marrou, *Education*, pp. 451–52.

63. Soz. 9. 1. 8, Joh. Chrys. *De inani gloria* 78, 83.

64. Recommended in Joh. Chrys. *De inani gloria* 28, 38–43.

to St. John Chrysostom the greatest hazard in the pathway of a young man seeking perfection.[65]

Socrates, Sozomen, and other sources thus reveal continuity between the notion of *basileía* that Pulcheria imposed on her siblings and those advertised for Flaccilla and Eudoxia. In one respect, however, she broke sharply with Theodosian tradition. Sozomen reports that in her fourteenth year (before July 1, 413) Pulcheria "devoted her virginity to God" and impressed the same resolution upon her sisters. This was no private vow but one entered into in the full light of publicity. "Taking her subjects, the priesthood, and God himself to witness," Sozomen continues, she dedicated an altar decorated with gold and precious stones in the Great Church of Constantinople. She did it, he says, "on behalf of her own virginity and her brother's rule," ordering that these words be inscribed on the face of the altar "so that they might be visible to all."[66] With this act Eudoxia's daughter denied to herself and her sisters access to the power an imperial woman could acquire through childbearing. It must have had an even weightier motivation.

Presumably Sozomen knew the truth. Evoking first a "godly resolve" which Pulcheria acquired despite her youth, he adds a more telling explanation, that Pulcheria adopted virginity and imposed it on her sisters "to avoid bringing another male into the palace and to remove any opportunity for the plots of ambitious men."[67] Indelicacy might have touched an imperial nerve, so the historian omitted names. But the "godly resolve" of which he wrote manifested itself with the onset of pubescence just as ambitious men expected Pulcheria to marry, and within a few years the same physiological change would come to Arcadia and Marina. The "plots," therefore, were proposals of marriage, requiring vows in stone "visible to all" in order to preclude attempts to repeat them.[68]

65. *Ibid.* 53, 59–62. Chrysostom, who believed that the passion for women struck a young man suddenly after his fifteenth birthday (76), recommended early marriage as the surest defense (81–82). For reasons of her own Pulcheria avoided this strategy: *infra,* p. 120.

66. Soz. 9. 1. 3–4.

67. *Ibid.*: σοφώτατον καὶ θεῖον ἔλαβεν νοῦν ... τὴν αὐτῆς παρθενίαν τῷ θεῷ ἀνέθηκε καὶ τὰς ἀδελφὰς ἐπὶ τὸν αὐτὸν ἐπαιδαγώγησε βίον, ὅπως μὴ ἄλλον ἄνδρα ἐπεισαγάγῃ τοῖς βασιλείοις καὶ ζήλου καὶ ἐπιβουλῆς πᾶσαν ἀνέλῃ ἀφορμήν.

68. In 364 a law of the emperor Jovian threatened with capital punishment those who solicited virgins for marriage (*CTh* 9. 25. 2); in 420 Honorius prescribed confiscation of property and exile (*CTh* 16. 2. 44, *Const. Sirm.* 10).

Those who imposed themselves on Pulcheria in 412–13 did so because they understood how readily the *basileía* could be communicated through *kedeia*. In the case of Rufinus the prospect alone had sufficed to produce rumors of imperial ambition.[69] In 434 Justa Grata Honoria was to infect her paramour, although he was only the steward of her estates,[70] with distinction enough to warrant a hasty excision. Pulcheria understood this. In addition, if she or one of her sisters married, inevitably the new consort would bring into the palace the baggage of new kin and unwanted obligations, along with competition for influence over Theodosius. On its surface Pulcheria's "godly resolve" looks suspiciously like mature enjoyment of rank and distance, joined with a child's unwillingness to share it.

Sozomen's compunctions can no longer discourage efforts to identify those involved in the "plots." After extended service Pulcheria displaced Antiochus in 412, at least within months of her public dedication and perhaps simultaneously with it. The congruence of these two events suggests a causal connection between them, that Antiochus lost his office because he resisted Pulcheria's "godly resolve." Such resistance implied of course that in 412 Antiochus favored a marriage, and if he did the benefactor of the proposed *kedeia* may be identified. The power of Anthemius and the stability of his government presuppose excellent relations with the palace, where Antiochus had held sway since about the time the great prefect came to power. Now, a case of imperial pubescence threatened this arrangement with the likelihood of an extraneous marriage connection, so Anthemius, with the eunuch's support, undertook to claim it for himself. The scenario unfolds with remarkable ease. Married long since and many years Pulcheria's senior, Anthemius naturally proposed a descendant or close relative, a grandson perhaps, a young man like the attested Flavius Anthemius Isidorus Theophilus, born a few years earlier than Pulcheria and an excellent prospect for her hand.[71]

A grandson of Anthemius did carry a great deal of baggage. Bathed in the glory of the great man's prefecture, he would have outshone Theodosius in aristocratic eyes. The family boasted other

69. Sources in Demougeot, *Division*, p. 157 n. 194; cf. Alan Cameron, *Claudian*, pp. 91–92.

70. Joh. Ant. frg. 199 (*FHG*, IV, 613), Marcell. com. *a.* 434 (*MGH: AA*, XI, 79).

71. On this Isidorus, unknown to Keil, see *St. Pal. Pap.*, XIV, 12a; *POxy*, XVI, 1879; Holum, "Pulcheria's Crusade," p. 160 n. 30; *PLRE*, II, 1109.

outstanding figures, such as the prefect's son Flavius Anthemius Isidorus, proconsul of Asia *ca.* 405–10 and city prefect of Constantinople in 410–12, at the height of his father's power.[72] Conjunction of these two prefectures in the same family must have convinced many in the dynastic city that Theodosius was losing importance. At about the same time, Anthemius revealed independent imperial pretensions, marrying a daughter to a military man named Procopius who claimed descent from Constantine the Great.[73] When Anthemius attempted to impose such a marriage on Pulcheria he may indeed have triggered a "godly resolve"—and also a lasting hatred for himself and his family.

In the works of Socrates, of Sozomen, and of Theodoret, a third ecclesiastical historian who wrote during the reign of Theodosius II, there is striking confirmation that Pulcheria hated Anthemius. Throughout their works all three historians stressed the theory that the emperor could secure victory and other good things for his subjects by piety alone.[74] But they differed in explaining how the East survived the perilous early years of Theodosius II. Sozomen and Theodoret found this an excellent opportunity to point out the fruits of piety, which Theodosius and his sisters practiced in exemplary fashion. It was divine care which preserved the rule of the young emperor and restrained usurpers, so that the East remained peaceful and prosperous while the West was undergoing its greatest trials. In particular, Uldin's invasion failed because God's providence protected the reigning monarch.[75] Socrates, however, gave full credit to Anthemius, as was observed above. He broke with his underlying thesis to give the view of cultured circles he had encountered in his youth. At the time he wrote (not long after 439)[76] men of such sympathies enjoyed the patronage of the empress Eudocia, who in 421 succeeded to first place in the palace. Thus Socrates was free to ignore Pulcheria and her sisters, whom he never mentioned by name.[77] But when

72. *CTh* 8. 17. 2–3 (= *CI* 1. 19. 6); *CTh* 15. 1. 50; Keil, "Familie," pp. 192, 196, 199–200, 202 (stemma); *PLRE,* II, 631–33.

73. Sid. Ap. *Carm.* 2. 68–69: "cui prisca propago Augustis venit a proavis," 94; Keil, "Familie," pp. 191, 202 (stemma); *PLRE,* I, 742–43, "Procopius 4," II, 920, "Procopius 2."

74. *Supra,* Chap. 2, n. 12.

75. Soz. 9. 1. 2, 3. 3, 5. 3, 6. 1, Thdt. *HE* 5. 36. 2–4.

76. W. Eltester, *RE,* VA (1927), 894, "Sokrates Scholasticus."

77. Soc. 7. 22. 4–6 attributes the court's ascetic tinge to Theodosius himself, admitting only that the emperor's sisters joined him in rising early to chant the hours.

Theodoret and Sozomen composed their histories (both probably after 443),[78] Eudocia had retired in disgrace and rebellion to the Holy Land, and the favor of Pulcheria might have been worth cultivating once more. As a result, both historians adopted the standard theory, and neither so much as mentioned the great prefect Anthemius, so offensive was his name to the woman who had clashed with him in the palace thirty years earlier.[79]

The attitudes of Socrates, Sozomen, and Theodoret close the circle, proving beyond reasonable doubt that Pulcheria's vow emerged from a threat to the independence of the dynasty, that her "godly resolve" had essentially political origins despite her youth. In the next two years she went on to reassert the Theodosian house as a political force. By March, 413, Isidorus had given up the city prefecture, and Anthemius himself is last attested April 18, 414.[80] He may simply have died, but the context suggests that not long after her vow Pulcheria ordered a change of government. To replace Anthemius she recalled her mother's associate Aurelian, although he had been living in retirement for more than a decade and was by now a very old man. Aurelian received both the praetorian prefecture of the East and the distinction *patricius*.[81]

78. Theodoret, *Kirchengeschichte*, ed. L. Parmentier and F. Scheidweiler, 2nd ed. (Berlin, 1954), pp. xxv–xxvi; Sozomenus, *Kirchengeschichte*, ed. J. Bidez and G.C. Hansen (Berlin, 1970), pp. lxv–lxvii; W. Eltester, *RE*, VA (1927), 1240, "Sozomenos."

79. Among others, Seeck concluded: "dass man in den Kreisen der neuen Regentin von den Verdiensten ihres Vorgängers nicht gern reden hörte," *Geschichte*, VI (Stuttgart, 1920), 401 *ad* 69. 8.

80. *CTh* 9. 40. 22. Among others Bury, *Later Roman Empire*, I, 214; Zakrzewski, *Parti*, p. 177; and Jones, *Later Roman Empire*, I, 179, believe that Anthemius died shortly after; Seeck, *Geschichte*, VI, 69, that Pulcheria forced him to lay down his office. There is no way of knowing.

81. For Aurelian's second praetorian prefecture and the distinction *patricius* see Jones, "Collegiate Prefectures," p. 81, and *PLRE*, I, 129. They are recorded under December 30 in *Chron. pasch. a.* 414 (p. 571 Bonn): ἀπὸ Αὐρηλιανοῦ δὶς ἐπάρχου τῶν ἱερῶν πραιτωρίων καὶ πατρικίου; in *CTh* 3. 12. 4, 9. 28. 2, etc.: "Aureliano PPO II"; and are at least alluded to in *Anth. graec.* 16. 73: ὃν τρισέπαρχον καὶ πατέρα βασιλῆες ἐκαλέσαντο μέγιστοι. Seeck, "Studien," p. 449, and (following him) von Haehling, *Religionszugehörigkeit*, pp. 82–83, identify the praetorian prefect of 414–16 with another Aurelian attested as *proconsul Asiae* in 395, *PLRE*, I, 129, "Aurelianus 4," but the language of the *Chron. pasch.* is decisive against them. In the list of praetorian prefects of the East for 395–414 it is difficult to find a place for the second Aurelian. The word τρισέπαρχος in *Anth. graec.* 16. 73 confirms Jones and the *PLRE*, because here the type of prefecture is not specified and thus the city prefecture the first Aurelian held in 393 must be counted. Cf. Monax-

On July 4, 414, about the time Anthemius disappeared, Theodosius proclaimed his sister Augusta.[82] As usual, the literary sources do not describe the ceremony or suggest how ideologues conceived its significance, but coins from the first period of Pulcheria's reign do indicate continuity, faithfully reproducing the types and legends of Flaccilla and Eudoxia along with the latter's *dextera Dei* (fig. 12).[83] Like her mother, Pulcheria was *a Deo coronata,* and she possessed sacral *basileía.* More clearly than that of her mother, Pulcheria's distinction had nothing to do with childbearing or the woman's function but expressed in official ceremonial, costume, and iconography the paradoxical but acceptable dominion of an imperial woman. Aurelian certainly found it acceptable, as he had during the tangle of 399–400. On December 30, 414, he dedicated a portrait bust of Pulcheria in the senate house of Constantinople; it was grouped with those of Honorius and Theodosius, her fellow Augusti.[84] Again official iconography assimilated the distinction of an Augusta with that of her male counterparts.

Unquestionably Pulcheria was a politician, an imperius young woman of her mother's stamp. Sozomen assured readers who might have found her shocking that she modestly attributed her exploits to her brother, but he also emphasized direct intervention: "she took control of the government, reaching excellent decisions and swiftly carrying them out with written instructions."[85] From the events of 414–21 and from contemporary reaction to them, some notion can be gleaned of the content of these instructions. Like its predecessor, the Pulcheria regime apparently reached decisions with some sensitivity for the traditional avenues to influence. Aurelian himself symbolized continuity, as did his location of imperial portraiture in the senate house, a traditional *locus* for the display of prestige. Some traditionalists even applauded the demise of Anthemius. During Aurelian's

---

ius, city prefect twice and praetorian prefect once in the period 416–20, called τρὶς ἔπαρχος γενόμενος: Call. *V. Hyp.* 21. 11 (ed. Bartelink).

Aurelian was perhaps seventy-five by 414, since Syn. *De prov.* 2. 5 (p. 123 Terzaghi) (referring to 400) calls him γηρῶν.

82. *Chron. pasch. a.* 414 (p. 571 Bonn): Πουλχερία . . . ἀνηγορεύθη; Marcell. com. *a.* 414. 1 (*MGH: AA,* XI, 71): "Pulcheria . . . Augusta appellata est."

83. Tolstoi, *Monnaies,* I, 104 no. 31; Kent and Carson, *Bronze,* p. 90 no. 2226.

84. *Chron. pasch. a.* 414 (p. 571 Bonn).

85. 9. 1. 5–6; cf. similar (but independent) language in Philostorg. 12. 7.

second praetorian prefecture the senate offered him the singular honor of a golden statue "for ending its distress."[86] The nature of this "distress" is unclear, but a good guess is Anthemian domination of the prefectures, which other great men must have resented until the new regime brought it to an end.[87]

Despite this show of confidence in Aurelian, sufficient evidence exists to prove that in general Pulcheria broke with the values and traditions of the ruling class. As her "godly resolve" reshaped life in the palace, it also produced broader innovation. The new line does not come through clearly in legislation against heresy, for even Anthemius had devoted the resources of government to support of the dynastic faith.[88] Pulcheria's treatment of the Jews is more revealing. Traditional policy had recognized synagogues as private property entitled to protection against the attacks of Christian fanatics. In 415 Theodosius II issued a constitution to Aurelian which for the first time forbade construction of new synagogues and in addition required the destruction of synagogues "in desert places, if it can be accomplished without riots."[89] While not directly reversing traditional policy, this constitution was an invitation to fanatics to go about their work of intimidation and destruction. Its implications can be measured from an outbreak that took place at about this time in Alexandria, where the new bishop Cyril led a Christian mob against the synagogues, drove the Jewish population from the city, and invited his followers to seize their property. The augustal prefect (civil governor) Orestes, recognizing that Cyril's conduct challenged imperial authority, objected to the court in Constantinople, but Cyril also related his version of the conflict and escaped the emperor's anger with the somewhat lame justification that the Jews were at fault. In his account of these events Socrates attacked Cyril openly for violence and "rebel-

86. *Anth. graec.* 16. 73; cf. Alan Cameron, *Porphyrius the Charioteer* (Oxford, 1973), p. 217.

87. Yet the new regime promoted the previously unknown Helio to master of offices in 414 and kept him on until 427: O. Seeck, *RE,* VIII (1913), 46–47, "Helion 2"; *PLRE,* II, 533, "Helion 1."

88. *CTh* 9. 35. 7, 16. 5. 48–49, 6. 6–7, *CI* 1. 3. 16; cf. Zakrzewski, *Parti,* p. 176, calling this legislation "une concession sans doute sincère à l'esprit de son temps." Thus Seeck, *Geschichte,* VI, 69, and W. Ensslin, *RE,* XXIII (1959), 1955, "Pulcheria 2," are overzealous in discerning the special influence of Pulcheria behind *CTh* 3. 12. 4 and 16. 5. 57–58 (both to Aurelian 415). Lippold, *RE,* suppl. XIII (1973), 1015, "Theodosius II," judiciously stresses continuity.

89. *CTh* 16. 8. 22; contrast esp. 16. 8. 9 (393): "Iudaeorum sectam nulla lege prohibitam esse constat"; M. Avi-Yonah, *The Jews of Palestine* (Oxford, 1976), pp. 208–20, 227–28.

lion" (*dynasteia*), language that implied harsh criticism of the regime for not standing up to him.[90]

Socrates went on to describe other episodes in the "truceless war" which raged at this time between Cyril's followers and the local authorities of Alexandria. Monks from the desert of Nitria abused Orestes as a "Hellene and sacrificer" and nearly killed him. In March of 415 other fanatics led by a minor cleric murdered Hypatia, the Alexandrian Neoplatonist and revered teacher of Synesius.[91] Socrates expressed the outrage of a traditionalist and admirer of Anthemius: "for killings, rioting, and like conduct are utterly foreign to those who have the mind of Christ."[92]

Apparently the court of Pulcheria did not agree, at least when violence contributed to the advance of Christianity. In September, 416, a legation from the Alexandrian city council approached Monaxius, Aurelian's successor as praetorian prefect of the East, asking that Cyril's excesses be checked. In his response the emperor denied most of the legation's request as *inutilia,* granting relief only from the "terror of those called *parabalani,* " hospital attendants who served as Cyril's shock troops for intimidating his enemies. In the future *parabalani* were not to attend the council or the courts en masse, and the emperor limited their strength to five hundred, with vacancies to be filled by the augustal prefect.[93] Two years later, however, the

90. Soc. 7. 13, apparently based on the relations of Cyril and Orestes. Criticism of the court is implicit in Socrates' words Ὀρέστης δὲ καὶ πρότερον μὲν ἐμίσει τὴν δυναστείαν τῶν ἐπισκόπων, ὅτι παρηροῦντο πολὺ τῆς ἐξουσίας τῶν ἐκ βασιλέως ἄρχειν τεταγμένων (7. 13. 9) and in his insistence that Orestes had kept the court informed of Cyril's conduct (7. 13. 19; cf. 14. 8). Contemporaries—at least those who agreed with Socrates—would have found the lack of imperial response unsettling.

91. Soc. 7. 14–15; cf. J. M. Rist, "Hypatia," *Phoenix* 19 (1965), 221–25.

92. 7. 15. 6.

93. *CTh* 16. 2. 42; cf. 12. 12. 15. On the *parabalani* cf. A. Philipsborn, "La compagnie d'ambulanciers «parabalani» d'Alexandrie," *Byzantion* 20 (1950), 185–90. Seeck, *Geschichte*, VI, 404–5 *ad* 78. 29 (following Mommsen-Meyer and Godefroid), recognized a lacuna at the beginning of 16. 2. 42: "quia inter cetera Alexandrinae legationis inutilia hoc etiam decretis scribtum est, ut reverentissimus episcopus de Alexandrina civitate aliquas . . . . non exire, quod quidem terrore eorum, qui parabalani nuncupantur, legationi insertum est." Seeck proposes "etwas zugunsten des Bischofs Cyrillus," but in my view the emperor would hardly have called such a provision *inutile*. I suggest a restoration like "ut r. e. de Alexandrina civitate aliquas [relationes] non [faciat] exire." Apparently, the emperor was outraged that the various *decreta* of the Alexandrian council submitted for imperial action included a particularly noxious one inhibiting Cyril. The court realized, however, that terrorism had compelled the countil to act, and that peace between the bishop and local authorities depended on limiting the political intervention of the *parabalani*.

regime withdrew even this concession to the traditional ideal of law and order. In a constitution of 418 Theodosius permitted the *parabalani* to increase to six hundred and returned them to the control of Cyril, "whose commands and dispositions they are to obey."[94] Socrates' criticism of Pulcheria's court applied here as well.

Evidence also exists that Pulcheria broke with her predecessor's receptiveness toward Hellenes. In 415 Aurelian received a constitution which excluded "those polluted from the error or, rather, the crime of pagan worship" from the army and administration.[95] Some men accused of Hellenism or tainted by excess devotion to culture probably were excluded, unless they could claim like Orestes to have received baptism from the bishop of Constantinople himself. Those who could not would read with approval the bitter comments of Eunapius, the sophist of Sardes, the only opponent of Christianity whose opinion of Pulcheria's regime has survived. Writing about 423, he charged that "in the time of Pulcheria" provincial governorships and offices of vicar and proconsul were auctioned off to the highest bidders, who then recovered their investments by brutal extortion. The praetorian prefect himself understood the system and could be bribed to deny relief to the victims—at such a price that the guilty magistrates saw their profits wasted, and their personal fortunes as well.[96] Of course, venal *suffragium* (sale of offices) was a well-established, thoroughly Roman practice, so much so that legislation had even defined the contractual obligations of the parties involved.[97] It was also an abuse, however, and offered enemies of a regime more than one point of attack.[98] The sophist's charge that under Pulcheria "the wretched

94. *CTh* 16. 2. 43.

95. *CTh* 16. 10. 21; cf. Seeck, *Regesten*, p. 331. Von Haehling, *Religionszugehörigkeit*, pp. 600–605, argues (correctly, in my opinion) that this was the first general exclusion of pagans from the imperial service. He also employs quantitative method to demonstrate that the law had an effect: according to his statistics, only three men attested in high office during the reign of Theodosius II (from 408) can be identified positively as pagans, all three of them *magistri militum*!

96. Eunap. frg. 87 (*FHG*, IV, 52–53); cf. Paschoud, *Cinq études*, pp. 169–75, for the fragment's date.

97. *CTh* 2. 29. 1–2 (362, 394) with the discussion of W. Goffart, "Did Julian Combat Venal *Suffragium*?" *CP* 65 (1970), 145–51. Cf. Jones, *Later Roman Empire*, I, 391–96; G. E. M. de Ste. Croix, "Suffragium: From Vote to Patronage," *British Journal of Sociology* 5 (1954), 33–48; C. Collot, "La pratique et l'institution du suffragium au Bas-Empire," *Revue historique de droit français et étranger* ser. 4, 43 (1965), 185–221.

98. For other near-contemporary examples of such invective see Zos. 4. 28 (*infra*) and Claud. *In Eutr.* 1. 190–210, 2. 585–90; cf. Alan Cameron, *Claudian*, pp. 190–91.

decrees [of the emperors] perished with the laws" paralleled the criticism implicit in Socrates, but Eunapius also went further: "What stands in your way, most curious fellow? Why do *you* not govern cities and provinces?" In Eunapius' view, venal *suffragium* opened high office to all comers, creating among the unworthy a craving for power more deadly than the thirst-producing venom of the *dipsas* snake.[99] The converse of this invective is that genuine merit, in the traditional forms of previous service, aristocracy, literary taste, and intellectual distinction, no longer guaranteed a man's promotion "in the time of Pulcheria."[100]

Already Pulcheria's new directions are clear enough, but the reactions of Socrates and Eunapius should be read in the light of other evidence that is less partisan and thus more spectacular. Above all, the Pulcheria regime took seriously the emperor's claim to be "master of victory."[101] Effete, bookish, and like his father palace-bound, Theodosius II necessarily depended on reliable generals to exert the claim. Some among them were Romans—the pious and orthodox Anatolius, for example, *magister militum* on the eastern frontier around 420.[102] By this time, however, two barbarians of Arian faith held the more prestigious commands "in the emperor's presence." Plinta the Goth, consul in 419, impressed Sozomen as "most potent of all around the emperor," and the Alan Ardaburius, Plinta's kinsman by marriage, founded a powerful military family which would

99. Eunap. *loc. cit.*

100. This aspect of Eunapius' invective comes through more directly in the attack on Theodosius I in Zos. 4. 28. 3 (probably based on Eunapius). In the case of Pulcheria's regime, prosopography tends to support the charge. Only two men attested in high office under Anthemius advanced their careers during the period 414–21: Monaxius MO 408–9, PUC 414, PPO *Or* 416–20; and Strategius CRP 410, PPO *Ill* 415 (*PLRE*, II, 764–65, 1033). Monaxius may have broken with Anthemius following a bread riot in 409 (*Chron. pasch.*, p. 571 Bonn; Marcell. com. *a.* 409 [*MGH: AA*, XI, 70]; Keil, "Familie," p. 200), while the Illyrican prefecture was not a praesental office and thus not so much an object of competition among those who hoped to influence the emperor. So far as is known, the powerful Helio (*supra*, n. 87) was a new man.

101. The thesis of my essay "Pulcheria's Crusade."

102. Recent scholarship (e.g., *PLRE*, II, 84–85, "Anatolius 10") has ignored this Anatolius attested independently by Cyril. Scyth. *V. Euth.* 10 (*TU*, XLIX:2, 18–19), Movsēs Xorenaçi *Hist. of Armenia* 3. 56–59 (II, 164–67 Langlois), Procop. *B. Pers.* 1. 2. 11–15, and Theoph. *a.m.* 5921 (p. 87 de Boor). See, however, O. Seeck, *RE*, I (1894), 2072–73, "Anatolius 9," and Holum, "Pulcheria's Crusade," pp. 156, 167–69. He may have been a relative (father?) or possibly even identical with the Anatolius known as *mag. mil. per Orientem* from *ca.* 437 and later as *praesentalis*: Demandt, *RE*, suppl. XII (1970), 751–52, "Magister Militum."

serve the Theodosian *basileía* faithfully until its extinction.[103] Memory of the Gaïnas revolt had induced Anthemius, Aurelian, and similar politicians to withdraw behind the new land walls of Constantinople and to insist that the emperors not employ such intimidating men. Through nearly two decades (401–18) no Germanic or associated barbarian name is attested among the *magistri*.[104] But when Pulcheria began to assert her brother's independence, she broke with the politicians in this respect too and returned to the traditional practice of her dynasty.

Pulcheria then put the generals to use in the interest of the dynasty. Far away in Persian Khuzestan, sometime in 419 or early 420, a Christian bishop destroyed a fire-altar of the Zoroastrian state religion, forcing Yazdgard I to execute him and those of his co-religionists who chose to remain defiant. When the king died late in 420, his son and successor Vahram V intensified the attack, breaking completely with Yazdgard's conciliatory policy.[105] The Romans responded quickly and with even greater fanaticism. War was already in the air months before Yazdgard's death, by May, 420, when the emperor ordered property-holders in border provinces to fortify their estates in case of a Persian invasion.[106] When refugees from the persecution appeared in Constantinople soon afterward to plead that their sufferings not be ignored, they found the court, in the words of Socrates, "ready to do anything for the sake of Christianity."[107] In 421 Roman troops undertook a major two-pronged offensive. Theodosius ordered Anatolius northward to support a revolt in Persian Armenia. At the same time Ardaburius, who had led his praesental army from Europe to the Mesopotamian frontier, struck plundering into enemy territory and besieged Nisibis, a major Persian stronghold.[108] When Vahram had been sufficiently chastized, hardheaded generals must have reasoned, diplomats could take over and negotiate

---

103. W. Ensslin, *RE*, XXI (1951), 457–58, "Plinta"; O. Seeck, *RE*, II (1896), 606–7, "Ardabur 1"; Demandt, *RE*, suppl. XII (1970), 746–48, "Magister Militum"; also Soz. 7. 17. 35 on Plinta's influence, and for his kinship with Ardaburius the so-called Silver Shield of Aspar, Delbrueck, *Konsulardiptychen*, pp. 154–56 no. 35.

104. Lippold, *RE*, suppl. XIII (1973), 1014, "Theodosius II," observes the re-emergence of Germans and related barbarians under Theodosius II but incorrectly traces it back to 410. Cf. *supra*, Chap. 2, n. 79.

105. Holum, "Pulcheria's Crusade," pp. 155–56.

106. *CI* 8. 10. 10.

107. 7. 18. 7.

108. Movsēs Xorenaçi *Hist. of Armenia* 3. 59 (II, 166–67 Langlois), Soc. 7. 18. 9–15, 19–20, Holum, "Pulcheria's Crusade," pp. 162–63, 167–68.

a halt to the persecution. The emperor's ability to secure victory would be vindicated.

Sometime in 420 or early 421[109] the court set in motion a sequence of events that paralleled the efforts of the hardheaded generals. As Eunapius might have objected, it "belittled the emperor's courage, the strength of his troops, and the conditions of real battle."[110] The chronicler Theophanes Confessor (ninth century) preserved a circumstantial narrative:

> Under the influence of the blessed Pulcheria, the pious Theodosius sent a rich donation to the archbishop of Jerusalem for distribution to the needy, and also a golden cross studded with precious stones to be erected on Golgotha. In exchange for these gifts, the archbishop dispatched relics of the right arm of Stephen Protomartyr, in the care of St. Passarion. When this man had reached Chalcedon, in that very night the blessed Pulcheria saw St. Stephen in a vision saying to her: "Behold, your prayer has been heard and your desire has come to pass, for I have arrived in Chalcedon." And she arose taking her brother with her and went to greet the holy relics. Receiving them into the palace, she founded a splendid chapel for the holy Protomartyr, and in it she deposited the holy relics.[111]

The narrative fits neatly into its context. As a contemporary *inventio* narrative reveals, the bones of St. Stephen had appeared outside Jerusalem in December, 415, and had come under the control of the bishop.[112] Naturally, gifts were required to inspire his generosity, and Passarion, a prominent ascetic of episcopal rank,[113] was a natural choice to escort the holy treasure. The date of the court's request, five years or so after the bones first came to light, was more than coincidental. As Roman armies marched to their positions, the court did well to procure the alliance of the saint whose very name (*Stephanos*) promised the victor's crown.[114] In like manner Theodosius the Great had rallied St. John the Baptist for the Frigidus campaign, and thus the emperor Leo I a generation later would seek translation to Con-

109. Holum, "Pulcheria's Crusade," p. 163 n. 46, for the correct date.

110. *Supra*, p. 51.

111. Theoph. *a.m.* 5920 (pp. 86–87 de Boor).

112. S. Vanderlinden, "*Revelatio Sancti Stephani* (BHL 7850–6)," *Revue des études byzantines* 4 (1946), 178–217.

113. F. Delmas, "Saint Passarion," *EO* 3 (1900), 162–63.

114. E.g., Proclus *Or.* 17. 2 (*PG*, LXV, 809) spoken the day after Christmas: χθὲς ἐτέχθη, καὶ σήμερον αὐτῷ Στέφανος προσηνέχθη· Στέφανος, ὁ φερώνυμος μάρτυς· Στέφανος, ὁ ἔμψυχος στέφανος· Στέφανος, τὸ αὐτόπλεκτον διάδημα· Στέφανος, τὸ αὐτοχάλκευτον περίθεμα; cf. Gagé, "ΣΤΑΥΡΟΣ ΝΙΚΟΠΟΙΟΣ," p. 381.

stantinople of the corpse of Simeon Stylites, so that "by his prayers" the pillar saint could guard the *basileia*.[115] "Living and present" like the prophet Samuel, St. Stephen would intercede with the divine protector and help the emperor's armies defeat Persia.

Correct so far as it goes, this interpretation is incomplete and therefore misleading. Like the prophet Samuel, St. Stephen arrived in Chalcedon with his episcopal escort. When he reached the urban shore, perhaps crowds of the faithful thronged in like manner to celebrate his *adventus*. But, if so, Theophanes consigned these joyous faithful to oblivion, a striking omission which calls for an explanation. Read in the light of contemporary *adventus* ceremonial, it indicates that this was not a normal *adventus* like that of Samuel but a highly unusual one which finds its closest parallel in a visual document, in the well-known Translation of Relics Ivory of the Trier Cathedral Treasure (fig. 15). The object itself is controversial. Art historians do not agree on its provenance or on the date of its manufacture. Again, the most fruitful method of interpretation is to read its iconography in the light of *adventus* ceremonial. This procedure reveals sufficient convergence with the Theophanes *adventus* to permit the conclusion that text and ivory narrate the same event.[116]

The Trier cortege enters the scene from the left. On a decorated imperial wagon two figures in episcopal garb somewhat possessively hold St. Stephen's right arm, contained in a gabled box. Although two stocky mules still draw the wagon vigorously to the right, the head of the procession has already reached its destination. Leading it is the emperor, wearing the diadem and the *paludamentum* secured on his right shoulder with a jeweled imperial *fibula*. High officials flank him, similarly clad in the *paludamentum* but with less elaborate *fibulae*. Like Theodosius these officials carry large candles, part of the expected apparatus of *adventus* ceremonial. As in the *adventus* of Samuel, the presence of the emperor and high officials leaves an impression of social order.

115. *V. Sym. syr.* 136 (*TU*, XXXII: 4, 179).

116. For complete discussion see K. Holum and G. Vikan, "The Trier Ivory, *Adventus* Ceremonial, and the Relics of St. Stephen," *DOP* 33 (1979), 113–33. See also J. Wortley, "The Trier Ivory Reconsidered," *GRBS* 21 (1980), 381–94, responding to Holum and Vikan with the view that the translation recorded by the Trier Ivory was "a fictitious event" for which "the earliest and almost the only evidence . . . is the testimony of Theophanes" (p. 382). Unfortunately, Wortley has ignored the St. Stephen encomium quoted *infra* (and in Holum and Vikan, p. 131). This text permits no reasonable doubt that the translation in question was historical.

Figure 12
Solidus of Pulcheria,
minted Constantinople 414–*ca.* 420 (2X),
Dumbarton Oaks

Figure 13
Solidus of Pulcheria,
minted Constantinople *ca.* 420–22 (2X),
Dumbarton Oaks

Figure 14
Solidus of Justa Grata Honoria,
minted Ravenna 438–50 (2X),
Dumbarton Oaks

Figure 15
Translation of Relics Ivory, 13.1 x 26.1 cm,
Trier, Domschatz

But the Trier Ivory parallels Theophanes in omitting the joyous crowds who normally greeted the arrival of relics in Constantinople. The figures that populate the architectural curtain in the background observe instead the etiquette of the court. Some stand at wooden attention, others cense the procession before them and chant the usual acclamations to honor the imperial presence and the saint.[117] These figures lend the scene a pervasive courtly atmosphere and invite the viewer to associate the architecture itself with the imperial palace —a three-story arcade surrounding an interior court, or perhaps a structure along the *mesē* where it approached the palace complex. In the interests of effective design the artist may have sacrificed precise architectural relationships; thus, the imposing portal at the left with its lunette icon of Christ may comfortably be identified with the Chalke gate.[118]

The most obtrusive parallel between the Trier Ivory and the Theophanes text is common focus on the pious acts of the empress. In Theophanes the emperor initiates the transaction, but does so "under the influence of the blessed Pulcheria." On the Ivory Theodosius wears distinctive costume and inclines slightly forward, but essentially he remains only part of the cortege and thus of the ceremonial context. The direction of the wagon's movement and the posture and gaze of other participants direct the viewer's attention inexorably toward the scene at the right, toward the diminutive woman clothed in the rich costume of an Augusta.[119] As in Theophanes, Pulcheria has founded a chapel in the palace complex. Workmen on its superstructure apply the finishing touches, showing by their feverish activity that they have constructed it at her command especially to receive these relics. The dramatic moment has arrived. "Receiving them into the palace," Theophanes concluded, ". . . in it she deposited the holy relics." With the gesture of the Augusta's right hand, the Ivory achieves a clarity of expression unavailable in the colorless narrative of the chronicler. The palace is Pulcheria's

117. The hand-to-ear gesture of the figures in the second register indicates singing: A. Hermann, "Mit der Hand Singen," *JfAC* 1 (1958), 105–8.

118. Mango, *Brazen House*, p. 104, refrained from using the Trier Ivory as evidence for the Chalke because of uncertain "origin, date, and subject matter." At least some uncertainties have now been removed.

119. The diadem of this Augusta does not correspond closely with those from late fourth- to early fifth-century coins and full-plastic portraiture (e.g., figs. 5–7, 9, 11–14, 19), indicating that the Ivory was created a century or so later with updated costume. See *infra*, n. 125.

home and into it she is welcoming the saint, to a permanent abode with her in the haunts of *basileía*.

The force of Pulcheria's gesture could emerge with equal transparency in evocative verbal language:

ἐν βασιλείοις στέφανος· ἐθαλάμευσε γὰρ αὐτὸν ἡ βασιλὶς καὶ παρθένος.

Stephen / the victory crown is in the palace, for the virgin empress has brought him into her bride-chamber.[120]

From an encomium of St. Stephen spoken only a few years after his translation, these words prove that in the eyes of contemporaries, as for the carver of the Trier Ivory, the saint's *adventus* brought him into a dynamic and intimate union with Pulcheria.

The conclusion to be drawn from both Theophanes and the Trier Ivory is that St. Stephen arrived in Constantinople in principle to intercede not for Theodosius but for Pulcheria herself. Since the translation may comfortably be associated with the Persian war, an additional conclusion likewise seems justified, that Pulcheria conceived the war to be a test and confirmation of her own ability to inspire victory.

She could claim that ability, to judge from the Trier Ivory, for its iconography includes one element which has yet to be explained. As she extends her right arm to receive St. Stephen, Pulcheria cradles in her left a long, crudely fashioned cross. This object makes good sense as part of the apparatus of *adventus* ceremonial, like the candles of the emperor and officials or the chanting and incense which greeted the procession. When Bishop Porphyry returned to Gaza in 402, for example, the faithful came to meet him "carrying the sign of the precious cross . . . and singing hymns."[121]

But this interpretation does not explain why Pulcheria alone should hold the cross. It may indeed honor St. Stephen, but, more importantly, this cross draws attention to the empress, to a personal quality that sets her off from the other persons in the tableau. As is well known, the cross was the most potent victory symbol available in the vocabulary of Christian art, evoking the victory of Christ on Golgotha over death, the devil, and the enemies of faith.[122] Thus it was an appropriate instrument with which to honor the *adventus* of a

120. *PG*, LXIII, 933; cf. Leroy, *Homilétique*, p. 158, identifying the text as a work of Proclus of Constantinople.
121. Marc. Diac. *V. Porph.* 58 (ed. Grégoire-Kugener).
122. For references see Holum, "Pulcheria's Crusade," p. 164 n. 49.

holy man or of the relics of St. Stephen, whose martyrdom repeated the victory of Christ and proved that it was a living and present reality.[123] The cross applied equally to Pulcheria, for she too repeated Christ's victory on Golgotha: in her "godly resolve," in "devoting her virginity to Christ"—thus depriving herself of the benefits of childbearing—in "exhausting her wealth by pious works and making her body dead to its passions."[124] Pulcheria's ascetic achievement contained the promise that the Roman armies would defeat Persia. This was her claim to inspire victory, and this she put to the test in 421.

The court's alacrity in attacking Persia has been explored thus far only from literary evidence and from an art object of apparently liturgical character.[125] It is therefore gratifying to discover the same themes in contemporary productions of official propaganda. The Theophanes text already confirms imperial preoccupation with Christian victory symbolism. Like the cross of the Ivory, the "golden cross studded with precious stones" Theodosius erected on Golgotha "under Pulcheria's influence" evoked Christ's victory and suggested that it would be repeated in imperial victory over present enemies of faith. At roughly the same time (*ca.* 420–22) the mint of Constantinople initiated a new solidus type with the same victory symbolism (fig. 13):[126]

Reverse. VOTXX MVLTXXX Victory standing left, holding a long jeweled cross. CONOB in the exergue.

Struck to celebrate the twentieth anniversary of Theodosius' elevation (hence VOTXX MVLTXXX), these coins reveal two significant innovations. For the first time numismatic art, the most conservative medium of official propaganda, presented a patently Christian explanation for imperial victory, one which, like the *adventus* of St. Stephen and official response to the defeat of Gaïnas in 400, openly

123. See esp. Basil of Seleucia *Or.* 41 (*PG,* LXXXV, 472), declaring that the cross rightly adorns St. Stephen because it "firmed him up" for his own passion: νευρώσας τῆς σῆς προθυμίας τὰ αἰσθητήρια.
124. Proclus *Or.* 12. 1 (*PG,* LXV, 788), paralleling the ascetic achievement of Pulcheria with the martyrdom of St. Stephen, quoted in full *infra,* pp. 137–38.
125. The Trier Ivory may well have decorated one side of a relic box, serving to authenticate the relics contained within by tracing visually the history of their translation. Leroy, *Homilétique,* p. 158, believes that Proclus *Or.* 12. 1 refers to mosaic decorations of Pulcheria's palatine chapel, a likely source of the iconography of the Trier Ivory.
126. For full discussion see Holum, "Pulcheria's Crusade," pp. 153–57, 165–67.

belittled the emperor's strength and the efforts of hardheaded generals. For the first time also, coin designers abandoned the traditional distinction, expressed through distinct reverse types, between male and female holders of *basileía*. The Long-Cross solidi appeared with identical reverses from the mint of Constantinople and with obverses of Theodosius II, of his western colleague Honorius, and of Pulcheria. Like Aurelian's dedication of portrait busts in the senate house, these coins assimilated the Augusta with her male counterparts. Like the cross of the Trier Ivory, they declared that a woman might claim to be "master of victory."

Within a few years after the Romans invaded Persia in 421, the court ordered its architects to raise a new victory column at the Hebdomon, a primary *locus* of victory propaganda, where the armies paraded ceremonially before setting out for battle. A monolithic granite column approximately seventeen meters in height supported a statue of Theodosius II, probably equestrian. The statue has perished, but excavations turned up fragments of its base now preserved in the Archeological Museum, Istanbul:[127]

> D(ominus) N(oster) Theodo[sius pius felix August]us
> Imperator et [fortissimus triumfato]r
> [gentium barbararum, pere]nnis [et ubiqu]e
> [victor, pro] votis sororum, pacato
> [orbe rom]ano celsus exultat

Although the surviving letters do not demand them, the excellent restorations of R. Demangel, drawn mainly from contemporary coinage, permit an attempt at translation:

> Our lord, the gracious and fortunate Theodosius Augustus
> Commander-in-chief, very mighty, triumphant
> Over barbarian nations, always and everywhere
> Victor, through the vows of his sisters, having pacified
> The Roman world, rejoices on high

Even without Demangel's restorations the sense would come through clearly enough. Theodosius has won military victories bringing peace to the Empire. Surviving letters identify the source of that victory— "[through] the vows of his sisters." The nature of these "vows" is not specified, but the inscription should be read with the Trier Ivory cross in mind and in the light of Sozomen's contemporary interpre-

---

127. Demangel, *Contribution*, pp. 33–43; cf. B. Croke, "Evidence for the Hun Invasion of Thrace in A.D. 422," *GRBS* 18 (1977), 365–66, associating the victory column (like Demangel) with the events of 421–22.

tation. In his view, when Pulcheria devoted her virginity to God and imposed the same vow on her sisters, she secured God's favor, causing "every threat and war raised against her brother to disperse spontaneously."[128] More impressively than in propaganda response to the events of 400, "in the time of Pulcheria" the longstanding dichotomy between the official ideology of imperial victory and Christian reaction to the same phenomenon was made to evaporate.

Diverse strands of evidence and interpretation may now be drawn tightly together. During the minority of Theodosius II the military and religious foundations of Theodosian *basileía* nearly gave way before an assault of civilians and politicians, traditionalists who placed their confidence in the genius of Anthemius. Pulcheria recognized the threat, responded with her "godly resolve," and prevented its perpetuation. In the years after 412/13, the virgin Augusta did not lay her hands, openly at least, on her brother's magisterial powers. Atop the Hebdomon column Theodosius II still appeared as commander-in-chief. With admirable modesty and due respect for tradition and law, Pulcheria attributed her exploits to her brother, satisfied, it seems, if decisions were made and executed "under her influence." But law and tradition mattered little, because in a pious court Pulcheria exerted influence that could hardly be resisted. Like her mother before her, Pulcheria exercised real power. Her vow, moreover, produced an unheard-of claim to imperial legitimacy, that of ascetic achievement. Together the Trier Ivory, the Long-Cross solidi, and the Hebdomon inscription demonstrate that the virgin empress claimed to be master of victory. In Pulcheria's version the sacral *basileía* of empresses approached perilously near to the fullness of sovereignty.

128. Soz. 9. 3. 3.

CHAPTER FOUR

Aelia Eudocia Augusta

A girl of wit and intellect . . .

Imbued with her mother's imperiousness, drawing on a female form of *basileía* now two generations old, Aelia Pulcheria had employed influence and power in ways that alarmed traditionalists. The invective of Eunapius proves that her ascendancy deprived many eastern aristocrats of hope of advancement and the means to satisfy their ambition. In the early 420s these aristocrats struck back. Adopting the methods of their enemy, they selected an Athenian maid, one who perfectly embodied their cultural biases, and married her to Theodosius II. When she had received a new name, Aelia Eudocia, and the distinction Augusta, her backers exploited her influence and power to gain high office and resist Pulcherian innovation, for in the East even old-fashioned men accepted the *basileía* of women. Ironically, the efforts of these men only induced Pulcheria to reinforce her own *basileía* with new resources, available to her because she was a virgin. In her competition with Eudocia the virgin empress brought the Theodosian phenomenon of female dominion to completion.

The Athenian Maid

The traditionalists chose a maid originally called Athenaïs. A century ago Ferdinand Gregorovius told her story in an exquisite book, but left much of its significance unrecognized because he accepted uncritically the charming legend of her marriage.[1]

At the age of twenty, this legend claimed, the emperor Theodosius II desired to marry. He discussed the matter with his older

---

1. F. Gregorovius, *Athenaïs, Geschichte einer byzantinischen Kaiserin*, 3rd ed. (Leipzig, 1892), pp. 61–64, surveys the story's tradition and concludes that it is authentic: "Sie enthält nichts, was nicht wirklich geschehen sein kann."

sister Pulcheria, who then began to search among maidens of patrician
or imperial blood. But while rank was desirable, Theodosius assured
his sister, if a girl of surpassing beauty could be found low birth
would be no hindrance. This was a passionate young man indeed!
Pulcheria dutifully extended her search, sending messengers throughout the Empire. Paulinus, the companion of Theodosius' childhood
and still his loyal friend, also joined in the search.

At this time, the legend continued, a girl named Athenaïs had
come to Constantinople. She was the child of the Athenian sophist
Leontius, who had recently died, leaving his large estate to his two
grown sons, Valerius and Gesius, but remembering his daughter with
only a hundred coins, "because her good fortune, surpassing that of
all other women, will be enough." The two brothers had refused to
set aside their father's will and share his wealth with their destitute
sister. Thus her mother's sister had brought her to Constantinople,
and her father's sister, who resided there, was able to arrange an
audience with the empress. When Pulcheria received the girl in the
palace, she was astonished at her beauty and at the intelligence and
sophistication with which she presented her grievance. Assured by the
two aunts that Athenaïs was indeed a virgin, and, moreover, that she
had received an excellent classical education from her father, the
empress hastened to report to her brother. She had found "a young
girl, a Greek maid, very beautiful, pure and dainty, eloquent as well,
the daughter of a philosopher." "Enflamed with desire, as any youth
would have been," Theodosius sent for Paulinus and demanded that
the girl be brought to his apartments, where he and his friend could
observe her from behind a curtain. Immediately he fell in love, and
Paulinus too found the girl charming. After converting her to Christianity—Athenaïs had been raised a pagan—Theodosius renamed
her Eudocia and made her his wife.

When word reached the two brothers that their sister was now an
empress, they fled in terror. But Eudocia recalled them to Constantinople, and Theodosius even rewarded them, making Gesius praetorian
prefect of Illyricum and Valerius master of offices, for it was Eudocia's
happy destiny, not their own evil dispositions, that had caused them
to mistreat her. Theodosius also honored his friend Paulinus for
bringing about the marriage, promoting him through the higher
positions until he too became master of offices. As "groomsman"
Paulinus remained on familiar terms with the emperor, and even
enjoyed frequent visits with Eudocia.

This account of Eudocia's marriage is preserved in a number of Byzantine chronicles and has found general acceptance among modern scholars.[2] Yet it strikes the suspicious reader at once as a romance of the rags-to-riches type, with the same appeal as the Cinderella tale or the story of Esther.[3] It does indeed bespeak an artless naïveté. From the hieratic isolation of Pulcheria's court, Theodosius emerges charmingly in the guise of a moonstruck lover. To provide a motive for the sophist's harsh treatment of his child, the romance fits him out with clairvoyance. It justifies the promotion of the wicked brothers through casuistry, as if their selfishness would have appeared less reprehensible because of its fortunate outcome. Thus the tale plays in a sub-philosophical way with the popular notion of irreversible destiny.

The story's claims to authenticity seem singularly ill-founded. The earliest version to have survived appeared a century after the death of Eudocia in the *World Chronicle* of John Malalas, an author who did not always distinguish between authentic history and a popular memory of events infused with folk-tale motifs.[4] Later authors for the most part adopted Malalas's version,[5] but elaboration was bound to creep in. The seventh-century *Easter Chronicle,* for example, made Eudocia even more enticing: "a Greek maid, a pure young thing, with slim and graceful figure, a delicate nose, skin as white as snow, large eyes, charming features, blonde curly tresses, and dancing feet, a girl of wit and intellect."[6]

Sources nearer the events indicate that Malalas, or whoever concocted the story, did have facts at his disposal. Among the ecclesiastical historians of the reign of Theodosius II, neither Sozomen nor Theodoret mentions Eudocia, perhaps because they wrote after 443, when she had fallen into disgrace. But Socrates (writing in 439 or

2. The chronicle sources are Joh. Mal. 14 (pp. 352–56 Bonn, paraphrased above); Evagr. 1. 20; *Chron. pasch. aa.* 420–21 (pp. 575–79 Bonn); John of Nikiu 84. 25–37 (trans. Charles); Theoph. *a.m.* 5911 (p. 83 de Boor); Cedren., p. 590 Bonn; Zon. 13. 22, pp. 40c–41a; Niceph. Call. *HE* 14. 23 (*PG*, CXLVI, 1129). For typical modern reactions see (besides Gregorovius) Seeck, *Geschichte,*VI, 82; Bury, *Later Roman Empire,* I, 220; Stein, *Histoire,* I, 281. J. W. van Rooijen, *De Theodosii II moribus ac rebus politicis* (Leiden, 1912), pp. 77–88, comes closest to my thesis; for an alternative see Alan Cameron, "Empress and Poet," pp. 270–79.
3. I expand here on my article "Family Life in the Theodosian House," *Kleronomia* 8 (1976), 280–92.
4. W. Weber, "Studien zur Chronik des Malalas," *Festgabe für Adolf Deissmann* (Tübingen, 1927), pp. 20–66, shows how Malalas combines "freischwebende Motive des Sagenschatzes der antiken Welt" with "ganz reale Geschehnisse" (p. 36).
5. Holum, "Family Life," p. 282 n. 17.
6. *Chron. pasch. a.* 420 (pp. 577–78 Bonn).

shortly thereafter) introduced her, praising her skill at versifying and confirming that she was the daughter of the Athenian sophist Leontius; that she was educated "in all genres of literature"; that the bishop of Constantinople had "made her a Christian" shortly before her marriage; and that originally she bore the name Athenaïs.[7] Another contemporary historian, Priscus of Panion, also preserved this name and added that Eudocia employed it even as empress.[8] The name of the girl's father survives in a distich once inscribed in a book she wrote, a verse which also boasts that Leontius came from a prominent family.[9] A chronographer gives the date of the wedding as June 7, 421—information probably taken from the consular chronicle of Constantinople—and reports that Theodosius celebrated his wedding with chariot races in the hippodrome; another confirms simply that the bride was an "Achaean."[10] Conspicuously absent from these early sources is any hint that Pulcheria fostered the union, a feature of the romance popular tradition might easily have supplied from awareness of her importance in the palace.

Another contemporary source, one generally overlooked by modern scholars, suggests an alternative to this part of the romance and to the notion that destiny caused Athenaïs to arrive in Constantinople when Theodosius was looking for a wife. Olympiodorus, a native of Thebes in upper Egypt during the reign of Theodosius II, wrote a history dedicated to the emperor. The work itself has been lost but important passages survive, chosen as they struck the fancy of the Byzantine patriarch Photius (ninth century) and summarized in his *Bibliotheca*.[11] To judge from these summaries, Olympiodorus' history mainly related events in the West between 407 and 425,[12] but in a number of digressions the author described personal adven-

7. Soc. 7. 21. 8–9.

8. Prisc. frg. 8 (*FHG*, IV, 94).

9. Phot. *Bibl.* cod. 183 (II, 196 Henry): Εὐδοκίη βασίλεια Λεοντιὰς εὐπατέρεια. The adjective εὐπατέρεια is immodest, in Homer an epithet for Helen whose father was Zeus (*Il.* 6. 292, etc.).

10. *Chron. pasch. a.* 421 (p. 578 Bonn); Marcell. com. *a.* 421. 1 (*MGH: AA*, XI, 75); on the so-called *Konsultafelannalen* cf. A. Freund, *Beiträge zur antiochenischen und zur konstantinopolitanischen Stadtchronik* (Jena, 1882); and O. Holder-Egger, "Die Chronik des Marcellinus Comes und die oströmische Fasten," *Neues Archiv* 2 (1877), 50–109.

11. Cod. 80 (I, 166–87 Henry), also *FHG*, IV, 58–68.

12. In general W. Haedicke, *RE*, XVIII (1939), 201–7, "Olympiodorus (von Theben)"; E. A. Thompson, "Olympiodorus of Thebes," *CQ* 38 (1944), 43–52; J. F. Matthews, "Olympiodorus of Thebes and the History of the West (A.D. 407–25)," *JRS* 60 (1970), 79–97.

tures and events from his own career. From summaries of these it becomes clear that Olympiodorus had connections with the government of Anthemius, which sent him on a diplomatic mission to the Huns on the Black Sea about 412,[13] and that he was a pagan who leaned toward mystical Neoplatonism and thaumaturgy.[14] In one of his most intriguing digressions, Olympiodorus told of his journey to Athens about 415. While there he used his influence to secure a public teaching position in rhetoric for a man named Leontius, who was, however, "not willing" (οὔπω ἐθέλοντα).[15] Unless two sophists of the same name held forth in Athens after *ca.* 415, this Leontius must have been the father of Athenaïs.[16]

There was more in Olympiodorus, and the summary of Photius invites an attempt to reconstruct what he omitted. The historian did not appear in Athens by accident. The Athenian chair in rhetoric, theoretically in the emperor's gift since the time of Marcus Aurelius, was during the fourth and fifth centuries in practice filled by the city council of Athens, though at times the proconsul of Achaea, his superior the praetorian prefect of Illyricum, or even the emperor himself might intervene for a favored candidate.[17] Since Theodosius and Pulcheria would not have concerned themselves with such matters, initiative for the appointment presumably came from the proconsul or the prefect, and Olympiodorus acted as a representative of higher authority.

But why was Leontius "not willing"? These words of Photius have long been interpreted to mean that Leontius did not want the Athenian position,[18] but why would Olympiodorus have exerted

13. Frg. 18 (*FHG*, IV, 61) dated to 412/13 by its position among the fragments. Haedicke, *RE*, XVIII (1939), 201, "Olympiodorus (von Theben)," followed by Maenchen-Helfen, *Huns*, p. 74, assumes that Olympiodorus was in the service of the western court at the time, a hypothesis the argument presented here will tend to refute.

14. Frgg. 1, 27, 38 (*FHG*, IV, 58, 63, 66); Zos. 5. 35. 5; cf. Thompson, "Olympiodorus," p. 43, and Matthews, "Olympiodorus," p. 79.

15. Frg. 28 (*FHG*, IV, 63).

16. An identification accepted, e.g., by Gregorovius, *Athenais*, p. 14; Seeck, *Geschichte*, VI, 82; *PLRE*, II, 668–69, "Leontius 6"; and Alan Cameron, "Empress and Poet," p. 274.

17. J.W.H. Walden, *The Universities of Ancient Greece* (New York, 1909), pp. 134–35, 138–42. The case of Prohaeresius, who established himself in the sophistic chair in Athens *ca.* 340–50 is particularly instructive. See Eunap. *V. soph.*, pp. 487–90 Boissonade, and Walden, *Universities*, pp. 152–58.

18. See the translations of Müller, *FHG*, IV, 63, Henry, I, 177; also Alan Cameron, "Empress and Poet," p. 275.

himself and why did Leontius after all accept the appointment? Another look at the summary of Photius provides an alternative explanation. In the same passage Olympiodorus described the initiation rite anyone, but "especially a foreigner" (καὶ μάλιστα ξένον), had to undergo to gain admission to the company of scholars. "All newcomers, whether young or mature men" (ὅσοι νεήλυδες, ἄν τε μικροί, ἄν τε μεγάλοι), faced a degrading game of tug and pull in front of the public baths before they could be admitted to the ritual washing and don the philosopher's cloak (τρίβων).[19] Olympiodorus seems to have described this rite with a specific "foreigner" in mind, and if that man was also "mature" he may well have been "unwilling" to face the indignity. That man was Leontius, it appears, and he was not an Athenian at all but an ambitious "newcomer" who secured the prized sophistic chair in Athens through connections in high places.

Confirmation of this interpretation and further precision come from a famous display of Eudocia's eloquence. In 438, on her way to fulfill a vow in the Holy Land, she delivered an encomium of Antioch before the senate of the city, casting it in Homeric hexameters. In it she included the line:

Ὑμετέρης γενεῆς τε καὶ αἵματος εὔχομαι εἶναι

Of your proud line and blood I claim to be.

Influenced by the traditional story of Eudocia's origin, the sixth-century author who recorded this verse explained it as a flattering hint at the tradition that Athenians were included among the first colonists of Antioch.[20] Stripped of this antiquarian lore, the words of Eudocia speak for themselves. Athenaïs, it appears, hailed not from Athens but from Antioch.

Thus she later showered favors on her ancestral city. She persuaded Theodosius to extend the walls of Antioch to take in a large

---

19. Greg. Naz. *Or.* 20 (43). 15–16 (*PG*, XXXVI, 513–17) gives another account of the same rite; cf. *ibid.* 17 (col. 517) and Liban. *Ep.* 301 (X, 282 Foerster) for teachers and students wearing the philosopher's cloak, and Soc. 7. 37 for the rhetor Silvanus, who refused to wear it after becoming a Christian.

20. Evagr. 1. 20. The verse is an adaptation of *Il.* 6. 211, 20. 241. Cf. Joh. Mal. 8 (p. 201 Bonn) and G. Downey, *A History of Antioch in Syria* (Princeton, 1961), pp. 79, 451, for the Athenian colonists. Alan Cameron ("Empress and Poet," p. 278) declares correctly "on the face of it [Eudocia's verse] might look like a claim to *Antiochene* blood." Thus it would also have looked to Eudocia's audience, which was presumably less erudite than Evagrius.

suburb—an appropriate project for the city's most prominent daughter.[21] Among Eudocia's literary interests, moreover, was St. Cyprian, a pagan magician who embraced Christianity when the lovely Justina, with Christ's assistance, successfully resisted his advances, then became bishop of Antioch and suffered martyrdom in the Diocletianic persecution. Eudocia turned a preexisting prose text of his *vita* into laborious hexameters.[22] Her concern for Antioch and its Christian mythology was more than accidental. Eudocia had left her native city in childhood when Leontius, like other literati of the day, traveled abroad to seek advancement.[23] Her pagan name of Athenaïs indicates not nationality but her father's devotion to Attic culture, a devotion which accounts for his efforts to secure the sophistic chair in Athens, and which Eudocia / Athenaïs continued to share (as Priscus confirmed) even after her baptism.[24]

There is still more in the summaries of Olympiodorus. In another digression[25] the historian reported that some inhabitants of Thrace had discovered three silver statues that had been buried there earlier as fetishes to ward off barbarian invaders. Olympiodorus accepted their efficacy for this purpose, as did the Roman "governor" (ἄρχων) of Thrace who reported the discovery to Theodosius II and had them dug out by imperial command. The "governor" himself informed Olympiodorus that within a few days after the statues were removed Goths had overrun all of Thrace, and that not long thereafter the Huns and Scythians had invaded both Illyricum and Thrace.[26] His name was Valerius, and the combination of his confidence in an ancient pagan rite and his acquaintance with Olympiodorus argues that he was Athenaïs' brother. That the bride of Theodosius had a brother so named is confirmed by an independent hagiographical

21. Joh. Mal. 14 (pp. 346–57 Bonn); Evagr. 1. 20; G. Downey, "The Wall of Theodosius at Antioch," *AJP* 62 (1941), 207–13.

22. *Eudociae Augustae Procli Lycii, Claudiani carminum graecorum reliquiae*, ed. A. Ludwich (Leipzig, 1897), pp. 16–79.

23. Alan Cameron ("Empress and Poet," pp. 274–75) proposes the alternative that Eudocia's father was the Leontius who was apparently professor in Alexandria *ca.* 400 but gave up his post and "went home" when he embraced Christianity (Damasc. *V. Isid.* 46 [ed. Zintzen]). Since Athenaïs / Eudocia remained pagan until shortly before her marriage (Soc. 7. 21. 9, *supra*, p. 115), Cameron's candidate could not have been her father, unless the man permitted his teenage daughter to retain the old beliefs for at least five years after his own conversion.

24. Cf. *infra*, pp. 123, 125–26, 220–21.

25. Frg. 27 (*FHG*, IV, 63).

26. Croke, "Evidence," pp. 358–65, has recently given this account its correct interpretation and date; cf. *Anth. pal.* 9. 805 for a statue of Ares buried in Thrace to ward off the Goths.

source, which also reveals that nearer the end of his life the man became an orthodox Christian.[27] There is, moreover, no reason to doubt the tradition of the romance that Valerius served as master of offices. A man of that name held the position in 435, apparently after receiving the consulship of 432 and serving as *comes sacrarum largitionum* in 427 and *comes rerum privatarum* in 425.[28] This career accords well with the honors of a man who began in the lesser posts of the Illyrican prefecture, then advanced to praesental office when his sister became the emperor's consort and could employ the bond of *kedeia* to establish members of her family in high places.

Olympiodorus tends to disprove another element in the romantic tradition, that the wicked brothers fled when they learned of their sister's good fortune and began their political careers only after she recalled them to Constantinople. The historian dated the discovery of the statues, their removal, and the "governorship" of Valerius precisely to the period between February 8 and September 2, 421.[29] The weeks between June 7 (the marriage) and September 2 leave too little time for the brothers' flight and recall and for the subsequent promotion of Valerius and the discovery and removal of the statues. It thus becomes likely that Valerius received his "governorship" even before the marriage. The language of Olympiodorus/ Photius does not permit exact identification of the office, but certainly it involved the rank *clarissimus* and membership in the senatorial class.[30]

Now that the romantic tradition concerning the existence of Valerius and the office he held has been confirmed, no doubt need remain, even though this man is not mentioned in contemporary sources, that Athenaïs had a second brother named Gesius. Nor is it surprising that Gesius should have received the prefecture of Illyricum. This office seems to have been the focus of ambition among traditionalists and those sympathetic to paganism, perhaps because the Illyrican prefect, stationed at Thessalonica,[31] could escape the immediate attention of the court.[32] Herculius, who held that prefecture between 407

27. Cyril. Scyth. *V. Euth.* 30 (*TU*, XLIX: 2, 47).
28. *PLRE*, II, 1145, "Valerius 6."
29. The reign of the western emperor Constantius III: Croke, "Evidence," p. 359.
30. *Ibid.*, p. 358. *PLRE*, II, 1144, "Valerius 4," suggests *consularis*.
31. Thdt. *HE* 5. 17. 1; E. Stein, "Untersuchungen," pp. 358–59.
32. A. Frantz, "Herculius in Athens," *Akten des VII. Internationalen Kongresses für Christliche Archäologie, Trier, 5–11 September 1965* (Vatican City-Berlin, n.d.), p. 530, suggests that it was, rather, the men who were chosen with the nature of their constituency in mind.

and 411, supported pagan sophistic and Neoplatonic studies in the schools of Athens, and was rewarded for his generosity with a statue on the Acropolis beside the image of Athena Promachos.³³ About 415, someone in the government of the Illyrican prefecture took a similar interest in the Athenian schools, appointing the pagan Leontius to the sophistic chair through the agency of Olympiodorus. In 420–21, when Athenaïs/Eudocia was betrothed and was married to Theodosius, the praetorian prefect of Illyricum was a man named Philippus who has been plausibly identified as a relative of Anthemius.³⁴ Not long after the imperial marriage, the great prefect's son emerged in high office for the first time since 412, again in the prefecture of Illyricum.³⁵ It begins to look as if the "good fortune" of Athenaïs did not precede the advancement of Valerius, and others like him, but paralleled it.

Evidence from independent and near-contemporary sources thus confirms the purely objective material contained in the romantic Byzantine account of Theodosius' marriage. Athenaïs did come from Athens, perhaps after her father's death, to Constantinople, where she may indeed have resided with relatives. There she received Christian baptism, adopted an appropriate Christian name,³⁶ and married the emperor. As a result, her brothers Valerius and Gesius acquired praesental offices. The shadowy Paulinus may have played some role in the affair, one that would justify the generous rewards assigned him in the Byzantine legend and again confirmed by an imperial constitution preserved in the contemporary *Theodosian Code*.³⁷

Olympiodorus and other sources provide an alternative to the fictional elements in the Byzantine romance—the humble origins of the girl, the father's testament, the cruelty of the brothers, and, above all, the role of Pulcheria. It is impossible to believe that the virgin empress would have approved "a young girl, a Greek maid, very beautiful, pure and dainty, eloquent as well, the daughter of a philosopher," even if she could have brought herself to introduce into the palace a competitor for her own influence. The real contrivers

33. *IG*, II², 4225; Frantz, "Herculius," also her "From Paganism to Christianity in the Temples of Athens," *DOP* 19 (1965), 190–91; *PLRE*, II, 345, "Herculius 2."

34. *CTh* 16. 2. 45, 8. 21; *CI* 11. 21; *PLRE*, I, 1145, stemma 25.

35. *CTh* 11. 1. 33; cf. Seeck, *Regesten*, p. 88.

36. Meaning the goodwill or grace of God which caused Him to dwell among men, especially in Jesus, Luke 2:14.

37. *CTh* 6. 27. 23; *PLRE*, II, 846, "Paulinus 8."

of the wedding were Pulcheria's enemies, men like those known from the correspondence of Synesius, pagans as bitter toward her as Eunapius and Christians like Socrates who favored toleration—men united, however, by family ties and ambition as well as by common commitment to Hellenic culture.[38] The associations of Olympiodorus with the family of Leontius prove conclusively that Athenaïs was known among such men in the prefecture of Illyricum and could serve them as Eudoxia had served the enemies of Rufinus many years before. These men must also have had a connection in the palace, one who enjoyed the confidence of Theodosius just as Eutropius had that of Arcadius. This was Paulinus, whose importance in the Byzantine tradition is thus explained.

Some critics may prefer the Byzantine sources for Eudocia's marriage, late as they are and interlarded with folk-tale themes, to an hypothesis based on no direct evidence at all. Other weapons exist with which to assault such credulity, for the marriage did work against Pulcheria's interests. The emergence of Athenaïs/Eudocia coincided in time with the outbreak of war against Persia and with St. Stephen's *adventus* in Constantinople, events contrived to strengthen the ideological underpinnings of Pulcheria's *basileía*. With her Attic eloquence Eudocia could present counter-arguments in the palace,[39] and Theodosius listened more readily because through Eudocia he experienced the pleasures of married life and looked forward to begetting an heir to strengthen the dynasty.

At the same time the course of the fighting weakened Pulcheria's hand. As Ardaburius besieged Nisibis in 421, King Vahram appeared with the bulk of his troops, raised the siege, and brought the Roman offensive quickly to an end.[40] His Saracen allies attacked toward the Euphrates, striking for Syria, it was said, and for Antioch itself.[41] Vahram likewise crossed the border to besiege Theodosiopolis, deep in Roman Mesopotamia. From a military point of view the most Pulcheria could claim by the end of the year was stalemate.

In 422 Theodosius decided to make peace, "out of generosity," Socrates asserted, and "even though his side had been successful."[42]

38. Cf. van Rooijen, *De Theodosii II moribus*, pp. 81–82, for a similar interpretation.

39. Cf. the oration she delivered in 422: *infra*, p. 123.

40. Soc. 7. 18. 21, 24, Thdt. *HE* 5. 37. 6–10, Holum, "Pulcheria's Crusade," p. 168.

41. Soc. 7. 18. 22.

42. Soc. 7. 20. 1–3.

In reality an emergency in Europe forced the Romans to call praesental units committed to the eastern front back to their usual
stations. *Hunni Thraciam vastaverunt:* three words in a chronicle
record another terrifying Hun invasion of Thrace, made especially
dangerous by the weakness of Roman defenses there.[43] The emperor
did well to begin heeding other advisers. Anatolius had initiated
talks with Vahram, but during 422 Procopius took over as *magister
militum per Orientem* and negotiated with Persia a treaty that recognized the *status quo.*[44] The appearance of this Procopius, the son-in-
law of Anthemius,[45] proves that the marriage of Theodosius had
already affected the distribution of high commands and the conduct
of war.

When genuine victory eluded a Roman emperor on the battlefield he could still claim it and celebrate in Constantinople. Reaction
there to the two-front war of 421–22 took on a revealing diversity. On
the one hand, the Hebdomon column attributed to the ''vows of his
sisters'' the ability of Theodosius to defeat his enemies everywhere
and to establish universal peace. The Long-Cross solidi, with their
related propaganda line, remained part of the mint repertoire during
the ensuing years.[46] The historian Socrates, who likewise presented
a Constantinopolitan view, stressed heavenly interference at every
turn—angels dispatched to be ''arbiters'' of the fighting, an ''irra-
tional terror'' that caused the Saracens of Vahram to cast themselves
fully armed into the Euphrates, and an ''act of providence'' visible in
a successful flank attack that mauled the entire corps of Persia's
elite ''Immortals.''[47]

But Socrates also gave evidence for a conflicting interpretation,
with somewhat questionable logic. ''Referring to God all hope for the
outcome,'' Theodosius nonetheless ''ordered to the front a mighty
array of reinforcements.'' ''When God had granted the victory,''
Socrates wrote inconsequentially, men of literary attainment composed and delivered encomiums in praise of Theodosius (βασιλικοὶ
λόγοι).[48] Although none of these orations survives, their content
may be inferred from the tradition of imperial panegyric and from

43. Croke, ''Evidence.''
44. Holum, ''Pulcheria's Crusade,'' pp. 169–71.
45. *Supra,* Chap. 3, n. 73.
46. J.P.C. Kent, '''*A21ream monetam . . . cum signo crucis,*''' *Num.
Chron.* ser. 6, 20 (1960), 130–31.
47. Soc. 7. 18. 23, 20. 8–10.
48. 7. 18. 15, 20. 1, 21. 7–8.

Socrates himself, who apparently heard them performed or had them at his disposal in written form. To judge from his account, the orators stressed not divine interference but, in Homeric fashion, man-to-man combats of champions, the individual exploits of Roman commanders and especially of Procopius, whose tactical genius proved that the "Immortals" could be slaughtered like any other Persians.[49] Among the literati Socrates mentioned specifically the emperor's consort, author of an encomium in hexameters. Eudocia's poem may have pleased the sophist Eunapius, for to judge from Socrates and panegyric tradition it spoke of "the emperor's courage, the strength of his troops, and the conditions of real battle." Here again the marriage of Theodosius worked to Pulcheria's disadvantage.

Between June 19, 422, and February 14, 423, a man named Asclepiodotus advanced from the office of *comes sacrarum largitionum* to the praetorian prefecture of the East.[50] The man, Eudocia's maternal uncle,[51] surely owed his promotion at least in part to the advantages of imperial *kedeia*. In addition, Theodosius designated Asclepiodotus consul for 423, and on January 2 of that year, the day after Eudocia's uncle entered his consulship, the emperor proclaimed Eudocia Augusta.[52] These were two good days for Eudocia, her kin, and those who had introduced her into the palace. She had given her husband a child in the previous year, a girl named Licinia Eudoxia,[53] but there was as yet no heir, so again her distinction may best be explained as politically motivated. From the time of Eudocia's coronation, the mint of Constantinople issued Long-Cross solidi of the new Augusta with reverses identical to those of Pulcheria—with the same costume, the same *nomen* AEL(IA), and the same *dextera Dei* crowning her from above.[54] Buttressed with the ideology of sacral *basileía*, her authority would equal that of Pulcheria.

Eudocia's coronation definitely affected policy during the three years of Asclepiodotus' prefecture (423–25). Directions emerged that contrasted with those of Pulcheria's regime but had clear affinities with Anthemian traditionalism. At first glance, the religious legisla-

49. 7. 18. 25, 20. 6–11; Holum, "Pulcheria's Crusade," p. 171.
50. *CTh* 6. 20. 23, 7. 4. 35; *PLRE*, II, 160, "Asclepiodotus 1."
51. *V. Sym. syr.* 130–31 (*TU*, XXXII: 4, 174–75); *infra*, p. 125.
52. *Chron. pasch. a.* 423 (p. 580 Bonn): ἀνηγορεύθη ... Αὐγούστα.
53. Marcell. com. *a.* 422. 1 (*MGH: AA*, XI, 75); O. Seeck, *RE*, VI (1909), 925–26, "Licinia Eudoxia 2"; *PLRE*, II, 410–12, "Licinia Eudoxia 2." The name Licinia presumably came from her mother's family.
54. Kent, "'*Auream monetam*,'" p. 130.

tion of the prefecture might suggest continuity.[55] Asclepiodotus sought no change in state policy toward most heretics, since, as before, Nicene orthodoxy would be the principal bond between the Roman people and the Theodosian dynasty. In order, however, were concessions for pagans and Jews—at least the right to practice non-Christian worship unobtrusively while enjoying traditional legal protection of person and property. In a constitution (or group of constitutions) addressed to Asclepiodotus on April 9, 423,[56] Theodosius confirmed penalties against a miscellaneous group of heresies—Manichaean, Priscillianist, Arian, Macedonian, Novatian, and Sabbatian—and against pagans and Jews. But by bringing before the emperor the "pitiable supplications" of the Jews[57] Asclepiodotus won a provision that Christians should "refrain from injuring and persecuting them, and that now and henceforth no person [should] seize or burn their synagogues." And by assuring Theodosius that all pagans had finally disappeared, the prefect elicited a remarkable but unfounded imperial declaration: "The regulations of constitutions formerly promulgated shall suppress any pagans who survive, although We now believe that there are none." For the good of the Empire, Theodosius hoped that this was true, but his words betray gullibility[58] and suggest that Asclepiodotus purposely misled him in order to prevent further legislation against paganism.

Two months later, on June 8, 423, Theodosius addressed another constitution (or group of them) to his praetorian prefect. Again he confirmed existing law against various heresies, and, for some, punishment by exile and proscription. The same penalties threatened pagans who sacrificed to demons, "although they ought to be subjected to capital punishment." But at the same time Asclepiodotus won a major concession. In language reflecting the tolerant attitude of men like Socrates, Theodosius commanded

55. So, e.g., Lippold, *RE*, suppl. XIII (1973), 1015–17, "Theodosius II"; Avi-Yonah, *Jews*, p. 219.

56. *CTh* 16. 5. 59, 8. 26, 9. 5, 10. 22.

57. The occasion of these *miserabiles preces* may have been an anti-Jewish campaign of the Syrian archimandrite Barsauma, who rampaged through the Holy Land about this time, destroying and burning Jewish and Samaritan synagogues and pagan temples. See F. Nau, "Résumé de monographies syriaques," *ROC* 18 (1913), 382–86; and *idem*, "Sur la synagogue de Rabbat Moab (422) et un mouvement favorisé par l'impératrice Eudocia (438) d'après la vie de Barsauma le Syrien," *Journal asiatique* 210 (1927), 189–90.

58. J. Geffcken, *Der Ausgang des griechisch-römischen Heidentums*, 2nd ed. (Heidelberg, 1929), pp. 178–223; W. Kaegi, "The Fifth-Century Twilight of Byzantine Paganism," *Classica et mediaevalia* 27 (1968), 243–75.

those persons who are truly Christians or who are said to be, that they shall not abuse the authority of religion and dare to lay violent hands on Jews and pagans who are living quietly and attempting nothing disorderly or contrary to law.

Any who did attack the persons or property of such law-abiding pagans and Jews would have to make triple or quadruple restitution, and governors, their staffs, and anyone else who connived in such crimes faced the same penalty.[59] In the hands of a determined praetorian prefect such a law had a chance to be effective.

Independent evidence proves that over the next two years (423–25) Asclepiodotus worked to enforce the law. In the Syriac version of the anonymous *Life of St. Simeon the Stylite,* an account appears of a "storm" that rose against the church because of the "villain and sinner" Asclepiodotus, brother of the Augusta's mother. The constitution of June 8, 423, and the prefect's decrees enforcing it were eventually promulgated everywhere. Pagans and Jews rejoiced. But soon bishops brought copies of the documents to St. Simeon, a famous holy man who had attracted attention and admiration by living for years atop a pillar near Antioch.[60] Filled with his usual zeal, Simeon addressed a violent letter to Theodosius, refusing to call him Augustus and threatening him with God's wrath:

Since your heart has grown arrogant and you have forgotten the Lord your God who gave you your diadem and the throne of empire, and since you have become friend, comrade, and protector of the faithless Jew, know now that you will soon face the punishment of divine justice, you and all who share your view in this affair. You will raise your hands to heaven and woefully cry: "Truly because I have denied the Lord God has he brought this judgment upon me."

This letter apparently terrified Theodosius. He withdrew his law favoring pagans and Jews, the *Life* reports, and dismissed Asclepiodotus in shame (425), letting joy return to the church.[61]

Scholars have long associated Eudocia with another famous event in the reign of Theodosius II—the reorganization and expansion of the so-called university of Constantinople.[62] Centuries later a tra-

---

59. *CTh* 16. 5. 60, 8. 27, 10. 23–24.

60. Cf. generally P. Brown, "The Rise and Function of the Holy Man in Late Antiquity," *JRS* 61 (1971), 80–101.

61. *V. Sym. syr.* 130–31 (*TU*, XXXII: 4, 174–75).

62. F. Fuchs, *Die höheren Schulen von Konstantinopel im Mittelalter,* Byzantinisches Archiv no. 8 (Leipzig-Berlin, 1926), p. 3; P. Lemerle, *Le premier hu-*

dition existed that with Eudocia (or her brothers) seven philosophers journeyed from Athens to Constantinople, where they interpreted sculptures in the hippodrome as foreshadowings of a dismal future without paganism.[63] Not only late but fanciful, the story does correctly interpret the cultural importance of Eudocia's origins and of her rise to power. The traditional classical education, hitherto fostered especially in the schools of Antioch, Alexandria, and Athens, was to emerge in Constantinople under imperial patronage and take on a more Christian stamp. It is likely that Eudocia herself, as well as Asclepiodotus and others behind her, took an interest in stabilizing academic life in the dynastic city and in honoring successful teachers.[64]

Near the end of Asclepiodotus' ascendancy (February–March, 425), Theodosius issued to the city prefect three constitutions on education. The first threatened punishment for any private teacher who attempted to compete with official professors and fixed the number of the latter who would be permitted to hold forth on grammar, rhetoric, philosophy, and law in the lecture rooms of the Capitol.[65] The second specified which structures would be used, even ordering that neighboring properties be seized to ensure large and well-appointed facilities. And the third granted certain professors the high rank of *comes primi ordinis,* providing that others of equal skill and moral stature would be decorated similarly when they had served twenty years.[66] For the present the Christian tone of official education would not be emphasized.

It is instructive that one of the men honored with the *comitiva primi ordinis* in 425 was the Greek grammarian Helladios. Earlier he

manisme byzantin (Paris, 1971), p. 62; also review of the foregoing by P. Speck, *BZ* 67 (1974), 387 n. 7.

63. *Script. orig. Const.*, pp. 61–64, 192–93 Preger.

64. Based on Tzet. *Chil.* 10. 49–52 (pp. 388–89 Leone) some scholars have identified the grammarians Orion and Hyperechius as Eudocia's teachers in Constantinople and members of the academic circle she fostered; see, e.g., F. Schemmel, *Die Hochschule von Konstantinopel vom V. bis IX. Jahrhundert* (Berlin, 1912), p. 5, and C. Wendel, *RE*, XVIII (1939), 1083-84, "Orion 3." Little further is known of Hyperechius (*PLRE*, II, 581), but Eudocia probably came in contact with Orion during her Jerusalem period (*infra*, p. 220).

65. *CTh* 14. 9. 3; cf. Lemerle, *Humanisme*, pp. 63–64, with Speck's review, pp. 385–87, giving the best interpretation of all three constitutions: "Der Kaiser ist der Protektor 'seiner' Schule und setzt für dieses Protektorat alle staatlichen Mittel ein . . . im Bewusstsein des Gründers wird ein anderer Gesichtspunkt im Vordergrund gestanden haben: das kaiserliche Renommee. . . . Die Schule diente also dem Kaiser zu einer Selbstdarstellung als eines Förderers des Geisteslebens in der Hauptstadt seines Reiches."

66. *CTh* 15. 1. 53, 6. 21.

had been the teacher of Socrates, who reported that Helladios had fled to Constantinople in the time of Theodosius I after a clash between pagans and Christians in Alexandria, where he had been a priest of Zeus. He used to boast, Socrates related, that in the fighting he had slaughtered nine Christians with his own hands. Yet in the time of Asclepiodotus and Eudocia such a man could pursue a career teaching in Constantinople, retiring with distinction.[67]

The honor shown Helladios and other professors indicates that Eudocia's presence in the palace after 421 benefited men of literary distinction, who once again had an effective claim to influence and promotion. According to Socrates, those who delivered encomiums in 422 to extol the victory of Theodosius did so "because they wished no one to be ignorant of the culture they had acquired through hard work," neither prospective students who might acquire the same valuable skill for a price nor the emperor himself, who was now inclined both to heed eloquence and to reward it.[68] To judge from the invective of Eunapius, this inclination had not existed "in the time of Pulcheria." It was part of the restored Anthemian-style traditionalism evident at once when men like Isidorus and Procopius returned to power, and with the emergence of Eudocia's kin Valerius and Asclepiodotus. These men had seen their opportunity in 420–21, when Pulcheria's godly resolve entangled the eastern Empire in a dangerous and futile war. They also had a proper instrument—an eloquent "Athenian" maid. Correctly explained, the "good fortune" of Athenaïs came not from the ineluctable working of destiny but from the mundane frustrations of ambitious men.

The elevation of Eudocia in 421 thus proves that in the East even traditionalists considered the distinction Augusta to be appropriate for an imperial woman, especially when it worked to their political advantage. Remarkably, at the same time official acceptance of female *basileía* first manifested itself in the West. There no empress had been recognized Augusta since the time of Constantine, not Justina, the powerful mother of Valentinian II, or even the fecund and pious Flaccilla. When Arcadius dispatched *laureatae* of Eudoxia to Ravenna, expecting to elicit official recognition from the western court, Honorius had responded by condemning strenuously this

67. Soc. 5. 16; A. Gudeman, *RE*, VIII (1913), 102–3, "Helladios 3," and O. Seeck, *ibid.*, cols. 103–4, "Helladios 8" (the same man); *PLRE*, II, 534, "Helladius 2." For other pagans among the Constantinople professors see Schemmel, *Hochschule*, pp. 5–7, and Fuchs, *Schulen*, pp. 3–4.

68. Soc. 7. 21. 10.

"innovation," which "raised voices of objection around the world." Although mints in both *partes imperii* struck simultaneously for all legitimate Augusti, emphasizing by this practice the ideal indivisibility of *basileía*, since the death of Helena no western mint had issued coins of an Augusta, not even of Pulcheria, whose portrait stood with those of Theodosius and Honorius in the senate house of Constantinople.

In 421 the western court abandoned its reservations and emulated the East. On February 8 of that year Honorius elevated Constantius, husband of his half-sister Galla Placidia, to the imperial distinction, and then Honorius and Constantius together made Placidia an Augusta.[69] Her elevation had a specific dynastic purpose. It would reinforce a decision to settle the succession in the West on the issue of Placidia's marriage, the child Flavius Placidus Valentinianus, born July 2, 419.[70]

This decision of 421 displeased the eastern court. Theodosius had not been consulted, but, more importantly, the prospective heir bore a name that emphasized his descent from the old dynasty of Valentinian,[71] while the eastern emperor was about to enter a union with Eudocia which might produce a proper Theodosian successor to Honorius. Thus when *laureatae* of Constantius III reached Constantinople—none of Placidia are mentioned—the eastern court refused to accept them.[72]

Within months Constantius III was dead, and on August 15, 423, Honorius himself succumbed with symptoms of edema, his

69. Olymp. frg. 34 (*FHG*, IV, 65, and *supra*, Chap. 1, n. 88), Theoph. *a.m.* 5913 (p. 84 de Boor), and the other sources cited by Oost, *Placidia*, p. 164 n. 78.

70. Oost, *Placidia*, pp. 162–68; W. Ensslin, *RE*, VIIA (1948), 2232–33, "Valentinianus III."

71. A few years later Galla Placidia based her son's right to rule in the West on claims the eastern branch of the Theodosian house could not make. In 423 she vowed a church to St. John in return for protection from a storm at sea. When she built the church she commemorated her rescue in inscriptions declaring that she had "fulfilled the vow on behalf of all of these. . . ." Among those included were Placidia's own family, and also Constantine, Valentinian I, and her mother's half-brother Gratian, through whom the house of Valentinian traced a connection with the house of Constantine. See *ILS* 818; R. Farioli, "Ravenna paleochristiana scomparsa," *Felix Ravenna* 83 (1961), 41–50; esp. F. Deichmann, *Ravenna, Hauptstadt des spätantiken Abendlandes*, I: *Geschichte und Monumente* (Wiesbaden, 1960), p. 156, II: *Kommentar* pt. 1 (Wiesbaden, 1974), pp. 93–98, 107–24. Two decades later Merobaudes, a poet of the western court, would stress that Valentinian III had been born to empire and that when Theodosius II restored him in the West in 424–25 (*infra*) he simply returned to him what was his by nature: *Carm.* 1. 9 (*MGH: AA*, XIV, 3), with Holum, "Honoria" (forthcoming).

72. Olymp. frg. 34 (*FHG*, IV, 65), Philostorg. 12. 12.

father's son only in susceptibility to this disease. Before his death Honorius had driven Galla Placidia into exile under suspicious circumstances, rumors of incest and of collaboration with rebellious Goths; and she had taken refuge in Constantinople (early 423) with young Valentinian and her daughter Justa Grata Honoria, born in 418. Since it appeared that the Theodosian dynasty had abandoned Italy, the West naturally proclaimed a new Augustus, John, a man of little substance. Word of this usurpation presumably reached the eastern government by late in the year.[73]

The loss of the West forced Theodosius early in 424 to withdraw his objections to the elevations of 421. As Olympiodorus expressed it precisely, Galla Placidia "took up again the distinction Augusta."[74] Theodosius did not elevate her a second time but recognized as valid the act of Honorius and Constantius III. Eastern mints now included Placidia obverses among the Long-Cross solidi, with the usual costume, the *nomen* AEL(IA), and the *dextera Dei*,[75] and Theodosius added more substance to his recognition by granting *kedeia* with his own branch of the family, betrothing to Valentinian his daughter Licinia Eudoxia, who would of course remain with her mother until she reached marriageable age.[76] In 425 the eastern emperor dispatched an army under Ardaburius and his son Aspar to restore Placidia and her children; and when it had destroyed the ephemeral rule of John at Ravenna, Helio, the eastern master of offices, arrived in Italy with the diadem and imperial *paludamentum*. As the eastern emperor's representative, he conferred these insignia on Valentinian at Rome on October 23, 425.[77]

This sequence of events transplanted the sacral *basileía* of empresses from East to West. From 425 western mints struck Long-Cross solidi for Galla Placidia with reverses copied from those of Constantinople and obverses modified only slightly:

73. Oost, *Placidia*, pp. 169–82.
74. Frg. 46 (*FHG*, IV, 68); Marcell. com. *a.* 424. 1 (*MGH: AA*, XI, 76); Oost, *Placidia*, p. 182 n. 48.
75. Kent, "'*Auream monetam*,'" p. 130. A. A. Boyce, *Festal and Dated Coins of the Roman Empire*, American Numismatic Society: Numismatic Notes and Monographs no. 153 (New York, 1965), p. 60, followed by Oost, *Placidia*, p. 49, takes the appearance of AELIA on Placidia's coins in place of Galla to mean that the latter caused offense in the East, but it should now be clear that the usual *nomen* was adopted as part of Augusta titulature.
76. Marcell. com. *a.* 424. 2 (*MGH: AA*, XI, 76); Oost, *Placidia*, pp. 184–85.
77. Sirago, *Placidia*, pp. 249–54; Oost, *Placidia*, pp. 183–93; Matthews, *Aristocracies*, pp. 379–81.

D(OMINA) N(OSTRA) GALLA PLA—CIDIA P(ERPETVA) F(ELIX) AV-G(VSTA) Bust right, diademed, wearing *paludamentum,* chi-rho visible on right shoulder, crowned by a hand.[78]

Apparently the *nomen* AEL(IA) made no sense in the West, so coin designers adopted the common legend of Augusti. Otherwise these obverses carried the same ideological burden as those struck in the East, but with greater charge, for since they came from Aquileia, Rome, and Ravenna, they impressed westerners as a dramatic innovation. In 425 or shortly thereafter, the same western mints began striking solidi with the image and legend of Justa Grata Honoria, and with obverse and reverse iconography identical to that of Placidia's coins (fig. 14). At the age of seven or eight, Honoria too had received the distinction Augusta, apparently from her brother Valentinian III, who, some years later, would deprive her of the "scepter of empire."[79]

Pulcheria's Special Resources

In Constantinople, meanwhile, raconteurs displayed irreverent wit when they talked of Theodosius and his two Augustae:

Theodosius was unsure of himself, carried along by every breeze. Often he signed documents that had not been read to him first. Once Pulcheria, a very clever woman, placed a contract of gift before him granting her his wife Eudocia to be sold into slavery. He signed it unread, and Pulcheria gave him a mighty scolding.[80]

No doubt apocryphal, the story perhaps went back to contemporary gossip. If so, the gossipers managed a good characterization of Theodosius, who emerges from the history of his mature years as a man of intelligence and sincerity but little backbone.[81] They also did well

78. J. F. W. de Salis, "The Coins of the Two Eudoxias, Eudocia, Placidia, and Honoria, and of Theodosius II, Marcian, and Leo I, Struck in Italy," *Num. Chron.* n.s. 7 (1867), 211; H. Cohen, *Description historique des monnaies frappées sous l'Empire romain,* 2nd ed., VIII (Paris and London, 1892), p. 196. 13; Boyce, *Festal,* pp. 64–65.

79. Salis, "Coins," pp. 213–14; Cohen, *Description,* VIII, pp. 219–20. 1, 4; Ulrich-Bansa, *Moneta,* pp. 227, 232, 234–35; Holum, "Honoria" (forthcoming); *supra,* pp. 1–2.

80. Theoph. *a.m.* 5941 (p. 101 de Boor).

81. E. A. Thompson, "The Foreign Policies of Theodosius II and Marcian," *Hermathena* 76 (1950), 58–75; and C. Luibheid, "Theodosius II and Heresy," *JEH* 16 (1965), 13–38, attribute too much of Theodosian policy to Theodosius himself.

with Pulcheria—for she did retain the ability to intimidate her brother—and with the implied rivalry between the emperor's sister and his wife.[82]

Surely that rivalry and contention existed from the day Eudocia entered the palace. Pulcheria's daily presence was bound to spoil the emperor's conjugal bliss, so Asclepiodotus and his associates presumably worked to limit it, aware also that her domineering personality might outweigh Eudocia's eloquence. Thus Pulcheria took up regular quarters at the suburban palaces of the Hebdomon and the Rufinianai, the latter (also called The Oak) formerly the villa of Rufinus but imperial property since his death.[83] In addition, Pulcheria personally owned two *domūs* within the city and her sisters Arcadia and Marina three more. These seem to have been not ordinary "dwellings," as the word *domus* implies, but elaborate private palaces with marble-paved courts, porticos, and luxurious formal dining rooms.[84] Nor would Pulcheria lack other trappings of *basileía*. It was probably when Theodosius married and his sister no longer lived principally in the imperial palace that he set up a distinct *sacrum cubiculum* for her, with a large staff and at its head a *praepositus augustae,* an official or quasi-official eunuch analogous to the *praepositus* of the emperor.[85] Elements of the palace guard were detached to provide security and a

---

The best recent treatment is Lippold, *RE*, suppl. XIII (1973), 961–1044, "Theodosius II," esp. his balanced assessment, cols. 1040–42.

82. Contrast Dagron, *Naissance*, p. 384 n. 4.

83. See Janin, *Constantinople*², pp. 139–40, 504–5, on the palaces, and for Pulcheria's residence in them *infra*, pp. 134, 136, 192, 196.

84. *Not. urb. Const.* 2. 12, 4. 8, 10. 7, 11. 13, 12. 9 (*Not. dig.*, ed. Seeck, pp. 230, 232, 237, 238); *CTh* 13. 1. 21; *Chron. pasch. a.* 396 (p. 566 Bonn); for the meaning of *domus* in this case C. Strube, "Der Begriff Domus in her Notitia Urbis Constantinopolitanae," *Studien zur Frühgeschichte Konstantinopels*, ed. H.-G. Beck, Miscellanea byzantina monacensia, vol. XIV (Munich, 1973), pp. 121–34; and for instructive examples *V. Olymp.* 5 (ed. Malingrey) with Dagron, *Naissance*, pp. 503–4 (the *domus* of Olympias); and Naumann and Belting, *Euphemia-Kirche*, pp. 13–15 (the private palace of Antiochus).

85. In 431 Pulcheria had her own *praepositus*, the Paulus mentioned in *ACO*, I, 4, 224, and in 441 Eudocia, who had none of her own, tried to take Pulcheria's, *infra*, pp. 191–92. The *Not. dig. Or.* 17. 8 (ed. Seeck) lists the *tabularius dominarum augustarum*, probably reflecting the situation *ca.* 395; see Jones, *Later Roman Empire*, III, 347–51, and G. Clemente, *La "Notitia Dignitatum,"* Saggi di storia e letteratura no. 4 (Cagliari, 1968), pp. 98–101. In 400–401 Eudoxia had a *castrensis* but apparently no *praepositus*, since the Amantius known from Marc. Diac. *V. Porph.* seems to have been her chief eunuch (*supra*, pp. 54–55). Thus the most attractive date for introduction of the *praepositus augustae* becomes *ca.* 421–23, when Theodosius married and faced the problem of what to do with his sister.

fitting escort for her travels about the city and suburbs.[86] Also in her court were numerous *cubiculariae*, women who waited on Pulcheria and added distinction to her retinue. Four or five names are known, and they seem to have been highborn, wealthy, and able to exercise influence.[87]

Yet, until the end of her brother's reign (450) distance was to deprive Pulcheria of ready access to his magisterial powers, reducing her by and large to her own resources. These, however, were not inconsiderable. Although the direct evidence is slight, she and her sisters must have possessed properties in the suburbs and provinces more extensive even than those of Olympias, made over to them by their father or brother out of the imperial domains.[88] The properties within Constantinople likewise produced substantial incomes from baths, bakeries, workshops, and dependents' dwellings that surrounded the palatial *domūs*.[89] Some of these establishments were extensive enough to give the names of their proprietors to entire quarters of the city, such as the "Marina quarter" in the second region and the Pulcherianai in the eleventh.[90] They also incorporated numerous

86. This is the most comfortable explanation for the troops with which Pulcheria protected the archimandrites Hypatius and Alexander *ca.* 427: *infra*, p. 136.

87. *ACO*, I, 4, 223–24, mentions Marcella and Droseria, two *cubiculariae* of Pulcheria, and also an Olympias who may have belonged to her household. Call. *V. Hyp.* 44. 1–3 (ed. Bartelink) tells of a very pious Christian *cubicularia* named Euphemia whom St. Hypatius cured of demon-possession—presumably the same Euphemia *cubicularia* who was wealthy enough to dedicate a *martyrium* to St. Christopher in 452: H. Grégoire, "Inscriptions historiques byzantines," *Byzantion* 4 (1927/28), 461–65, suggesting that Euphemia belonged to Pulcheria's household. Most interesting is the case of Eleuthera Stephanis, identified in the anonymous *Vie de St. Auxence* 29 (ed. Clugnet) and in Sym. Metaphr. *V. S. Auxentii* 61 (*PG*, CXIV, 1429–31) as a *cubicularia* of Pulcheria and perhaps typical of the women around her. Of high birth, righteous disposition, and great piety, Eleuthera came to St. Auxentius with a gift of relics and asked to be taught the monastic life. Auxentius established a cloister for her near his own, and soon other female ascetics came to join her. This seems to have taken place after Pulcheria's death (453).

88. *CTh* 10. 25 speaks of properties of Arcadius' daughters placed under procurators in the various provinces. Part of Marina's estates retained their separate existence long after her death: Grégoire, *Recueil*, no. 308; cf. K. Amantos, "Zu den wohltätigen Stiftungen von Byzanz," *OCP* 21 (1955), 16–17. In 402 Synesius (*Ep.* 61) spoke of an οἰκία (*domus*) of Galla Placidia in Constantinople that had once belonged to Ablabius, presumably the praetorian prefect of Constantine: *PLRE*, I, 3–4, "Fl. Ablabius 4." It may well have passed from Ablabius to the imperial estates and thence to Placidia before the death of her father Theodosius I; cf. S.I. Oost, "Some Problems in the History of Galla Placidia," *CP* 60 (1965), 2–3, 9 n. 14; *idem*, *Placidia*, p. 54.

89. *V. Olymp.* and Dagron cited *supra*, n. 84.

90. Janin, *Constantinople*[2], pp. 385, 415; J. Papadopulos, "L'église de Saint-Laurent et les Pulchérianae," *Studi byzantini* 2 (1927), 59–63.

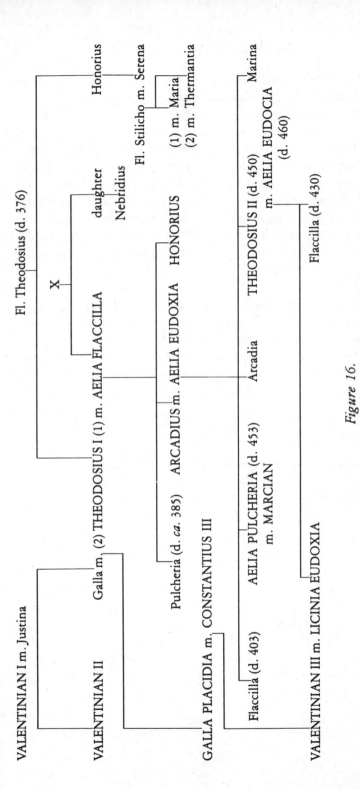

Figure 16.

The Theodosian House: Genealogical Table

[Simplified. Names of female and male Augusti in capital letters.]

personnel, another tangible asset. The stewards whom Sozomen questioned about Pulcheria's philanthropy, the *conductores* in charge of the farms, and tradesmen pursuing humble occupations in the shelter of the urban properties all received employment and expected patronage from their mistresses. In 416 the praetorian prefect secured a constitution from Theodosius ordering that such patronage not lead to illegal exemptions from the *collatio lustralis*, the periodic tax on the capital of tradesmen, "even if they belong to the *domūs* of our lady the venerable Augusta Pulcheria our own sister, or of the other most noble sisters of our piety."[91] The exercise of patronage, even when unsuccessful, evoked devotion among those who bene-fited, and they were sufficient in number to make an impression in the dynastic city.

Pulcheria's massive wealth also financed other impressive loyal-ties. According to Sozomen, her philanthropy "for the least of these" extended to the monks, whose charitable labors paralleled her own and attracted similar popular sympathy. Personal contact strength-ened this link with St. Hypatius, for example, archimandrite of a monastic community near Chalcedon in the time of Theodosius II:

Longing to see the famous Hypatius, the three princesses, sisters of the emperor, came to the palace near the Apostles Church. From there they sent word to him: come so that we can see you. If you do not, we will come to you for your blessing. Feeling himself compelled because they loved Christ, Hypatius went to them. He heartened them with exhortation, uttered a prayer, and having blessed them took his leave.[92]

This passage from the pen of Callinicus, a disciple of St. Hypatius, illustrates well how Pulcheria profited from such contact and the monk's blessing. The palace mentioned was the Rufinianai, the church one Rufinus had dedicated nearby to saints Peter and Paul.[93] The imperial sisters resided there often, presumably imposing more than once on the goodness of Hypatius. At first he hesitated to meet them, because the Augusta and her "most noble" sisters embodied the established social order, while the strength of the ascetic movement came partly from its revolutionary character, from that mass appeal which had brought the monk Isaac into competition with John

91. *CTh* 13. 1. 21.
92. Call. *V. Hyp.* 37. 3–4 (ed. Bartelink).
93. R. Janin, "La banlieue asiatique de Constantinople," *EO* 22 (1923), 184–85.

Chrysostom, the establishment bishop.[94] With their compelling piety —"because they loved Christ"—the emperor's sisters could bridge the gap, drawing Hypatius and other monks into their own imperial orbit and acquiring for themselves some of the movement's revolutionary appeal.

Not long after St. Simeon's fulminations brought Asclepiodotus down, the establishment of Constantinople clashed with another holy man, the archimandrite Alexander who came from Antioch to the dynastic city *ca.* 425 bringing his disciples, the *akoimetai* or "sleepless ones," so named from their discipline of perpetual prayer.[95] The company soon grew to more than three hundred as monks abandoned other archimandrites to share in Alexander's spectacular asceticism, and he attracted a large and potentially disorderly following outside his community by adopting the usual revolutionary hostility toward "the authorities" (οἱ ἄρχοντες).[96] In 426 the establishment moved against him, raising a charge of heresy to be tried by an episcopal tribunal.[97] When the bishops could not reach a decision, they handed Alexander's case to the city prefect,[98] who at first likewise hesitated to act. Mobs, presumably aroused by jealous rival archimandrites, attacked the "sleepless ones." They were beaten and chained, bringing the perpetual liturgy temporarily to an end. Finally Alexander received an order to dismiss his followers and return to Syria (*ca.* 427).[99]

The holy man did not give up easily. Alexander crossed the Propontis and took refuge with the remnant of his followers in the Apostles Church near the Rufinianai. Again the establishment

94. *Supra*, p. 70.

95. In general *Vie d'Alexandre l'Acémète*, ed. E. de Stoop, *PO*, VI, 641–706; G. Dagron, "La vie ancienne de Saint Marcel l'Acémète," *An. Boll.* 86 (1968), 271–321; J. Pargoire, "Un mot sur les Acémètes," *EO* 2 (1898–99), 304–8, 365–72; *idem*, "Les débuts du monachisme à Constantinople," *Revue des questions historiques* n.s. 21 (1899), 129–43. See *Vie d'Alexandre*, *PO*, VI, 696–99, and Call. *V. Hyp.* 41. 1–20 (ed. Bartelink) for the events described here.

96. Call. *V. Hyp.* 41. 2.

97. *Vie d'Alexandre* 48 (*PO*, VI, 697); Nil. *De vol. paup.* 21 (*PG*, LXXIX, 997a). On the date I follow Pargoire, "Débuts," p. 134, against R. P. V. Grumel, *Les regestes des actes du patriarcat de Constantinople*, I, 1 (Constantinople, 1932), p. 24 n. 49. The charge against Alexander was Messalianism, exuberant rejection of episcopal and other forms of authority; see H. Dörries, "Die Messalianer im Zeugnis ihrer Bestreiter: Zum Problem des Enthusiasmus in der spätantiken Reichskirche," *Saeculum* 21 (1970), 213–27.

98. *Vie d'Alexandre* 49 (*PO*, VI, 698).

99. *Ibid.* 49–50 (pp. 697–99); Call. *V. Hyp.* 41. 3 (ed. Bartelink).

attacked. Ordered by "the authorities" (διὰ τὸ κέλευσμα τῶν ἀρχόντων), the local bishop Eulalius of Chalcedon dispatched "deacons, beggars, laborers, and minor clerics" from his own episcopal establishment to expel the "sleepless ones" with violence. St. Hypatius took them in and tended their wounds, but the next day the bishop's roughnecks appeared again with two mules to carry away the two troublesome archimandrites. The threat to Hypatius provoked his following in the countryside, and angry peasants quickly arrived to defend their spiritual adviser. Since bloodshed appeared inevitable if he resisted, Hypatius prepared to leave quietly with his brothers.

Just then a horseman, an attendant of the empress, rode up from the nearby palace. Pulcheria and her court had happened to be in residence at the Rufinianai when Alexander was expelled from Constantinople. The horseman asked for a scribe and paper and demanded names: "The empress has sent me to discover who these men are that persecute the servants of God." This intimidated the bishop's roughnecks, who covered their faces and fled. Pulcheria sent a troop of soldiers to guard the monastery of Hypatius in case Eulalius should make further attempts, but in a few days Alexander and the "sleepless ones" felt secure enough to leave Hypatius and found their own convent some distance away.[100] In this episode Pulcheria had intervened effectively against both the episcopacy and the government, aligning herself with archimandrites whose conduct clearly challenged the social order. It will be worth remembering how easily the establishment gave way.

According to Sozomen again, the accounts of Pulcheria's stewards documented lavish expenditures on "houses of prayer."[101] Like Constantine's basilica in Jerusalem, the "lofty and beautiful achievement of a truly imperial mind," her churches in Constantinople did convey an impression of her majesty.[102] But Pulcheria, unlike Constantine, devoted her resources to housing relics and memorializing the saints, to structures that expressed in monumental architecture the same intimacy between herself and the holy dead which

100. *Ibid.* 4–20.

101. Soz. 9. 1. 10; *supra*, p. 91. Cf. Ensslin, *RE*, XXIII (1959), 1961–62, "Pulcheria 2," for a survey of attested Pulcheria foundations.

102. Euseb. *LC* 11. On the motives of imperial construction cf. R. Krautheimer, "The Constantinian Basilica," *DOP* 21 (1967), 125, 130; D.J. Geanakoplos, "Church Building and 'Caesaropapism,'" *GRBS* 7 (1966), 185–86; and C. Capizzi, "L'attività edilizia di Anicia Giuliana," *Collectanea byzantina* = *Orientalia christiana analecta* 204 (1977), 124–30.

the Trier Ivory captured in miniature. Her Church of Saint Stephen established the pattern, but it was a palatine structure inaccessible to the people of the dynastic city. Building projects in the Pulcherianai in the decades after 421 give a better notion of her motivation. There she constructed a Church of St. Lawrence, a Roman deacon martyred in the third century, and one for the prophet Isaiah.[103] She founded both structures to receive newly translated relics, as in the case of St. Stephen, but both saints came to dwell amid the populace and in the vicinity of Pulcheria's own palatial *domus*. Clearly, relics preoccupied her in these years, as did her efforts to let the public know of her association with them.

These efforts could take other forms. In the time of the bishop Proclus (434–46), St. Thyrsos, another third-century martyr, came to Pulcheria three times in dreams to report that the Forty Martyrs of Sebaste—military saints who had lost their lives in the persecutions of Licinius—lay concealed near his own shrine. If the dreaming was genuine it had a perfectly natural explanation, for Pulcheria had learned in advance the exact position of the Forty Martyrs, from an aging priest and a monk who had known earlier inhabitants of the site. Still, some excited digging followed, and then Pulcheria herself presided with Proclus as the sacred treasure was brought to light. Ordering the relics placed in a costly chest and deposited beside St. Thyrsos, she celebrated the discovery with a public procession of the usual type.[104]

Thus Pulcheria employed her tangible resources to amass vast intangible ones—the potent friendship of living holy men and of dead saints. As Augusta divinely placed at the head of the social order, she also profited from the alliance of bishops, who with one notable exception abandoned John Chrysostom's objections to the sacral *basileía* of women. Proclus, for example, used the occasion of a Resurrection sermon to extol Pulcheria:[105]

When we see the trophies, there can be no doubt that the victory has been won. We wonder at the great soul of the empress, a brimming source of

103. Marcell. com. *a.* 439. 2, 453 (*MGH: AA*, XI, 80, 85); Theod. Anag. *Epit.* 363 (p. 102 Hansen); *Script. orig. Const.*, p. 241; Janin, *Eglises*, pp. 139–40, 301–4.

104. Soz. 9. 2. The Caesarius who originally owned the site was certainly the praetorian prefect of 395–97, *PLRE*, I, 171, "Fl. Caesarius 6"; Tiftixoglu, "Die Helenianai," pp. 57–58.

105. *Or.* 12 (*PG*, LXV, 788–89).

spiritual blessings for all. As long ago the Jews flung stones at Stephen, wishing to cast down the matchless preacher and first athlete of the Crucified One—so she devoted her virginity to Christ, exhausting her wealth in pious works and making her body dead to its passions, bringing the Crucified One into her bride-chamber, beautifying the heaven which we see on earth.

In these words the bishop highlighted for his congregation some essentials of Pulcheria's sacral *basileía,* declaring that her ascetic achievement repeated the victory of Christ celebrated in the Resurrection and drawing a parallel between it and the martyrdom of St. Stephen. The trophies by which one could recognize her victory were her pious works, especially her churches, the "heaven which we see on earth."

Proclus then went on to exploit Pulcheria as John Chrysostom had her mother, making her a spectacular paradigm of *eusebeia:*

She confesses that the tomb is the treasury of salvation. She finds her glory in the cross, through which the old covenant was torn up. She embraces the death that sets us free from ancient bondage. She proclaims the Resurrection, the greatest gift of the Crucified One. She wonders at the baptismal waters, virginal though mother of so many, from which the bright ones rise. She marvels at the mystery by which the devil suffered unexpected shipwreck. Such are the gifts of the Crucified One.

In these words Proclus offered Pulcheria's response to the mystery of the Resurrection as a model for those neophytes—the "bright ones" —who had just received baptism. It is likely that Pulcheria observed the baptismal rite that day and heard Proclus deliver this sermon. His words would have had special force if delivered in her presence.

The alliance between Pulcheria and the Constantinopolitan episcopacy pre-dated this sermon by at least a decade, going back to the time of John Chrysostom's second successor, Atticus (406–25).[106] This man was remembered neither for eloquence nor for learning, but he did compose one treatise that survived long enough to be included in the literary catalogue of Gennadius of Marseilles (*ca.* 480):

Atticus the bishop of Constantinople wrote a very fine book *On Faith and Virginity,* addressing it to the princesses, the daughters of Arcadius. In it Atticus attacked in advance the teaching of Nestorius.[107]

106. In general G. Bardy, "Atticus de Constantinople et Cyrille d'Alexandrie," *Histoire de l'église depuis les origines jusqu'à nos jours,* ed. A. Fliche and V. Martin, IV (Paris, 1937), 149–55, 158–62.
107. Gennad. *De script. eccl.* 53 (ed. Herding).

Although the treatise of Atticus has been lost, it is safe to assume that the bishop of Constantinople was among those who counseled Pulcheria when she embraced virginity, and that his counsel appeared in this treatise in written form. The words of Gennadius permit limited speculation on its content. The "teaching" he had in mind was certainly the attack on those who called the Virgin Mary *Theotokos* ("mother of God"), because posterity remembered Nestorius as the heretic who denied her that title. Since the *Theotokos* controversy had not broken out before the death of Atticus, presumably Gennadius did not find a systematic defense of the title in the treatise but simply observed with satisfaction that Atticus, a bishop of good reputation, had employed it.[108]

More can be extracted from Gennadius. If Mary *Theotokos* appeared in the treatise, and if it set forth the aims of the virgin life, surely Atticus presented Mary as the archetypal virgin whose chastity the three imperial sisters should emulate. Virgins had adopted Mary as their model as early as the third century.[109] Moreover, Atticus must have specifically urged the sisters to achieve Mary's purity and certainty of faith. This was also traditional teaching.[110] If they did, Christ would be born in them mystically just as the Divine Word had taken flesh in Mary's womb:

And you also, women, you who have been renewed in Christ, who have cast off every stain of sin and have partaken of blessing in the most-holy Mary: you also may receive Him in the womb of faith, the one who is born today of the Virgin. For even the blessed Virgin Mary first opened herself through faith, and not until she had made her body worthy of the kingdom did she receive the king of the universe in her womb.[111]

These words come not from the treatise in question but from a Christmas sermon Atticus delivered before the faithful of Constantinople. But if he connected faith and virginity in his treatise *On Faith*

108. Cf. *ACO*, I, 1, 1, 98; 5, 66.

109. T. Camelot, *Virgines Christi: la virginité aux premiers siècles de l'église* (Paris, 1944), p. 34; C.W. Neumann, *The Virgin Mary in the Works of Saint Ambrose* (Freiburg, Sw., 1962), pp. 5–35; J.-M. Demarolle, "Les femmes chrétiennes vues par Porphyre," *JfAC* 13 (1970), 46.

110. H. Rahner, "Die Gottesgeburt: Die Lehre der Kirchenväter von der Geburt Christi im Herzen des Gläubigen," *Zeitschrift für katholische Theologie* 59 (1935), 333–418, esp. 373–76.

111. J. Lebon, "Discours d'Atticus de Constantinople «Sur la Sainte Mère de Dieu»," *Muséon* 46 (1933), 190 = M. Brière, "Une homélie inédite d'Atticus, Patriarche de Constantinople (406–25)," *ROC* 29 (1933–34), 181.

and Virginity, he must have treated them in the traditional manner and as he himself did on other occasions.

This exhausts Gennadius, but Atticus did express himself on Mary and virgins elsewhere, and Pulcheria and her sisters must have learned of his views whether or not they formed part of the treatise. Some of his statements touched on the dignity of women. Despite St. Paul's teaching that "there is neither Jew nor Greek, nor slave nor free, nor male nor female,"[112] women had occupied a secondary position in Christian society from the outset. Encouraged to labor in charitable occupations such as care for the sick, destitute, and aged, they had been categorically excluded from the priesthood and any office of teaching or leadership.[113] Their subordination found concrete expression when the people of Constantinople gathered in the Great Church; women were physically separated from men and generally restricted to the galleries or *gynaikeia*, the "women's section," and no female might ever enter the sanctuary.[114] Whatever the origins of these attitudes and practices, dogma had a convenient explanation: woman was the daughter of Eve, and through Eve sin had entered the world.

As early as the second century, Christian teachers had also discerned a contradiction between the universality of their religion and the subordination of women. To explain this contradiction and establish the equal dignity of the female sex, they explored the antithesis of Eve and the New Eve.[115] As sin had entered the world through

112. Gal. 3:28; cf. G.B. Caird, "Paul and Women's Liberty," *Bulletin of the John Rylands Library* 54 (1972), 268–81, for a recent defense of St. Paul.

113. J. Leipoldt, *Die Frau in der antiken Welt und im Urchristentum* (Leipzig, 1954), pp. 186–210; J.G. Davies, "Deacons, Deaconesses and Other Minor Orders in the Patristic Period," *JEH* 14 (1963), 1–15; R. Gryson, *Le ministère des femmes dans l'église ancienne*, Recherches et synthèses, Section d'histoire, no. 4 (Gembloux, 1972).

114. H. Holtzinger, *Die altchristliche Architektur in systematischer Darstellung* (Stuttgart, 1889), pp. 175–77; T.F. Mathews, *The Early Churches of Constantinople: Architecture and Liturgy* (University Park-London, 1971), pp. 130–32. To the texts and monuments cited in these works add Joh. Ruf. *Pler.* 36 (*PO*, VIII, 82): The wife of a praetorian prefect attacked Nestorius "du haut des portiques (στοά) supérieurs."

115. M.-J. Nicolas, "La doctrine mariale et la théologie chrétienne de la femme," *Maria: études sur la Sainte Vierge*, ed. H. du Manoir, vol. VII (Paris, 1964), pp. 341–62; E. Guldan, *Eva und Maria* (Graz-Cologne, 1966), pp. 26–35; R. Murray, "Mary, the Second Eve, in the Early Syriac Fathers," *Eastern Churches Review* 3 (1971), 372–84; H.C. Graef, "The Theme of the Second Eve in Some Byzantine Sermons on the Assumption," *Studia patristica* 9 (1966) = *TU*, XCIV, 224–30, esp. 225 on the "mystical synopsis of Greek theology": Eve—New Eve—women in general.

the disobedience and weakness of Eve, so the Divine Word took flesh through the faith or "obedience" of Mary. As Eve had set creation at odds with its Lord, so Mary cooperated in the redemption of the universe by opening herself to the interpenetration of the divine. As Eve had brought women under a curse, so the New Eve embodied the glory and rank of her sex:

Through Mary all women are blessed. The female can no longer be held accursed, for the rank of this sex surpasses even the angels in glory. Now Eve is healed, the Egyptian woman passed over in silence. Delilah is sealed in a tomb, Jezebel given to oblivion. Even Herodias herself is no longer mentioned. Now behold the catalogue of admirable women: All praise Sarah, the fertile field of the people. Rebekah is honored, a capable provider of benedictions, and Leah too they admire as mother of the ancestor in the flesh. Deborah wins praise because she led in battle despite her sex. Elizabeth also they call happy, for she carried the precursor in her body, and he leaped in delight at the approach of grace.[116]

Atticus spoke these words in the Christmas sermon quoted earlier, once again adhering to traditional themes. The same Eve/New Eve antithesis found its way into other sermons of the period as well, into Christmas homilies or the Mary encomiums of Theodotus of Ancyra, for example, a principal opponent of Nestorius, and of Proclus,[117] who also contributed to the Mariological statements of Atticus. The historian Socrates, who knew Atticus well, related that early in his career Proclus had "assisted Bishop Atticus constantly as the ghostwriter [ὑπογραφεύς] of his discourses."[118]

Because she was herself a virgin, Pulcheria could not resist the Mariology of contemporary preaching and the treatise of Atticus. She embraced Mary as a paradigm for her own asceticism, in the belief that by emulating the *Theotokos* she would receive the Divine Word in her own body, or, as Proclus expressed it, would "bring the Crucified One into her bride-chamber." She believed that this reception confirmed the dignity of her sex.[119] If she, like other virgins, forfeited the traditional advantages of childbearing, she did so only to

116. Proc. *Serm.* 5 (*PG*, LXV, 720) = Lebon, "Discours," p. 189 = Brière, "Homélie," p. 180; cf. Lebon "Discours," pp. 167–75.

117. Theod. Anc. *Serm.* 6 (*PG*, LXXVII, 1427–28) = M. Jugie, "Homélies mariales byzantines," *PO*, XIX (1926), 329–31; *idem, Serm.* 5 (*PG*, LXXVII, 1418) = M. Aubineau, "Une homélie de Théodote d'Ancyre," *OCP* 26 (1960), 232; Proc. *Serm.* 1. 1–2 (*ACO*, I, 1, 1, 103–4). On Theodotus see Aubineau, "Homélie," pp. 221–24, and on Proclus *infra*, pp. 148, 155–57, 182–83, 188, 197.

118. Soc. 7. 41. 1; cf. Lebon, "Discours," pp. 173–74.

119. *Infra*, pp. 145, 153–54.

repeat mystically an even more glorious female function. As Atticus put it, she would "receive the king of the universe in her womb."

But Pulcheria was also an Augusta; inevitably, contemporary Mariology entered the ideological framework of her sacral *basileía*. In the last decades of her life, she undertook construction of three Mary churches, those of the Blachernai, the Hodegoi ("Guides"), and the Chalkoprateia, which was, in typical fashion, raised over the ruins of a synagogue.[120] Like her other building projects, these three impressed

120. Theod. Anag. *Epit.* 363 (p. 102 Hansen). The early history of all three churches is obscure, but Theod. Anag. provides the most reliable evidence for their foundations, and other, apparently contradictory evidence can be reconciled with his notice readily if it is assumed that later "founders" in reality undertook rebuilding or restoration. On this and these churches in general see J. Ebersolt, *Sanctuaires de Byzance* (Paris, 1921), pp. 44–60; Janin, *Eglises*, pp. 169–79, 208–16, 246–51; Mathews, *Churches*, pp. 28–33; A.M. Schneider, "Die Blachernen," *Oriens* 4 (1951), 102–5; W. Kleiss, "Neue Befunde zur Chalkopratenkirche in Istanbul," *Akten des VII. Internationalen Kongresses für Christliche Archäologie, Trier, 5–11 September 1965* (Vatican City-Berlin, n.d.), pp. 587–94.

On the relics and icon of the three Pulcherian foundations—the famous Virgin's cincture of the Chalkoprateia; the icon of Mary "the Guide," later thought to have been painted by St. Luke himself; and the Virgin's shroud of the Blachernai—see also C. Cecchelli, *Mater Christi*, I (Rome, 1946), pp. 200–233. No early source confirms that Pulcheria discovered the Virgin's cincture, but see Niceph. Call. *HE* 14. 2, 49, 15. 14 (*PG*, CXLVI, 1061, 1233, CXLVII, 41). An obscure work called *Euthymiac History* quoted by Joh. Damasc. *De dorm. Virg.* 2. 18 (ed. Voulet) claims that Bishop Juvenal of Jerusalem sent the Virgin's coffin and shroud to Pulcheria; but the account also speaks of the Virgin's dormition, a tradition that did not take shape until the seventh century, and it is therefore held to be apocryphal by (e.g.) M. Jugie, *La mort et l'assomption de la Sainte Vierge*, Studi e testi no. 114 (Vatican City, 1944), pp. 92–93, 159–67; and A. Wenger, *L'assomption de la t. S. Vierge dans la tradition byzantine du VIe au Xe siècle* (Paris, 1955), pp. 136–39; cf., however, E. Honigmann, "Juvenal of Jerusalem," *DOP* 5 (1950), 267–70, who argues that the *Euthymiac History* drew upon Theod. Anag. Wenger, *Assomption*, pp. 293–303, publishes the best text of the so-called "Legend of Galbius and Candidus," which recounts, on the contrary, how two patricians found Mary's funerary vestment in the Holy Land and brought it to Constantinople, where Leo I (457–74) and his consort Verina founded the Blachernai church to house it. Wenger, *Assomption*, pp. 113–32, 432–36, dates the original form of this text to the sixth century and argues for its accuracy. This evidence, however, should not be allowed to stand against the testimony of Theod. Anag. Some imaginative author seems to have constructed the "Legend of Galbius and Candidus" in the sixth century from mosaics and inscriptions then visible in the church. As for Luke's portrait, Theod. Anag. *Epit.* 353 (p. 100 Hansen) says that Eudocia sent it from the Holy Land to Pulcheria. Jugie, *Mort*, pp. 93–95, accepts this notice, but scholars have often considered it to be an interpolation from the Iconoclastic period. I am inclined to believe that Pulcheria "discovered" the cincture and the shroud. The analogy of her other foundations suggests that she would have searched out some physical witness to the saint's presence for her Mary churches as well. On the other hand, if Eudocia had indeed "discovered" St. Luke's portrait she would hardly have given it over to her sister-in-law, for the two were enemies (*infra*, Chaps. 6 and 7, *passim*).

the people of Constantinople as "achievements of a truly imperial conception" and at the same time emphasized in monumental architecture the association between the Virgin *Theotokos* and the virgin Augusta.

These were not, however, the earliest Mary churches of the dynastic city. In his *De ceremoniis,* Constantine Porphyrogenitus (tenth century) mentioned a *Theotokos* church called "First-Founded" (πρωτόκτιστος) located in the Daphne complex of the imperial palace in close proximity to Pulcheria's Church of St. Stephen.[121] Another text, this one from late in the fifth century, reports that members of the imperial court worshiped in a Mary church before the Council of Ephesus,[122] perhaps the same structure mentioned in the *De ceremoniis* but in any case proof that St. Mary's "First-Founded" antedated 431. The date of this church, its location near St. Stephen's in the Daphne complex, and Pulcheria's devotion to the Virgin's cult argue strongly that she built the *Theotokos* "First-Founded" as well. If this is so, clearly she intended its function to be imperial, to bring the Virgin, like St. Stephen, into physical intimacy with the *basileía.*[123]

It is also certain that Pulcheria's devotion to Mary was shared by her two sisters; their lives and Mary piety induced contemporaries to call the three "the ever-virginal chorus of princesses."[124] After the marriage of Theodosius, when Pulcheria received her own *cubiculum* and a distinct staff, inevitably the same piety and common life extended to her *cubiculariae,* who presumably likewise embraced virginity and thus resembled a convent of nuns with Pulcheria at their head. This group of women recalls the "holy choir" that surrounded John Chrysostom's friend Olympias and the "angelic life-style of these holy women," some of them high-born relatives of Olympias, some her own *cubiculariae*—all, however, "ornamented with the crown of virginity."[125] There were other parallels. Each day Chrysostom visited the women of Olympias to strengthen them with his teaching, and Olympias herself prepared his meals.[126] Atticus strengthened Pulcheria and her sisters similarly with his treatise *On Faith and*

121. *De caer.* 1 (I, 1, 5 Vogt), the only certain notice of this church. Vogt (note *ad loc.* I, 2, 38) and Cecchelli, *Mater,* I, 234–35, take πρωτόκτιστος to mean that this was the first Mary church in Constantinople, earlier than the famous Pulcheria foundations (*supra*).
122. Joh. Ruf. *Pler.* 1 (*PO,* VIII, 11–12).
123. *Supra,* pp. 103, 107–108.
124. Thdt. *HR* 17 (*PG,* LXXXII, 1424); *ACO,* I, 1, 2, 104.
125. *V. Olymp.* 6–8 (ed. Malingrey); Dagron, *Naissance,* p. 505.
126. *V. Olymp.* 8.

Virginity, and either he or his successor Sisinnius (425–27) invited Pulcheria's "nuns" to dine with him in the episcopal palace on Sundays following communion. Atticus or his successor accepted Pulcheria's robe, one she actually wore, for use as the altar-covering during communion in the Great Church,[127] an honor, appropriate to women of distinction and spectacular piety, also granted by Chrysostom to Olympias.[128] As Gilbert Dagron put it neatly, Pulcheria "c'est Olympias devenue impératrice!"[129]

Equally instructive contrasts must be kept in mind. Olympias lived with her women in a "monastery" she had constructed adjacent to Chrysostom's episcopal palace,[130] Pulcheria and her "nuns" in suburban palaces belonging to the state or in her own palatial *domūs*, where she would be unquestioned mistress. Olympias made her wealth over to Chrysostom to use at his discretion. Pulcheria kept her estates intact and her wealth under personal control, for Sozomen could investigate the accounts of her stewards to confirm the scale of her philanthropy. Olympias and the more prominent members of her group accepted ordination as deaconesses, a clerical function which brought a woman under the bishop's authority and which Pulcheria, later in life, would categorically refuse.[131] In each case the empress, unlike Olympias, kept the episcopacy at a safe distance. Strictly speaking, Pulcheria remained an Augusta, her sisters and the *cubiculariae* around her not nuns but the members of her court. As the parallel with Olympias suggests, however, she acquired the authority of a holy woman. It came from "the fame of her virginity," which another bishop (Cyril of Alexandria) held up "like an image bearing an inscription . . . before everyone in every city and province."[132] Similarly, the bishop of Constantinople (either Atticus or Sisinnius)

127. *Infra*, p. 153.
128. Pall. *HL* 61 (p. 156 Butler). The practice seems extravagant but is also attested for Melania the Younger and for Eudocia, Geront. *V. Mel. Iun.* 19 (ed. Gorce); F. Nau, "Résumé de monographies syriaques," *ROC* 19 (1914), 117. To judge from Isid. Pel. *Ep.* 1. 1. 123 (*PG*, LXXVII, 264–65) it was a liturgy that recalled Joseph of Arimathea, who provided the linen shroud in which the crucified body of Christ was wrapped; cf. F.J. Dölger, "Die eigenartige Marienverehrung der Philomarianiten oder Kollyridianer in Arabien," *Antike und Christentum* 1 (1929), 129.
129. *Naissance*, pp. 506–7.
130. *V. Olymp.* 6, 8 (ed. Malingrey); Mango, *Brazen House*, pp. 54–56.
131. Soz. 8. 9. 1; Pall. *Dial.* 117 (p. 110 Coleman-Norton); *V. Olymp.* 6–7 (ed. Malingrey); Dagron, *Naissance*, pp. 490–91, 502; *infra*, p. 192.
132. *ACO*, I, 1, 5, 62.

employed that fame to instruct the faithful, by having an image of Pulcheria painted above the altar in the Great Church.[133] This image, like the Resurrection sermon of Proclus but in visual language, offered the virgin empress as a paradigm of faith.

Thus while drawing living holy men, dead saints, and the episcopacy into her orbit, Pulcheria adopted a spectacular form of imperial cenobitism much like the regimen she had imposed on her brother after 412,[134] but female in character and infused with devotion to Mary. That devotion offered special advantages. By no means limited to Pulcheria and her circle, Mary piety had already become one of the major enthusiasms of all Christendom. Either Atticus or Sisinnius responded to popular enthusiasm for Mary by including in the liturgical cycle of the Great Church the earliest Constantinopolitan festival of Mary, a "memorial" (μνήμη) observed annually on December 26, a "celebration of virginity" exalting women because the Virgin *Theotokos* had erased the sin of Eve.[135] The conclusions Pulcheria herself drew from her emulation of Mary and from the Eve / New Eve synthesis emerge from another liturgical practice introduced under Sisinnius. On Easter she entered the sanctuary of the Great Church to take communion within in the company of priests and of Theodosius her brother, an expression of her claim to the priestly character possessed by an Augustus. She defended this practice against the objection that she was a daughter of Eve by evoking the mystical birth of Christ in her own flesh and her consequent Marial dignity.[136] Echoing as it did a popular new enthusiasm, this claim to Marial dignity added a potent element to Pulcheria's sacral *basileía*.

With their "Athenian" maid, men of traditionalist persuasion had hoped to defeat Pulcheria. Exploiting for themselves the weapons of *kedeia* and of female *basileía*, they had driven their antagonist from the palace and forced her to relax her grip on her brother's magisterial powers. Their initial success forced Pulcheria to deploy her own legions in the dynastic city, to make known through visible monuments the strength of her special resources. Saints both living and dead lined her battlements, and she commanded a regiment of bish-

133. *Infra*, p. 153.

134. *Supra*, pp. 91–93.

135. Proc. *Serm*. 1. 1–2 (*ACO*, I, 1, 1, 103–4) dated 428 by Theoph. *a.m.* 5923 (p. 88 de Boor); cf. Jugie, *Mort*, pp. 175–77. I quote from the sermon *infra*, pp. 155–56.

136. *Infra*, pp. 153–54.

ops. Above all she brought Mary into her camp, her own exemplar, the archetypal virgin. Those who resisted Pulcheria resisted Mary as well. Any who challenged Pulcheria's *basileía* on the ground that she was a woman risked insulting the New Eve. This was the gravest risk, for, like Pulcheria, the pious multitudes of Constantinople and the Empire believed that Mary was *Theotokos*, the "Mother of God."

CHAPTER FIVE

The Controversy Over the Mother of God

The heresiarch Nestorius occupied the see of Constantinople for less than four years (428-31), but his unhappy episcopacy and fall merit detailed investigation. On the question of Nestorius and of his attack on the *Theotokos*, traditional *basileía* with the accouterments of magisterial power stood against the independent *basileía* of a woman, Theodosius against Pulcheria with her less tangible resources. The outcome permits an estimate of their respective strengths; remarkably, Pulcheria defeated both the bishop and her brother the emperor.

Born near Germanicia in northern Syria, Nestorius traveled as a youth to Antioch,[1] no doubt aiming at a public career, and received there the usual literary and rhetorical training. Soon he experienced the attraction of the spiritual life, just as John Chrysostom had, and felt compelled to enter the monastery of Euprepius outside of Antioch.[2] Nestorius read theology, falling naturally under the influence of the Antiochene school in exegesis and Christology; and his asceticism, along with his learning, dialectical ability, rhetorical style, physical attractiveness, and especially his clear, high-pitched, almost feminine voice, began to win recognition. Nestorius was ordained a priest and appeared often as preacher in the churches of Antioch.[3] His reputation grew, extending as far as Constantinople.

---

1. For his origins and early life see Soc. 7. 29. 2; Thdt. *Haer. fab. comp.* 4. 12 (*PG*, LXXXIII, 433); M. Brière, "La légende syriaque de Nestorius," *ROC* 15 (1910), 17; also (with fanciful information) Dionysius bar Salibi in *PO*, VIII, 162-63; and J. Tixeront, "La lettre de Philoxène de Mabboug à Abou-Niphir," *ROC* 8 (1903), 624-25. Cf. M. Jugie, *Nestorius et la controverse nestorienne* (Paris, 1912), pp. 18-22.

2. Evagr. 1. 7.

3. Thdt. *loc. cit.*; Soc. 7. 29. 3; *Lettre à Cosme* 9 (*PO*, XIII, 280); Barhadbeshabba 20 (*PO*, IX, 517-20); Joh. Ruf. *Pler.* 1 (*PO*, VIII, 12); Brière, "Légende syriaque," p. 18; cf. L. Abramowski, *Untersuchungen zum Liber Heraclidis des Nestorius*, CSCO, Subsidia, vol. XXII (Louvain, 1963), p. 73.

Meanwhile, the see of the dynastic city passed through a time of difficulty. After Bishop Atticus died on October 10, 425,[4] a contest lasting several months ensued over the succession. Some favored Proclus the secretary of Atticus, others Philip of Side, a church historian and associate of Chrysostom, who vented his disappointment at defeat in scurrilous attacks upon the winner, the holy and gentle Sisinnius.[5] Though popular as a benefactor of the poor, Sisinnius may have been acceptable among the powerful mainly because his advanced age or peaceful nature guaranteed that he would be ineffectual, and that another election would soon give the competing factions a new occasion to test their strength.

Sisinnius died on December 24, 427.[6] Theodosius pleaded with Dalmatius, chief of the archimandrites, to accept the episcopal dignity, and when he refused tried to persuade another (unknown) ascetic.[7] The emperor's efforts confirm the importance of placating these leaders of public opinion. Neither Proclus nor Philip survived the abuse the partisans of each heaped upon the other. In this impasse, which apparently again lasted several months, Nestorius seemed to the emperor and his most influential advisers to be a reasonable alternative.[8] He had a reputation for asceticism that might attract the admiration of the monks. If he failed to gain their confidence, his oratorical powers promised to win him a popular following to counteract monastic influence. His learning and rhetorical skill appealed to the cultured aristocrats, even those on the fringes of Christianity. His origins and personal qualities powerfully recalled the memory of Chrysostom,[9] whose followers remained numerous and impassioned at Constantinople two decades after his death. Since Nestorius' views on Mary were as yet unknown, there is no reason to think that Pulcheria and her followers objected to his candidacy.[10] Thus Nestorius came forth from his monastery. Theodosius ordered

---

4. See Soc. 7. 25. 21, 26. 1–4 for the death of Atticus and the election of Sisinnius.

5. Soc. 7. 27. Philip boasted to be a relative of the sophist Troïlus (7. 27. 1).

6. On him *ibid*. 7. 26. 2–4, 28; Coelest. *Ep*. 13. 1 (*PL*, L, 470–72).

7. Nest. *Heracl.*, pp. 242–43 Nau.

8. Soc. 7. 29. 1–3; cf. Nest. *loc. cit*. on the electioneering.

9. Joh. Cass. *De incarn. Dom*. 7. 30. 2 (*CSEL*, XVII, 388); Dionysius bar Salibi, *PO*, VIII, 163.

10. *Infra*, p. 154. Nestorius claims (*Heracl.*, p. 89 Nau) that before they clashed Pulcheria had been his friend.

the *magister militum* Dionysius to escort him to the capital,[11] underscoring the fact that the emperor had made the choice. On April 10, 428, the people of Constantinople acclaimed their new bishop and witnessed his consecration.[12]

Despite impressive personal qualifications and the trust and love of the emperor, which he enjoyed until the very end of his episcopacy,[13] Nestorius failed miserably as bishop of Constantinople. His failures may have been partly doctrinal, although some modern scholars have argued that Nestorius was thoroughly orthodox.[14] But far more serious was his inability to cope with politics in the dynastic city, to understand where power and influence lay and when conflict, however justified it might be, had to be avoided in order to preserve orthodoxy and order. Reportedly, Nestorius antagonized the populace by suppressing the circus, theater, mimes, games, and dancers,[15] and he also clashed with the monks. Finding many of them at large in public places and residential quarters of Constantinople, where they both ministered to the people and rallied opposition to incompetent or vicious authorities, Nestorius tried to insulate them safely behind their cloister walls. Any who refused to return he excommunicated.[16]

This policy appealed to the great men and civil authorities of Constantinople because it made the city easier to govern successfully, but it also provoked a dangerous response. The monk Hypatius, among the earliest enemies of Nestorius, effaced his name on the diptychs of the Apostles Church near the Rufinianai, so that he would be omitted from the prayer of offering.[17] Within Constantinople, Basil, a former deacon of Antioch and famous ascetic, inter-

11. Call. *V. Hyp.* 32. 1 (ed. Bartelink); Brière, "Légende syriaque," p. 18.

12. Soc. 7. 29. 1, 4; Vinc. Lir. *Comm.* 1. 11 (*PL*, L, 651), Thdt. *Haer. fab. comp.* 4. 12 (*PG*, LXXXIII, 433); Call. *V. Hyp.* 32. 2 (ed. Bartelink); Nest. *Heracl.*, p. 244 Nau; Barhadbeshabba 20 (*PO*, IX, 518–20); Brière, "Légende syriaque," p. 18.

13. Nest. *Heracl.*, p. 242 Nau; Barhadbeshabba 20 (*PO*, IX, 520, 523); *infra*, pp. 171–73.

14. E.g., F. Loofs, *Nestorius and His Place in the History of Christian Doctrine* (Cambridge, 1914); and M. V. Anastos, "Nestorius Was Orthodox," *DOP* 16 (1962), 117–40. The traditional view is found, for example, in Jugie, *Nestorius,* and (more recently) G. S. Bebis, "'The Apology' of Nestorius: A New Evaluation," *Studia patristica* 11 (1972) = *TU*, CVIII, 107–12.

15. Barhadbeshabba 20 (*PO*, IX, 522–23); Brière, "Légende syriaque," p. 19.

16. Nest. *Heracl.*, pp. 239–40 Nau; Barhadbeshabba 21 (*PO*, IX, 528–29); *Lettre à Cosme* 3 (*PO*, XIII, 277); cf. Dagron, "Moines," pp. 253–61.

17. Call. *V. Hyp.* 32 (ed. Bartelink).

rupted Nestorius and denounced him during a sermon. The master of offices ordered Basil arrested, beaten, and exiled (just as Alexander had been earlier), but a mob carried him to the Church of St. Euphemia and he continued his tirades.[18] Nestorius was to find to his dismay that such outbursts played into the hands of monastic leaders like the archimandrite Dalmatius, whose way of life the emperor greatly admired.[19]

Furthermore, Nestorius alienated or antagonized some among the powerful and aristocratic—including those whose views paralleled the views of Socrates the historian—by adopting a hard line against heresy. In a sermon delivered shortly after his installation Nestorius declared to Theodosius: "Give me the earth free of heretics, O Emperor, and I will give you heaven in return. Help me destroy the heretics, and I will help you destroy the Persians."[20] This statement of imperial victory ideology could not fail to win a positive response from Theodosius. Apparently Nestorius himself dictated the terms of a constitution against a long list of heresies issued to the praetorian prefect on May 30, 428, less than two months after he received the episcopal throne.[21] This was a harsh law, providing stiff penalties both for heretics and for those who connived in their sin by failing to punish them. It was also strictly enforced. Socrates lamented the sufferings of Quartodecimani (who celebrated Easter on the Jewish Passover) in Asia, Lydia, and Caria, and the deaths of many believers in Sardes and Miletus because of the unrest Nestorius had caused. In Constantinople attacks on Novatians, Borborians (a gnostic sect), Manichaeans, and Arians are mentioned.[22]

Nestorius had tried to seize a church from the Arians of the city only four days after his installation. The heretics set fire to it rather

18. Joh. Ruf. *Pler.* 35 (*PO*, VIII, 78–81), probably not the same incidents recorded in *ACO*, I, 1, 5, 8–9 (see, however, Dagron, "Moines," p. 266).

19. On Theodosius' admiration for Dalmatius and other monks see Call. *V. Hyp.* 37. 1–2 (ed. Bartelink); Nest. *Heracl.*, pp. 241–42 Nau; Barhadbeshabba 27 (*PO*, IX, 567); *ACO*, I, 1, 2, 65, 68; and esp. the texts published and discussed by F. Nau in *PO*, VIII, 166–74.

20. Soc. 7. 29. 4–5. Socrates goes on to state (6–7) that these words revealed at once Nestorius' superficial, impetuous, and vainglorious character.

21. *CTh* 16. 5. 65; F. Loofs, ed., *Nestoriana: Die Fragmente des Nestorius* (Halle, 1905), p. 205 = *ACO*, I, 4, 26: "qui certe legem inter ipsa meae ordinationis initia contra eos, qui Christum purum hominem dicunt, et contra reliquas haereses innovavi." Also Barhadbeshabba 21 (*PO*, IX, 530).

22. Soc. 7. 29. 8–13; Loofs, *Nestoriana*, p. 183; Barhadbeshabba 21 (*PO*, IX, 530–31).

than give it over, and the flames quickly engulfed several neighboring dwellings. From this Nestorius won the epithet "firebrand" even, as Socrates reports, among the orthodox. Such enthusiasm was dangerous because the Arians involved were mainly Germans and associated barbarians from among the praesental armies, the emperor's guard, and, especially, the most prominent generals.[23] These men had acquired the right to worship in their own churches, both within the capital and in the suburbs, in the ten years or so since they again reached the high command.[24] Without another convenient source of recruits and capable generals, Theodosius could not support Nestorius' efforts. The emperor and his advisers urged the bishop to cool his zeal, but apparently without success.

Nestorius also blundered into a conflict with Bishop Cyril of Alexandria. At the outset of his episcopacy he had neglected to send his Egyptian colleague the gifts or "benedictions" that men in positions of influence customarily accepted as indications of obedience, sympathy, and the hope of good relations. Whether it was a declaration of policy or a simple oversight, this omission soon induced a few of Cyril's many enemies to step forward with accusations against him.[25] The Alexandrian clerics Chairemon, Victor, and Sophronas brought before Nestorius an obscure dispute concerning property. Though they were "the dung of the city" (Cyril's words), Nestorius took their case to the emperor, who discussed the conduct of the bishop of Alexandria with his advisers and then returned the matter to Nestorius for investigation.[26] The possibility emerged that Cyril

23. Barhadbeshabba 21 (*PO*, IX, 529) and the *Lettre à Cosme* 3 (*PO*, XIII, 277–78) identify these Arians as soldiers, the latter specifically as σπαθάριοι (*scholares?*). The *magistri militum praesentales* at this time were apparently the Goth Plinta and either Ardaburius, an Alan, or Areobindus, another Goth: Demandt, *RE*, suppl. XII, 746–48, 752–53, "Magister Militum." Cf., however, *PLRE*, II, 137–38, "Fl. Ardabur 3," 144–45, "Fl. Ariobindus 2."

24. Soc. and Barhadbeshabba (*locc. citt.*) speak of an oratory within the city, the latter stating that the Arians had built churches and formed a clergy after extracting permission from the emperor and great men in the time of Sisinnius.

25. Nest. *Heracl.*, p. 92 Nau; on *eulogiai* or *benedictiones* see *infra*, pp. 180–81, and P. Batiffol, "Les présents de S. Cyrille à la cour de Constantinople," *Etudes de liturgie et d'archéologie chrétienne* (Paris, 1919), pp. 173–76.

26. *ACO*, I, 1, 1, 25–26 (Cyril. *Ep.* 4), 111; 3, 88; Nest. *Heracl.*, pp. 92–93, 97 Nau; Barhadbeshabba 22 (*PO*, IX, 536–37); *Lettre à Cosme* 4 (*PO*, XIII, 278). Loofs, *Nestorius*, pp. 32–41, dates the accusations against Cyril before the outbreak of the Mary controversy, but they may have come later; see, e.g., B.J. Kidd, *A History of the Church to A.D. 461*, III (Oxford, 1922), pp. 210–11; G. Bardy, "Les débuts du Nestorianisme (428–433)," *Histoire de l'église*, ed. Fliche and Martin, IV, 175.

152 · Theodosian Empresses

might be ordered to answer the charges before an ecclesiastical tribunal, and that the judge might be the bishop of Constantinople. In this capacity Nestorius would appear to the world as the champion of Antioch, where he had received his training in theology and exegesis and had first won prominence. At once the longstanding struggle over the primacy of episcopal sees broke out again.[27] Faced with humiliation, Cyril began to cast about for issues and allies.

He must have realized at once the importance of a sympathetic hearing at court, but his prospects in that quarter were far from encouraging. Theodosius stuck by his bishop despite the controversy Nestorius had aroused. Nestorius' supporters even persuaded the emperor to introduce an annual memorial of the martyred Antiochene John Chrysostom "at court" (*apud comitatum*), with the first celebration on September 26, 428.[28] Faced with this situation, Cyril resolved to stir up the muddy waters of dogma, and to enlist Pulcheria.

The latter had not gotten on well with the new bishop, who considered her a "contentious female."[29] Like Chrysostom, Nestorius aimed to keep the prominent women of Constantinople under control; he put an end to female participation in evening psalms and prayer and in watches for the dead, claiming that this led to promiscuity.[30] One of the first to attack Nestorius openly was a pious and generous woman named Heleniana, wife of an important politician, who shouted out against him from the women's gallery of the Great Church.[31] Like Chrysostom also, Nestorius foolishly clashed with an empress while attempting to put women in their place. In his apologetic work known as the *Bazaar of Heracleides,* Nestorius admitted his indiscretion—while implying that Pulcheria, in spite of her vow

27. Both ancient and modern observers have considered this the key to understanding the controversy. See Barhadbeshabba 21, 26 (*PO*, IX, 526, 558–62); Nest. *Heracl.*, p. 250 Nau; Loofs, *Nestoriana*, p. 300; Isid. Pel. *Ep.* 1. 310 (*PG*, LXXVIII, 361); E. Schwartz, *Cyrill und der Mönch Viktor*, Sitzungsberichte der Akademie der Wissenschaften in Wien, Philosophisch-historische Klasse vol. CCVIII, no. 4 (Vienna-Leipzig, 1928), pp. 3–4; N.H. Baynes, "Alexandria and Constantinople," *Byzantine Studies and Other Essays* (London, 1955), pp. 107–9; R. Sellers, *The Council of Chalcedon* (London, 1953), pp. 3–4. On the conflicting Christological traditions of Antiochenes and Alexandrians cf. *ibid.*, pp. 132–81; A. Grillmeier, *Christ in Christian Tradition from the Apostolic Age to Chalcedon (451)*, trans. J.S. Bowden (London, 1965), pp. 361–495; W.H.C. Frend, *The Rise of the Monophysite Movement* (Cambridge, 1972), pp. 4–5, 13–14, 104–42.
28. Marcell. com. *a.* 428. 2 (*MGH: AA*, XI, 77).
29. Nest. *Heracl.*, p. 89 Nau: "une femme belliqueuse."
30. Barhadbeshabba 21 (*PO*, IX, 528).
31. Joh. Ruf. *Pler.* 36 (*PO*, VIII, 81–82).

of chastity, had enjoyed adulterous sexual relations with numerous men. The bishop did not announce the scandal publicly, but because of this "weakness typical of a young woman" he would not honor Pulcheria as the bride of Christ in his prayers for the imperial house. Since his predecessors had used that formula, people could not fail to notice and to draw the appropriate conclusion.[32] Another source reveals that Nestorius refused to continue Sisinnius' practice of entertaining Pulcheria and her women after Sunday communion for dinner in the episcopal palace, and that he effaced Pulcheria's portrait above the altar of the Great Church and removed her robe from the holy table, where it had served as an altar-covering during communion.[33]

Most dramatic, however, was the confrontation that may have introduced Nestorius to the problem of women at Constantinople. On an Easter Sunday, probably April 15, 428,[34] only five days after Nestorius was ordained bishop of Constantinople, Pulcheria appeared at the gate to the sanctuary of the Great Church, expecting to take communion within in the presence of the priests and her brother the emperor. The archdeacon Peter informed Nestorius of her custom, and the bishop hurried to bar the way, to prevent the sacrilege of a lay person and woman in the Holy of Holies. Pulcheria demanded entrance, but Nestorius insisted that "only priests may walk here." She asked: "Why? Have I not given birth to God?" He replied: "You? You have given birth to Satan!" And then Nestorius drove the empress from the sanctuary.[35] He had certainly faced the issue squarely. In his view Pulcheria could not claim Marial dignity—that

32. Nest. *Heracl.*, p. 89 Nau; also Theod. Anag. *Epit.* 340 (p. 97 Hansen), who confirms that Nestorius charged Pulcheria with unchastity, identifying the lover as Paulinus, and that the bishop reported the matter only to Theodosius. Barhadbeshabba 27 (*PO*, IX, 565) claimed that Pulcheria had no fewer than seven lovers.

33. *Lettre à Cosme* 5–7 (*PO*, XIII, 278); Barhadbeshabba 27 (*PO*, IX, 565–66); cf. Abramowski, *Untersuchungen*, p. 70.

34. The date is not given, but if Pulcheria habitually took communion in the sanctuary on Easter the confrontation occurred on the first Easter of Nestorius' episcopacy.

35. *Lettre à Cosme* 8 (*PO*, XIII, 279). On the nature, historicity, and date of the *Lettre à Cosme* see O. Braun, "Ein syrischer Bericht über Nestorius," *Zeitschrift der Deutschen Morgenländischen Gesellschaft* 54 (1900), 380–81; Nau in Nest. *Heracl.*, pp. 361–62 Nau and in *PO*, XIII, 273–74; Loofs, *Nestoriana*, pp. 86–87; and Abramowski, *Untersuchungen*, pp. 15–20. Abramowski has doubts about cc. 1–10 but admits that the original document came from Constantinople ca. 436 and that sections of it possess "ein gewisses Lokalkolorit." It must have resembled a memoir preserved in the Ephesine *acta* describing the Dalmatius affair: *ACO*, I, 1, 2, 65–66, *infra*, p. 169.

she had (mystically) "given birth to God"—to justify ceremonial equality with her brother. Like any woman, Pulcheria was a daughter of Eve, through whom sin had come into the world.

Not long after this confrontation Nestorius challenged the dignity of Mary herself. He stumbled into a doctrinal quarrel over Mariology and Christology that made it possible to cast him as hostile to the cult of the Virgin. Apparently his views on the title *Theotokos* were unknown or considered of no consequence when he was selected to be bishop of Constantinople. Shortly after his arrival, members of two factions came to Nestorius in the bishop's palace, some calling Mary "Mother of God," the others insisting on "Mother of Man." Both must have expected a fair hearing. Nestorius ended their contention, he claimed, by recommending to both the title *Christotokos,* "Mother of Christ."[36] This formula, of course, begged the more profound Christological question of the relation of man and God in Christ, but Nestorius' enemies probably devoted their efforts to whispering about that it was a slur against Mary. They were helped when Anastasius, the new bishop's domestic chaplain, declared in a sermon in the Great Church: "Let no one call Mary *Theotokos.* She was a human being, and it is impossible that God was born of a human."[37] Because Mary gave birth to Christ, wrote Socrates, and because Christ was known as God, these words seemed heretical and created a furor.[38] They must have enraged Pulcheria and others who shared her devotion, because they denied Mary her due. It was in large part this excessive worship and near-deification of Mary that Nestorius feared in the title *Theotokos.*[39]

Thus the new bishop did not withhold his support from Anastasius but again faced the issue squarely. Beginning in the last months of 428, Nestorius preached on the title *Theotokos.* In the first of his controversial sermons he asked rhetorically, "Has God a mother?" and then went on to explain his reservations:

If so we may excuse paganism for giving mothers to its deities. . . . No, Mary was not *Theotokos.* For that which is born of flesh is flesh. A creature

36. Nest. *Heracl.*, pp. 91–92 Nau; *ACO*, I, 4, 5; Evagr. 1. 7; Loofs, *Nestoriana*, pp. 251–52; for the date Thdt. *Haer. fab. comp.* 12 (*PG*, LXXXIII, 436) and Loofs, *Nestorius*, pp. 28–31.
37. Soc. 7. 32. 1–2; *ACO*, I, 1, 1, 110; 7. 96; Theoph. *a.m.* 5923 (p. 88 de Boor).
38. 7. 32. 3.
39. Loofs, *Nestoriana*, pp. 252 (quoted *infra*), 353. In another sermon, however, Nestorius claimed that the title *Theotokos* concealed Trinitarian and Christological heresies: *ibid.*, pp. 272–73; cf. p. 179.

did not bring forth Him who is uncreated; the Father did not beget by the Virgin a new God.[40]

On one occasion (probably late in 428) an utterance like this provoked a heated response from a man named Eusebius, at this time of the laity—apparently an imperial official (*agens in rebus*) and advocate —but later bishop of Dorylaeum and a pillar of orthodoxy at the Council of Chalcedon. He shouted out in the Great Church that God in the person of the Divine Word had indeed undergone a second birth in the flesh of a woman.[41] The same Eusebius seems to have authored an anonymous propaganda sheet displayed in Constantinople as early as the end of 428. It openly branded Nestorius a heretic, equating his views with those of the notorious Paul of Samosata, who had been condemned in the third century for denying Christ's divinity.[42]

Eusebius may have created the greatest stir, but he was probably only the chief among numerous lay persons of prominence who joined Pulcheria in outrage against Nestorius and in defense of Mary's prerogatives. His counterpart on the ecclesiastical side was Proclus. Ordained bishop of Cyzicus by Sisinnius, he had been unable to enter his see because the local clergy and populace elevated their own candidate.[43] Therefore Proclus resided in Constantinople. His episcopal dignity meant that he could not be muzzled, and he had already won Pulcheria's respect as a Mariologist. Thus it is not surprising that Proclus appeared, undismayed by the presence of Nestorius himself, in the Great Church of Constantinople, probably on the Sunday before Christmas in 428, to deliver a panegyric on the Virgin Mary *Theotokos:*[44]

A virginal assembly, my brothers, calls the tongue today to fair speech, and the present feast promises benefits for those who have gathered. This is most fitting. For the object of this feast is purity. The mystery it celebrates is the boast of the whole race of women and the glory of the feminine, on her account who was at once mother and maiden. This coming together is lovely

---

40. *Ibid.*, p. 252; for the date *ACO*, I, 5, 29: "eius primus impietatis in ecclesia ad populum sermo."

41. Cyril. *Adv. Nest.* 1. 5 (*ACO*, I, 1, 6, 25–26); on Eusebius G. Bareille, *DTC*, V, 2 (1939), 1532–37, "Eusèbe de Dorylée"; *PLRE*, II, 430–31, "Eusebius 15."

42. *ACO*, I, 1, 1, 101–2; Leont. Byz. *Contra Nest. et Euty.* 3 (*PG*, LXXXVI: 1, 1389); cf. Loofs, *Nestoriana*, p. 49, for the date.

43. Soc. 7. 28. 1–3. On Proclus see F. X. Bauer, *Proklos von Konstantinopel* (Munich, 1919).

44. *ACO*, I, 1, 1, 103–7 (103 for the passage quoted). Theoph. *a.m.* 5923 (p. 88 de Boor) gives the date; cf. *supra*, p. 145.

to see. For behold earth and sea attend the Virgin, the sea gently smoothing her billows for the passage of ships, the earth hurrying along the feet of the traveler. Let nature leap in delight, and women are honored. Let humankind dance with joy, and virgins win glory. For where sin multiplied, Grace has abounded even more. It is the blessed St. Mary who has called us together.

These words begin one of the most famous Mary sermons of the early medieval church, one which was often quoted, copied, and, for wider distribution, translated into several languages.[45] But there has never been a complete explication of the introductory passage. These words prove (as was pointed out earlier) that a memorial of Mary had become part of the liturgical year by the time of Nestorius's episcopacy, and that this Mary festival honored virgins and women in the most blessed exemplar of their sex. To judge from the language of Proclus, the gathering consisted largely of women, for they would "benefit" the most. Among them, no doubt, were the female ascetics of the capital and vicinity, prominent women of the great families, and at their head the Augusta Pulcheria with her sisters Arcadia and Marina. It is not unreasonable to suppose that the opening words of Proclus reveal Pulcheria's own view of the issues at stake. The sermon and the Mary festival must be seen against the background of her quarrels with Nestorius and her rising anger over his attacks on the title *Theotokos*.

When Proclus had finished speaking, the assembly applauded enthusiastically as Nestorius acknowledged when he stood up to comment on his colleague's views. "It is not surprising," Nestorius admitted, "that you who love Christ should applaud those who preach in honor of the blessed Mary, for the fact that she became the temple of our Lord's flesh exceeds everything else worthy of praise." With his audience in mind, Nestorius adopted a polite tone,[46] but as he continued he spoke his mind more clearly: "Whoever claims without qualification that God was born of Mary prostitutes the reputation of the faith," for the pagan will reply, "a god who was born, died, and was buried I cannot adore."[47] Such utterances enraged the gathering so much that Nestorius was interrupted and prevented from finishing—or so at least one scholar explains the truncated ending of this sermon as it has been preserved.[48]

45. Bauer, *Proklos*, pp. 23 n. 3, 24 n. 1.
46. M. Richard, "L'introduction du mot 'hypostase' dans la théologie de l'incarnation, II," *Mélanges de science religieuse* 2 (1945), 257.
47. Loofs, *Nestoriana*, pp. 337–38.
48. Bauer, *Proklos*, p. 31.

Clearly, Proclus had won the day and established himself as a major antagonist of Nestorius. He was called upon again to speak for the opposition,[49] and Pulcheria probably had a hand in it. On one day after Christmas (presumably 428–30) Proclus preached an Incarnation sermon "in the Pulcheria quarter" (ἐν ταῖς Πουλχεριαναῖς).[50] This may confirm cooperation between the bishop and the empress, who seems to have opened one of the churches near her *domus* so that an authoritative statement of orthodox Mariology and Christology could be heard.

Excitement over the *Theotokos* apparently reached a climax in Constantinople in the first few months of 429. About that time Bishop Dorotheus of Marcianopolis declared in the Great Church that any who called Mary "Mother of God" would be anathema. From his episcopal throne Nestorius at once admitted Dorotheus to communion, thereby embracing his statement as well. Enraged priests and people—among them, perhaps, Pulcheria and her sisters—began to hold separate services in private places.[51] When the archimandrite

49. Soc. 7. 28. 3 says that when the Cyzicenes chose their own bishop (*supra*) Proclus remained in Constantinople without his own church but active in preaching, ἐν δὲ ταῖς ἐκκλησίαις τῆς Κωνσταντινουπόλεως κατὰ τὰς διδασκαλίας ἀνθῶν. Migne published a number of his sermons in *PG*, LXV, 679–850, and others have been identified more recently, especially among the *spuria* and *dubia* of Chrysostom; see B. Marx, *Procliana* (Münster, 1940), and Leroy, *Homilétique*. Those belonging to the Nestorian period probably include (a) Migne's *Serm*. 1, the famous Mary sermon (*supra*, pp. 155–56); (b) Migne's *Serm*. 3 (next note); (c) the *Sermo de dogmate incarnationis*, C. Martin, "Un florilège grec d'homélies christologiques des IVe et Ve siècles sur la nativité (Paris. Gr. 1491)," *Muséon* 54 (1941), 44–48; (d) the *Sermo de nativitate Domini*, Martin, "Florilège," pp. 40–43 = *PG*, LXV, 843–46, also C. Moss, "Proclus of Constantinople Homily on the Nativity," *Muséon* 42 (1929), 61–73; (e) a Palm Sunday sermon published by E. A. Wallis Budge, *Coptic Homilies in the Dialect of Upper Egypt* (London, 1910), pp. 235–40. Richard "Introduction," pp. 260–61, demonstrates that (a), (c), and (d) formed a series. Since Theophanes dates (a) (*supra*, n. 44), the series should be placed in 428–29, rather than 430–31, as Richard argues.

50. Phot. *Bibl.* cod. 229 (IV, 170 Henry) certainly referring to Migne's *Serm*. 3, *PG*, LXV, 704–8. The contents do not require the Nestorian period, but it was probably then that Proclus most often preached in churches other than the Great Church. The *Sermo de dogmate incarnationis* (preceding note) was delivered in the Church of Anthemius.

51. *ACO*, I, 1, 1, 98, 109; 5, 11–12. See also Joh. Ruf. *Pler.* 1 (*PO*, VIII, 11–12): According to Peter the Iberian, a member of the court, Nestorius preached in the church called Maria blaspheming against Mary and denying that she was *Theotokos*. This caused many to break with him, especially among those in the palace. Since Theodosius continued to support Nestorius, presumably this means Pulcheria and her following.

Basil appeared at the episcopal palace to remonstrate with Nestorius, the bishop had him and his companions beaten, jailed, and handed over to the city prefect for further punishment.[52]

But by this time wider areas of the Roman Empire were also being drawn in, and the controversy began to look like a dispute among bishops over Christology. Antiochus, the former praetorian prefect of the East, dispatched some of Nestorius' works to Celestine, the bishop of Rome.[53] Cyril's agents in Constantinople sent Nestorius' controversial sermons to Alexandria as soon as they were delivered,[54] and by Easter, 429, heated debates had erupted among the volatile Egyptian monks. This was the handle Cyril needed against Nestorius. He composed his long *Epistle to the Monks of Egypt* in defense of the *Theotokos* title and the Christological doctrines it implied.[55] It was only the first of several series of "letters" between the disputants, most of them really tracts intended to rally opinion among a wider readership than their addresses suggest.[56] Cyril repeatedly admonished Nestorius, who replied with growing truculence. Nestorius tried to explain himself to Celestine, who, having asked Cyril for enlightenment, received a dossier including Cyril's own refutation of Nestorius (poorly translated into Latin)[57] along with Cyril's letters and a catalogue of Nestorian errors.

By the summer of 430, positions were clear. Cyril might still face a tribunal, but more likely an ecumenical council, first proposed a year earlier by Basil and his associates and more recently favored by Nestorius, would grapple with the broader Christological issue.[58] This still seemed dangrous, because Theodosius remained firmly behind his bishop. Nestorius could boast that the emperor and empress (Eudocia!) delighted in his teachings; an imperial chamberlain carried one of Nestorius' letters to Rome; Cyril did not yet dare allow his men

52. *ACO*, I, 1, 5, 8–9.
53. *ACO*, I, 1, 1, 24, 114; 2, 8; cf. *PLRE*, II, 1034, "Antiochus (Chuzon I) 7," for his career.
54. *ACO*, I, 1, 1, 24; 2, 7–8; 5, 11; cf. I, 1, 1, 110–12, and Nest. *Heracl.*, p. 92 Nau, for Cyril's agents in Constantinople.
55. *ACO*, I, 1, 1, 10–23; cf. Kidd, *History*, III, 210, for the date.
56. *ACO*, I, 1, 1, 23–28, 33–42 (Cyril. *Epp*. 1–3 to Nestorius); Loofs, *Nestoriana*, pp. 165–82 (Nest. *Epp*. 1–2 to Cyril, 1–3 to Celestine); *ACO*, I, 1, 5, 10–12; 7, 171–72 (Cyril's communication to Celestine). Cyril's *Epistle to the Monks* provoked excitement in Constantinople, *ACO*, I, 1, 1, 24, 110; 5, 11; Nest. *Heracl.*, p. 96 Nau. Cyril's letters became part of his dossier to Celestine, *ACO*, I, 1, 5, 12.
57. *ACO*, I, 1, 5, 12.
58. *ACO*, I, 1, 1, 111–12; 5, 9–10; Loofs, *Nestoriana*, pp. 185–86; Nest. *Heracl.*, p. 244 Nau; Barhadbeshabba 22 (*PO*, IX, 540–41).

in Constantinople to accuse Nestorius of heresy before the emperor.[59] Alexandria might be certain of the bishop of Rome, but Constantinople was the center of power. Even so, Cyril was not afraid, for he knew "what to write and to whom."[60]

In the late summer or autumn of 430 the bishop of Alexandria undertook an unusual and risky diplomatic demarche. He composed a treatise known as the *Address to the Pious Emperor Theodosius on the Correct Faith* and sent it to the court of Theodosius and Eudocia.[61] In it Cyril praised the emperor for fearing God as his ancestors did. Still, he saw fit to recount the salutary story of King Hezekiah, who knew (according to Cyril's free interpretation of the biblical texts)[62] that it was not Sennacherib's troops that threatened Jerusalem but the blasphemies of Sennacherib's officer Rabshakeh. Cyril refused to believe that dangerous impieties could be heard in the emperor's presence.[63] Even so, he continued with an exposition of "orthodox" incarnation teaching, keeping in mind various Christological heresies, and especially that of Nestorius.

At the same time, Cyril prepared another treatise, this one known as *Address to the Most Pious Princesses*[64] and often thought in antiquity and among modern scholars to have gone to Arcadia and Marina.[65] In reality Cyril probably addressed this work simply "to the holy virgins" and dispatched it to the court of Pulcheria and her sisters.[66] It amounts to a plea that they intercede with Theodosius in Cyril's favor. The work is not without rhetorical pretensions. It begins with an elaborate prologue in which Cyril praises "the sacred and wholly pure brides of Christ" for their famous ancestry and for their virginity, which glorifies the court and keeps

59. *ACO*, I, 1, 1, 32, 112; I, 2, 15.
60. *ACO*, I, 1, 1, 112.
61. *Ibid.* pp. 42–72. At p. 44 Cyril announces that he is sending this "gift" to the emperor but also to both Eudocia and Pulcheria. The preserved version probably reflects editing after Cyril's imperial scolding: *infra*, p. 165.
62. II Kings 18:13–19:36, Isa. 36–37, II Chron. 32:1–21.
63. Pp. 43–44.
64. *ACO*, I, 1, 5, 62–118.
65. Pusey in Cyril, *De recta fide ad imperatorem, etc.*, ed. P.E. Pusey (Oxford, 1877), p. xi; O. Bardenhewer, *Geschichte der altkirchlichen Literatur*, IV (Freiburg i. B., 1924), p. 50; and J. Quasten, *Patrology*, III (Utrecht-Antwerp, 1966), p. 126, assume that the addressees given in the superscription, *ACO*, I, 1, 5, 62, are the correct ones. These superscriptions were provided in later centuries by compilers of *acta* and *florilegia*, and thus do not represent dependable evidence.
66. F. Loofs, *Realencyclopädie für protestantische Theologie und Kirche*, XIII (1903), 743, "Nestorius"; Seeck, *Geschichte*, VI, 214–15; Ensslin, *RE*, XXIII (1959), 1957, "Pulcheria 2."

the image of the sisters brilliant throughout the world. He urges them
to add the adornment of correct doctrine, which would not be difficult for those whose "sharp eye of intelligence" could pierce behind
the pious words of any who would mislead them.[67]

Such flattery introduced the less appetizing meat of Cyril's discourse. Cyril briefly catalogued a number of bishops (including John
Chrysostom and Atticus of Constantinople) who had employed the
term *Theotokos* before the time of Nestorius,[68] and then went on at
much greater length with the real doctrinal issue, collecting and
explicating in a few words each more than two hundred New Testament texts that proved *contra* Nestorius that the one Mary bore was
God.[69] Pleasant reading was not the object. Cyril collected "the heart
of the matter" for Pulcheria and her sisters so that "you might
embellish your own intellects but also decorate your holy heads with
apostolic laurels by leading whomever you decide to help to the
correct faith."[70] He had Theodosius in mind.

When Cyril had completed his *Address to the Most Pious Princesses,* a labor that cannot have lasted many days, he devoted more
time and deeper thought to still another treatise, the *Address to the
Most Pious Empresses on the Correct Faith.*[71] Misled again by the
conventional title, most scholars have identified Pulcheria and Eudocia
as the joint addressees.[72] More likely this treatise also went to the
court of the emperor's sisters, but it was dedicated to Pulcheria herself.[73] This explains the artful language of Cyril's again elaborate
prologue, in which he ignored virginity to develop an analogy on the
imperial diadem. "It becomes you," he declared, "you who are holy
and God-beloved, to bind on with the supernal ornaments of *basileia*
also the victory wreath of love for Christ."[74] The same thesis accounts

67. *ACO*, I, 1, 5, 62–64.
68. Pp. 65–68.
69. Pp. 69–118.
70. P. 69.
71. *Ibid.*, pp. 26–61.
72. Pusey, Bardenhewer, and Quasten, cited *supra*, n. 65.
73. This treatise complements the *Address to the Princesses* as part of the
same diplomatic effort in the late summer or autumn of 430, as Cyril himself stated
in *ACO*, I, 1, 3, 77, written in late 431 (*infra*, p. 176). If this dating is correct,
the *Address* cannot have been sent to Eudocia and Pulcheria jointly, because in
November of 430 Theodosius scolded Cyril for dispatching separate treatises to them
and attempting to sow discord (*infra*, p. 165). Loofs and Seeck (*supra*, n. 66)
choose Eudocia, but it is unlikely that Cyril would have directed the deeper elements
of his argument to a youthful convert from paganism, while hoping to satisfy the
pious senior Augusta with "all that is easiest to grasp."
74. *ACO*, I, 1, 5, 26–27.

for the less patronizing tone of this treatise. Having exhausted "all that is easiest to grasp" in his discourse to the holy virgins, Cyril now proposed to expound "whatever is less clear," for "your God-beloved sovereignty could not be ignorant of the former and must know the latter as well."[75]

In the discussion that followed Cyril laid bare what he considered to be the principles of orthodox Christology, clearly directing his polemic against the bishop of Constantinople, whose name, however, did not appear. According to Cyril, the correct teaching was that in Christ the Divine Word voluntarily debased Himself and made human flesh His Own so that He could suffer and overcome death. Cyril argued that those who denied the divinity of Mary's child really divided Christ in two, separating the Divine Word in Him from the human flesh, and in so doing they made redemption impossible. Whether this was in fact the teaching of Nestorius is debatable,[76] but there is no doubt that Cyril expected his arguments to convince Pulcheria of Nestorius' Christological error—and to give her further ammunition against their common enemy. The discussion was more technical than that in the *Address to the Princesses,* but once again Cyril anchored every argument firmly in New Testament passages with which Pulcheria could plague her brother.

While Cyril's three treatises traveled to Constantinople and presumably contributed to the ferment there, Celestine introduced what the see of Rome expected would be the decisive maneuver in the bishops' war against Nestorius. He consulted with his suffragans in a Roman synod early in August, then dispatched a letter of excommunication through Cyril, who was to act as his representative in the affair.[77] Nestorius would have to disavow his heretical teachings publicly and in writing within ten days of receiving the letter or be cut off from communion with the universal church. Cyril, in turn, assembled his own local synod late in November, and with its approval sent four Egyptian bishops to Constantinople to deliver Celestine's ultimatum. The contest was over, in Cyril's view; any need for an ecumenical council had passed.[78] Suspected and in some quarters

75. P. 28.
76. Cf. the works cited *supra*, n. 14.
77. *ACO*, I, 1, 1, 33–34, 92; I, 2, 5–12, 20, 22; *PL*, L, 457; Nest. *Heracl.*, p. 250 Nau; Kidd, *History*, III, 222–26.
78. *ACO*, I, 1, 1, 33–34, 113–14; 2, 37; 5, 12–13; Nest. *Heracl.*, p. 250 Nau; Kidd, *History*, III, 226–28. Cyril was working against a council in the autumn of 430, *ACO*, I, 1, 1, 74; Nest. *Heracl.*, p. 253 Nau.

already convicted of heresy, Nestorius, Cyril might hope, could no longer threaten the bishop of Alexandria.

This maneuver by Celestine and Cyril had already been out-flanked, however, when the four bishops arrived in Constantinople. They found Nestorius on Sunday, December 7, in his episcopal palace, where he had come with the clergy and high officials after celebrating divine worship. Nestorius accepted the documents with a promise to meet the bishops the next day, but when they appeared he had the door closed in their faces.[79] Far from being intimidated, Nestorius could ignore Cyril's bluster with cool determination. His response came in a sermon the following Saturday, December 13. It was another incarnation sermon, and in it Nestorius chided Cyril for trying to avoid a council. "Let us face the issues between us," he urged, "allowing the purity and piety of each man to argue for or against him. . . . Why not let the debate begin?" As for himself, Nestorius declared that the episcopal office had been only a burden to him anyway, that "as long as I have breath I will seek only to protect the faith." These were brave words—but only superficially so, because Nestorius did not expect to lose. "The emperor is pious," he said, "and the empresses love the Lord."[80] His words seem to mean that Theodosius and Pulcheria, though their purposes and expectations were opposite, had now joined in support of Nestorius' proposed council.

In fact, of course, on November 19, 430, while Cyril was still preparing his decisive blow, an imperial letter had already gone out from the imperial palace convoking the Third Ecumenical Council.[81] "From zeal that the condition of the church might honor God and contribute to the safety of the Empire" Theodosius ordered metropolitan bishops from everywhere to gather with a few suffragans each on the next Pentecost, June 7, 431, at Ephesus in Asia. There the bishops would "resolve according to the canons the confusion which has arisen from these disagreements, correct the failures of the past, and provide firm guidance toward piety before God and the good of the state." In the meantime nothing was to be done individually; no "innovations" were to be introduced to alter the existing situation.

On its surface this document left to the bishops complete freedom to deliberate on the truth, uncoerced by the emperor or any special

79. *ACO*, I, 1, 2, 36–37.
80. Loofs, *Nestoriana*, pp. 297–313, 299–300 for the passages quoted.
81. *ACO*, I, 1, 1, 114–16. On the emperor's powers to convoke an imperial council, supervise its deliberations, and enforce its decisions cf. *supra*, pp. 17–18.

interests. Even so, in the intense disputes that must have preceded the call of November 19 the partisans on either side cannot have ignored the realities of power. There was a reason for Nestorius' confidence. The emperor's order to avoid "innovations" meant that Cyril's intrigues were to end.[82] The specification that each metropolitan should come with only a few suffragans would also help to protect Nestorius from Cyril, who was sole head of the numerous bishops of Egypt and like Athanasius a century earlier "a rich and powerful man, able to do anything."[83] Moreover, Theodosius appointed a military man to represent him at Ephesus. Count Candidian was co-commander of the elite praesental *domestici*. Theodosius commissioned him to set the proceedings in motion and to secure the council from violent outside pressure, without, however, taking part in the discussions; but his actions at Ephesus nonetheless confirm that he was a partisan of Nestorius.[84] Others whose influence would likewise be diminished if the emperor lost confidence in his bishop must also have worked to secure a favorable outcome. Among these was certainly Count Irenaeus, who owed his promotion to the rank of *illustris* to his friendship with Nestorius and who accompanied the beleaguered bishop to Ephesus with no commission but simply as a powerful friend.[85] Despite his protests of impartiality, Theodosius had no reason to doubt that with such support Nestorius would quickly be vindicated.

There were others among the archimandrites, high clergy, and prominent lay men and women of Constantinople who hated their bishop bitterly and no doubt attempted to influence the arrangements for the council. Among them was Pulcheria. A tradition on both sides of the question said that it was she who brought down Nestorius,[86] and there is truth in this tradition. It existed as early as 432, within a year or two of Cyril's victory, when Epiphanius, the *synkellos* or domestic chaplain of the bishop of Alexandria, expressed

82. Kidd, *History*, III, 229–30, who believes that "the hand of Nestorius is traceable in it [the letter of convocation]."

83. Athan. *Apol. contra Arian.* 9. 4 (II: 1, 95 Opitz), also Soc. 7. 7. 4.

84. An imperial letter, *ACO*, I, 1, 1, 120–21, contains his instructions. Cf. *PLRE*, II, 257–58, "Candidianus 6."

85. *ACO*, I, 1, 1, 93, 121; *Koptische Akten*, pp. 6, 50–53 = *Koptische Akten zum ephesinischen Konzil vom Jahre 431*, trans. W. Kraatz, *TU*, XXVI: 2; Loofs, *Nestoriana*, p. 184. The office he held, if any, is unknown: *PLRE*, II, 624–25, "Irenaeus 2."

86. E.g., Nest. *Heracl.*, p. 89 Nau; Barhadbeshabba 27 (*PO*, IX, 565–66); *Histoire nestorienne* 1. 70 (*PO*, V, 326); *ACO*, II, 4, 12–15, 37 (Leo to Pulcheria); Joh. Ruf. *Pler.* 3 (*PO*, VIII, 14).

the hope that Pulcheria would "*once again* devote herself to the cause of the Lord Christ."[87]

The precise nature of Pulcheria's earlier intervention is not specified, but it appears that she influenced the arrangements. Though few modern scholars seem to have recognized it, the choice of Ephesus was crucial. Theodosius himself explained that this spot was chosen because the bishops could reach it easily, either by land or sea, and it could be provisioned for large numbers if the council should last for weeks or months.[88] Perhaps some did argue this in the emperor's presence, but the same persons must have known that Ephesus was the see of Memnon, a mighty competitor of the bishop of Constantinople for influence in Asia and thus a natural ally of Cyril.[89] He would lead a powerful group of anti-Nestorius suffragans in the council and, equally important, his lower clergy, monks, and other roughnecks would be available for service as shock troops to intimidate the opposition. Moreover, Ephesus, the ancient center of the virgin goddess Artemis, had already devoted itself to the cult of the Virgin *Theotokos*. Memnon's episcopal palace abutted on a splendid church to the west that was dedicated to the Virgin, and there the council would be held.[90] The choice of Ephesus placated the enemies of Nestorius, Pulcheria among them. If the bishops gathered in Mary's church, she must have thought, surely with Mary's help and guidance they would punish Nestorius.[91]

Thus the letter of convocation implies backstage controversy and eventual compromise. This process was a fact of political life, but one

87. *ACO*, I, 4, 223; cf. *infra*, pp. 179–81, for the date and content of this letter.

88. *ACO*, I, 1, 3, 31.

89. R. Janin, *DHGE*, XV (1963), 556–57, "Ephèse," discusses the powers of the bishop of Ephesus during this period and his relations with Constantinople. That the choice of Ephesus was contrary to the interests of Nestorius and his supporters is underscored by their pleas during the council that it be moved elsewhere: *ACO*, I, 1, 5, 130, 134. After the council Theodoret of Cyrrhus declared that he hated even the name of the place: *ACO*, I, 4, 86. On Memnon *infra*, pp. 166–68, 171, 173.

90. On the episcopal palace and the church of the council see R. Krautheimer, *Early Christian and Byzantine Architecture* (Baltimore, 1965), pp. 80–81; and esp. E. Reisch, F. Knoll, and J. Keil, *Die Marienkirche in Ephesos*, Österreichisches Archäologisches Institut: Forschungen in Ephesos vol. IV, no. 1 (Vienna, 1932). Reisch et al., *Marienkirche*, p. 9, question whether the church had been dedicated to Mary before the council, but their doubts are unfounded. It is referred to as such repeatedly in Ephesine letters and *acta*, e.g., *ACO*, I, 1, 1, 117; 2, 67, 70, 102; 3, 4; 7, 118. Although the documentation is copious, no dedication during the proceedings is mentioned. On the significance of the site cf. Cecchelli, *Mater*, I, 191–99.

91. Cf. the role assigned to St. Euphemia at Chalcedon, *infra*, p. 213.

the emperor usually obscured behind the pretentious language of his pronouncements.[92] In the wake of Cyril's demarche of summer, 430, and the bargaining that led to the November policy, the veil slipped a bit to allow a fascinating glimpse of the real situation.

Cyril's treatises had reached their addressees, but they must also have circulated widely, because Theodosius became concerned at the unflattering impression they left of relations between himself and his sister—an impression which was doubly embarrassing because it was true. Along with the letter of convocation he sent another letter to Cyril, this one containing an imperial reprimand.

Theodosius was not surprised that a man bold enough to bring confusion upon the church would also believe something unworthy of the emperor. For Cyril had addressed writings (ἕτερα) to Theodosius and Eudocia, and other writings (ἕτερα) to Pulcheria, as if he knew them to be at odds or expected them to fall into disagreement because of his intervention.[93] The emperor did not deny that such disagreement existed, but chided Cyril for knowing of it if it did and in any case for hoping to create it. "Your goal and purpose are the same in seeking to separate members of the church from its body and also members from the one body of the emperors [τά τε τῶν βασιλέων μέλη χωρίζειν], as if there were no other way to win a reputation." Now he wished Cyril to know that in both church and *basileía* perfect unity had been achieved (καὶ τὰς ἐκκλησίας ἴσθι καὶ τὴν βασιλείαν ἡνῶσθαι). This seems to mean that Pulcheria and Theodosius had both adopted the suggestion of Nestorius that an ecumenical council should be called to examine the doctrinal question, a council, Theodosius continued, that no one would coerce and whose judgment no one could escape. The tone of the letter leaves no doubt that disputes with his sister had distressed Theodosius and that he considered Cyril to be responsible.

Six months passed. Not long after Easter, 431, metropolitan bishops, many of them no doubt aging and infirm,[94] undertook the laborious journey to Ephesus. Their troubles, sadly, were in vain, for Pulcheria's efforts had guaranteed that the Ephesine synod would be a farce. Cyril "seized Ephesus as if he were attacking a citadel."[95]

92. Cf. R. MacMullen, "Roman Bureaucratese," *Traditio* 18 (1962), 364–78.
93. *ACO*, I, 1, 1, 73–74.
94. Bishops on both sides complained later of fatigue and other ailments, *ACO*, I, 1, 2, 8; 3, 3, 6, 46, 52–53, 64; 5, 125; 7, x; I, 3, 178; Nest. *Heracl.*, pp. 97–98, 100, 110, 113, 118 Nau; Evagr. 1. 3.
95. *ACO*, I, 1, 5, 130.

The Cyrillians introduced into the city a crowd of lower clergy, rustics, Egyptian sailors, vagrant monks from Constantinople, and perhaps Cyril's famous bath attendants, all apparently based in the monasteries and provisioned like an army by the ships of the Alexandrian grain fleet. Memnon employed these roughnecks to intimidate the opposing party, closing off to Nestorius and his allies the churches and martyr shrines of the city, accosting and threatening them in the streets, and even marking their dwellings for easier identification of the enemy.[96] When the bishops finally gathered in the Church of Mary, the Cyrillians tricked Candidian into reading the emperor's charge officially constituting the council, then drove the emperor's officer and the enemy bishops from the assembly.[97] After a day-long session on June 22 the adherents of Cyril found the teachings of Nestorius heretical and declared him excommunicated and deposed.[98] The people of Ephesus rejoiced as they escorted Cyril and his friends to their quarters. Women swinging censers led the way, for this was a victory of the Virgin *Theotokos.* In her honor incense and candle illumination decorated the evening.[99]

In the face of this Egyptian attack, Nestorius was by no means defenseless. Candidian had imperial soldiers, Irenaeus no doubt some personal retainers, and Nestorius apparently commanded his own bath attendants, the Zeuxippitai from the Baths of Zeuxippos near the imperial palace.[100] But these were outgeneraled and overwhelmed. The allies of Nestorius lamented a few days later that they were "prey to the tyrant" and besought the emperor to reconvene the council somewhere nearby — but not in Ephesus.[101]

96. *ACO*, I, 1, 1, 120; 3, 50; 5, 14, 121, 124, 126–33; Nest. *Heracl.*, pp. 119–20, 236–37, 255 Nau; *Koptische Akten*, pp. 12, 17 Kraatz.

97. *ACO*, I, 4, 32; I, 1, 2, 9; 5, 119–21, 132; Nest. *Heracl.*, pp. 100–101, 108–9, 119–20 Nau; *Koptische Akten*, pp. 18, 54–55 Kraatz; Schwartz, *Cyrill*, pp. 30–31.

98. *ACO*, I, 1, 2, 3–64; cf. Kidd, *History*, III, 242–43; Bardy, "Débuts," pp. 180–82.

99. *ACO*, I, 1, 1, 118. Seeck, *Geschichte*, VI, 222, and W.H.C. Frend, "Popular Religion and Christological Controversy in the Fifth Century," *Popular Belief and Practice*, ed. G.J. Cuming and D. Baker, Ecclesiastical History Society: Studies in Church History vol. VIII (Cambridge, 1972), p. 22, are certainly correct in identifying Mary as the object of this popular demonstration, although Cyril does not mention her.

100. *ACO*, I, 1, 2, 10, 67; 3, 4, 11–12, 46; *Koptische Akten*, p. 17 Kraatz; cf. Schwartz, *Cyrill*, p. 35, and Janin, *Constantinople²*, pp. 222–24, on the Zeuxippitai and the Baths of Zeuxippos.

101. *ACO*, I, 1, 5, 130; cf. 133, *supra*, n. 89.

They did not regain their composure until at long last John, the bishop of Antioch, arrived with his suffragans. Like Cyril, he was a powerful man, and unlike Nestorius, he understood politics.[102] Candidian and the anti-Cyrillian bishops had already protested to the emperor concerning the proceedings of June 22.[103] Now, "before he had even shaken the dust from his feet," Bishop John set about providing a result more to the emperor's liking. On June 26 he convened a counter-synod, smaller in numbers but allegedly legal and orthodox and therefore greater in authority than the violent followers of Cyril. This counter-synod examined Cyril's anti-Nestorian writings and the conduct of Cyril and Memnon, and promptly condemned and deposed both.[104]

Though Pulcheria had probably not foreseen how effectively John of Antioch could intervene, she had good reason to be encouraged by events thus far. Whatever the theory of church-state relations, the outcome now depended on which results Theodosius would accept and enforce, and Pulcheria would have new arguments with which to challenge her brother. Nestorius had been shown, at least to the satisfaction of the assembled bishops, to be a heretic. He had suffered excommunication and deprivation of episcopal office according to the canons.

Knowing how effective such arguments could prove, supporters of Nestorius took immediate steps to hinder their use. Candidian had felt compelled to send Theodosius a copy of the decree deposing Nestorius,[105] but apart from this he and his colleagues hoped to control the government's apprehension of what had happened. Thus Candidian stationed soldiers at all land and sea exits from Ephesus, while some sympathetic authority in Constantinople ordered guards to watch the Bosporus and Propontis for Cyrillian messengers.[106] Since

102. Cf. esp. Schwartz, *Cyrill*, pp. 12, 15, 41.

103. *ACO*, I, 4, 27–33; I, 1, 5, 13–15.

104. *ACO*, I, 1, 5, 119–24; cf. Kidd, *History*, III, 243–44; Bardy, "Débuts," pp. 183–84; and for the date Schwartz, *Cyrill*, p. 36 with n. 3; and P. Batiffol, "Un épisode du concile d'Ephèse (Juillet 431) d'après les actes coptes de Bouriant,"*Mélanges . . . Gustave Schlumberger* (Paris, 1924), I, 29 n. 1. Only 43 (or 53, *ACO*, I, 4, 37–38) bishops signed the decree against Cyril and Memnon, while 197 had condemned Nestorius (*ACO*, I, 1, 2, 55–64), but John's adherents claimed greater authority nonetheless, in *ACO*, I, 1, 5, 130; cf. Nest. *Heracl.*, pp. 114–15 Nau.

105. *ACO*, I, 1, 5, 120.

106. *ACO*, I, 1, 2, 65, 68; 3, 11–12; *Koptische Akten*, pp. 20, 47–49 Kraatz. The blockade was still maintained as late as August: *ACO*, I, 1, 3, 43–44, 51.

further details of Nestorius' situation were bound eventually to filter through, Candidian and the Nestorian bishops also protested Cyril's conduct at once to the emperor,[107] and after its session the counter-synod hastened to write to Theodosius and to the clergy, people, highest officials, and senate of Constantinople presenting its version of the critical events.[108]

An explanation of the counter-synod's position also went to the empresses,[109] perhaps because John of Antioch recognized how crucial Pulcheria's attitude might be. This document presented typical arguments. Cyril and his allies had not waited for all of the bishops. They had assembled their "tyrant synod" despite Candidian's objections and the terms of convocation. They had also closed the churches and martyr shrines, prevented the celebration of the Pentecost festival, and by threats and violence had forced bishops to condone or subscribe to their actions. Thus Cyril and Memnon had been deposed and those with them excommunicated until they should repent and join the legally constituted synod.

Since everything now depended on the emperor, each side acted hurriedly to lay its arguments before him.[110] Nothing could demonstrate more vividly than their pell-mell haste that they expected the imperial will to prevail in governing the church as well as the state. Candidian's reports on the Cyrillian council must have reached the palace about July 25, and within a day or two, rumors of Nestorius' deposition brought monks into the thoroughfares of the dynastic city to demonstrate with antiphons, shouts in praise of Cyril "the gift of God," and curses upon Nestorius "the Jew."[111] Documents from the

107. *ACO*, I, 1, 3, 9; 5, 13–15; *Koptische Akten*, pp. 14, 22 Kraatz.

108. *ACO*, I, 1, 5, 124–25, 127–29, 132–33.

109. *Ibid.*, pp. 131–32.

110. My reconstruction of the chronology from late June to early July, 431, depends on the *Koptische Akten*, pp. 47–55 Kraatz. It reveals a few days of intense crisis, immediately after the separate councils met, during which each side raced to make its decisions and arguments known before the other. Soc. 7. 19 reports that the *magistrianos* Palladius, one of the imperial messengers used during the Council of Ephesus (*ACO*, I, 1, 8, 40, index *s.v.* Παλλάδιος), could ride to the Roman-Persian frontier in only three days. If this is anywhere near accurate, post horses can have had little difficulty covering roughly three hundred miles to or from Constantinople in two or three days. There is striking confirmation in *ACO*, I, 1, 3, 9–12: an imperial letter dated June 29 and carried to Ephesus by Palladius, and a letter of Cyril's synod said to have been dated July 1 and dispatched to Constantinople with the same Palladius, who was in such a hurry that he could not wait for all of Cyril's allies to sign it. Cf. A. M. Ramsay, "The Speed of the Roman Imperial Post," *JRS* 15 (1925), 60–74, suggesting that times such as that of Palladius were unusual but not impossible.

111. *Koptische Akten*, pp. 40, 47–48 Kraatz; *ACO*, I, 1, 2, 65; Nest. *Heracl.*, pp. 239–41 Nau.

Cyrillians penetrated the blockade, including one concealed in a beggar's staff,[112] and the chief archimandrite, Dalmatius, who had kept himself locked up in his cell for forty-eight years, came forth to deliver them to the emperor.[113] This impressed Theodosius. Though refusing to believe that Nestorius was guilty, and disclaiming like Pilate any responsibility on the part of himself or his sister for innocent and holy blood, he did agree that messengers from Cyril's synod would be admitted.[114] But this was only a temporary deviation. On July 29, within two or three days after Dalmatius' triumphal intervention, Theodosius dispatched an imperial letter to Ephesus in which he condemned Cyril's procedure in strong terms, declaring that the dogmatic question still had not been properly examined and announcing that he would send another commissioner to cooperate with Candidian in preventing further disturbances.[115]

The revelations the counter-synod hoped would rescue Nestorius must have reached Constantinople by about July 1, but that was the very day on which the Cyrillian messengers entered the city according to the emperor's command and laid their full story before him.[116] Pulcheria probably saw her opportunity and went to work on her brother. Soon "the lion" began to doubt, and when he did "his thousand whelps"[117] hastened to withdraw their support from the emperor's bishop. Within a few days many of the leading men in the government, including *illustres* like the praetorian and city prefects, the master of offices, the *magistri militum,* and the influential palace eunuch Scholasticius, had abandoned open support of Nestorius.[118] When Count Irenaeus arrived on Friday, July 3,[119] to argue Nestorius'

112. *ACO*, I, 1, 2, 65. The "letter of the hollow staff" was probably *ACO*, I, 1, 2, 66–68 = *Koptische Akten*, pp. 40–46 Kraatz.

113. On Dalmatius and his role at Ephesus see *ACO*, I, 1, 2, 65–69; 3, 14–15; 7, x–xi; I, 4, 223; Nest. *Heracl.*, pp. 240–47 Nau; Barhadbeshabba 27 (*PO*, IX, 566–67); *Koptische Akten*, p. 48 Kraatz; Dagron, "Moines," pp. 267–68.

114. Nest. *Heracl.*, p. 245 Nau; *ACO*, I, 1, 2, 68–69. Nestorius wrote that Dalmatius had persuaded Theodosius to confirm the decree against him (*loc. cit.*, Barhadbeshabba 27 [*PO*, IX, 566–67]), but his memory had failed him. The emperor's letter of July 29 (*infra*) proves that he had not changed his mind.

115. *ACO*, I, 1, 3, 9–10.

116. *Ibid.*, 5, 135 (Irenaeus arrived three days after the "Egyptians"; see *infra*, n. 119).

117. *ACO*, I, 1, 5, 136, Irenaeus to the Cyrillians describing a session of the *consistorium.* He recalls II Tim. 4:17.

118. *ACO*, I, 1, 5, 135. On Scholasticius cf. *ACO*, I, 1, 5, 133; I, 4, 223–24; *PLRE*, II, 982, "Scholasticius I."

119. Irenaeus arrived three days after the Cyrillian envoys (*supra*, n. 116), who appeared four days before the crowd first gathered in the Great Church, Saturday, July 4 (*infra*, n. 122).

case in person at the imperial palace, he found the great men uniformly hostile. His pessimism may have been exaggerated, but there can be no doubt that another shift had taken place.

Even more threatening to Nestorius and his adherents were signs of rebellion in the dynastic city. Fanatics on either side battled in the streets and squares.[120] On July 4 a crowd occupied the Great Church, constituting itself in the usual way as the Roman people of Constantinople. The people demanded that the council's decree against Nestorius be read before them (i.e., promulgated) and enforced. They were still there the next day, Sunday, July 5, and the next, insisting that their acclamations, the *voces populi,*[121] be delivered to Theodosius. Mary the Virgin had deposed Nestorius! Christ and the cross had won the victory! Nestorius "the Jew" should be burned, and Anastasius with him! Irenaeus the "sorcerer," "Hellene," and "shameful creature" should be thrown from the palace and likewise delivered to the flames! The treasures with which Hellenes and Jews had worked against the orthodox should be returned, or distributed among the poor.

The crowd assembled in the Great Church also identified and acclaimed the one who fought for orthodoxy:

Many years to Pulcheria! She it is who has strengthened the faith! . . . Many years to Pulcheria! Many years to the empress! Many years to Pulcheria! She has strengthened the faith! . . . Many years to Pulcheria! Many years to the orthodox one![122]

In effect, Pulcheria brought her special resources to bear through these *voces populi.* The crowd in the Great Church certainly included her many dependents. It also encompassed those who responded to

120. *Koptische Akten*, p. 49 Kraatz.
121. On the *voces populi* see *supra*, pp. 10–11.
122. *ACO*, I, 1, 3, 14; *Koptische Akten*, pp. 49–55 Kraatz (representative excerpts); perhaps also Nest. *Heracl.*, pp. 246–47 Nau, where, however, the gathering in the Great Church is not mentioned specifically. The date of this popular demonstration is crucial to my interpretation because it anchors chronologically the account of the *Koptische Akten*, pp. 47–55 (*supra*, nn. 110, 116, 119). The demonstration took place on a Saturday, Sunday, and Monday after word of the deposition of Cyril and Memnon had reached the emperor but apparently before the condemnation of John of Antioch (July 17) and the arrival of the Roman legates (July 10) had been announced. These events, especially the former, could not have been ignored in the acclamations, had the people known of them. Thus only July 4–6 remain, a dating confirmed by the unlikelihood that the deposition of Cyril and Memnon could have remained unknown to the people and clergy as long as two weeks after it took place (*infra*). Cf. Batiffol, "Episode," pp. 28–31.

the visible monuments of her philanthropy and piety, to her links with the monastic community, and to her Marial dignity. "Many years to Pulcheria," the crowd acclaimed. "Many years to the empress!" In these words the Roman people spoke, insisting that Pulcheria's *basileía* was authentic.

Apparently the emperor's court could not easily ignore these *voces,* so Theodosius gave in. On the evening of July 5 his messenger brought the Cyrillian decree against Nestorius to be read in the Great Church. But the crowd's delight changed to fury when the messenger also read the conciliar letters deposing Cyril and Memnon. Despite the opposition of the great men, Irenaeus had gained access to the emperor and restored his confidence in Nestorius.[123] As a result, the dramatic events of early July resulted only in stalemate. Some persons around Theodosius recommended that all three conciliar depositions be enforced, others that all three be lifted, still others that bishops representing the two sides come to Constantinople to be reconciled under imperial duress.[124] Nothing happened. In Ephesus the Cyrillians assembled in six more sessions in July, then they and their opponents rotted in the heat and famine.[125] Late in August Theodosius sent John *comes sacrarum largitionum* to take command from Candidian. This officer placed Nestorius, Memnon, and Cyril under arrest and tried to force negotiations toward reconciliation, but the two sides refused so much as to enter the presence of those each had condemned, and John reported that he even had difficulty keeping the holy bishops from using their fists against one another.[126]

Finally the court adopted the third approach. Eight bishops from each side traveled to Chalcedon early in September, and the emperor came to the Rufinianai palace to meet with the legates and

---

123. *ACO,* I, 1, 5, 135–36 (Count Irenaeus to Nestorius' supporters in Ephesus); *Koptische Akten,* pp. 50–51 Kraatz. Irenaeus reports that the deposition of Cyril was dispatched to be announced in the Great Church. The *Koptische Akten,* apparently deriving from a source near the Constantinopolitan clergy, reveal that on Sunday, July 5 (preceding note), the *referendarius* Domitian brought and read the deposition of Cyril and Memnon, and that of Nestorius as well. This juxtaposition ties the arrival of Irenaeus (*supra,* n. 119) into the chronology of the *Koptische Akten.*

124. *ACO,* I, 1, 5, 136.

125. Sources *supra,* n. 94, esp. *ACO,* I, 1, 3, 52–53; I, 3, 178.

126. *ACO,* I, 1, 2, 100; 3, 31–33, 50–51, 65–66; 7, 67–70, 74; Nest. *Heracl.,* pp. 247–49 Nau. The dates and duration of John's mission are uncertain; Bardy, "Débuts," p. 186, and Kidd, *History,* III, 249, suggest August. Cf. *PLRE,* II, 596, "Ioannes 12."

press for agreement (September 11–12).[127] This too proved futile. Theodosius himself demonstrated support for Antiochene theological principles, starting back in horror and shaking out his cloak when informed that Cyril and his followers taught of a God who had suffered.[128] But even so it became clear that once again the emperor had changed his position, and that now the cause of Nestorius was hopeless. The bishop's supporters found that if they so much as mentioned his name in the presence of courtiers they were accused of disloyalty, and Theodosius himself was heard to say: "Let no one speak of this man to me, for in what concerns him I have already made my decision."[129]

The emperor had abandoned Nestorius late in August, but only because Nestorius himself had lost courage. When it became clear to him that Count John's mission would fail, Nestorius began to think less of the difficulties of the episcopacy and more of the peace with recognition he had once enjoyed in the monastery of Euprepius near Antioch.[130] Not daring to disappoint the emperor, he wrote instead to the *cubicularius* Scholasticius and to Antiochus, praetorian prefect of the East, asking them to intervene.[131] During the first week in September Antiochus notified Nestorius of the emperor's response: he would be returned, with the assistance of the imperial post, to his former dwelling near Antioch.[132] As his friends recognized, this served to confirm whatever accusations had been made against him.[133] The defense of Nestorius collapsed, and the emperor's attachment gave way to the resentment evident in his remarks at Chalcedon. There being no further impediment, Theodosius permitted the Cyrillian legates to enter Constantinople about October 1, 431, and to enthrone the aging and ascetic priest Maximian as Nestorius' successor.[134]

127. *ACO*, I, 1, 3, 33–42, 65–66; 7, 82–84; Nest. *Heracl.*, pp. 251–52 Nau; Thdt. *Ep.* 112 (III, 52 Azema). For the date see *ACO*, I, 1, 7, 76–77.

128. *ACO*, I, 1, 7, 77; Nest. *Heracl.*, p. 252 Nau; Barhadbeshabba 25 (*PO*, IX, 554).

129. *ACO*, I, 1, 7, 80–81.

130. Nest. *Heracl.*, pp. 248–49 Nau; *ACO*, I, 1, 7, 71; Loofs, *Nestoriana*, p. 194.

131. Loofs, *Nestoriana*, p. 194; also Barhadbeshabba 25 (*PO*, IX, 555–56); cf. Abramowski, *Untersuchungen*, p. 62.

132. *ACO*, I, 1, 7, 71. Antiochus' brief letter is distant and cold. For its date see *ibid.*, pp. 76–77: the imperial decision had been announced eight days before the Nestorian legates reached Chalcedon.

133. *ACO*, I, 1, 7, 76–77: the Nestorian legates express their consternation at Nestorius' withdrawal ὅτι τὰ ἀκρίτως καὶ ἀθέσμως γεγενημένα τέως δοκεῖ κρατεῖν.

134. Soc. 7. 35. 3, 37. 19; *ACO*, I, 1, 3, 67; 7, 75, 137; Nest. *Heracl.*, p. 252 Nau.

Not long thereafter, an imperial letter dissolved the Council of Ephesus. Theodosius permitted the bishops, including the theoretically deposed Cyril and Memnon, to return to their sees, but declared with vehemence that "as long as we live we shall never be able to condemn the Orientals [i.e., the group around John of Antioch], for they were not convicted in our presence, there being no one willing to undertake an examination."[135] The emperor's position had changed, but not his mind.

In the denouement Theodosius II again stood forth as a man of principle but little will. Determined from the outset that the bishops would reach their own decision, he had nonetheless acquiesced in arrangements that gave the advantage to Cyril, then reacted with befuddlement when he received not one decision but two, and depended on time and a hot summer to produce unanimity. Equally striking, in the denouement as in the entire proceeding, is the fact that despite their theoretical independence in matters of doctrine, bishops of both persuasions recognized that the court alone could make a decision effective. At Ephesus in 431 a divided episcopacy combined with imperial indecision to create a logjam, broken when Nestorius, the principal log, removed himself.

What of this man Nestorius? Theodosius had chosen him to be another Chrysostom, for manifest holiness and oratorical ability, because such a man promised to be an effective support for the dynastic faith. Like his exemplar, Nestorius clashed terribly with an imperious woman, but the parallel must not be pressed too far. John Chrysostom had a bond with the people of Constantinople that even exile could not break. When Eudoxia drove him away, "the people raised an intolerable tumult." "We are one body," he said, and "what God has joined no man may put asunder." Remarkably, on July 5, 431, the people of Constantinople cursed their bishop in the Great Church, his own body in his own episcopal see: Nestorius "the Jew" should be given to the flames, and with him should go his Hellenic friends. Even in Ephesus the erstwhile heir to Chrysostom's mantle could draw the appropriate conclusion—that the necessary bond had been destroyed forever.

Remarkably also, the *voces populi* of July 5 identified a new source of victory: the Virgin Mary had deposed Nestorius, repeating again Christ's triumphant death. In Constantinople the Virgin had been the crux from the beginning, since Nestorius first challenged her

135. *ACO*, I, 1, 7, 142.

right to the title *Theotokos* and embroiled himself in public debate. The *voces* likewise declared a victory of the virgin empress: "Many years to Pulcheria! She it is who has strengthened the faith." Indisputable evidence places this woman in opposition to both Nestorius and her brother, and hypothetical though it may be, her intervention at various points in the controversy should not be doubted. But Pulcheria had a more important function in the *Theotokos* controversy than backstage maneuvering and attempts to exert influence. More than anyone else in Constantinople, she embodied the fullness of Mary piety—in her womanhood, in her spectacular asceticism, and in her claims to Marial dignity. The *voces populi* of July 5 prove that the people of Constantinople responded to her piety, and that this response contributed to their hatred for Nestorius. Thus Mary's victory became her victory as well. In contemporary thinking this victory conferred legitimacy as effectively as any battlefield success. To judge from the *Theotokos* controversy, Pulcheria's sacral *basileía* encompassed resources better emulated than resisted by an imperial person of either sex.

CHAPTER SIX

Two Empresses Who Refused to Be One

Pulcheria's victory at Ephesus tightened her grip on the people of Constantinople, reinforcing an emotional attachment not shared by her sister-in-law. Traditionalists had designed Eudocia's *basileía* for their own narrow purposes: to regain access to high office and nurture enthusiasm for classical culture. It would be unreasonable to think that baptism for convenience instantly made the former Athenaïs an impassioned Christian and altered her priorities.[1] It is unlikely that she took much interest in the wranglings over Mary and Christ which exercised Theodosius, Pulcheria, and the people of Constantinople.[2]

Even so, appearances had to be maintained. The potency of *basileía,* and with it peace and order in the Empire, depended on the fiction that all holders of dominion, female as well as male, acted from a single imperial will.[3] Whether or not the Nestorian quarrel concerned Eudocia, Bishop Cyril had felt compelled to name her as co-recipient of the *Address to the Emperor* he dispatched to the court of Theodosius in 430. His parallel treatise to Pulcheria and her separated court had left an appearance of disharmony, provoking the emperor's wrath against Cyril for knowing of disagreement (if it existed) and for "seeking to separate members from the one body of the emperors." This imperial scolding taught the bishops surrounding John of Antioch a lesson, so they addressed their pleas to the

---

1. Forced to accept Christianity during the reign of the emperor Zeno (474–91), the physician Gesius of Petra exclaimed as he rose from the baptismal waters: Αἴας δ'ἐξαπόλωλεν ἐπεὶ πίεν ἁλμυρὸν ὕδωρ, Sophron. *Nar. mir. SS. Cyr. et Ioh.* 30 (*PG*, LXXXVII: 3, 3513–16). Adapted from *Od.* 4. 509, 511, the verse meant something like "That is a bath which takes one's breath away." Eudocia's baptism need not have affected her more profoundly, although presumably she showed greater respect.

2. Cf., however, Gregorovius, *Athenais*, pp. 103–4; Seeck, *Geschichte*, VI, 83–84.

3. Thus imperial constitutions appeared in the names of all reigning Augusti (females excluded, of course), although only one was the actual origin. Note also the common legend CONCORDIA AVGVSTORVM in the coinage.

emperor and "the most pious empresses," as protocol demanded. After the Council of Ephesus, Cyril escaped from the emperor's arrest and on October 30, 431, he entered the see of Alexandria in triumph. To justify his conduct over the past year, the bishop then composed a lengthy *Apology to the Emperor on the Correct Faith*, addressing it to Theodosius and to both the empresses. In it he denied any intention of creating discord at court. How could he hope to do so when everyone recognized the emperor's piety and that of Eudocia and Pulcheria also, "the two empresses who appear to be one"?[4]

Cyril's words protested too much. Despite appearances and protocol, the two empresses of Theodosius II remained at odds after 431. For nearly two decades the imperial house was plagued with discord between the Augustae. In the early 440s, despite appearances and despite the imperatives of marriage and blood, both of them even broke openly with the emperor and he with them. Pulcheria withdrew from Constantinople to a more solitary abode in its suburbs, Eudocia to permanent exile far away in the Holy Land. For a time others—politicians and generals, monks and palace eunuchs—controlled Theodosius. Early in 450, however, shortly before Theodosius died, Pulcheria returned to power and to harmony with her brother. This restoration of harmony in the *basileía* allowed Pulcheria to arrange a smooth succession and to engineer the victory of orthodoxy in the Council of Chalcedon (451). That council, whose bishops acclaimed Pulcheria as the "New Helena," was her most glorious triumph and the last great monument of the Theodosian dynasty.

The Apple of Discord

According to John Malalas, a remarkable apple was the source of the discord that ruined Eudocia's marriage. Although the chronicler did not provide a date for the events he described, those which were genuine probably commenced early in 443.[5]

On the Epiphany feast, Malalas wrote,[6] the emperor emerged from his palace to celebrate in the Great Church. He left behind the master of offices, Paulinus, who excused himself from attending the

4. *ACO*, I, 1, 3, 77, 79–80.
5. *Infra*, pp. 192–94.
6. Joh. Mal. 14 (pp. 356–57 Bonn); cf. *Chron. pasch. a.* 444 (pp. 584–85 Bonn); Theoph. *a.m.* 5940 (p. 99 de Boor); Cedren., p. 601 Bonn; Zon. 13. 23, p. 44c–d; Niceph. Call. *HE* 14. 23, 49 (*PG*, CXLVI, 1129–32, 1232); *Script. orig.*

emperor because of an injured foot. As it happened, a poor man had brought to the palace a Phrygian apple of such unusual size that it amazed the emperor and all the great men in his company. Theodosius had presented this apple to Eudocia, and she now gave it innocently to Paulinus, "because he was the emperor's friend." Not knowing the apple's origin, Paulinus in turn dispatched it to Theodosius as he reentered the palace, and at once the emperor recognized his gift. When questioned Eudocia swore that she had eaten the apple, but her protests only confirmed the emperor's fears. An apple, of course, was a token of love, and his wife's denials were intended to conceal her adulterous passion for Paulinus. Theodosius ordered the execution of Paulinus, whose youthfulness and manly beauty served to confirm the appearance of guilt. This action offended Eudocia, for the public concluded that she too was at fault. Angrily she demanded that Theodosius dismiss her, and when he agreed the Augusta left him and Constantinople, to pray in the holy places of Jerusalem.

Malalas' version of these events, unlike his account of Eudocia's marriage, has inspired little confidence either in antiquity or among modern scholars.[7] Here the chronicler transmitted popular tradition, in a tale patently invented to save the reputation of an amiable figure. The tale employed a familiar folk-tale device[8] to demonstrate that an unfortunate accident had produced the evil whisperings that surrounded Eudocia's departure. It also had a deeper purpose: to maintain appearances under pressure of the facts that the Augusta did leave her husband and Theodosius did execute Paulinus. A popular audience would respond best to a sanitary explanation for stress within the imperial household, one that did not tinge the *basileía* with the scandal of adultery or a profound division of wills.

Like Eudocia's departure and the execution of Paulinus, the discord implied in the Malalas tale was genuine enough.[9] It originated not in an accident in 443, as Malalas supposed, but in Eudocia's

---

Const., pp. 261–63 Preger; John of Nikiu 87. 1–13 (trans. Charles). The later accounts seem to depend on Malalas, except that Theophanes and Nicephorus add the information that Paulinus was executed in Cappadocia, an item which must have been transmitted independently (cf. Marcell. com. *a*. 440. 1[*MGH: AA*, XI, 80], *infra*, n. 83).

7. In antiquity Evagr. 1. 21 expressed skepticism; for characteristic modern reactions see Bury, *Later Roman Empire*, I, 229–30; and van Rooijen, *De Theodosii II moribus*, pp. 88–91; and now Alan Cameron, "Empress and Poet," pp. 258–59.

8. Cf. A.R. Littlewood, "The Symbolism of the Apple in Byzantine Literature," *Jahrbuch der österreichischen Byzantinistik* 23 (1974), 33–59.

9. Cf. also the report that Pulcheria tricked Theodosius into giving Eudocia to her as a slave: *supra*, p. 130.

efforts during the preceding years to make her *basileía* more effective. Here again Cyril of Alexandria had focused attention on the problem. In his *Address to the Emperor* he had observed a distinction between the two empresses of Theodosius II. Cyril had contrasted Pulcheria, "who takes part in the care and administration of your empire," with Eudocia, "who exults in the offspring you have prayed for" and "permits the hope that your dynasty will last forever."[10]

If Eudocia read the *Address to the Emperor,* Cyril's words must have distressed her profoundly. She might "exult in offspring," but thus far she had presented her husband only with girls, with Licinia Eudoxia (b. 422) and a second daughter, Flaccilla. Nor would she meet with greater success in the future. Flaccilla died early in 431,[11] and thereafter Licinia Eudoxia remained an only child. Since together Theodosius and his consort had managed two successful pregnancies, presumably the difficulty was not physiological. More likely the example of Pulcheria and the emperor's well-known admiration for monks,[12] both of which the Mary victory at Ephesus can only have reinforced, persuaded him to return to the regimen he had followed before his marriage. As a later source indicates,[13] in the years after 431 the eastern court may well have produced the incredible phenomenon of an emperor who had abandoned conjugal relations with his wife. In any event, Eudocia would never bear a son to confirm Cyril's hope that "your dynasty will last forever."[14] She could no longer claim to emulate the namesakes of her daughters, neither the

10. *ACO*, I, 1, 1, 44; cf. *supra*, p. 159.

11. Holum, "Family Life," p. 291 n. 62.

12. E.g., for the archimandrite Dalmatius, *ACO*, I, 1, 2, 65. See also the texts published by Nau in *PO*, VIII, 166–74.

13. Cod. Paris. gr. 881 published by Nau, *ibid.*, 173; cf. John of Nikiu 87. 14–16 (trans. Charles).

14. Cf. the desperate reaction of Eusebia, wife of Constantius II, who was likewise denied the advantages of childbearing (*supra*, p. 28). A son of Eudocia named Arcadius has now made his way into *PLRE*, II, 130, "Arcadius 1," and Alan Cameron, "Empress and Poet," pp. 266–67, but the evidence adduced refers to the emperor who died in 408. *ILS* 818 (*supra*, p. 128, n. 71) paired "d. n. Arcadius" and "d. n. Eudoxia Aug." with "d. n. Theodosius" and "d. n. Eudocia," obviously the familiar imperial couples. The verse dedication of a presentation copy of Proba's *Cento* (ed. Schenkl, *CSEL*, XVI, 568) addresses an eastern emperor who is "spes orbis fratrisque decus," obviously Arcadius, rather than Theodosius II, who had no brother (so Schenkl, *CSEL*, XVI, 515). It urges Arcadius to pass the *Cento* on to an awaited but as yet unborn and hence unnamed heir, "Arcadius Junior," who in turn will transmit the work to his imperial descendants: "haec relegas servesque diu tradasque minori / Arcadio, haec ille suo semini, haec tua semper / accipiat doceatque suos augusta propago." Eudocia's son vanishes.

earlier Eudoxia, who had exploited childbearing so effectively, nor the original Flaccilla, whose image depended on it.

Deprived of this resource, Eudocia confronted Pulcheria, who, as Cyril put it, "takes part in the care and administration of your empire." If the virgin empress had suffered effacement after her brother's marriage, Cyril's words confirm that even before 431 she had returned to prominence in the government. Pulcheria's victory at Ephesus further strengthened her position. As the resignation of Nestorius had demonstrated, resistance could be hazardous.

Within a few months of that resignation, the eastern government initiated a campaign to restore the unity of the church. The vigor of this campaign contrasted so sharply with the emperor's helplessness in 431 that Pulcheria's more resolute hand must have been in control.[15] Immediately after the new bishop Maximian occupied the see of Constantinople, he and a synod of episcopal colleagues deposed several other bishops who refused to break with Nestorius, including Dorotheus of Marcianopolis in Moesia Inferior.[16] Dorotheus would not give way, so the government ordered the *magister militum praesentalis,* Plinta, to install a successor by force.[17] A few months later (about early summer of 432) Theodosius dispatched the "respectable tribune and notary Aristolaus"[18] to Antioch, where he urged Bishop John and his allies to withdraw support from Nestorius; then on to Alexandria to dissuade Cyril from extreme doctrinal positions which offended the Antiochenes; then to Antioch again and back to Constantinople. Aristolaus traveled as a diplomat, urging concessions in the interests of peace, but he could also apply coercion. A *magister militum* stood by with orders to use force ("praeceptum habet ut nobis violentus insistat") in case John of Antioch proved recalcitrant.[19]

The mission of Aristolaus worried Cyril so much that he suffered an attack of melancholy—so wrote Cyril's archdeacon Epiphanius in a letter (*ca.* autumn of 432) to Maximian, bishop of Constantinople. This letter survives and is a most illuminating document.[20] Epiphanius

15. Schwartz, *Cyrill*, p. 42 n. 2.

16. *ACO,* I, 1, 3, 70; 4, 32; 7, 153–54, 164.

17. *ACO,* I, 4, 88, 155; cf. Demandt, *RE,* suppl. XII (1970), 746, "Magister Militum" (with the wrong date).

18. *ACO,* I, 1, 4, 6, 8, 21, 31, 33; 7, 146, 150, 154–55, 158, 160, 162; Nest. *Heracl.,* pp. 255–59, 289–90 Nau; Kidd, *History,* III, 254–62; *PLRE,* II, 146–47; esp. Schwartz in *ACO,* I, 1, 8, 12–13, for chronology.

19. *ACO,* I, 4, 91; Barhadbeshabba 27 (*PO,* IX, 564); cf. Demandt, *RE,* suppl. XII (1970), 741–42, "Magister Militum."

20. *ACO,* I, 4, 222–25.

confirmed that Aristolaus pressured Cyril to accept the new imperial policy ("insistebat ei ut divinitus sancita perageret"), expressed Cyril's displeasure that Constantinople was not working in concert with him, and in particular complained that Maximian had not yet secured the withdrawal of Aristolaus from Alexandria. Epiphanius also recommended means by which Cyril's aims could be accomplished. Cyril had written earlier to "Our Lady the Handmaid of God and Most Reverent Pulcheria, to [her] *praepositus* Paul and [her] *cubicularius* Romanus, to Lady Marcella [her] *cubicularia,* and to Droseria."[21] Now Maximian himself should hasten to beseech Pulcheria to devote herself as she had before to the cause of Alexandria, "for I think," Epiphanius wrote, "that she does not concern herself sufficiently for your brother the most holy Cyril." Maximian was also to ask Lady Olympias for assistance; this woman (otherwise unknown) could enlist Marcella and Droseria, who were open to her influence. Finally, Epiphanius urged the bishop to plead with Pulcheria to "have Lausus enter [the palace] and become [the emperor's] *praepositus* so that the power of Chryseros might be dissolved . . . , because otherwise our troubles will continue forever."

After these recommendations, Epiphanius appended a list of "benedictions," presents Alexandria had sent to Constantinople to win the favor of the mighty. The purpose of the list was to impress Maximian with the volume of bribes Cyril had delivered in their common interest. For example, Paul, the *praepositus* of Pulcheria, had received:

four large woolen carpets, two small woolen carpets, four cushions, four fine tablecloths, six large curtains, six small curtains, six seats, twelve door curtains, two large embroidered cloths, four chairs decorated in ivory, four *persoina* [?], two large *tabulae* [paintings?], and two peacocks.[22]

Cyril had also sent Paul fifty pounds of gold "so that he would cooperate," and the same amount in presents and gold had gone to Droseria and to Marcella, to induce them "to plead with the Augusta and to persuade her." Even the domestic of Paul had received his share, although it was smaller, as befitted his rank.

21. Paul, Romanus, Marcella, and Droseria are not identified explicitly as members of Pulcheria's *cubiculum,* but they appear in close association with her name, while the *cubicularii* of Theodosius are mentioned elsewhere. Romanus later won promotion in the service of Pulcheria or Theodosius. He must be the former *praepositus* Romanus who attended the Council of Chalcedon (*ACO,* II, 1, 1, 55; 2, 70, 84; *PLRE,* II, 947, "Romanus 3").

22. Cf. Batiffol, "Présents," pp. 169–73.

Apart from the unflattering picture it gives of politics in the proto-Byzantine court, Epiphanius' letter proves that Pulcheria did not obediently follow the bidding of either Cyril or Theodosius but had a will and policy of her own. Presumably she expressed that policy through the mission of Aristolaus and the effort to impose unity on the eastern bishops. It is clear that, even so, Cyril placed much confidence in Pulcheria, since he was aware that she possessed enough power to place sympathetic persons (e.g., Lausus)[23] in positions close to her brother and to secure convenient imperial decisions. Epiphanius did mention other powerful individuals in the government and court of Theodosius whose influence, he thought, might benefit the Alexandrian cause. Some of them had received "benedictions" greater in value than those directed to members of Pulcheria's staff. This does not mean that Cyril expected Pulcheria's support to be of smaller consequence than theirs, but only that her *cubicularii* ranked lower than those of the emperor and would be easier to persuade.[24] More significantly, the letter reveals that late in 432 the emperor's *praepositus* Chryseros, who had received as many presents as anyone, still opposed Cyril. Epiphanius, moreover, urged Maximian to have the monk Dalmatius correct the emperor by "binding him with a terrible oath . . . that no mention shall be made of the impious person again." Obviously the person in question was Nestorius. Cyril had to depend on Pulcheria because powerful individuals in the emperor's presence, and thus probably Theodosius himself, still considered renewing support for Nestorius!

Yet within a few months the campaign for unity took on a new harshness. About March, 433, Aristolaus brought his pressure diplomacy to fruition. John of Antioch abandoned Nestorius, and Cyril dispatched to his Antiochene colleague a joyful letter of communion: "The heavens rejoice and earth is made glad. For the wall of separation has broken down, our pain is ended, every source of discord has been removed."[25]

This was a joy, however, which only those could share who agreed that Nestorius had been properly condemned and deposed. Although the emperor had said late in 431 that "we shall never be able to condemn the Orientals," by 435 at least seventeen bishops had lost their sees. Some found themselves exiled—Dorotheus of

23. *PLRE*, II, 660–61, "Lausus 2."
24. Contrast Jones, *Later Roman Empire*, I, 346.
25. *ACO*, I, 1, 4, 15.

Marcianopolis to Cappadocia, for example, and the stiff-necked
Alexander of Hieropolis to the mines of Egypt. In the eastern provinces
the *magister militum* Dionysius and his vicar Titus, count of the
domestics, carried out an imperial persecution.[26] It struck Count
Irenaeus as well. Deprived of his rank and property, the friend of
Nestorius faced exile at Petra in the Egyptian desert.[27] By an imperial
letter of August 3, 435, Nestorius himself suffered the same penalty,
and he was soon relegated to the even more remote Great Egyptian
Oasis.[28] The heresiarch blamed Pulcheria for this harshness.[29] He was
far away and bitter, but probably correct. The letter of Epiphanius
supports the view that it was she who directed the emperor or secured
his consent for the campaign to impose unity upon the church.

Pulcheria also exerted herself to find effective support to conclude
the campaign. The aged Maximian, bishop of Constantinople, obli-
gingly died on Holy Thursday (April 12), 434.[30] Alleging the threat
of disorder, but more likely afraid that a drawn-out election amid
popular disturbances would permit Nestorian sympathizers to rally
the emperor's support for his restoration,[31] some of Theodosius'
advisers persuaded him to turn the matter over to a few bishops
present in Constantinople. They promptly selected and enthroned
Proclus,[32] the same man who had preached on Mary in the Pulcherianai and who as bishop of Constantinople was to extol Pulcheria's
virginity. A late source reports that the empress herself was responsible for his selection;[33] more securely attested is the role of the
patrician and praetorian prefect Taurus, the son of Aurelian and like
his father no doubt a trusted associate of Pulcheria. Not long after the
election, John of Antioch wrote to Taurus to congratulate him on
Proclus' victory: he had been elected ''by your efforts and the concern

26. *ACO*, I, 4, 166–204; R. Devreesse, "Après le concile d'Ephèse," *EO* 30
(1931), 271–92.
27. *ACO*, I, 4, 203.
28. *ACO*, I, 1, 3, 67–70; *CTh* 16. 5. 66 (with the date); Evagr. 1. 7; Soc. 7.
34. 11; *Coll. Avell.* 99. 2 (*CSEL*, XXXV: 1, 440); Thdt. *Haer. fab. comp.* 4. 12 (*PG*,
LXXXIII, 436); Jugie, *Nestorius*, pp. 56–62.
29. Barhadbeshabba 27 (*PO*, IX, 567–68); cf. Abramowski, *Untersuchungen*,
p. 68.
30. Soc. 7. 40. 1–2.
31. *ACO*, I, 4, 173–74. Nestorius' supporters could also organize demonstrations.
32. Soc. 7. 40. 3–5; cf. Bauer, *Proklos*, pp. 38–40.
33. Niceph. Call. *HE* 14. 37 (*PG*, CXLVI, 1185).

of the emperor," who, as John made clear, had needed persuading.[34] The victory consolidated the strength of Nestorius' enemies and gave them a forceful advocate for the final campaign, which may have commenced soon afterward.[35]

Eudocia shared in none of this. Her name does not appear in Epiphanius' letter, and there is no indication that her views, if she had any, counted at all. The persecuted bishops of Euphratensis did address a supplication *ad Augustas* about 435; they dispatched it with some clerics and monks who were to beg the empresses to lay the situation before the emperor and convince him to check the excesses of John of Antioch.[36] Bishops in distant provinces knew that in religious matters Pulcheria guided the will of her brother, but this letter does not prove that Eudocia possessed a similar reputation; protocol required that both be addressed, that the two empresses "appear to be one."

Then a new Eudocia emerged, shortly after her daughter's wedding. Betrothed since infancy to the western emperor Valentinian, the girl Licinia Eudoxia at last reached a marriageable age, and Constantinople celebrated the union on October 29, 437.[37] The western court had sent a prominent figure to the East to complete the arrangements—the senator and former prefect Rufius Antonius Agrypnius Volusianus.[38] Surprisingly, the man was still a pagan. Even so, he willingly listened to his niece, the famous Christian ascetic Melania (St. Melania the Younger), who had settled near Jerusalem some years earlier in a convent on the Mount of Olives, and who now traveled to Constantinople and assisted her uncle to a last-minute conversion. On the Epiphany feast, January 6, 438, Volusian died.[39] According to the priest Gerontius, a contemporary who later com-

---

34. *ACO*, I, 4, 154: "per studium vestrum et curam deo amicissimi principis, qui cum bene viderit, velociter quoque deliberata complevit. . . ." On Taurus *PLRE*, II, 1056–57, "Fl. Taurus 4."

35. Bauer, *Proklos*, pp. 58–63.

36. *ACO*, I, 4, 162–63.

37. Soc. 7. 44 (with the wrong year); Marcell. com. *a.* 437 (*MGH: AA*, XI, 79); *Chron. pasch. a.* 437 (p. 582 Bonn); Oost, *Placidia*, pp. 242–45.

38. A. Chastagnol, "Le sénateur Volusien et la conversion d'une famille de l'aristocratie romaine au Bas-Empire," *REA* 58 (1956), 241–53; *PLRE*, II, 1184–85.

39. Geront. *V. S. Mel. Iun.* 50–56 (ed. Gorce). Chastagnol, "Volusien," p. 253; Oost, *Placidia*, p. 243; P. Devos, "Quand Pierre l'Ibère vint-il à Jérusalem?" *An. Boll.* 86 (1968), 342–44; and Gorce in his edition of the *V. S. Mel. Iun.*, pp. 44, 224 n. 1, 237 n. 4, all (apparently) follow M. Rampolla del Tindaro, *Santa Melania*

posed an account of her life, Melania remained in the city during the customary forty days of mourning, sharing her spiritual gifts with its inhabitants "but especially with the Christ-loving empresses." Like Cyril of Alexandria and the bishops of Euphratensis, Gerontius thus paired Pulcheria with Eudocia,[40] but he did not include the latter simply to observe protocol. As Gerontius wrote, Melania also edified Theodosius and urged him to "release his consort because she desired to worship in the Holy Places."[41] Apparently Eudocia had succumbed to the engaging personality of this woman and intended to visit her at her home in Palestine.

Theodosius did "release" his wife, and she did depart for the Holy Land about February or March, 438. In view of Eudocia's background, her new receptiveness to Melania's influence and her "desire" to undertake an arduous journey require elucidation. Writing a few years later, the historian Socrates spoke of a vow, of Eudocia's pious intention to give thanks in the Holy Places for the divine favor manifest in her daughter's splendid marriage.[42] An admirer of Eudocia, Socrates naturally transmitted a sanitary explanation, one that would enhance the public image of the empress while countering the natural assumption that Theodosius released her because of disharmony at court.

Other evidence suggests that the disharmony was genuine, and that at this time the court of Theodosius was even willing to admit it. During the previous year Bishop Proclus of Constantinople, who was anxious to reunite with his see the still schismatic adherents of John Chrysostom, had persuaded the emperor to order the return of Chrysostom's bones. On January 28, 438, Proclus deposited these bones with those of the Christian emperors and empresses in the Apostles Church of Constantinople. Theodosius participated in the relic *adventus,* and, as protocol demanded, Pulcheria appeared at his

---

Giuniore senatrice romana (Rome, 1905), p. 230, in dating the arrival of Melania in Constantinople to late 436 and her return to Palestine in February of 437. This is impossible. Eudocia did not depart for her pilgrimage until after the wedding (*infra*), while the *V. S. Mel. Iun.* 56–58 makes it clear that Melania reached Jerusalem only a few weeks before Eudocia arrived in Antioch. Thus Volusian died in 438.

40. Gorce in his note on Geront. *V. S. Mel. Iun.* 56 (p. 238 n. 2) identifies τὰς φιλοχρίστους βασιλίδας whom Melania counseled as Eudocia and Eudoxia, but if my dating is correct the latter was in Thessalonica, wintering there with her new husband: Marcell. com. *a.* 437 (*MGH: AA*, XI, 79).

41. Geront. *V. S. Mel. Iun.* 56 (ed. Gorce).

42. Soc. 7. 47. 2.

side, but the sources do not mention Eudocia.[43] Their silence may well be significant. Melania was still mourning Volusian at the time, and thus Eudocia had not yet departed for the Holy Land. If the emperor's consort did not join with the other Augusti during the ceremonial *adventus* of Chrysostom's bones, it was presumably because the court did not wish to equate her position in the dynastic city with that of the emperor and his sister. This indicates that Eudocia left Constantinople under a cloud, out of frustration that her *basileía* still lacked the resources of Pulcheria's.[44]

Whatever the motives for it, Eudocia's departure certainly eased her frustrations. No virgin herself, during the subsequent journey she emulated Pulcheria's piety as best she could, by demonstrating devotion and friendship for a famous holy woman. As Gerontius wrote, Melania had returned through winter storms to Jerusalem in time to celebrate Easter, and had busied herself for a few days constructing a small martyr shrine. Soon news arrived that Eudocia was on her way to Jerusalem, having already visited Antioch. When Melania hastened to Sidon to meet her, the empress greeted the holy woman with the profound respect due a spiritual parent. "I fulfill a double vow," she declared, "both to kneel at the holy places and to behold you, my own mother." Eudocia then visited the convent on the Mount of Olives, treating Melania's virgins with admirable humility as her own sisters. She attended the translation of relics into the small shrine Melania had just constructed, spraining her foot by the devil's malignity, but finding relief through Melania's prayers. The two remained inseparable until they reached Caesarea, then "with difficulty tore themselves from one another." Eudocia returned in safety to Theodosius, protected by Melania's intercessions and with potent rewards from their intimacy. As Gerontius put it succinctly, "in honoring the one who truly glorified Heaven's King, the empress found glory herself."[45]

Other sources confirm the chronology of Gerontius and add illuminating detail. Gerontius reported correctly that before meeting Melania at Sidon the empress had visited Antioch. As part of the

43. Soc. 7. 45; Thdt. *HE* 5. 36. 1–2; Marcell. com. *a*. 438. 2 (*MGH: AA*, XI, 79); Theoph. *a.m.* 5930 (pp. 92–93 de Boor); Proc. *Or*. 20 (*PG*, LXV, 827–34); Baur, *Chrysostomus*, II, 458–60.

44. However, Gregorovius, *Athenais*, p. 139, believed that, on the contrary, with the marriage of her daughter Eudocia reached preeminence.

45. Geront. *V. S. Mel. Iun.* 58–59 (ed. Gorce).

traditional *adventus* ceremonial, the eloquent Augusta delivered an imperial address (*adlocutio*) before the city's senate,[46] seated on a throne decorated "imperially" with gold and precious stones. This was her famous encomium of Antioch, which included the verse: "Of your proud line and blood I claim to be."[47] Eudocia flattered her audience by recalling a common background and delighted them with her clever use of Homeric diction, a demonstration that she shared their devotion to classical culture.[48] The Antiochenes responded with acclamations of the empress and dedicated statues of her in significant places, one of gold in the senate house itself and a bronze statue in the sanctuary of the Muses. Eudocia responded in turn, "showering her wealth upon the Antiochenes for use in feeding the population."[49] Unlike Helena, Flaccilla, and the other Theodosian empresses, she directed her philanthropy not "to the least of these" but, following ancient imperial practice, to the inhabitants of Antioch "the Great," one of the proudest cities of the Empire.[50] While exhibiting new-found enthusiasm for the Theodosian image of imperial womanhood, Eudocia also exploited her journey to acquire prestige by more traditional methods.

Then Eudocia resumed her imperial itinerary, going on to Jerusalem, where she arrived, as Gerontius implied, in the spring of the year. On May 15, 438, Cyril of Alexandria consecrated a church of St. Stephen in her presence, and he also attended the translation of relics into Melania's shrine, which apparently took place the next day.[51] Eudocia did hurt her foot, as Gerontius claimed, and her left knee as well. But despite Melania's prayers, the injuries continued to bother her.[52] Eudocia did consort with Melania, but she also encountered Barsauma, a wild, illiterate Syrian archimandrite.

46. Evagr. 1. 20, *Chron. pasch. a.* 444 (p. 585 Bonn) (with the wrong year); cf. S. MacCormack, "Change and Continuity in Late Antiquity: The Ceremony of *Adventus*," *Historia* 21 (1972), 748 n. 158.

47. *Supra*, p. 117.

48. Liban. *Or.* 11 (I, 499 Foerster) stated that the treasures of Hellenism were in his day divided between Athens and Antioch.

49. *Chron. pasch. a.* 444 (p. 585 Bonn).

50. Dagron, *Naissance*, pp. 56–60.

51. *V. Petr. Hib.*, p. 37 Raabe; cf. E. Honigmann, "Juvenal of Jerusalem," pp. 225–26.

52. In an epigram, now lost but once inscribed in the church of St. Stephen at Zapharambolou, Eudocia thanked St. Stephen for healing her; see G. Doublet, "Inscriptions de Paphlagonie," *BCH* 13 (1889), 294–99; cf. F. Halkin, "Inscriptions grecques relatives à l'hagiographie, IX," *An. Boll.* 71 (1953), 96.

Barsauma's long hair reached to the ground. He wore no shoes but donned an iron tunic in which he froze in winter and roasted in summer. He ate only fruit and roots which grew without cultivation, and never sat or rested prone but slept standing supported by his elbows. When they traveled abroad from his monastery (near Samosata in Euphratensis), he and his *montagnard* followers used cudgels to terrorize pagans, Samaritans, and Jews, and Barsauma's pyrotechnic skill to destroy synagogues and sanctuaries. Frequently his appearance alone convinced his victims to embrace Christianity.[53] This holy man appeared at Jerusalem during Eudocia's sojourn, and naturally the empress wished to meet him. According to the Syriac *Life of Barsauma*, he persuaded her to distribute her largesse more generously among the poor. She requested his mantle as a souvenir of their encounter, and pleaded that in return he accept her veil "of great price" and use it to cover the altar of his monastery church.[54]

Above all, Eudocia did pray at the empty tomb of Christ in the Resurrection Church. Like countless other men and women from all over the Empire,[55] she came as a pilgrim to worship at the spot where God had revealed on earth his power to conquer death. For an empress an effort of this type offered special rewards. Arriving in a vehicle decorated with gold and precious stones, escorted by a contingent of the imperial guard, clothed in the insignia of *basileía*, the "mistress of the inhabited world" made an impression when she humbled herself:

> Like a servant girl she kneels before His tomb,
> She before whom all men bend the knee.[56]

Later, when Eudocia had returned to Constantinople, an unknown artist painted the scene or reproduced it in mosaic on the wall of an unknown church. Later still, an unknown poet described the artist's work in a surviving verse *ekphrasis*.[57] Both artist and poet appreciated

53. E. Honigmann, *Le couvent de Barsauma et le patriarcat jacobite d'Antioche et de Syrie*, CSCO, Subsidia, vol. VII (Louvain, 1954), pp. 6–23, discusses the sources, but is too skeptical regarding the value of the Syriac *Vita*.
54. See the Syriac *Vita*, published in Nau's excerpts, "Résumé de monographies syriaques," *ROC* 19 (1914), 115–16.
55. For an excellent example see E.D. Hunt, "St. Silvia of Aquitaine: The Role of a Theodosian Pilgrim in the Society of East and West," *JThS* n.s. 23 (1972), 351–72.
56. *Anth. pal.* 1. 105.
57. Ensslin, *Gottkaiser*, p. 79, misinterprets the poem as a description of Eudocia kneeling before the tomb of her husband.

the significance of the scene. For those who visited the church, Eudocia had now equalled Flaccilla's exalted humility, and the scene also evoked an earlier empress of even greater fame—Constantine's mother Helena, the first empress who traveled on pilgrimage to the Holy Land and knelt at Christian holy places.[58] Eudocia exploited her journey to establish herself as a latter-day Helena.

In Constantinople, meanwhile, Pulcheria "lorded over her brother"—τὸν ἀδελφὸν αὐθεντήσασα. On January 31, 438, a few days after the ceremonial *adventus* of Chrysostom's bones and not long before Eudocia left the dynastic city, Theodosius issued his last great constitution against pagans, Samaritans, and Jews.[59] Apparently the government enforced this law, causing communal strife between Christians and Jews in Palestine and the vicinity, especially in Caesarea, and the deaths not only of Jews but also of some Christians. When Pulcheria and Theodosius (οἱ βασιλεῖς) heard of it, they ordered the local authorities to punish the miscreant Jews. There were reports of bribery and of the escape of some of the accused, so Pulcheria ordered the officials responsible dismissed from office and half of their properties confiscated.[60] It is not surprising that she stood behind such a drastic and one-sided reaction: Pulcheria had long nursed a special hatred for Jews, and the Nestorian heresy, which appeared to contemporaries to be of Jewish origin, no doubt had served to confirm that hatred.[61]

Another episode, again during Eudocia's absence from Constantinople, likewise reveals Pulcheria ruling alongside her brother. On September 25, 438, an earthquake struck the dynastic city, terrifying the people and causing them to flee for safety to the open country outside the walls. As Bishop Proclus led supplications for deliverance at the Hebdomon, a child was miraculously lifted into the air and received the words of a new litany from God Himself: "Holy God, Holy and Mighty, Holy and Immortal, have mercy upon us!" When Proclus led the people in this prayer, the earth ceased quaking. "Rejoicing at this miracle, the blessed Pulcheria and her brother issued a constitution [ἐθέσπισαν] ordering that this sacred hymn be

58. *Supra*, pp. 24, 26–27.
59. *NTh* 3; *CI* 1. 5. 7, 1. 7. 5, 1. 9. 18.
60. Theod. Anag. *Epit.* 336 (p. 96 Hansen), dated to about 439 by its position at the beginning of the *Epitome*.
61. *Supra*, pp. 98–99 (Pulcheria and the Jews), 170 (their supposed affinities with Nestorius' teaching).

chanted throughout the world.''[62] The role of the child is transparently a contrivance invented within the next century to lend the hymn additional authority.[63] But there is no reason to doubt the rest of the story, or that Pulcheria took pains to establish forms of worship that would conciliate the divine protector.[64]

Early in 439 Eudocia returned to Constantinople in triumph. Her oration in Antioch had been a smashing success. Her intimacy with Melania and her exchange of gifts with Barsauma proved that she was indeed a woman of imperial piety. She had, like Helena, visited the holy places, and had prayed at Christ's tomb. Moreover, when she returned she brought with her not only Barsauma's cloak but also additional remains of Stephen Protomartyr, the saint whose very name evoked victory. The emperor and the people of Constantinople received both Eudocia and the relics in a public *adventus* celebration.[65] As E.D. Hunt has demonstrated, to come home blessed with relics compounded the authority normally acquired in one's community as a result of the exertion of a pilgrimage.[66] Thus for the first time Eudocia commanded resources like those of Pulcheria's sacral *basileía*.

One result was the brief but astonishing political career of the poet Cyrus.[67] A native of Panopolis in Egypt, this man was one of a school of Egyptian versifiers who regarded their skill as an excellent

62. Theoph. *a.m.* 5930 (p. 93 de Boor); Cedren., pp. 599–600 Bonn; Niceph. Call. *HE* 14. 46 (*PG*, CXLVI, 1216–20); Georg. Mon., pp. 604–5 de Boor; *Script. orig. Const.*, p. 150 Preger, all probably going back to Theod. Anag.; H.G. Opitz, *RE*, VA (1934), 1874, "Theodoros 48." Cf. also Nest. *Heracl.*, pp. 317–21 Nau, apparently describing the same event.

63. See, e.g., Paulin. *V. Ambr.* 6 (ed. Kaniecka), Marc. Diac. *V. Porph.* 66–68 (ed. Grégoire-Kugener), for similar application of the adage "there is truth in children."

64. Cf. Theodosius in *NTh* 3 against the Jews (*supra*, p. 188): "For why has the spring renounced its accustomed charm? Why has the summer, barren of its harvest, deprived the laboring farmer of his hope of a grain harvest? Why has the intemperate ferocity of winter with its piercing cold doomed the fertility of the lands with the disaster of sterility? Why all these things, unless nature has transgressed the decree of its own law to avenge such impiety?" (trans. Pharr). This constitution may also have reflected Pulcheria's thinking.

65. Marcell. com. *a.* 439. 2 (*MGH: AA*, XI, 80). The precise date of Eudocia's return is not recorded, but she probably entered Constantinople before the promotion of Cyrus to the city prefecture (*infra*). For the relics see also *supra*, n. 52.

66. Hunt, "St. Silvia," pp. 354, 362, 365.

67. On Cyrus see now *PLRE*, II, 336–39, and esp. Alan Cameron, "Empress and Poet." The main sources are remains of his poetry (Cameron, pp. 225–35); a series of imperial constitutions dated March 23, 439–August 18, 441 (*PLRE*); two passages in the *V. Dan. Styl.* (31, 36, *An. Boll.* 23 [1913], 150–51, 154); and brief notices in

qualification for a public career. In the past his fellow Egyptians Claudian of Alexandria and Olympiodorus of Thebes had achieved some prominence, but no poet of this type had yet risen to the pinnacle of a praetorian prefecture, nor would Cyrus in all likelihood have reached it without the patronage of Eudocia and the prestige she had acquired from her pilgrimage. Cyrus is first attested as city prefect of Constantinople in a constitution he received from Theodosius on March 23, 439,[68] probably about the time of Eudocia's dramatic *adventus*. By the end of the year he had won promotion to the praetorian prefecture of the East, but he remained city prefect during his tenure of the higher office. Cyrus also received the distinction *patricius* and the consulship for 441. Early in the next year an otherwise unknown Thomas succeeded him as praetorian prefect, but Cyrus retained the city prefecture until early in 443.[69] Thus he held the prefect's rank for nearly four years, with the enthusiastic support of Eudocia. According to a reliable source, she admired him because of his poetry.[70] This was clearly no minor qualification in a court where Eudocia exercised power.

During his prefectures Eudocia's man Cyrus acquired immense popularity as a benefactor of Constantinople. He apparently brought the city's Anthemian fortifications to completion, providing sea walls for protection from naval attack.[71] The Constantinopolitans remembered Cyrus also as the prefect who had ordered that lighting be provided along their streets and who secured an imperial constitution permitting wills and judicial decisions in Greek,[72] the language of

---

later sources derived mainly from Priscus: Joh. Mal. 14 (pp. 361–62 Bonn); Joh. Lyd. *De mag.* 2. 12, 3. 42 (ed. Wuensch); *Chron. pasch. a.* 450 (pp. 588–89 Bonn); Theoph. *a.m.* 5937 (pp. 96–97 de Boor); *Suda s.vv.* Θεοδόσιος, Κῦρος (II, 695, III, 220 Adler). Apart from the constitutions, these sources provide no valid absolute dates for his career. I prefer my chronology (and that of *PLRE*) to Cameron's because, while respecting the Priscan tradition, it makes better sense of politics in the period.

68. *CI* 11. 18. 1 = 1. 2. 9. *CI* 2. 7. 5, addressed to Cyrus as city prefect in 426, must be redated to 439: Seeck, *Regesten*, p. 369.

69. Joh. Mal. and the *Chron. pasch.* (from Malalas) say he held *both* offices "for four years." This positive statement, presumably Priscan tradition, must be partly correct. In my view Cyrus would not have won promotion while Pulcheria "lorded over her brother" (*supra*), so the four years must have commenced in early 439, corresponding with Eudocia's *adventus*.

70. *Suda s.v.* Κῦρος: Εὐδοκία . . . ὑπερηγάσθη τὸν Κῦρον, φιλοεπὴς οὖσα. This presumably came from Priscus.

71. *Chron. pasch. a.* 439 (p. 583 Bonn); Meyer-Plath and Schneider, *Landmauern*, II, 3.

72. *Chron. pasch.*, Joh. Lyd. (*supra*, n. 67); cf. *NTh* 16. 8 on the language question with G. Dagron, "Aux origines de la civilisation byzantine: Langue de culture et langue d'Etat," *Revue historique* 241 (1969), 41–42.

poets, perhaps, but, more importantly, the language of the people. Indeed, his construction and other achievements made him so popular that in the emperor's presence the hippodrome echoed with dangerous acclamations: "Constantine founded the city; Cyrus renewed it."[73] This was a juxtaposition which could turn the head of any man, or might be thought to have done so.

The danger in the hippodrome acclamations was the same which had brought the fall of Anthemius and his government a generation earlier. Again a traditionalist sought to protect Constantinople from dependence on the military. A civilian magistrate once more devoted himself to efficient administration, winning popular acclaim. This acclaim touched a most sensitive nerve, for Cyrus threatened to make Theodosius and the imperial blood irrelevant in the dynastic city. Again the palace struck back, directed this time not by a princess but by a politician who outmaneuvered them all. Chrysaphius, surnamed Tzumas, had emerged about 440 as imperial *spatharius* (sword-bearer) and perhaps *praepositus sacri cubiculi* as well. He became the next eunuch to put to use his personal hold over Theodosius and to exploit the need of a weak-willed emperor to establish distance from his subjects.[74]

Chrysaphius had quickly removed Pulcheria, his most formidable rival.[75] In 441 Chrysaphius employed Eudocia's newly discovered taste for power, and the disharmony that existed between the two empresses, to break the influence of the emperor's sister.[76] "Finding that he could accomplish nothing while Pulcheria ruled," the eunuch

73. Joh. Mal., *Chron. pasch.*, Theoph. (*supra*, n. 67).

74. On Chrysaphius in general see O. Seeck, *RE*, III (1899), 2485–86, "Chrysaphius"; *PLRE*, II, 295–97, "Chrysaphius *qui et* Ztummas"; Stein, *Histoire*, I, 297–98; P. Goubert, "Le rôle de Sainte Pulchérie et de l'eunuque Chrysaphius," *Das Konzil von Chalkedon*, ed. A. Grillmeier and H. Bacht, 3 vols. (Würzburg, 1951–54), I, 305–12. Near-contemporary sources agree that he was *spatharius*. The functions of that office in the early period are unknown, but later a corps of *spatharii* served as part of the emperor's bodyguard; see R. Guilland, *Recherches sur les institutions byzantines*, Berliner byzantinische Arbeiten, vol. XXXV: 1, 2 (Berlin-Amsterdam, 1967), pt. 1, 283–85. The office *praepositus* is not attested, but Chrysaphius probably held it as well from *ca.* 443. No other incumbent is recorded, and Chrysaphius is not likely to have tolerated a rival.

75. Another victim fell about the same time. John the Vandal revolted in 441, was defeated by his rival Arnegisclus, and then executed upon orders of Chrysaphius; see Marcell. com. *a.* 441. 2 (*MGH: AA*, XI, 80); Theoph. *a.m.* 5938, 5943 (pp. 97, 103 de Boor); Joh. Ant. frg. 206 (*FHG*, IV, 616–17); *PLRE*, II, 597; Demandt, *RE*, suppl. XII (1970), 744–45, "Magister Militum."

76. Theoph. *a.m.* 5940 (pp. 98–99 de Boor). Theophanes dated the event to 447 because he counted the regnal years of Theodosius from 408 rather than 402 and took 447 instead of 441 to be the fortieth; cf. Holum, "Pulcheria's Crusade," p. 163

surreptitiously spurred the jealousy of Eudocia, "who was inexperienced." He suggested that she persuade her consort to assign Pulcheria's *praepositus* (and thus her separated imperial court) to herself. Despite Eudocia's "nagging," Theodosius refused: "Do not trouble yourself over this, for it is not possible that you have a *praepositus*, nor will I dismiss my sister, who governs well, with skill and piety." When his first attempt failed, Chrysaphius contrived a new ploy which would have the same effect. Instructed by the imperial eunuch, Eudocia convinced Theodosius that since his sister had adopted the ascetic life she could not properly take part in worldly affairs but should be made a deaconess. Accepting this argument, the emperor ordered the bishop of Constantinople to carry through the ordination. That bishop, however, was Proclus, long an ally of Pulcheria.[77] To avoid conniving at her removal from power, he warned Pulcheria in writing not to enter his presence, if she wished to retain her freedom and avoid a confrontation. Pulcheria therefore dismissed her *praepositus* and staff and retired to a more private existence outside Constantinople, in the Hebdomon palace. She did not withdraw because she foresaw the eventual fall of Chrysaphius, as later authors maintained, or to preserve the appearance of harmony in the *basileía*, but because she had been outmaneuvered.

Other victims soon followed. In 443 and 444, in fact, the penalties of exile, confiscation of property, and execution were inflicted upon at least five persons connected with the court of Constantinople and the government of Theodosius II, and all probably owed their fates to Chrysaphius. Early in 443 Cyrus of Panopolis gave up his city prefecture. Some months later Theodosius confiscated his property and imposed upon him exile and a kind of penal ordination, as bishop of Cotyaeum, an unhappy Phrygian see where the people had murdered four previous episcopal appointees.[78] Contemporaries alleged paganism and excessive ambition as the reasons for his political demise; the author of the dependable *Life of Daniel the Stylite* identified Chrysaphius as the plotter and also blamed the prefect's "excessive cleverness" (διὰ τὴν ἄγαν ἀγχίνοιαν). If these words hinted at Cyrus' poetic gift, as seems likely, it appears that a commit-

---

n. 46, for a similar error. The year 447 is clearly impossible because by then Eudocia had departed to stay permanently in Palestine.

77. Theophanes presumably found Proclus at this point in his source, but thinking the year was 447 (preceding note) he felt obligated to insert Flavian instead.

78. On Cotyaeum see Joh. Mal. 14 (p. 362 Bonn), and D.J. Constantelos, "Kyros Panopolites, Rebuilder of Constantinople," *GRBS* 12 (1971), 454-55, 463.

ment to traditional culture could still damage a man severely during political infighting, implicating charges of devotion to traditional religion.[79]

Significantly, the ruin of Eudocia's favorite occurred shortly after that of the Augusta herself. Paulinus, the former master of offices, had been a friend of Theodosius since boyhood. He had enjoyed such intimacy with the imperial family that Nestorius had once identified him as the object of Pulcheria's affection, when he accused her of illicit sexual relations.[80] In a similar effort to break the power of an Augusta, Chrysaphius apparently charged Eudocia with adultery about early 443, implicating the same paramour.[81] Malalas' sanitized version of Eudocia's fall conceals discord of the nastiest variety. The charge of adultery implied inevitably that Eudocia intended to make Paulinus emperor, to challenge her husband, and perhaps to assassinate him. Whether or not the charge was true, this time Theodosius believed it, so great was his eunuch's hold over him

79. On the fall of Cyrus see Joh. Mal., *Chron. pasch.*, Theoph., *Suda*, and the *V. Dan. Styl.* cited *supra*, n. 67; also *Anth. pal.* 9. 136, in which Cyrus attributes his fall to "pernicious drones," presumably hinting at Chrysaphius. As for the charge of paganism, scholars now agree that at the time of his public career Cyrus was a Christian; see Constantelos, "Kyros," pp. 458–64; T. Gregory, "The Remarkable Christmas Homily of Kyros Panopolites," *GRBS* 16 (1975), 317–24; von Haehling, *Religionszugehörigkeit*, pp. 87–90; and now Alan Cameron, "Empress and Poet," pp. 239–54; proposing in addition that he was a theologian, Mariologist, and hagiographer, an interpretation I find extravagant and poorly attested. In my view the man's Christianity was probably more "practical" (Gregory, "Homily," p. 324) than profound. The thirty-second-long Christmas sermon recorded by Joh. Mal. 14 (p. 362 Bonn), in which Cyrus declared that the birth of Christ should be celebrated "in silence" even as Mary conceived him "through hearing alone" is remarkable mainly for its flippancy. (Gregory, "Homily," p. 323, correctly calls it "a clever—one might even say wily—statement of orthodox theology.") Especially instructive is the fact that after the death of Theodosius, who had sentenced him, Cyrus abandoned his vows and the episcopacy and took up the life of a Byzantine aristocrat once again (*V. Dan. Styl.* 31 [p. 150]). Although it is hazardous to search his heart, the probability is high that Cyrus remained essentially a traditionalist, whose devotion to Hellenic culture sufficed to make a charge of "excessive cleverness" and paganism credible.

80. Theod. Anag. *Epit.* 340 (p. 97 Hansen), *supra*, p. 153, n. 32.

81. Sources *supra*, n. 6, the story of the apple of discord. As for the date, we know for certain only that Eudocia had reached Palestine by the time Theodosius exiled Cyrus, *Suda s.v.* Κῦρος (III, 220 Adler) presumably from Priscus. Cameron's chronology ("Empress and Poet,"pp. 256–70: Eudocia's departure, 440, fall of Cyrus, 441) rests on an entry in Marcellinus' chronicle (*infra*, n. 83) and on Nest. *Heracl.*, p. 331 Nau, which actually does not help at all. Nestorius does state correctly that the alleged adultery occurred after the death of Eudocia's daughter Flaccilla in 431 ("après celle-là") but provides no relative chronology for the alleged adultery and Vandal attacks in 439. Adhering to Priscan tradition, I maintain chronological continuity between Cyrus' career of 439–43 and that of Eudocia.

and so readily did he conclude from the effective breakdown of his marriage that his wife was prepared to replace him. Soon the empress Eudocia departed "in shame and embarrassment" for Jerusalem, never to return.[82] The "prince of adultery" who had cast her down suffered banishment to Cappadocia, where about a year later his erstwhile friend Theodosius ordered him put to death.[83]

The legend of Eudocia's Phrygian apple came from a conflict far deadlier than Malalas had imagined. Even far off in the Holy Land, Eudocia still seemed so great a threat that Theodosius ordered the count of domestics, Saturninus, to Jerusalem to deal with her. This powerful general executed two of the empress' entourage, the priest Severus and John the Deacon, "because they had been her confidants in Constantinople." Not to be outdone in brutality, Eudocia struck Saturninus down with her own hands. For this offence Theodosius deprived her of her imperial ministers,[84] presumably the *praepositus* and court she had recently acquired from Pulcheria. At about this time the imperial mints ceased striking coins with her image, an indication that the apparatus of imperial propaganda no longer equated her *basileía* with that of her fellow Augusti.[85] Yet so far as is known Theodosius did not withdraw her imperial distinction. Unlike the western emperor Valentinian III, who a decade earlier had deposed his sister Justa Grata Honoria, Theodosius left his errant wife with the "scepter of empire."

82. Nest. *Heracl.*, p. 331 Nau.

83. *Chron. pasch. a.* 444 (p. 585 Bonn), perhaps dating the entire affair from the execution of Paulinus; Marcell. com. *a.* 440. 1 (*MGH: AA*, XI, 80) with the wrong date. I cannot explain the error in Marcellinus, but an error it surely is. The entry implies that Cyrus received the consulship for 441 *after* his champion Eudocia had been accused of adultery and presumably of plotting to overthrow Theodosius, and that Cyrus continued to hold both great prefectures for at least a year *after* the execution of Eudocia's alleged lover. *PLRE*, II, 846–47, accepts 444 "perhaps."

84. Marcell. com. *a.* 444. 4 (*MGH: AA*, XI, 81): "Eudocia nescio quo excita dolore Saturninum protinus obtruncavit, statimque mariti imperatoris nutu regiis spoliata ministris, apud Aeliam civitatem moritura remansit"; Theoph. *a.m.* 5942 (p. 102 de Boor); Prisc. frg. 8 (*FHG*, IV, 93–94). The treatment of Severus and John indicates that they had been implicated in Eudocia's "plotting" with Paulinus.

85. A.A. Boyce, "Eudoxia, Eudocia, Eudoxia," *American Numismatic Society: Museum Notes* 6 (1954), 134–39, attempted to date Eudocia's banishment from court using a worthless chronicle passage (Cedren., p. 601 Bonn, dated from Theoph.) and a frequency count of dated solidi first issued early in 443, the IMPXXXXII COSXVII type of Theodosius II and the other Augusti. Although Boyce's sampling was minuscule—she identified a total of only 62 pieces out of presumably thousands originally struck—her statistics gain some authority from the relative frequency of types representing the various imperial figures. Eastern mints

The New Helena

The fates of Cyrus, Paulinus, and Eudocia reveal the good sense of Pulcheria, who yielded and therefore survived to take revenge on Chrysaphius. Discord continued between herself and her brother, now firmly in the eunuch's control, but Pulcheria did not share fully in Eudocia's demise.

Although Pulcheria had forfeited her *praepositus* and court, the mints continued to strike coins with her image during the succeeding period.[86] During this period also (*ca.* 449), the ecclesiastical historian Sozomen brought his work to completion, including in it a miniature encomium of Pulcheria. Apparently such an expression seemed at least perfectly safe, and eventually might bring rewards.[87] About 446 Bishop Theodoret of Cyrrhus (in Euphratensis) even addressed a letter of petition to Pulcheria, part of a series in which he begged prominent persons in Constantinople, including the praetorian prefect and Bishop Proclus, to secure confirmation of tax advantages already enjoyed by the provincials under his pastoral care for a decade. Theodoret approached the Augusta who "embellishes her *basileía* with piety and by her faith glorifies the imperial purple" because he knew that she paid honor to the priesthood. The bishop urged the empress, whom he called "Your Sovereignty" (τὸ ὑμέτερον κράτος), to indulge his land by "ordering" that its rights be confirmed. His city, he declared, would not survive without care received from the healing hands of "Your Piety"; but if "Your Serenity should tend these wounds" Pulcheria could add more more to her catalogue of successes.[88] Theodoret may have been ignorant of the political situ-

would indeed have struck more coins for the eastern Augusti Theodosius, Pulcheria, and Eudocia (46 specimens in all) than for their western counterparts Valentinian III, Galla Placidia, and Licinia Eudoxia (16 specimens). (For the eastern origin of COMOB as well as CONOB types in this issue see J. P. C. Kent, "Gold Coinage in the Later Roman Empire," *Essays in Roman Coinage Presented to Harold Mattingly*, ed. R. A. G. Carson and C. H. V. Sutherland [Oxford, 1956], pp. 202–3.) Similarly, in the Boyce sampling Theodosius II specimens appeared more frequently (29) than those of the two eastern empresses (17), as one would expect. Hence the fact that Boyce identified 15 Pulcheria solidi but only 2 of Eudocia may well be statistically significant. These tentative figures indicate that Eudocia possessed the *Münzrecht* early in 443 but lost it relatively soon thereafter, and that the mints continued to strike IMPXXXXII COSXVII solidi for Pulcheria well into the period 443–50.

86. Preceding note.
87. *Supra*, pp. 95–96.
88. Thdt. *Epp.* 42–47 (II, 106–24 Azema); cf. Azema's notes *ad locc.* for the date, also Jones, *Later Roman Empire*, I, 355.

ation in Constantinople, or he may have written to Pulcheria simply as a matter of protocol. His letter does not prove that the empress could intervene effectively with her brother. Yet its terms of address do indicate that for Theodoret, as for the imperial mints, Pulcheria's *basileía* still included the same sovereignty as that of an Augustus.

During these years Pulcheria lived apart at the Hebdomon palace with her circle of ascetic women.[89] Her two sisters apparently died there, Arcadia in 444 and Marina five years later. Both had lived pious and charitable lives, but neither established a reputation independent of their impressive senior.[90] In this period Pulcheria presumably devoted their wealth and hers to philanthropy "for the least of these," and to construction of her church of St. Lawrence in the Pulcherianai, where she deposited some of the relics of St. Stephen that her sister-in-law had brought from Jerusalem.[91] In this way Pulcheria turned Eudocia's downfall to her own profit.

During these years also, the discordant Augusta Pulcheria joined with the archimandrite Manuel[92] and other dissidents in the suburbs to rally the faithful against a sharp departure in imperial ecclesiastical policy. That departure had profound roots in the varied attitudes and experiences of eastern Roman Christians. Conflict had erupted over a

89. Theoph. *a.m.* 5940 (p. 99 de Boor); Zon. 13. 23, p. 44a; Niceph. Call. *HE* 14. 47 (*PG*, CXLVI, 1224).

90. *PLRE*, II, 129, "Arcadia 1," 723, "Marina 1."

91. Theoph. *a.m.* 5945 (p. 106 de Boor); Georg. Mon., p. 610 de Boor; *Script. orig. Const.*, p. 239 Preger; Constantelos, *Philanthropy*, pp. 212, 224, 274 (Pulcheria's charitable projects); Theod. Anag.(?) 2. 64 (*PG*, LXXXVI: 1. 216); Marcell. com. *aa.* 439. 2, 453. 5 (*MGH: AA*, XI, 80, 85); *Script. orig. Const.*, p. 241 Preger (the St. Lawrence church; also *supra*, p. 137). Following Theod. Anag.(?), Ebersolt, *Sanctuaires*, pp. 87–88, assumed that Pulcheria began the church late in Theodosius' reign. The relevant passage appears in a chronological summary which concludes with excerpts of Theod. Anag. in Cod. Barocc. 142 (cf. Opitz, *RE*, VA [1934], 1876, "Theodoros Anagnostes"). Hansen has not included this summary in his edition, but I see no reason to doubt the information.

92. Manuel signed the deposition of Eutyches in 448 (*ACO*, II, 1, 1, 146, *infra*, p. 201); received letters of exhortation from Pope Leo in 449 and 450 (*ACO*, II, 4, 25–26, 31–32); and witnessed against Eutychian monks in session IV of the Council of Chalcedon (*ACO*, II, 1, 2, 114, 119). This evidence led E. Schwartz, *Der Prozess des Eutyches*, Sitzungsberichte der Bayerischen Akademie der Wissenschaften, Philosophisch-historische Abteilung, Jahrgang 1929, Heft 5 (Munich, 1929), p. 56 n. 1, followed (apparently) by Sellers, *Council*, pp. 34, 75–76, to theorize that Pulcheria came under the influence of Manuel. Since the empress was residing at the Hebdomon this theory is probably correct, despite the doubts of H. Bacht, "Die Rolle des orientalischen Mönchtums in den kirchenpolitischen Auseinandersetzungen um Chalkedon (431–519)," *Das Konzil von Chalkedon*, ed. Grillmeier and Bacht, II, 219.

side issue when Nestorius attacked the title *Theotokos,* but contro-
versialists on either side had devoted most of their energy to the
problem of how God joined man in Christ. Their differences on that
profounder question had been merely papered over in the union of
433. All agreed that Christ was both man and God, but the Antiochenes insisted on Christ's full humanity, the Alexandrians on his full
divinity. The Alexandrians argued that Jesus was God incarnate, the
manifestation of divine power to protect human beings from demons,
illness, and other terrors of everyday life and to secure them from
mortality. The Antiochenes, on the other hand, thought of a God-
man, of a person who could suffer in his humanity without implying
the monstrous doctrine of a passible deity, and whose perfection
could serve as a model for the perfectibility of his fellow men.[93]
Thus the Antiochene Christology combined Hebrew theology more
carefully with Greek metaphysics and moral philosophy, while Alexandria spoke a simple language which could more readily assuage the
anxieties of ordinary men and women.[94]

More important, however, were the persons who championed
the various points of view.[95] Bishop John died in 441/42, bequeathing
the episcopal throne of Antioch to his nephew Domnus, a man of no
great ability[96] who depended for advice on Theodoret of Cyrrhus,
now the principal Antiochene theologian. At the death of Proclus in
446, the see of the dynastic city went to the priest Flavian; like his
predecessor, he aimed to follow a moderate or independent line,
favoring neither the Antiochene nor the Alexandrian school.[97]

The Alexandrian school was represented by Dioscorus, a "violent" man who came from the Alexandrian opposition, from among
those who had rejected Cyril's accommodation with John of Antioch

93. For the opposing Christological positions see the works cited *supra*, p.
152, n. 27.

94. Frend, "Popular Religion," pp. 19–29.

95. On the successions of Flavian, Dioscorus, and Domnus to the great sees
and the dramatic change that resulted see Theod. Anag. *Epit.* 341–43 (p. 97
Hansen); Kidd, *History*, III, 278–81; E. Schwartz, "Über die Reichskonzilien von
Theodosius bis Justinian," *Zeitschrift der Savigny-Stiftung für Rechtsgeschichte,
Kanonische Abteilung*, 11 (1921), 230–31; A. Grillmeier and H. Bacht,
"Einleitung," *Das Konzil von Chalkedon*, ed. Grillmeier and Bacht, I, 248.

96. Cyrill. Scyth. *V. Euth.* 20 (*TU*, XLIX: 2, 33); Schwartz, *Prozess*, p. 53;
Bacht, "Rolle," p. 203.

97. Bauer, *Proklos*, p. 116, speaks of Proclus' "union theology"; Grillmeier,
Christ, p. 453, of the *via media* of Proclus and Flavian. On the latter cf. J. Liébaert,
DHGE, XVII (1971), 390–96, "Flavien 13."

and Theodoret. Immediately upon his election in 444, Dioscorus turned on the relatives and favorites of Cyril, persecuting them and extorting money which he used to win popularity by distributions of bread and wine among the people of Alexandria.[98] With such a man in the ring, the old struggle among the major sees was bound to break out again, and, indeed, in the spring of 448 Dioscorus revealed both his policy and his ruthlessness. He wrote twice to Domnus demanding the condemnation and deposition of Theodoret,[99] and agents of Dioscorus probably persuaded dissident bishops in the province of Osrhoene to seek support in Constantinople for their efforts to unseat their metropolitan, the Antiochene partisan Ibas of Edessa.[100]

In Constantinople the first year or so of Flavian's episcopacy apparently passed without serious incident. But early in 448, about two months before Dioscorus began to intervene openly in Antioch, a remarkable imperial letter came from the court.[101] In it Theodosius in effect set aside the agreement of 433 as the foundation of doctrinal unity, thus obtruding the imperial power into the dogmatic sphere, and he also interfered in church discipline by ordering the removal of the bishop of Tyre. The emperor had been surprised to find the former Count Irenaeus occupying that see. In contravention of an imperial sentence, the friend of Nestorius had not only escaped exile but—"I know not how," declared Theodosius—had become a prince of the church.[102] The emperor also struck the new Nestorianizing trend at its source. While Dioscorus of Alexandria was demanding that Domnus of Antioch discipline his theologian Theodoret, the latter received a peremptory command from Zeno, *magister militum per Orientem,* not to leave his own see because his activities in Antioch were causing confusion among the faithful.[103]

Constantinople was obviously working in concert with Alexandria, and the "violence" of Dioscorus had now become state policy.

98. *ACO*, II, 1, 2, 20–22; Liberat. *Brev.* 10 (*ACO*, II, 5, 113); Theod. Anag. *Epit.* 342 (p. 97 Hansen): ἄγριος . . . τις; Sellers, *Council*, p. 30; N. Charlier, *DHGE*, XIV (1960), 508–14, "Dioscore 3."

99. *Akt. ephes.* 449, pp. 133–39, 141–43 = *Akten der ephesinischen Synode vom Jahre 449*, ed. J. Flemming with trans. by G. Hoffmann, Abhandlungen der Königlichen Gesellschaft der Wissenschaften zu Göttingen, Philologisch-historische Klasse, n.s. XV, no. 1 (Berlin, 1917); Thdt. *Ep.* 83 (II, 204–19 Azema); Schwartz, *Prozess*, pp. 58–60; Sellers, *Council*, pp. 42–44, 46–47.

100. Schwartz, *Prozess*, p. 62.

101. *ACO*, I, 1, 4, 66; *CI* 1. 1. 3.

102. Cf. *supra*, p. 182.

103. Thdt. *Epp.* 79–81 (II, 182–99 Azema); Schwartz in *ACO*, I, 4, xii.

His agent at court was not, however, the bishop of Constantinople but the "bishop of bishops," Eutyches. An aging archimandrite and priest, this man had achieved many years of ascetic confinement and emerged after the death of Dalmatius as a leader of the monastic communities in and near the dynastic city.[104] The man's purity inspired the emperor's respect, but Eutyches had an even stronger connection, for it was he who had received Chrysaphius fresh from the baptismal waters. As the eunuch's "god-parent"[105] Eutyches advised the emperor's powerful minister. Long an ardent supporter of Alexandria—one of those, in fact, who had joined Dalmatius in defiance of Nestorius[106]—Eutyches was a natural ally of Dioscorus, and the radical new Alexandrian policy of the eastern court should be laid at his feet.

Pulcheria meanwhile lived on the fringes of Constantinopolitan court intrigue, no doubt developing her own views on the emerging struggle, instructed by the holy men of the suburban monasteries. The virgin empress prayed to Mary, but if she was a child of her age she prayed more fervently to Christ, and like her contemporaries she required an Alexandrian Christ whose power could protect her. On the other hand, she must have shuddered like her brother when she heard God blasphemed in her presence, as if the Divine could be born and die. Dogmatics did count in Pulcheria's thinking.

Nevertheless, personal interest and political instinct probably contributed as much as theological speculation to the new orthodoxy the empress now helped to impose on the Roman world. Pulcheria had long since adopted the 433 Formula of Union as the key to the Christological riddle: "For there has been a union of two natures; wherefore we confess one Christ, one Son, one Lord."[107] The empress, who had guided efforts to have this formula accepted, took credit for the union achieved, a union that represented another victory of her sacral *basileia*. Attacks on that union thus struck Pulcheria personally.

104. Nest. *Heracl.*, p. 294 Nau. On Eutyches see Bacht, "Rolle," pp. 206–9; Dagron, "Moines," p. 270; A. van Roey, *DHGE*, XVI (1967), 87–91, "Eutychès."

105. Liberat. *Brev.* 11 (*ACO*, II, 5, 114); more generally Nest. *Heracl.*, p. 295 Nau; *Coll. Avell.* 99. 5 (*CSEL*, XXXV: 1, 441).

106. *ACO*, I, 4, 223; II, 1, 1, 90. 155, 91. 157, 130. 417; *supra*, p. 169.

107. The formula was of Antiochene origin, but Cyril accepted it in 433 in his famous epistle *Laetentur coeli* to John of Antioch: *ACO*, I, 1, 4, 17 = II, 1, 1, 109, *supra*, p. 181; see Sellers, *Council*, pp. 16–20; and Grillmeier, *Christ*, pp. 430–32, for the genesis of the formula and its importance in the final Chalcedonian definition; and E. Caspar, *Geschichte des Papsttums von den Anfängen bis zur Höhe der Weltherrschaft*, I (Tübingen, 1930), p. 502, on Pulcheria's commitment to it.

Moreover, those who now fought resurgent Nestorianism were formidable precisely because they had the backing of Chrysaphius, the very person who had forced Pulcheria into retreat at the Hebdomon. "Ludens in orbe terrarum . . . Deus!" declares a prominent Roman Catholic scholar:[108] the nemesis of Nestorius would destroy his worst enemies as well. Nothing could demonstrate more clearly how the personal rancor and predilections of powerful men and women sometimes cause profound shifts in the theoretical underpinnings of society.

Thus from the first the affair of Eutyches involved high politics and the disharmony between Pulcheria and her brother. The man who stepped forth against the archimandrite was the same Eusebius who had opened the assault on Nestorius two decades before; he had since left the ranks of the *scholastici* to become bishop of Dorylaeum in Phrygia Salutaris, a suffragan see of the bishop of Constantinople. On September 8, 448, Eusebius, a man of such zeal that "to him even fire seems cool," accused Eutyches of heresy before a local synod in Constantinople.[109] No explicit evidence connects this move with Pulcheria, but all must have realized that if the reputation of Eutyches were destroyed Chrysaphius' credit with the emperor would be damaged, and he might even be brought down.

On November 12 Bishop Flavian opened the "trial" of Eutyches.[110] The emperor took the monk's side. An escort of soldiers protected Eutyches as he entered the episcopal palace, demonstrating by their presence that the government stood with the defendant.[111] Theodosius appointed the *patricius* and former prefect Florentius, "a trustworthy man of proven orthodoxy," to see that the bishops followed the proper trial form.[112] Even so, the result could not be in doubt. Eutyches refused to accept the words "two natures" required

108. Goubert, "Rôle," p. 304.
109. *ACO*, II, 1, 1, 100–101. 225, 230; cf. p. 131. 419 for Flavian's description of Eusebius and *supra*, p. 155, for his attack on Nestorius.
110. Schwartz, *Prozess*, is the standard treatment. He includes the relevant texts: pp. 11–49.
111. *ACO*, II, 1, 1, 137–38. 463–64.
112. *Ibid.* 468. Schwartz, *Prozess*, pp. 81–82, 85–86, develops the thesis that Florentius' mission was to secure the condemnation of Eutyches under conditions that would allow Dioscorus to intervene later and destroy his enemies while overturning their verdict. Bacht, "Rolle," p. 216, expresses justified reservations about this "wohl zu geistvolle Hypothese." The *Gesta de nomine Acaci* in *Coll. Avell.* 99. 5. (*CSEL*, XXXV: 1, 441) indicate that Florentius accepted the mission reluctantly and that his conduct of the trial displeased Theodosius: "offenditur imperator." Cf. *PLRE*, II, 478–80, "Fl. Florentius 7."

by the Formula of Union, so on November 22 all bishops present subscribed to his excommunication and deposition. Surprisingly, twenty-three archimandrites of Constantinople and its suburbs also signed the sentence,[113] demonstrating that these equally potent troops stood with their bishop, as they usually did not in such crises, and with Pulcheria. The empress had allied herself with a powerful bloc of those among whom she had been living.

Despite the monks' attitude, the emperor's faith in Chrysaphius and Eutyches remained unshaken. On March 30, 449, an imperial letter convened another general council, for August in Ephesus, to continue and complete the earlier council there.[114] As in 430–31, Theodosius once again committed himself in advance—though his commitment had undergone a complete reversal, and his orders now were "to extirpate every devilish root, to expel from the holy churches those who favor and further the impious blasphemy of Nestorius."[115] Dioscorus received the presidency,[116] while the emperor forbade Theodoret, the ablest theologian and politician of the Antiochenes, to leave Cyrrhus.[117]

On August 8 about one hundred and fifty bishops assembled once again in the famous Mary church.[118] Ignoring the Formula of Union, they restored Eutyches, then deposed both Eusebius of Dorylaeum and Flavian of Constantinople, in effect for adding the Formula to the definition of Ephesus.[119] Counts Elpidius and Eulogius, sent by Theodosius to create order, introduced troops to force the reluctant.[120] Even the hapless Domnus approved the condemnation of

113. *ACO*, II, 1, 1, 145–47. 552. Some signed under episcopal duress, according to Eutyches himself: *ACO*, II, 4, 144.

114. *ACO*, II, 1, 1, 68–69. 24. Theodosius does not state why he again chose Ephesus, but see *Akt. ephes. 449*, pp. 160–62 Flemming-Hoffmann. On Ephesus II see the accounts in Kidd, *History*, III, 301–7; G. Bardy, "Le «brigandage» d'Ephèse et le concile de Chalcédoine," *Histoire de l'église*, ed. Fliche and Martin, IV, 220–24; Sellers, *Council*, pp. 70–87; Bacht, "Rolle," pp. 226–31; Honigmann, "Juvenal," pp. 233–37; and esp. J. Liébaert, *DHGE*, XV (1963), 561–74, "Ephèse (concile d')," 431."

115. *ACO*, II, 1, 1, 74. 51.

116. *Ibid.*, 74. 52.

117. *Ibid.*, 69. 24, 74. 52.

118. *Ibid.*, 77. 68; *Akt. ephes. 449*, p. 161 Flemming-Hoffmann.

119. *ACO*, II, 1, 1, 112. 261, 182–86. 883–84, 191–95. 962–1067; Sellers, *Council*, pp. 79–80.

120. *ACO*, II, 1, 1, 75–76. 60, 88. 134, 179–81. 851–62; cf. 72. 49 (Elpidius and Eulogius); also *ACO*, II, 2, 78; Liberat. *Brev.* 12 (*ACO*, II, 5, 118); Nest. *Heracl.*, pp. 308, 316 Nau.

Flavian and Eusebius, only to be deposed himself in a later session, along with Theodoret, Ibas of Edessa, and others of their school.[121] "Seduced by Chrysaphius," Theodosius issued another letter, confirming Ephesus II and commissioning Dioscorus as imperial agent to secure signatures of approval from bishops everywhere and to supervise the burning of heretical works such as those of Nestorius and Theodoret.[122] A few weeks later Flavian died, apparently from rough treatment on his way to exile,[123] while Domnus returned to the quiet of the monastic life.[124] Aided by a eunuch and an aged monk, Dioscorus had outdone Cyril, bringing down both of Alexandria's rival sees.

Supporters of the Formula of Union at first managed only "a feeble response."[125] When he found that he too would be a victim, Flavian objected "I beg you," but the Roman deacon Hilary interjected a more significant *contradicitur*.[126] Hilary was one of three legates at the council representing Pope Leo the Great (440–61).[127] Leo had been among those to whom Eutyches appealed after his trial and condemnation;[128] but when Leo examined the trial transcript,[129] he agreed with the sentence and in his celebrated *Tome*, addressed to Flavian on June 13, 449, announced to the world that the see of Peter, in which resided the full authority Christ had given to the Prince of the Apostles, would send legates to Ephesus to confirm the reality of two natures in Christ.[130]

Leo had no legions, however, and Hilary could accomplish nothing, so Leo's other initiatives for the Formula of Union were of greater consequence. On the same day he sent the *Tome* (June 13),

121. These depositions took place during the second session on August 22; see *Akt. ephes. 449*, pp. 7–151 Flemming-Hoffmann; *Nest. Heracl.*, pp. 304–5 Nau; Liberat. *Brev.* 12 (*ACO*, II, 5, 117–18); *Coll. Avell.* 99. 9 (*CSEL*, XXXV: 1, 443).

122. *Akt. ephes. 449*, pp. 150–54 Flemming-Hoffmann; *ACO*, II, 3, 2, 88–89, 105–6.

123. *Coll. Avell.* 99. 9 (*CSEL*, XXXV: 1, 443); Marcell. com. *a.* 449. 2 (*MGH: AA*, XI, 83); H. Chadwick, "The Exile and Death of Flavian of Constantinople," *JThS* n.s. 6 (1955), 17–34. Cf. *infra*, n. 145, for Chadwick's theory that Pulcheria conspired in the murder of Flavian.

124. Cyrill. Scyth. *V. Euth.* 20 (*TU*, XLIX: 2, 33).

125. Honigmann, "Juvenal," p. 236, citing *Akt. ephes. 449*, pp. 104, 122 Flemming-Hoffmann.

126. *ACO*, II, 1, 1, 191. 963–64.

127. On him T. Jalland, *The Life and Times of St. Leo the Great* (London, 1941).

128. *ACO*, II, 1, 1, 175. 819; 2, 1, 33–34. 6; 4, 144–45. 108.

129. *Ibid.*, pp. 9. 6 [Leo *Ep.* 27], 17. 4 [*Ep.* 36], also 2, 1, 24.

130. *Ibid.*, pp. 24–33 [*Ep.* 28].

Leo dispatched a letter to the archimandrites of Constantinople, hoping to confirm support for Flavian among those who had subscribed to the condemnation of Eutyches.[131] Another letter went to Pulcheria.[132] Her reputation, Leo explained, had invited him to address her:

We have proof from many examples that God has established a great defense of His church in Your Clemency, and if the labors of priests have achieved anything in our time against the enemies of universal truth, it goes to your glory. For as you have learned from the Holy Spirit to do, you subordinate your potency in everything to Him by whose protection you reign.

Leo then mentioned Eutyches, urging Pulcheria to add to her glory by doing away with his erroneous teaching, and continued with a detailed exposition of orthodoxy, explaining that even as Nestorius erred in denying the divinity of Mary's child, so Eutyches missed the mark in denying Christ's human nature. (The discussion was perhaps more technical than was normal for a theologian addressing a woman.)[133] In conclusion, Leo declared his full confidence in the legates he had sent to the eastern court, and his hope that Pulcheria would labor "as is habitual for Your Piety" that the doctrine of Eutyches might not win acceptance.

This letter marked the appearance of an alliance between Leo and Pulcheria, an arrangement which bore fruit and which has earned for Pulcheria, in the words of a prominent scholar, the distinction of "une 'Jeanne d'Arc' de la papauté."[134] The origins of this alliance are obscure. To judge from Leo's epistle of June 13th, the fame of Pulcheria's intervention against Nestorius had reached the West, and her reputation alone may have been enough to suggest that she would serve Rome as she had Alexandria two decades earlier. Leo did, however, have connections in the East. He also corresponded again with the archimandrites of Constantinople,[135] and with Bishop Julian of Coös,[136] who had attended the "trial" of Eutyches, signed the con-

---

131. *Ibid.*, 4. 11–12 [*Ep.* 32]; cf. Bacht, "Rolle," pp. 226–27.

132. *Ibid.*, pp. 12–15 [*Ep.* 31]; cf. 10–11 [*Ep.* 30], which Schwartz (*ibid.*, 4, xxi–xxii) proves to be a later, abbreviated version of *Ep.* 31.

133. Schwartz, *Prozess*, p. 92. Leo slips near the end of his letter when he says that women too can concern themselves in the case of Eutyches because the Apostles' Creed sufficiently refutes him—and even women can comprehend the Apostles' Creed.

134. Goubert, "Rôle," p. 321.

135. *ACO*, II, 4, 25–26. 24 [Leo *Ep.* 51].

136. *Ibid.*, 6–8. 5 [*Ep.* 35], 16–17. 13 [*Ep.* 34], 23. 22 [*Ep.* 48].

demnation, and then remained in Constantinople in close touch with the political situation there.[137] This man may well have informed Leo of Pulcheria's position and encouraged him to cultivate her support.

When Leo learned of the outcome of Ephesus II, and that his first letter had not even reached Pulcheria, he addressed her again on October 13, 449.[138] The pope announced his rejection of Ephesus II and proposed a new council to meet in Italy, asking Pulcheria to plead with Theodosius to this effect. She was herself "commissioned" for this purpose "as a special legate of the Blessed Apostle Peter [sibi specialiter a beatissimo Petro apostolo legatione commissa]." Apparently Leo had solid reasons for thinking Pulcheria would intervene. About October, 449, Deacon Hilary also addressed Pulcheria, apologizing for his failure to visit Constantinople and to deliver the pope's missive. Indeed, he had barely escaped the violence of Dioscorus and returned safely to Rome. He could only express the hope that despite a temporary setback Pulcheria "might not now abandon what she had willingly undertaken [in quibus libenter fecit initium, relinquere non debet], but might preserve it with pious zeal and purpose steadfast in the faith." These words hint at a Pulcherian intervention against Eutychianism, most likely in the initial attack of Eusebius of Dorylaeum.[139]

Again Pope Leo and his supporters were disappointed. For several months after the letters of October, 449, they received no response from the East, perhaps because Leo's letters failed once again to reach their destination.[140] In his *Bazaar of Heracleides* Nestorius blamed Pulcheria for being unwilling to support Flavian or "to show her power in anything in internal affairs,"[141] but Nestorius was far away in exile and harbored resentment. In reality, Pulcheria was unable to act effectively because her enemy Chrysaphius still controlled the emperor, and Chrysaphius backed Eutyches. Hoping to counteract the eunuch's power, Leo persuaded Valentinian III, his consort, Licinia Eudoxia, and his mother, Galla Placidia, early in 450 to write to the eastern emperor on behalf of Flavian and of Leo's theological position.[142] Galla Placidia also wrote to her niece Pulcheria, asking

137. Schwartz, *Prozess*, p. 92; Jalland, *Life*, pp. 229–30.
138. *ACO*, II, 4, 23–25. 23 [*Ep.* 45].
139. *Ibid.*, pp. 27–28. 26 [*Ep.* 46]. Schwartz, *Prozess*, p. 93, suggests, to the contrary, that Pulcheria brought Flavian, Julian, and the archimandrites into communication with Leo.
140. *ACO*, II, 4, 28. 27 [Leo *Ep.* 61]; Jalland, *Life*, p. 268 n. 28.
141. Nest. *Heracl.*, p. 300 Nau.
142. *ACO*, II, 1, 1, 5–6. 2–4.

her to take action.[143] According to a reliable source,[144] Chrysaphius dictated the responses. In letters to his relatives addressed in early or mid-March, 450, Theodosius declared the case closed: truth had been vindicated and Flavian suitably punished.[145] At about the same time, Leo received his first answer from Pulcheria. It apparently declared her support for his cause but offered little immediate hope that the eastern court would change its policy.[146]

It was shortly after this that extraneous forces again brought a decisive shift in Theodosian ecclesiastical policy. Like Eutropius four decades earlier, the eunuch Chrysaphius had provoked opposition among the great men. Their propaganda attacked him as an avaricious creature who permitted the acquisition of high office through bribery.[147] But Chrysaphius had also brought some of these great men to his side, including the powerful Nomos,[148] who as master of offices shared the eunuch's ascendancy over Theodosius and supported his policies.

One policy of Chrysaphius that appealed to men like Nomos was his effort to bridle the general Flavius Ardaburius Aspar. Son of Ardaburius, grandson of Plinta, and chief, therefore, of a formidable Alanic and German military dynasty, this man held a high command position as a *magister militum praesentalis*.[149] The government needed

143. *Ibid.*, pp. 49–50. 14. Oost, *Placidia*, p. 289 n. 131, believes that the imperial personages composed these letters themselves.

144. Theod. Anag. *Epit.* 350 (p. 99 Hansen).

145. *ACO*, II, 1, 1, 7–8. 5–7. These responses, which provide the last solid evidence that Chrysaphius was in power, unfortunately do not have dates. *ACO*, II, 1, 1, 5. 2, one of the letters to which they respond, was dispatched to the East after February 22 (Jalland, *Life*, pp. 268–69), so presumably Theodosius sent the responses dictated by Chrysaphius about mid-March at the earliest. Thus we acquit Pulcheria of Chadwick's charge (*supra*, n. 123) that she ordered Flavian murdered, because by Chadwick's own admission ("Exile," pp. 26, 31–34) the bishop died in February at the latest.

146. Pulcheria's letter has not been preserved, but Leo thanks her for it in *ACO*, II, 4, 29. 28 [*Ep.* 60] dated March 17, 450.

147. Theod. Anag. *Epit.* 354 (p. 100 Hansen); Marcell. com. *a.* 450. 3 (*MGH: AA*, XI, 83); Joh. Ant. frg. 191 (*FHG*, IV, 612); cf. *supra*, p. 62, for similar charges leveled against Eutropius.

148. W. Ensslin, *RE*, XVII (1937), 845–46, "Nomos 1"; *PLRE*, II, 785–86, "Nomus 1." For the man's power and relationship with Chrysaphius see Prisc. frg. 13 (*FHG*, IV, 97); Thdt. *Ep.* 110 (III, 40 Azema); *ACO*, II, 1, 2, 20–22; and esp. *NTh* 24 with Jones, *Later Roman Empire*, I, 203, 344, 369; and Demandt, *RE*, suppl. XII (1970), 758–59, "Magister Militum," on his successful efforts to exalt his office at the expense of the *magistri militum*.

149. O. Seeck, *RE*, II (1896), 607–10, "Ardabur 2"; *PLRE*, II, 164–69, "Fl. Ardabur Aspar"; Demandt, *RE*, suppl. XII (1970), 748–51, "Magister Militum"; *supra*, pp. 101–102.

the troops at his disposal because in the last decade of the reign of Theodosius II three powerful enemies, the Persians under Yazdgard II (438–57), the Vandal kingdom of Gaiseric, and especially the Hun empire of Attila, simultaneously threatened the eastern Empire.[150] Still, Chrysaphius had to keep him in check if he and his civilian colleagues wished to control the government. Caught between two necessities, the eunuch demonstrated the power of improvisation, calling in the Isaurians, a half-civilized and warlike mountain people of southeastern Asia Minor.[151] It was their chieftain Flavius Zeno who defended Constantinople from Attila's onslaught in 447.[152] Zeno received the consulship as a reward and as confirmation of his place in Chrysaphius' defensive plans, and in the next years he held the position of *magister militum per Orientem,*[153] while the power of Aspar declined.

Innovation, however, and even statesmanship could not save a eunuch. Zeno apparently turned on his backer soon after he realized that Theodosius depended on Isaurian arms. In the summer of 449 he embarrassed Chrysaphius acutely by carrying off a wealthy woman whom the eunuch had promised to one of Attila's associates and marrying her instead to one of his own Isaurian friends. When Theodosius ordered the woman's estates confiscated, making her less attractive as a bride, Zeno blamed Chrysaphius and demanded that the emperor deliver him over for punishment. Theodosius naturally refused to cooperate, so the general prepared to revolt, it was alleged, and to restore paganism—for Zeno and many of his following adhered to the ancient religion.

The government took this threat so seriously that it readied powerful land and naval forces to strike down the rebel, but these

150. Stein, *Histoire*, I, 291–93; Maenchen-Helfen, *Huns*, pp. 108–25; Thompson, "Foreign Policies," pp. 58–75 (cf. *supra*, Chap. 4, n. 81).

151. Stein, *Histoire*, I, 4, 64, 141–42, 238, 291; E. W. Brooks, "The Emperor Zenon and the Isaurians," *EHR* 8 (1893), 209–38, esp. 211 on the character of the Isaurians.

152. Prisc. frg. 8 (*FHG*, IV, 94). On this Zeno (not to be confused with the later emperor of the same name) see Demandt, *RE*, suppl. XII (1970) 742–43, 754, "Magister Militum"; *PLRE*, II, 1199–1200, "Fl. Zenon 6"; and esp. E. A. Thompson, "The Isaurians under Theodosius II," *Hermathena* 68 (1946), 18–31.

153. Prisc. frg. 8 (*FHG*, IV, 94); Damasc. *V. Isid.* frg. 303 Zintzen; *Akt. ephes.* 449, p. 17 Flemming-Hoffmann; Thdt. *Ep.* 71, and cf. 65 (II, 154–56, 144–46 Azema); Demandt, *RE*, suppl. XII (1970), 742–43, "Magister Militum" (Zeno *magister militum per Orientem*, securely dated 447). On the decline in Aspar's power see Prisc. frg. 8 (*FHG*, IV, 94–95) with Thompson, "Isaurians," p. 22, and *idem*, *A History of Attila and the Huns* (Oxford, 1948), pp. 98, 102, 219–20.

forces never moved against the enemy, and therefore the "revolt" of
Zeno looks suspiciously like a simple demand that the emperor dismiss Chrysaphius.[154] The allegations against him recall those against
Paulinus and Cyrus, who had fallen by the same hand that now
threatened Zeno. Although no source suggests it, Pulcheria may have
intervened also, persuading her brother that the faith of Eutyches and
Chrysaphius was wrong and dangerous. Angered in addition by the
violence done to Flavian, Theodosius ordered the wealth of Chrysaphius confiscated and the eunuch himself exiled to an island. At once
Pulcheria returned to assist her brother in governing the Empire.[155]

The fall of Chrysaphius apparently occurred between March and
early July of 450.[156] So far as is known, it did not bring a sudden
reversal in the ecclesiastical situation, but even so, the return of
Pulcheria to her brother's side proved to be crucial. It gave the
empress time to reinforce her position with military backing. The
great general Aspar, whom Chrysaphius had declined to recall despite
the "revolt" of Zeno, returned to favor soon after the eunuch's fall,[157]
and Pulcheria may well have sponsored him. On the barbarian question she had long since embraced the practical approach of her grandfather Theodosius the Great. It was she, of course, who had permitted
the promotion of the Goth Plinta in 419, thus initiating the ascendancy
of Aspar's military dynasty. By mid-July of 450 a new regime had
formed in Constantinople, one with a strong Pulcherian stamp and
with the might to overwhelm any opposition.

154. Prisc. frgg. 8, 12–14 (*FHG*, IV, 93–94, 96–98); Joh. Ant. frg. 199. 1
(*FHG*, IV, 613); Damasc. *V. Isid.* frg. 303 Zintzen; *ROC*, XIX, 127 (Nau's extracts
from the *Life* of Barsauma). Stein, *Histoire*, I, 298, is properly cautious regarding
Zeno's alleged plans; Joh. Ant. (from Prisc.) indicates that not much came of it: τὴν
παρασκευὴν ἀνεβάλετο [*sc.* Theodosius].

155. Theoph. *a.m.* 5942 (pp. 101–2 de Boor); Niceph. Call. *HE* 14. 49 (*PG*,
CXLVI, 1232); Zon. 13. 23, p. 44a. These sources confuse chronology and events
hopelessly, but it is nonetheless likely that Theodosius exiled Chrysaphius and that
Pulcheria returned to power before the emperor's death. Contrast Seeck, *Geschichte*,
VI, 269; Stein, *Histoire*, I, 298, 570 n. 68; Goubert, "Rôle," pp. 315, 318.

156. See n. 145 *supra* for the *terminus post quem*. No *terminus ante quem*
can be established other than the death of Theodosius, but it is likely that Chrysaphius had fallen by early summer, when Aspar was again influential (next note). On
the other hand, letters Leo dispatched to Theodosius, Pulcheria, and the archimandrites of Constantinople on July 16 reveal no knowledge of any reversal in the
East: *ACO*, II, 4, 29–32 [*Epp.* 69–71].

157. Prisc. frg. 14 (*FHG*, IV, 98) reports that about early summer of 450
Theodosius(!) married the daughter of Plinta to Attila's Latin secretary Constantius
in place of the girl Zeno had stolen (*supra*, p. 206; cf. Thompson, *Attila*, p. 123,
for the date). The woman was, of course, a relative of Aspar, and her availability thus
depended on him and reflected his strong position at court.

On July 26, 450, the emperor Theodosius II, while hunting near Constantinople, injured his spine in a fall from horseback, and two days later he was dead.[158] For nearly a month thereafter Pulcheria reigned alone at Constantinople. None of her sovereign acts has been recorded, but presumably she led the people of the dynastic city in a public funeral for her brother, and she did take revenge on the fallen Chrysaphius, having him handed over to the son of a victim for execution.[159] Pulcheria was a child of the age, sharing its savagery as well as its enthusiasm for the religious life.

Then, since the Romans could not abide a woman reigning alone, the empress took a husband, one with significant connections. Aspar himself already had a wife;[160] moreover, his barbarian race excluded him from participation in the *basileia*. But a man of suitable age and character emerged from among the great general's close associates (*domestici*), a tribune named Marcian of Illyrian or Thracian origin.[161] Marcian was a man of little substance, with no ancient aristocratic or imperial blood. He was a Roman, however, and thus the bond of *kedeia* at once communicated eligibility for *basileia*. Soon after the wedding, on November 25, 450, Pulcheria herself conferred upon Marcian the imperial diadem and *paludamentum,* and the troops acclaimed him Augustus at the Hebdomon.[162] Although not without precedent,[163] coronation by an Augusta was highly unusual and

158. Theod. Anag. *Epit.* 353 (p. 100 Hansen), and for the date *idem*(?) in *PG*, LXXXVI: 1, 214–15 (cf. *supra*, n. 91); also Marcell. com. *a.* 450. 1 (*MGH: AA*, XI, 83); Evagr. 2. 1; Joh. Mal. 14 (pp. 366–67 Bonn); Cedren., pp. 602–3 Bonn; *Chron. pasch. a.* 450 (pp. 589–90 Bonn); Theoph. *a.m.* 5942 (p. 103 de Boor); Zon. 13. 24, p. 45c-d; Niceph. Call. *HE* 14. 58 (*PG*, CXLVI, 1271–72) on the death of Theodosius and the accession of Marcian. Reports that Theodosius had arranged the succession of Marcian before his death are, of course, not to be trusted.

159. Theod. Anag. *Epit.* 353 (p. 100 Hansen), where the position of the notice confirms (*contra* Joh. Mal. 14 [p. 368 Bonn]) that the execution of Chrysaphius came between the death of Theodosius and the accession of Marcian.

160. *PLRE*, II, 164–165, "Fl. Ardabur Aspar."

161. Procop. *B. Vand.* 1. 4. 7; Theoph. *a.m.* 5943 (p. 104 de Boor) (*domesticus*); *Chron. pasch. a.* 457 (p. 592 Bonn) (aged fifty-eight at accession); Theod. Anag. *Epit.* 354 (p. 100 Hansen) (Illyrian); Evagr. 2. 1 (Thracian); in general W. Ensslin, *RE*, XIV (1930), 1514–29, "Marcianus 34"; *PLRE*, II, 714–15, "Marcianus 8."

162. See esp. Theoph., Zon., and the *Chron. pasch.* cited *supra*, n. 158. On the question of who conferred the imperial insignia I follow W. Ensslin, "Zur Frage nach der ersten Kaiserkrönung durch den Patriarchen und zur Bedeutung dieses Aktes im Wahlzeremoniell," *BZ* 42 (1943–49), 101–15, 369–72, *contra* (e.g.) Treitinger, *Reichsidee*, p. 8 with n. 7.

163. In an emergency Constantine's daughter Constantia had created Vetranio Caesar in 350 to resist the usurper Magnentius: Philostorg. 3. 22; cf. 28, *supra*, Chap. 1, n. 90.

represented another case in which the eastern court assimilated an Augusta with her male counterparts, this time in the power to invest another with imperial dominion.

As a condition of his elevation, Marcian pledged to respect Pulcheria's vow of virginity.[164] No doubt he kept his pledge, but the marriage of a consecrated virgin was bound to raise eyebrows, especially when the virgin in question had based her claim to power in part on her celibate state. It is not surprising that Pulcheria's detractors contrived their own apple-of-discord romance to undermine her power and tarnish her reputation. In their version Theodosius presented the beautiful apple to Pulcheria, "the second Eve," and she sent it to her illicit lover, the young and handsome Marcian, whom she would shortly marry and raise to the *basileía*.[165]

In an effort to limit such adverse reaction, the court ordered its mints to strike a commemorative marriage solidus, perhaps for distribution at the wedding or at Marcian's subsequent coronation. On similar coins issued for the wedding of Valentinian III and Licinia Eudoxia (fig. 17), the emperor Theodosius had appeared as *Pronubus* between the bridal couple, drawing them together with his embrace to establish harmony in the marriage and, by extension, between the two imperial families thus joined in *kedeia*.[166] On the solidus of 450, however, the *Pronubus* is Christ, identified by a nimbus of cruciform type (fig. 18). He thus became the source of marriage harmony between Pulcheria, His own virgin "bride," and her new husband Marcian. This iconography declared that Christ Himself sponsored the union and that it therefore should not provoke shock or unjustified suspicions.[167] The solidi also emphasized that after two decades of conflict between Augustae and their male counterparts, Christ had at last restored harmony in the *basileía*.

The new rulers moved with deliberate haste to correct the ecclesiastical situation and restore harmony in the Empire as well. The new Augustus had little experience in dealing with bishops, but Pulcheria had engineered the defeat of Nestorius at Ephesus, had directed the

---

164. Evagr., Theoph., Zon. cited *supra*, n. 158.

165. F. Nau, "Histoire de Dioscore, Patriarch d'Alexandrie, écrit par son disciple Théopiste," *Journal asiatique* ser. 10, 1 (1901), 242–51; also Joh. Ruf. *Pler.* 3 (*PO*, VIII, 14–15); Mich. Syr. 8. 9, 10. 2, 14 (II, 36, 38, 122 Chabot).

166. E. Kantorowicz, "On the Golden Marriage Belt and the Marriage Rings of the Dumbarton Oaks Collection," *DOP* 14 (1960), 1–16, esp. 7–8.

167. H. Dressel, "Erwerbungen des Königlichen Münzcabinets in den Jahren 1890–97 (antike Münzen)," *Zeitschrift für Numismatik* 21 (1898), 249, suggests an interpretation along these lines.

Figure 17
Marriage Solidus of Valentinian III and Licinia Eudoxia,
minted Constantinople 437 (2X),
Dumbarton Oaks

Figure 18
Marriage Solidus of Marcian and Pulcheria,
minted Constantinople 450 (2X),
Glasgow, Hunterian Collection

Figure 19
Solidus of Pulcheria,
minted Constantinople 450–53 (2X),
Dumbarton Oaks

imperial effort to establish the Formula of Union, and had at least observed the unfolding Eutychian crisis at first hand. Thus it is reasonable to identify the new ecclesiastical policy of the autumn of 450 as Pulcheria's policy. Pope Leo acknowledged that it was indeed hers, in a letter he addressed to the empress on July 20, 451, when the outlines of the new policy and the identity of its initiators had become apparent to all. "I give thanks to God," Leo wrote,

when I see how you commit yourself to every concern of the universal church, so that whatever I think might contribute to justice and goodwill I confidently suggest to you, expecting that with Christ's help what has been accomplished faultlessly thus far through the zeal of Your Piety might be brought more swiftly to a welcome conclusion, most glorious Augusta.[168]

Leo's correspondence with other important personages bears out this assessment of the situation. He wrote to the monks, to Anatolius, the new bishop of Constantinople, to Julian of Coös, and of course to the emperor Marcian, always observing protocol and hoping to rally his supporters in the East.[169] But if he thought specific guidance desirable, that Eutyches be removed from Constantinople, for example, or that more care be devoted to reconciliation than to punishment, Leo made sure to bring his concern before Pulcheria.[170]

When Marcian appeared soon after his coronation in the Great Church of Constantinople, "the whole clergy, the monks, and the laity, a great crowd of them, all shouted forth, acclaiming the emperor and Pulcheria, demanding that the crimes of Dioscorus and Eutyches against Flavian be examined."[171] The scene resembled similar agitation on July 4–6, 431, and demonstrated that Pulcheria was able again to rally the dynastic city to her side and to act in concert with the sovereign Roman people.

Within a few months, on November 22, 450, the empress reported to Leo on the progress she had achieved. Her letter, which still exists,[172] reveals Pulcheria's conventional reverence for the great pope. "We received your epistle,"[173] she wrote, "with the reverence owed to every bishop." She assured Leo in typically pretentious court

168. *ACO*, II, 4, 50. 51 [Leo *Ep.* 95].
169. *Ibid.*, pp. 32–33, 38–45, 47–50 [*Epp.* 74, 75, 78, 80–83, 85, 86, 89–92, 94].
170. *Ibid.*, pp. 37–38, 43–44, 50–51 [*Epp.* 79, 84, 95].
171. Theod. Anag. *Epit.* 355 (p. 100 Hansen).
172. *ACO*, II, 3, 1, 18–19. 29 [Leo *Ep.* 77]; cf. *ACO*, II, 1, 1, 8. 8 [*Ep.* 76] for the date.
173. Pulcheria apparently refers to Leo's letter of July 16, *supra*, n. 156.

jargon that "I and my lord the most tranquil emperor my consort always have and do remain in the same faith, spurning all depravity, all pollution, and all evil." She was pleased to report that Anatolius, the new bishop of Constantinople, had willingly subscribed to Leo's *Tome;*[174] that by orders of the emperor the remains of Flavian had been brought back and deposited in the Apostles Church;[175] and that all bishops exiled for supporting Flavian could now return "by the force of an imperial pragmatic"[176] to await the judgment of a new general council restoring them to their sees. Pulcheria requested that Leo instruct the bishops of the Orient to gather for that council in a city to be designated by the emperor. In particular, the news that Anatolius had come over proved to Leo that a fresh wind blew in the eastern capital. This man had been an Alexandrian partisan, indeed, the spokesman (*apokrisiarios*) of Dioscorus in Constantinople, and had been installed "by violence" after the deposition of Flavian.[177] Even more striking was Pulcheria's request that Leo summon the Oriental bishops. With it she offered Leo a prerogative that had belonged to the emperor since the time of Constantine the Great.

Pulcheria's letter, however, marked Leo's apogee in the East, and his influence there soon began to decline. The pope first wished a council in Italy, and by the summer of 451, because he considered his *Tome* to be authoritative, no council at all.[178] But Pulcheria and Marcian, urged on by Theodoret and presumably by other eastern bishops, adhered to their plan of providing the Formula of Union with unassailable conciliar authority as a basis for harmony in the eastern Empire.[179] On May 23, 451, another imperial letter convened

174. Cf. Theod. Anag. *Epit.* 532 (p. 153 Hansen), reporting that Pulcheria had the *Tome* approved in a local synod at Constantinople under Anatolius' direction.

175. Cf. *ibid.* 357, 532 (pp. 100, 153) reporting that Pulcheria instructed Anatolius to restore Flavian's remains.

176. "Reverti robore pragmatici sui praecepit." Pulcheria stresses that, unlike the previous government, she and Marcian will proceed legally, leaving the final decision to the bishops. Cf. also *ACO*, II, 1, 1, 120. 337: ἡ σύνοδος μετὰ δικαιο-σύνης ἐπιτελεῖται; and Thdt. *Epp.* 139–41 (III, 142–52 Azema), in which Theo-doret asks the *patricius* Anatolius, Aspar, and Vincomalus, the master of offices, to thank Marcian "and the God-beloved and most pious Augusta" for his recall, and to urge upon them the project of a new general council.

177. Theod. Anag. *HE* frg. 2, *Epit.* 351 (p. 99 Hansen); Liberat. *Brev.* 13 (*ACO*, II, 5, 118); *ACO*, II, 4, 29. 29 [Leo *Ep.* 70]; cf. on Anatolius in general M. Jugie, *DHGE*, II (1914), 1497–1500, "Anatole."

178. *ACO*, II, 3, 1, 14. 19; 4, 29–31, 43, 47–50. 28–30, 41, 46, 48, 51 [*Epp.* 55, 60, 69, 70, 83, 89, 91, 95]; Jalland, *Life*, pp. 266–67; Sellers, *Council*, pp. 98–101.

179. See Pulcheria's own explanation for calling the council in *ACO*, II, 1, 1, 29. 15. She claims to have labored to arrange the council (πολλὴν ἐθέμεθα φρον-τίδα) and refers to the letter of convocation (next note) as τὸ ἡμέτερον θέσπισμα.

a general council.[180] Marcian ordered bishops from everywhere to meet at Nicaea on September 1 of the same year to complete the work begun there by the venerable council of Constantine the Great.[181]

In the summer and autumn of 451 Marcian found it necessary to take the field in person against a threatened Hun invasion.[182] Thus he apologized to the bishops who were gathering in Nicaea. Declaring that he would be unable to keep his promise to attend the council (as Constantine had done) if it were convened so far from Constantinople and the Illyrican provinces, Marcian asked them to come to Chalcedon, which lay directly across the Bosporus from the dynastic city.[183] Another reason for the transfer was a report that the Egyptian followers of Dioscorus planned to disrupt the council and that agitation had already begun. Since the emperor was absent, and because she knew well how to deal with the situation, Pulcheria herself issued an imperial letter to Strategius, the *consularis* (civil governor) of Bithynia.[184] He was to eject from Nicaea all turbulent clerics, monks, and lay persons who had no reason to be at the gathering council, and he should know, Pulcheria warned, "that if anyone of the other troublemakers turns up among those present, either before Our Serenity arrives or thereafter, you will be severely punished." Pulcheria did not act behind the scenes but took personal charge, as Sozomen had put it, "reaching excellent decisions and swiftly carrying them out with written instructions."[185]

On October 8, 451, about five hundred and twenty bishops gathered near Chalcedon in the basilica of St. Euphemia, a local martyr of the Diocletianic persecution. Pulcheria selected her martyr shrine because it was large enough to contain so numerous a gathering, but also because she trusted that this powerful female saint would protect the council and bring it to a salutary conclusion.[186] Pulcheria

180. *ACO*, II, 1, 1, 27–28. 13.
181. E. Schwartz, "Die Kaiserin Pulcheria auf der Synode von Chalkedon," *Festgabe für Adolf Jülicher* (Tübingen, 1927), pp. 205–6; R. Haacke, "Die kaiserliche Politik in den Auseinandersetzungen um Chalkedon (451–553)," *Das Konzil von Chalkedon*, ed. Grillmeier and Bacht, II, 104–5. For assimilation to Nicaea of 325 see esp. the acclamations quoted *infra*, pp. 215–16, and Tim. Ael. in *PO*, XIII, 205 (the Chalcedonians claimed exactly twice the bishops present at Nicaea).
182. Prisc. frg. 18 (*FHG*, IV, 99); Thompson, *Attila*, pp. 143–44.
183. *ACO*, II, 1, 1, 28–30. 14, 16.
184. *Ibid.*, p. 29. 15.
185. *Supra*, p. 97.
186. *ACO*, II, 1, 1, 55. 1; Evagr. 2. 3; A.M. Schneider, "Sankt Euphemia und das Konzil von Chalkedon," *Das Konzil von Chalkedon*, ed. Grillmeier and Bacht, I, 291–302. In *ACO*, II, 1, 3, 117. 21, the fathers of Chalcedon informed Leo that Euphemia had brought agreement out of confusion, confirming the votes of the

214 · *Theodosian Empresses*

gave Euphemia practical assistance by providing the council with a highly unusual presidency. Nineteen of the most prominent men in eastern Roman society, including the *magister militum praesentalis* Anatolius, the praetorian prefect, the city prefect, the master of offices, and others who had filled these offices in the past, sat before the bishops. They proposed which matters should be treated, guided discussions, and called for votes, according to instructions, presumably, from the imperial palace.[187]

With this display of prestige before them, there was little doubt how the fathers of Chalcedon would act. In sixteen sessions between October 8 and November 1, 451, they confirmed and wrote into the canons the ecclesiastical policy Pulcheria had adopted as her own.[188] They deposed Dioscorus and rehabilitated his victims. Despite the insistence of Leo that no credal statement was necessary beyond his *Tome*,[189] the fathers succeeded under imperial duress in producing a new definition to serve as the foundation of harmony, one that was essentially an expansion and explication of the Formula of Union.[190] Despite the spirited opposition of the Roman legates, the fathers also adopted their well-known Canon 28.[191] It gave to the see of Constantinople the privilege of consecrating metropolitans for Pontus, Asia, and Thrace, basing this privilege on the city's rank as "New Rome" among the cities of the Empire. With Pulcheria's support, Anatolius completed the work begun at Constantinople in the council of 381, elevating the see of the dynastic city to the first rank of the episcopacy.

During the council the assembled bishops repeatedly called out in unison their acclamations of the two Augusti, and stenographers

---

bishops, and had offered to Christ her bridegroom "the confession which she received from us and adopted as her own, through the agency of the most pious emperor and the Christ-loving empress."

187. For the full list of ἄρχοντες and σύγκλητος see *ACO*, II, 1, 1, 55–56. 2, and for the functioning of the presidents P. Batiffol, *Le siège apostolique (359–451)* (Paris, 1924), p. 537; and W. de Vries, "Die Struktur der Kirche gemäss dem Konzil von Chalkedon (451)," *OCP* 35 (1969), 73–78.

188. *ACO*, II, 1, 1, 55–3, 116; Kidd, *History*, III, 315–34; Bardy, "«Brigandage»," pp. 228–40; Sellers, *Council*, pp. 103–29; M. Goemans, "Chalkedon als 'Allgemeines Konzil,'" *Das Konzil von Chalkedon*, ed. Grillmeier and Bacht, I, 261–78.

189. *ACO*, II, 4, 51–52. 52 [Leo *Ep.* 93]; II, 1, 3, 95. 14, 99. 45.

190. *Supra*, n. 107.

191. T.O. Martin, "The Twenty-Eighth Canon of Chalcedon," *Das Konzil von Chalkedon*, ed. Grillmeier and Bacht, II, 433–58; Dagron, *Naissance*, pp. 477–82.

dutifully recorded these acclamations for inclusion in the official *acta*.[192] The bishops extolled Pulcheria for her firm stand in the past against heresy: "The Augusta cast out Nestorius! Many years to the orthodox one!" They registered their approval of the course that both Marcian and Pulcheria had now adopted: "The emperor believes thus! The Augusta believes thus! Thus we all believe!" And they expressed their obedience in the usual manner to the legitimate holders of *basileía*: "Many years to the emperor! Many years to the Augusta! Many years to the orthodox ones!" On at least two occasions the fathers of Chalcedon even reversed protocol, acclaiming the Augusta before her male counterpart: "Many years to the Augusta! Many years to the emperor!"[193] In this way, it appears, they officially approved the fact that despite tradition a woman had openly exercised a major political function, organizing and directing a general council to restore unity in the Empire.

Adulation of Pulcheria reached its peak on October 25, when the council formally adopted the new definition of faith and both the sovereigns appeared in person in the Church of St. Euphemia to accept the acclamations of the bishops.[194] For a woman to come before such a deliberative body was most unusual,[195] but it did not offend the fathers of Chalcedon. They saluted Marcian as "New Constantine, New Paul, New David," and praised Pulcheria enthusiastically because she had restored harmony:

Many years to the Augusta! You are the light of orthodoxy! Because of this there will be peace everywhere! Lord protect those who bring the light of peace, those who lighten the world!

Again they acclaimed her resistance to heresy, recognizing that it was traditional in her family:

God will protect her, for she inherited orthodoxy! God will guard the protectress of the faith, the ever-pious one! God will protect the pious one, the orthodox, she who was raised against the heretics! You have persecuted all heretics! You persecuted Nestorius and Eutyches!

192. *ACO*, II, 1, 1, 69. 31, 33, 70. 39, 111. 255, 143. 530; 2, 109. 11, 123–24. 12, 139. 3, 140. 5.
193. *ACO*, II, 1, 2, 124. 12, also 1, 70. 39; cf. Ensslin, *RE*, XXIII (1959), 1961, "Pulcheria 2."
194. *Coll. Avell.* 99. 11 (*CSEL*, XXXV: 1, 444); Schwartz, "Pulcheria auf der Synode," pp. 203–12.
195. Schwartz, "Pulcheria auf der Synode," p. 211.

And the fathers identified Pulcheria with the famous mother of Constantine the Great:

Marcian is the New Constantine, Pulcheria the New Helena! You have shown the faith of Helena! You have shown the zeal of Helena! Your life is the security of all! Your faith is the glory of the churches![196]

In these words the fathers insisted, in effect, that the council of Marcian and Pulcheria had introduced no innovations at all but had confirmed and renewed the work of Constantine's council of Nicaea. In their eyes this was no mean achievement but one that equalled the achievement of Constantine himself. Thus they acclaimed Marcian as the "New Constantine," a second founder of the Christian Empire, while for them Pulcheria revivified Helena, the perfect example of imperial womanhood.

No doubt the empress appreciated adulation that placed her in exalted company, but assimilation with Helena did not do justice to her work. Nor, in the end, did Leo's "Joan of Arc"—as a modern scholar has called her—prove a trustworthy instrument of papal authority. From the inception of the Eutychian crisis, this woman had acted more in the manner of her grandfather Theodosius, convinced that the Christological formula she had adopted was correct, and that to restore harmony she had to impose it on her subjects. For this reason she had returned from ascetic retreat and had married after her brother's death, that she might prolong her dynasty sufficiently and secure the necessary military backing. During the year of Chalcedon she directed preparations from the palace, and the council unfolded according to her plan. The fathers of Chalcedon admitted as much in the warmth of their acclamations, but they did not declare this to be Pulcheria's council or recognize in it the ultimate dynastic victory of the Theodosian house.

196. *ACO*, II, 1, 2, 155. 11; cf. 156. 13, 15, 157. 20.

CHAPTER SEVEN

From Dominion to Sainthood

The Augusta Eudocia broke with her husband and left him forever to dwell in the Holy Land, but she retained her imperial distinction. After 443 the sacral *basileia* of women thus made itself felt not only in the dynastic city but also in Palestine, where Christian pilgrims and monks had displaced other claimants to holy places, especially the Jews.[1] In the traditionalist spirit of her uncle Asclepiodotus, Eudocia respected Jewish claims.

Early in her permanent exile, members of the Jewish community in Palestine came to Eudocia requesting that she permit them to pray at the ruins of Solomon's Temple. According to the *Life of Barsauma*,[2] she granted that permission, so the Jews wrote to their co-religionists throughout the East, urging them to return at once for the Feast of Tabernacles, "because our kingdom will be restored at Jerusalem." The Diaspora responded enthusiastically, and many of the pious made their way to the Holy City. Eudocia had created a Zionist movement and an explosive situation. Far away in Euphratensis, the archimandrite Barsauma heard the news and set out at once with his rugged monks, arriving at Jerusalem in time for the first day of the Jewish feast. While Barsauma lurked in concealment, some of his monks confronted Jews praying at the Temple ruins and bludgeoned or stoned them to death.

"Eudocia had ordered that no harm befall the Jews," the *Life* reports, so this brutality outraged not only the Jewish pilgrims but also some Christian clerics and Roman soldiers of the Jerusalem garrison. Joining together, they appeared before the Augusta's palace at Bethlehem, honoring her with palm branches (as appropriate for an empress) and pleading that she punish these "robbers come from Mesopotamia, clad in the respectable garb of monks." Eudocia

1. Since Constantine, Jews had been permitted in Jerusalem only on the Day of Lamentation (9 Ab): Avi-Yonah, *Jews of Palestine*, pp. 165–66.
2. Nau, "Résumé," pp. 118–25, containing excerpts from the Syriac *Vita*.

ordered the soldiers to seize the guilty and cast them into prison, and that Barsauma's men face, without trial, death by cudgel or stoning, the same death they had inflicted on their victims.

By this time, however, word had spread in the Holy City that the monks were innocent, that no marks appeared on the corpses of the Jews, and that therefore divine judgment, not Barsauma's monks, had caused their deaths. Quickly "the Christians began to agitate." A huge mob of them, "the entire populace," surrounded Eudocia's palace, demanding that she allow the accused a normal trial. Some even threatened the empress herself: "She wishes to slay these Christians treacherously, so we will burn her and all those in her company." Eudocia wisely sent for the provincial governor, who came from Caesarea with his troops. Ignoring both the empress and the Jews, this magistrate instead asked Barsauma for an explanation. As the archimandrite began to speak, "thunder sounded from the bowels of the earth; roofs collapsed and colonnades fell apart; but no one died, and no building suffered complete ruin." At this point, presumably, the governor released the imprisoned monks. "The Cross has conquered," a herald shouted. "The Cross has conquered," responded the mob— "and the people's voice swelled and boomed like the roar of the breaking sea."

Replete as it is with reports of miracles, the *Life of Barsauma* nonetheless preserves an authentic glimpse, perhaps from eyewitnesses, of Eudocia's position in the Holy Land during the first years of her exile.[3] At odds with the reigning Augustus, in theory lacking his magisterial powers, this Augusta still reigned in a palace at Bethlehem and received there the petitions of her subjects, addressed with appropriate displays of adoration. She issued commands with sovereign assurance to both the soldiers and the people, expecting instant compliance and threatening death to those who would not obey. Stationed at Caesarea, the provincial capital, the governor who exercised the emperor's power did not interfere with the *basileía* of an empress until she invited him to do so. That invitation came when Eudocia, like other Christian Augusti, discovered that she could not rule from Bethlehem without the enthusiastic support of the Christian people and monks.

Eudocia had long since learned how to rally that support, and, fortunately, Theodosius had left intact not only her distinction, Au-

3. Contrast Honigmann, *Couvent*, pp. 17–18.

gusta, but also a vast personal fortune that included extensive land-holdings in Palestine.[4] During her Holy Land years Eudocia employed these tangible resources in typical imperial fashion. Emulating the works of Anthemius and Cyrus, she restored the walls of Jerusalem and added fortifications to encompass Mount Zion within the enceinte. She built an episcopal palace, shelters "too numerous to count" for pilgrims, the poor, and the aging, and especially churches in Jerusalem and its environs, decorating them lavishly with such objects as the enormous copper cross (three tons in weight) that she placed atop the Ascension Church. Benefactions to the monks, the clergy, and the needy brought the total of her expenditures to 20,480 pounds of minted gold.[5] She rebuilt on a grander scale the Church of St. Stephen which Cyril of Alexandria had dedicated in her presence (438), and claimed the alliance of saints by enclosing within its main altar a generous assortment of martyrs' bones.[6]

In this milieu of pilgrims and monks[7] the emperor's estranged wife might have surrounded herself with deaconesses and virgins, but she does not seem to have adopted the same kind of ascetic life as Olympias, Pulcheria, and her friend Melania the Younger. Not women but lesser male clerics appeared in her Jerusalem circle, men like the *chorepiscopus* (local bishop) Anastasius and Cosmas, a "guardian of the Cross" (*staurophylax*). Eudocia's patronage enabled her to place such men in convenient positions. She drew Gabriel and Chrysippus, brothers of Cosmas, from the monastic community of the famous archimandrite Euthymius and had them ordained priests of the Resurrection Church. Later she selected Gabriel to be archpriest of St. Stephen's.[8] These men did Eudocia's bidding in the Holy Land, much as the priest Severus and John the deacon had earlier in Constantinople—the two whom Theodosius had executed "because

4. Joh. Ruf. *Pler.* 20 (*PO*, VIII, 39); *V. vir. ap. monophys. celebr.*, *CSCO: SS*, XXV, 18; H. Vincent and F.-M. Abel, *Jérusalem, recherches de topographie, d'archéologie, et d'histoire*, II, fasc. 4 (Paris, 1926), p. 910.

5. Cyrill. Scyth. *V. Euth.* 35 (*TU*, XLIX: 2, 53); Vincent and Abel, *Jérusalem*, II: 4, 910–11; M. Avi-Yonah, "The Economics of Byzantine Palestine," *Israel Exploration Journal* 8 (1958), 44; Capizzi, "L'attività edilizia," pp. 128–29.

6. See Vincent and Abel, *Jérusalem*, II: 4, 743–804, for the church, *ibid.*, pp. 799–804, and *SEG*, VIII, 192, for the relics Eudocia assembled to dedicate its altar.

7. See esp. D.J. Chitty, *The Desert a City* (Oxford, 1966), pp. 82–100.

8. For these men and their association with Eudocia see Cyrill. Scyth. *V. Euth.* 16, 20, 22, 30, 35 (*TU*, XLIX: 2, 25, 32–33, 35, 47–49, 53–54).

they were her confidants." Also "confidants," presumably, were the "clerics" who had joined in accusing Barsauma's monks and thus in support of Eudocia's traditionalist Jewish policy. Significantly, the Jerusalem circle also shared an enthusiasm for learning. Eudocia attended the lectures of Orion, professor of literature (*grammaticus*) in nearby Caesarea Maritima, and in honor of their association Orion dedicated a collection of wise sayings to her.[9] The cleric Gabriel had mastered several languages. Chrysippus in particular left "many writings worth reading." And their brother Cosmas appeared among those who produced the *Homerocentones,* along with Optimus "the philosopher," a man named Simplicius, and Eudocia herself.[10]

Some of these *Homerocentones,* or "Homeric stitchings," survive. They are brief poems of fifteen to fifty hexameters each, relating simple biblical stories in verses lifted intact from the *Iliad* and *Odyssey.*[11] The effect is incongruous, to say the least. In the reader's mind God the Father becomes the philandering Zeus, Jesus a wily Odysseus. When the angel arrives to announce the approaching incarnation, he finds not the Blessed Virgin but Queen Arete of the Phaeacians

> sitting by the fireside with her attendant women
> turning sea-purple yarn on a distaff.[12]

H. Hunger has described this poetry as "a naive and moving attempt to clothe the history of salvation, which is of fundamental importance

9. Tzet. *Chil.* 10. 49–52 (pp. 388–89 Leone); *Suda s.v.* Ὠρίων (III, 623 Adler); *PLRE,* II, 812, "Orion 1"; Alan Cameron, "Empress and Poet," pp. 274–75, 280–81.

10. Eudocia *Homerocentones* titulus (ed. Ludwich, p. 87) lists as authors Eudocia, Cosmas "of Jerusalem," Optimus, and Patricius "the bishop." In the twelfth century (?) an otherwise unknown Moyses gave "Patricius Hierosolymorum praesul, Optimus, Cosmas atque Simplicius, nec non Eudocia philosophus Athenais, Leontii philosophi filia"; see *Moysi expositio,* ed. F. Gustafsson, Acta societatis scientiarum fennicae XXII, no. 3 (Helsingfors, 1897), p. 14. In her preface (ed. Ludwich, pp. 83–86) Eudocia declares that she revised the work of Patricius, "who was the first to undertake this glorious task" (i.e., composing Christian *Homerocentones*), so he presumably did not belong to her Jerusalem circle. Cosmas, however, may be identified comfortably with the man known from Cyril of Scythopolis. His appearance among these authors indicates that Eudocia labored at *Homerocentones* during her Jerusalem period, and that some or all of the other authors listed joined her labors.

11. Eudocia *Homerocentones,* ed. Ludwich, pp. 88–114, represents selections from the *Codex Mutinensis = Cod. Paris. gr.* 388.

12. Lines 95, 97 (ed. Ludwich) employing *Od.* 6. 52–53. I translate by "stitching" two lines from Lattimore's translation.

to every Christian, in that linguistic garb which was the most venerable to every Greek, namely, the verses of Homer.[13]

Hunger characterizes the *Homerocentones* aptly indeed, and
Eudocia as well and the school of poetasters that produced such
verses. But the incongruity apparent in them requires greater emphasis.
It repelled St. Jerome, who called these literary efforts *puerilia*, "like
the games of itinerant tricksters."[14] It emerges from a reading of the
poems, where one finds hardly a trace of genuine spirituality, and
especially from a verse preface, composed by Eudocia, containing the
boast that she and her school had surpassed a well-known predecessor
in the craft by adhering even more slavishly to precise Homeric diction. That predecessor was the pagan Tatianus, the praetorian prefect
of Theodosius I whom rhetoricians had praised two generations earlier
for his verse sequel to the *Iliad*.[15] Thus even in the Holy Land, in the
milieu of pilgrims and monks, Eudocia remained Athenaïs. Her boast
revealed profound affinities with the values of traditional culture,
and it also revealed the distance that still separated her brand of
imperial piety from Pulcheria's.

In the dynastic city, meanwhile, Pulcheria the "New Helena"
had once again established the authenticity of her sacral *basileía*. Not
unexpectedly, the mint of Constantinople adopted as its principal
issue in gold, 450–53, the same victory type she had inspired *ca.*
420–22, striking Long-Cross solidi with the reverse legend VICTORI—A
AVGGG and obverses of the imperial colleagues Marcian, Valentinian III, and the Augusta Pulcheria (fig. 19).[16] Implicated in a
conjugal union, the virgin Augusta still emphasized her Marial dignity
in this period, as she devoted her resources to construction of three
great *Theotokos* churches.[17] The effort was crucial because parts of the
Empire could not swallow the results of Chalcedon.

13. H. Hunger, "On the Imitation (ΜΙΜΗΣΙΣ) of Antiquity in Byzantine
Literature," *DOP* 23–24 (1969/70), 34.
14. *Ep.* 53. 7 (III, 16 Labourt) to Paulinus of Nola. Jerome may have had in
mind the Latin *Cento Vergilianus de laudibus Christi* composed by the illustrious
Christian poetess Faltonia Betitia Proba; see Schenkl's edition in *CSEL*, XVI; *PLRE*,
I, 732; and R.A. Markus, "Paganism, Christianity and the Latin Classics in the
Fourth Century," *Latin Literature of the Fourth Century*, ed. J.W. Binns (London-
Boston, 1974), pp. 3, 6. A dispute also occurred in the East on the value of such exer-
cises: Alan Cameron, "Empress and Poet," pp. 282–85.
15. *Supra*, p. 14.
16. Tolstoi, *Monnaies*, I, 104. 32–33.
17. *Supra*, p. 142 with n. 120.

When Pope Leo learned of the council's results, he took time to ponder the implications of Canon 28, then addressed himself to Marcian and Pulcheria in separate letters on May 22, 452, indignantly rejecting this innovation because it implied that episcopal rank depended on the rank of cities rather than on scripture and tradition.[18] To Pulcheria Leo expressed satisfaction that the universal faith had been defended and peace secured "by the holy and God-approved efforts of Your Clemency," especially since she had accomplished this without excessive harshness and unnecessary excommunications. The rest of the letter was reproachful. Anatolius had forgotten that he owed his elevation to "the benefit of Your Piety and my own support." Carried away by ambition, he had sought to overturn the decisions of the Council of Nicaea; in vain, however, because with his letter Leo canceled Canon 28. He also urged Pulcheria to hold Anatolius in check and declared in effect that she was to blame for recommending that Leo accept his succession to the see of Constantinople.

By the time Leo's letters reached their destinations, more serious blows had been struck in Palestine against the Chalcedonian decisions. Bishop Juvenal of Jerusalem, a backer of Dioscorus during Ephesus II and a supporter of his "violence," had, to avoid deposition, embraced the new orthodoxy at Chalcedon.[19] When he sought to return to Palestine, the local archimandrites refused to have him, and a revolt broke out against his apostasy.[20] Fanatic "monophysite" monks incensed by the "Nestorian" or "dyophysite" victory at Chalcedon murdered their enemies, looted, burned, and even raised one of their number, the archimandrite Theodosius, to the see of Jerusalem. Inevitably, Eudocia took their side,[21] perhaps from conviction but more clearly because Chalcedon had been a victory for her rival Pulcheria. With Eudocia's support, Theodosius and his fellow archimandrites closed the gates of Jerusalem to the local authorities, taking refuge behind fortifications Eudocia had provided for them.[22] This was an act of open rebellion, made especially dangerous by the parti-

18. *ACO*, II, 4, 55–59. 54–55 [Leo *Epp.* 104–5].
19. See Honigmann, "Juvenal," esp. pp. 240–47 for his conduct at Chalcedon.
20. On the monks' revolt see *ACO*, II, 1, 3, 125–26. 26; Zach. Rhet. *HE* 3. 3–9 (*CSCO: SS*, LXXXVII, 107–12); Cyrill. Scyth. *V. Euth.* 27–28 (*TU*, XLIX: 2, 41–45); Evagr. 2. 5; Theoph. *a.m.* 5945 (p. 107 de Boor); Niceph. Call. *HE* 15. 9 (*PG*, CXLVII, 29–32); Honigmann, "Juvenal," pp. 247–57; Bacht, "Rolle," pp. 244–52; Chitty, *City*, pp. 89–90; Frend, *Rise*, pp. 148–54.
21. *ACO*, II, 4, 69. 63 [Leo *Ep.* 117]; Cyrill. Scyth. *V. Euth.* 27, 30 (*TU*, XLIX: 2, 41, 47); Theoph. and Niceph. Call. *locc. citt.*
22. *ACO*, II, 1, 3, 124. 26; Niceph. Call. *HE* 15. 9 (*PG*, CXLVII, 32).

cipation of the Augusta who had herself been a rebel since 443. Eudocia and her supporters must have expected that Marcian would feel compelled to crush them utterly.

Hoping to escape imperial wrath, the threatened archimandrites and other monks addressed a petition to Pulcheria.[23] They apparently knew of her admiration for holy men and expected her because of it to mollify the emperor's response to their actions. The rebels blamed others for their outrages, in particular the Samaritans, whom they knew Pulcheria had previously attacked and punished. The monks also complained that soldiers had interfered with their monasteries, and they may even have gone so far as to question the orthodoxy not only of the recent council but of Marcian and Pulcheria themselves.[24]

Astonishingly, this directness bore fruit. Perhaps in autumn or early winter, 452, the emperor and empress responded in separate letters to the archimandrites and monks of Jerusalem.[25] Marcian chided the holy men for improperly broaching questions of dogma which should have been left to bishops and councils. But both Pulcheria and Marcian also defended their own "ancestral" faith, including in their letters vehement denials that they or their council were Nestorian and also reciting what amounted to personal confessions of Chalcedonian orthodoxy. Marcian rebuked the monks for rebellion, murder, arson; for mutilation of a victim's corpse, releasing imprisoned criminals, ravishing noble women; and for the gravest offense of all—imposing false doctrine by force, condemning the Council of Chalcedon, and attacking Pope Leo and other holy fathers. But in most cases the emperor reserved punishment for the Divine Judge, announcing his intention to act only to restore peace. The soldiers would no longer interfere, and the crimes of the Samaritans would be investigated and punished.

Pulcheria concluded her letter with a declaration that the monks owed this philanthropic treatment to her own efforts:

For the emperor believes with me that through such concern and exhortation you will regret your earlier actions, and that the universal church will be united in harmony, and the orthodox religion preserved in peace and unanimity.

23. This letter has not been preserved, but Marcian mentions it in his response (*ACO*, II, 1, 3, 124. 26), and this response plus the reply of Pulcheria (*ibid.*, pp. 124–29. 26–27) permit reconstruction of the contents of the monks' petition.

24. Although not mentioned explicitly in the responses of Marcian and Pulcheria, the presence of such a charge in the monks' petition would account for the insistent language with which Pulcheria and Marcian defend their orthodoxy.

25. Cited *supra*, n. 23; for the date Schwartz in *TU*, XLIX: 2, 363 n. 1.

The influence of Pulcheria was such that she could induce Marcian to eschew normal Roman severity in dealing with such uprisings and instead to adopt a policy of gentle persuasion. Eudocia also benefited from this philanthropy and from the reluctance of the eastern court to tamper with the independence of a legitimate Augusta. Ultimately the soldiers had to be unleashed. Eventually Count Dorotheus, the local military commander, drove out Theodosius and by force restored Juvenal to the see of Jerusalem.[26] But this happened about August, 453,[27] most probably a month or two after Pulcheria's death. Even then Marcian did not arrest Eudocia or inhibit her exercise of *basileía*. Not until two years later (about late 455), when notable holy men such as St. Euthymius, St. Simeon Stylites, and Pope Leo the Great had intervened with her in the interests of harmony and for the good of her soul, did Eudocia finally submit. She died October 20, 460, in communion with the Chalcedonian faith.[28]

Daughter of a pagan rhetorician, Eudocia had adopted Christianity for practical reasons, to provide her kin and associates access to power. Over the years she had also assumed the Theodosian image of imperial womanhood, for in this way she could make her *basileía* effective and employ it to encourage traditional values in government and culture. By 443 these efforts had failed. Her career in ruins, Eudocia brought female *basileía* with her into exile and at last took on the monophysite enthusiasm of her subjects.[29] In a life of successive

26. Zach. Rhet. *HE* 3. 5. (*CSCO: SS*, LXXXVII, 109); Niceph. Call. *HE* 15. 9 (*PG*, CXLVII, 32); cf. O. Seeck, *RE*, V (1905), 1570–71, "Dorotheus 11," identifying Count Dorotheus as *Dux Palaestinae*.

27. Bacht, "Rolle," pp. 251–52, says that Theodosius had been expelled from Jerusalem by the end of 452, but Theoph. and Niceph. Call. (*supra*, n. 20) claim that he held the city for twenty months, evidence confirmed by Cyrill. Scyth. *V. Euth.* 27–28 (*TU*, XLIX: 2, 42, 45). Even if the monks' revolt broke out in mid- or late November, 451, immediately after the council of Chalcedon, Theodosius therefore still held Jerusalem until mid- or late July of 453, and probability favors an interval of a month of so after the council before he seized the city. The same argument refutes the contention of Bacht, "Rolle," p. 252, that the *regina* who intervened in favor of the monophysite bishop Peter the Iberian (Zach. Rhet. *HE* 3. 5 [*CSCO: SS*, LXXXVII, 109]) was Pulcheria. On chronology cf. F.M. Clover, "The Family and Early Career of Anicius Olybrius," *Historia* 27 (1978), 178.

28. *ACO*, II, 4, 77 [Leo *Ep.* 123], Cyrill. Scyth. *V. Euth.* 30, 35 (*TU*, XLIX: 2, 47–49, 53–54); Chitty, *City*, pp. 91–92, 95, remarking (p. 91): "if she was to be converted, she must be converted in style"; Clover, "Anicius," pp. 178–79, for chronology.

29. Ignoring Eudocia's submission, monophysite tradition venerated her as a champion of the anti-Chalcedon movement; see, e.g., John of Nikiu 87. 45–46 (trans. Charles) and, for Eudocia in monophysite legend, H. Drake, "A Coptic Version of the Discovery of the Holy Sepulchre," *GRBS* 20 (1979), 381–92.

transformations, each no doubt embraced with energy and conviction, this woman certainly displayed one consistent trait—the will of a Theodosian empress to see her dominion taken seriously.

Pulcheria had died seven years before Eudocia, on the winning side. She had devoted the last months of her life to her usual preoccupations, seeing to it, for example, that the philanthropy evident in imperial treatment of the monks' revolt of 451–53 extended also to holy women. Pulcheria had been saddened to learn that consecrated virgins as well as monks had followed the false archimandrite Theodosius. Early in 453 she addressed a letter to Bassa, the prominent abbess (*hegumene*) of a women's cloister in Jerusalem.[30] She reported with satisfaction that after receiving her earlier letter and the response of her consort, the people of Jerusalem had sent a delegation to Constantinople to ask forgiveness. Now concerned that the distortions of Theodosius might mislead the weaker members of her own sex, Pulcheria also declared her orthodox confession to "all the women dedicated to God" and asked Bassa to pray more continuously for herself and her *basileia*. Pulcheria seems to have worried that she might lose the admiration of these virgins, especially since her recent entrance into nominal marriage would have made her appear to have left their ranks.

In March, 453, Pope Leo addressed two final letters to Pulcheria. In the first, dated March 10,[31] he complained once more of Anatolius and again held Pulcheria responsible for promoting his succession to the see of Flavian. The Constantinopolitan bishop had now ordained an unrepentant Eutychian named Andreas to be archdeacon of the dynastic city. In this matter Pulcheria was exhorted to heed Bishop Julian of Coös, who would act as Leo's legate in suggesting how Pulcheria might aid the universal faith. Leo's letter of March 21[32] was more benign. In the meantime Marcian had responded to the pope's protests regarding Anatolius and Canon 28;[33] although Leo had received no communication from Pulcheria, he declared in his letter that "even so when the most glorious princeps writes to me, I rejoice just as much at his condescension as if addresses had also been brought

---

30. *ACO*, II, 1, 3, 135–36. 31; cf. Cyrill. Scyth. *loc. cit.* 30 (p. 49) reporting that "the blessed Bassa" called a monk named Andreas from the laura of St. Euthemius and placed him in charge of a *martyrium* she had built. Apparently the woman was wealthy and aristocratic.

31. *ACO*, II, 4, 64–65. 59 [Leo *Ep.* 112].

32. *Ibid.*, pp. 68–69. 62 [*Ep.* 116].

33. *Ibid.*, pp. 67–68. 61 [*Ep.* 115].

to me from Your Serenity." The pope knew well that in ecclesiastical matters Marcian depended on his consort and that the emperor's words reflected Pulcheria's views as much as his own. Leo also expressed his thankfulness for the faith of the Augusta "because I recognize in the princes of our time not only imperial potency but also priestly learning." Again he attributed to a female holder of *basileía* the sacerdotal character possessed by her male counterpart.

Leo also indicated obliquely that he knew Pulcheria was ill:

I write in observance of my customary duty to assure you that I rejoice in the continued health of Your Clemency, and that I plead with God in ceaseless prayers that he may preserve you and the Roman state and the Christian church in all prosperity.

The same messengers who brought Marcian's letter apparently informed the pope that he could not count on Pulcheria's help much longer.

On an unknown day in July of 453, "Pulcheria Augusta, wife of Marcian the princeps, . . . brought her life to a blessed end."[34] Mention of her death in the chronicles confirms that her passing, like that of Flaccilla, struck like an earthquake in the dynastic city. Unlike Eudocia, she had lived out her life in Constantinople and its suburbs, forming a bond with its people which even death could not sever. In her will she reinforced that bond by instructing that all of her remaining wealth be distributed among the poor, "to the least of these."[35] Marcian presumably celebrated a public funeral, and then deposited her corpse—probably again at her own instructions—in a sarcophagus carved of porphyry, the imperial stone, located in the mausoleum of Constantine near the tomb of her grandfather Theodosius the Great.[36] Pulcheria wished to emphasize her nearness in descent and character to the founder of the dynasty, and to rest in death close to the life-giving relics of the adjacent Apostles Church.

When they recounted her death, Byzantine chroniclers marveled at Pulcheria's "successes,"[37] at the works of piety and philanthropy through which she embodied most completely the image of female

34. Hydat. *Cont. chron. Hier.* 157 (*MGH: AA*, XI, 27) ("mense Iulio"); Marcell. com. a. 453. 5 (*ibid.*, p. 85); esp. Zon. 13. 25, p. 48a; also Stilting in *AASS*, Sept., III, 536–37, for discussion of the date of Pulcheria's death.

35. Theod. Anag. *Epit.* 363 (p. 102 Hansen); Theoph. *a.m.* 5945 (p. 106 de Boor); Zon. *loc. cit.*

36. P. Grierson, "The Tombs and Obits of the Byzantine Emperors (337–1042)," *DOP* 16 (1962), 20–26, 44.

37. Theod. Anag. and Theoph. cited *supra*, n. 35.

basileía articulated in the previous century for Helena and Flaccilla. Like Helena she became a saint of the church, both in the West[38] and in the East, where centuries later the faithful of Constantinople celebrated her memorial each year on September 10, bearing in mind her piety and virginity, her works of philanthropy and construction, and especially her greatest triumph: "she caused the holy synod to take place at Chalcedon."[39]

Reaction is also attested nearer in time and in an imperial context. It is reported that when Marcian's successor, Leo I, occupied the palace, he composed a narrative passing in review Pulcheria's entire life. That work, written by an imperial hand, apparently belonged to the genre of *vitae sanctorum* and was designed to establish the sanctity of its heroine. Calling Pulcheria blessed, Leo also had her image carved and placed on her tomb, and he celebrated a "memorial [μνήμη] of her perfection." This was an imperial cult of a sainted virgin Augusta.[40]

The report regarding the Pulcheria cult should be read with another, with evidence that Leo and his consort, Verina, also constructed a chapel adjacent to Pulcheria's Blachernai church and deposited in it Mary's shroud, contained in a costly chest. Above the altar that enclosed the chest, they commissioned a mosaic of gold and precious stones showing the Virgin *Theotokos,* and flanking her the emperor, the empress, and their children. Upon the chest Leo and Verina inscribed the words: "By showing reverence here to the *Theotokos,* they secured the power of their *basileía.*"[41] Thus Leo and Verina embraced both the image of Pulcheria's *basileía* and the devotion that had been its most striking component. In this way, Pulcheria contributed after her death to an alliance of emperors with the Virgin, and through that alliance to the Virgin's preeminence in Byzantine civilization. As Norman Baynes wrote, "for the protection of Constantinople the constant pledge, the unfailing guarantee, was the succour and mediation of the blessed Virgin . . . the city was *her* city."[42]

38. T. Schnitzler, "Das Konzil von Chalkedon und die westliche Liturgie," *Das Konzil von Chalkedon*, ed. Grillmeier and Bacht, II, 737.

39. *Synax. Const.* Sept. 10 (*AASS*, Nov., *Propylaeum*, p. 32); D. Stiernon, *Bibliotheca sanctorum*, X (1968), 1254–55, "Pulcheria."

40. *Script. orig. Const.*, p. 52 Preger.

41. Wenger, "Notes inédites," pp. 54–59; also *idem, Assomption*, pp. 300–303; *supra*, Chap. 4, n. 120.

42. N.H. Baynes, "The Supernatural Defenders of Constantinople," *An. Boll.* 67 (1949), 171–72; also Averil Cameron, "The Theotokos in Sixth-Century

Imperial cult, the emulation of successors, eventual sainthood—such manifestations of approval confirm that Pulcheria's was authentic *basileía,* and they demonstrate more besides. The dominion Pulcheria held had emerged two generations earlier from the proclivities of the dynasty's founder, from the domestic side of the monarchy and the necessary bond between dynasty and dynastic city. Limited by their sex, Augustae had at first received authority from childbearing and the prospect of imperial *kedeia* with themselves or their offspring. Lacking magisterial powers, Pulcheria especially had to develop other resources that had nothing to do with traditional female functions, power acquired instead through spectacular piety, exalted humility, works of construction and philanthropy, and potent alliances with saints. Manifestations of approval such as those in the reign of Leo I indicate that by exploiting these resources Pulcheria transformed the *basileía* itself, showing the way to Byzantium.

Constantinople," *JThS* 29 (1978), 79–108, esp. pp. 97–98 on "the role of imperial patronage" in the emergence of *Theotokos* cult.

BIBLIOGRAPHY

Abramowski, L. *Untersuchungen zum Liber Heraclidis des Nestorius.* CSCO, Subsidia, vol. XXII. Louvain, 1963.

Aldama, J. A. de. *Repertorium pseudochrysostomicum.* Institut de Recherche et d'Histoire des Textes: Documents, études et répertoires vol. 10. Paris, 1965.

Alföldi, A. "Die Ausgestaltung des monarchischen Zeremoniells am römischen Kaiserhofe." *Mitteilungen des Deutschen Archäologischen Instituts, Römische Abteilung* 49 (1934), 3–118 = *Die monarchische Repräsentation im römischen Kaiserreiche.* Darmstadt, 1970. Pp. 1–118.

———. "Insignien und Tracht der römischen Kaiser." *Mitteilungen des Deutschen Archäologischen Instituts, Römische Abteilung* 50 (1935), 1–171 = *Die monarchische Repräsentation im römischen Kaiserreiche.* Darmstadt, 1970. Pp. 119–276.

Alföldi, M. R. *Die constantinische Goldprägung.* Mainz, 1963.

Alföldi-Rosenbaum, E. "Bemerkungen zur Porträtbüste einer jungen Dame justinianischer Zeit im Metropolitan Museum." *Jahrbuch für Antike und Christentum* 15 (1972), 174–78.

Amantos, K. "Zu den wohltätigen Stiftungen von Byzanz." *Orientalia christiana periodica* 21 (1955), 15–20.

Anastos, M. "Nestorius Was Orthodox." *Dumbarton Oaks Papers* 16 (1962), 117–40.

Anton, H. "Kaiserliches Selbstverständnis in der Religionsgesetzgebung der Spätantike und päpstliche Herrschaftsinterpretation im 5. Jahrhundert." *Zeitschrift für Kirchengeschichte* 88 (1977), 38–84.

Armstrong, G. "Fifth and Sixth Century Church Building in the Holy Land." *Greek Orthodox Theological Review* 14 (1969), 17–30.

Aubineau, M. "Une homélie de Théodote d'Ancyre." *Orientalia christiana periodica* 26 (1960), 221–49.

Avi-Yonah, M. "The Economics of Byzantine Palestine." *Israel Exploration Journal* 8 (1958), 39–51.

———. *The Jews of Palestine: A Political History from the Bar Kokhba War to the Arab Conquest.* Oxford, 1976.

Bacht, H. "Die Rolle des orientalischen Mönchtums in den kirchenpolitischen Auseinandersetzungen um Chalkedon (431–519)." *Das Konzil von Chalkedon,* ed. A. Grillmeier and H. Bacht. Vol. II. Würzburg, 1953. Pp. 193–314.

Baldwin, B. "'Perses': A Mysterious Prefect in Eunapius." *Byzantion* 46 (1976), 5–8.

Bardenhewer, O. *Geschichte der altkirchlichen Literatur.* 4 vols. Freiburg i. B., 1902–24.

Bardy, G. "Acace de Bérée et son rôle dans la controverse nestorienne." *Revue des sciences religieuses* 18 (1938), 20–44.

———. "Atticus de Constantinople et Cyrille d'Alexandrie." *Histoire de l'église depuis les origines jusqu'à nos jours,* ed. A. Fliche and V. Martin. Vol. IV. Paris, 1937. Pp. 149–62.

———. "Le «brigandage» d'Ephèse et le concile de Chalcédoine." *Histoire de l'église,* ed. A. Fliche and V. Martin. Vol. IV. Paris, 1937. Pp. 211–40.

———. "Les débuts du Nestorianisme (428–433)." *Histoire de l'église,* ed. A. Fliche and V. Martin. Vol. IV. Paris, 1937. Pp. 163–96.

Barnes, T.D. "*Patricii* under Valentinian III." *Phoenix* 29 (1975), 155–70.

Batiffol, P. "Un épisode du concile d'Ephèse (juillet 431) d'après les actes coptes de Bouriant." *Mélanges . . . Gustave Schlumberger.* Paris, 1924. I, 28–39.

———. "Les présents de S. Cyrille à la cour de Constantinople." *Etudes de liturgie et d'archéologie chrétienne.* Paris, 1919. Pp. 154–79.

———. *Le siège apostolique (359–451).* Paris, 1924.

Bauer, F.X. *Proklos von Konstantinopel: Ein Beitrag zur Kirchen- und Dogmengeschichte des 5. Jahrhunderts.* Munich, 1919.

Baur, P. Chrysostomus. *Der heilige Johannes Chrysostomus und seine Zeit.* 2 vols. Munich, 1929–30.

Baynes, N.H. "Alexandria and Constantinople: A Study in Ecclesiastical Diplomacy." *Byzantine Studies and Other Essays.* London, 1955. Pp. 97–115.

———. "Rome and the Early Middle Age." *History* 14 (1930), 289–98.

———. "The Supernatural Defenders of Constantinople." *Analecta Bollandiana* 67 (1949), 165–77 = *Byzantine Studies and Other Essays.* London, 1955. Pp. 248–60.

Bebis, G.S. "'The Apology' of Nestorius: A New Evaluation." *Studia patristica* 11 (1972) = *TU,* CVIII, 107–12.

Becatti, G. *La colonna coclide istoriata: problemi storici iconografici stilistici.* Rome, 1960.

Beck H.-G. *Senat und Volk von Konstantinopel.* Sitzungsberichte der Bayerischen Akademie der Wissenschaften, Philosophisch-historische Klasse, Jahrgang 1966, Heft 6. Munich, 1966. Pp. 1–75.

Bloch, H. "The Pagan Revival in the West at the End of the Fourth Century." *The Conflict between Paganism and Christianity in the Fourth Century,* ed. A. Momigliano. Oxford, 1963. Pp. 193–218.

Boyce, A. A. "Eudoxia, Eudocia, Eudoxia: Dated Solidi of the Fifth Century." *American Numismatic Society: Museum Notes* 6 (1954), 134–42.

———. *Festal and Dated Coins of the Roman Empire.* American Numismatic Society: Numismatic Notes and Monographs no. 153. New York, 1965.

Bregman, J. *Synesius of Cyrene: Philosopher-Bishop.* Berkeley-Los Angeles-London, 1982.

Brehier, L. "L'origine des titres impériaux à Byzance." *Byzantinische Zeitschrift* 15 (1906), 161–78.

Brooks, E. W. "The Emperor Zenon and the Isaurians." *English Historical Review* 8 (1893), 209–38.

Brown, P. "The Rise and Function of the Holy Man in Late Antiquity." *Journal of Roman Studies* 61 (1971), 80–101.

Browning, R. "The Riot of A.D. 387 in Antioch: The Role of Theatrical Claques in the Later Empire." *Journal of Roman Studies* 42 (1952), 13–20.

Bruns, G. *Der Obelisk und seine Basis auf dem Hippodrom zu Konstantinopel.* Istanbuler Forschungen vol. VII. Istanbul, 1935.

Bruun, P. "Notes on the Transmission of Imperial Images in Late Antiquity." *Studia romana in honorem Petri Krarup septuagenarii.* Odense, 1976. Pp. 122–31.

Bury, J. B. *History of the Later Roman Empire.* Vol. I. London, 1923.

———. "Justa Grata Honoria." *Journal of Roman Studies* 9 (1919), 1–13.

Caird, G. B. "Paul and Women's Liberty." *Bulletin of the John Rylands Library* 54 (1972), 268–81.

Calza, R. *Iconografia romana imperiale da Carausio a Giuliano (287–363 d.C.).* Quaderni e guide di archeologia vol. III. Rome, 1972.

Camelot, T. *Virgines Christi: la virginité aux premiers siècles de l'église.* Paris, 1944.

Cameron, Alan. *Circus Factions: Blues and Greens at Rome and Byzantium.* Oxford, 1976.

———. *Claudian: Poetry and Propaganda at the Court of Honorius.* Oxford, 1970.

———. "The Empress and the Poet: Paganism and Politics at the Court of Theodosius II," *Yale Classical Studies* 27 (1981) 217–89.

———. *Porphyrius the Charioteer.* Oxford, 1973.

———. "Theodosius the Great and the Regency of Stilico." *Harvard Studies in Classical Philology* 73 (1969), 247–80.

———. "Wandering Poets: A Literary Movement in Byzantine Egypt." *Historia* 14 (1965), 470–509.

Cameron, Averil. "Agathias on the Sassanians." *Dumbarton Oaks Papers* 23–24 (1969/70), 68–183.

———. Flavius Cresconius Corippus. *In laudem Iustini Augusti minoris.* Ed. and trans. with commentary by Averil Cameron. London, 1976.

———. "The Theotokos in Sixth-Century Constantinople." *Journal of Theological Studies* 29 (1978), 79–108.

Capizzi, C. "L'attività edilizia di Anicia Giuliana." *Collectanea byzantina = Orientalia christiana analecta* 204 (1977), 119–46.

Caspar, E. *Geschichte des Papsttums von den Anfängen bis zur Höhe der Weltherrschaft.* 2 vols. Tübingen, 1930, 1933.

Cecchelli, C. *Mater Christi.* Vol. I. Rome, 1946.

Chadwick, H. "The Exile and Death of Flavian of Constantinople." *Journal of Theological Studies* n.s. 6 (1955), 17–34.

Charlesworth, M.P. "Imperial Deportment: Two Texts and Some Questions." *Journal of Roman Studies* 37 (1947), 34–38.

Charlier, N. *DHGE,* XIV (1960), 508–14, "Dioscore 3."

Chastagnol, A. "Le sénateur Volusien et la conversion d'une famille de l'aristocratie romaine au Bas-Empire." *Revue des études anciennes* 58 (1956), 241–53.

Chitty, D.J. *The Desert a City.* Oxford, 1966.

Christensen, A. *L'Iran sous les Sassanides.* 2nd ed. Copenhagen, 1944.

Christophilopoulou, A. *Eklogē, anagoreusis kai stepsis tou Byzantinou autokratoros.* Pragmateiai tēs Akadēmias Athēnōn XXII, no. 2. Athens, 1956.

Clemente, G. *La "Notitia Dignitatum."* Saggi di storia e letteratura no. 4. Cagliari, 1968.

Clover, F.M. "The Family and Early Career of Anicius Olybrius." *Historia* 27 (1978), 169–96.

Collot, C. "La pratique et l'institution du suffragium au Bas-Empire." *Revue historique de droit français et étranger* ser. 4, 43 (1965), 185–221.

Constantelos, D.J. *Byzantine Philanthropy and Social Welfare.* New Brunswick, N.J., 1968.

———. "Kyros Panopolites, Rebuilder of Constantinople." *Greek, Roman and Byzantine Studies* 12 (1971), 451–64.

Croke, B. "Arbogast and the Death of Valentinian II." *Historia* 25 (1976), 235–44.

———. "Evidence for the Hun Invasion of Thrace in A.D. 422." *Greek, Roman and Byzantine Studies* 18 (1977), 347–67.

Dagron, G. "L'Empire romain d'Orient au IVe siècle et les traditions politiques de l'hellénisme: le témoinage de Thémistios." *Travaux et mémoires* 3 (1968), 1–242.

———. "Les moines et la ville: le monachisme à Constantinople jusqu'au concile de Chalcédoine (451)." *Travaux et mémoires* 4 (1970), 229–56.

———. *Naissance d'une capitale: Constantinople et ses institutions de 330 à 451.* Paris, 1974.

———. "La vie ancienne de Saint Marcel l'Acémète." *Analecta Bollandiana* 86 (1968), 271–321.

Daly, L. "Themistius' Concept of *Philanthropia.*" *Byzantion* 45 (1975), 22–40.

Davies, J. G. "Deacons, Deaconesses and Other Minor Orders in the Patristic Period." *Journal of Ecclesiastical History* 14 (1963), 1–15.

Deichmann, F. *Ravenna, Hauptstadt des spätantiken Abendlandes.* I: *Geschichte und Monumente.* Wiesbaden, 1960. II: *Kommentar.* Pts. 1–2. Wiesbaden, 1974.

Delbrueck, R. *Die Konsulardiptychen und verwandte Denkmäler.* Berlin and Leipzig, 1929.

———. *Spätantike Kaiserporträts von Konstantinus Magnus bis zum Ende des Westreichs.* Berlin and Leipzig, 1933.

Delmas, F. "Saint Passarion." *Echos d'Orient* 3 (1900), 162–63.

Demandt, A. "Der Tod des älteren Theodosius." *Historia* 18 (1969), 598–626.

———. "Die Feldzüge des älteren Theodosius." *Hermes* 100 (1972), 81–113.

———. *RE*, suppl. XII (1970), 553–790, "Magister Militum."

Demangel, R. *Contribution à la topographie de l'Hebdomon.* Recherches françaises en Turquie, fasc. 3. Paris, 1945.

Demarolle, J.-M. "Les femmes chrétiennes vues par Porphyre." *Jahrbuch für Antike und Christentum* 13 (1970), 42–47.

Demougeot, E. *De l'unité à la division de l'Empire romain 395–410.* Paris, 1951.

———. "Modalités d'établissement des fédérés barbares de Gratien et de Théodose." *Mélanges d'histoire ancienne offerts à William Seston.* Paris, 1974. Pp. 143–60.

Devos, P. "Quand Pierre l'Ibère vint-il à Jérusalem?" *Analacta Bollandiana* 86 (1968), 337–50.

Devreesse, R. "Les acts du concile d'Ephèse." *Revue des sciences philosophiques et théologiques* 18 (1929), 223–42, 408–31.

———. "Après le concile d'Ephèse: le retour des Orientaux à l'unité (433–37)." *Echos d'Orient* 30 (1931), 271–92.

Dölger, F. J. "Die eigenartige Marienverehrung der Philomarianiten oder Kollyridianer in Arabien." *Antike und Christentum* 1 (1929), 107–42.

Dörries, H. "Die Messalianer im Zeugnis ihrer Bestreiter: Zum Problem des Enthusiasmus in der spätantiken Reichskirche." *Saeculum* 21 (1970), 213–27.

Downey, G. *A History of Antioch in Syria.* Princeton, 1961.

———. "*Philanthropia* in Religion and Statecraft in the Fourth Century after Christ." *Historia* 4 (1955), 199–208.

———. "The Wall of Theodosius at Antioch." *American Journal of Philology* 62 (1941), 207–13.

Dressel, H. "Erwerbungen des Königlichen Münzcabinets in den Jahren 1890–97 (antike Münzen)." *Zeitschrift für Numismatik* 21 (1898), 245–49.

Dudden, F. Homes. *The Life and Times of St. Ambrose.* 2 vols. Oxford, 1935.

Dunlap, J.E. *The Office of the Grand Chamberlain in the Later Roman and Byzantine Empires.* University of Michigan Studies in the Humanities vol. XIV. New York and London, 1924. Pp. 165–324.

Dvornik, F. *Early Christian and Byzantine Political Philosophy.* 2 vols. Washington, D.C., 1966.

Ebersolt, J. *Sanctuaires de Byzance.* Paris, 1921.

Eltester, W. *RE*, VA (1927), 893–901, "Sokrates Scholasticus."

———. *RE*, VA (1927), 1240–48, "Sozomenos."

Ensslin, W. *Die Religionspolitik des Kaisers Theodosius des Grossen.* Sitzungsberichte der Bayerischen Akademie der Wissenschaften, Philosophisch-historische Klasse, Jahrgang 1953, Heft 2. Munich, 1953.

———. *Gottkaiser und Kaiser von Gottes Gnaden.* Sitzungsberichte der Bayerischen Akademie der Wissenschaften, Philosophisch-historische Klasse, Jahrgang 1943, Heft 6. Munich, 1943.

———. *RE*, XIV (1930), 1514–29, "Marcianos 34."

———. *RE*, XIV (1930), 1757, "Marina 4."

———. *RE*, suppl. VIII (1956), 556–67, "Praepositus sacri cubiculi."

———. *RE*, XXIII (1959), 1954–63, "Pulcheria 2."

———. "Zum Heermeisteramt des spätrömischen Reiches, III." *Klio* 24 (1931), 467–502.

———. "Zur Frage nach der ersten Kaiserkrönung durch den Patriarchen und zur Bedeutung dieses Aktes im Wahlzeremoniell." *Byzantinische Zeitschrift* 42 (1943–49), 101–15, 369–72.

———. "Zur Torqueskrönung und Schilderhebung bei der Kaiserwahl." *Klio* 35 (1942), 268–98.

Farioli, R. "Ravenna paleocristiana scomparsa." *Felix Ravenna* 83 (1961), 5–88.

Felletti Maj. B. "Contributo alla iconografia del IV secolo d.C.: il ritratto femminile." *Critica d'arte* 6 (n.s. 1) (1941), 74–90.

Frank, R.I. *Scholae Palatinae: The Palace Guards of the Later Roman Empire.* Papers and Monographs of the American Academy in Rome vol. XXIII. Rome, 1969.

Frantz, A. "From Paganism to Christianity in the Temples of Athens." *Dumbarton Oaks Papers* 19 (1965), 185–205.

———. "Herculius in Athens: Pagan or Christian." *Akten des VII. Internationalen Kongresses für Christliche Archäologie, Trier, 5–11 September 1965.* Vatican City and Berlin, n.d. Pp. 527–30.

Frend, W.H.C. "Popular Religion and Christological Controversy in the Fifth Century." *Popular Belief and Practice*, ed. G.J. Cuming and

D. Baker. Ecclesiastical History Society: Studies in Church History vol. VIII. Cambridge, 1972. Pp. 19–29.

———. *The Rise of the Monophysite Movement.* Cambridge, 1972.

Freund, A. *Beiträge zur antiochenischen und zur konstantinopolitanischen Stadtchronik.* Jena, 1882.

Fuchs, F. *Die höheren Schulen von Konstantinopel im Mittelalter.* Byzantinisches Archiv no. 8. Leipzig and Berlin, 1926.

Gagé, J. "ΣΤΑΥΡΟΣ ΝΙΚΟΠΟΙΟΣ: la victoire impériale dans l'Empire chrétien." *Revue d'histoire et de philosophie religieuses* 13 (1933), 370–400.

Geanakoplos, D.J. "Church Building and 'Caesaropapism.'" *Greek, Roman and Byzantine Studies* 7 (1966), 167–86.

Geffcken, J. *Der Ausgang des griechisch-römischen Heidentums.* 2nd ed. Heidelberg, 1929.

Goemans, M. "Chalkedon als 'Allgemeines Konzil.'" *Das Konzil von Chalkedon*, ed. A. Grillmeier and H. Bacht. Vol. I. Würzburg, 1951. Pp. 251–89.

Goffart, W. "Did Julian Combat Venal *Suffragium?*" *Classical Philology* 65 (1970), 145–51.

Goubert, P. "Le rôle de Sainte Pulchérie et de l'eunuque Chrysaphius." *Das Konzil von Chalkedon*, ed. A. Grillmeier and H. Bacht. Vol. I. Würzburg, 1951. Pp. 303–21.

Grabar, A. *L'empereur dans l'art byzantin.* Paris, 1936.

Graef, H.C. "The Theme of the Second Eve in Some Byzantine Sermons on the Assumption." *Studia patristica* 9 (1966) = *TU*, XCIV, 224–30.

Grégoire, H. "Inscriptions historiques byzantines." *Byzantion* 4 (1927/28), 437–68.

———, and M.-A. Kugener. "Quand est né l'empereur Théodose II?" *Byzantion* 4 (1927–28), 337–48.

Gregorovius, F. *Athenais, Geschichte einer byzantinischen Kaiserin.* 3rd ed. Leipzig, 1892.

Gregory, T. "The Remarkable Christmas Homily of Kyros Panopolites." *Greek, Roman and Byzantine Studies* 16 (1975), 317–24.

———. "Zosimus 5. 23 and the People of Constantinople." *Byzantion* 43 (1973), 61–83.

Grierson, P. "The Tombs and Obits of the Byzantine Emperors (337–1042)," *Dumbarton Oaks Papers* 16 (1962), 1–60.

Grillmeier, A. *Christ in Christian Tradition from the Apostolic Age to Chalcedon (451).* Trans. J.S. Bowden. London, 1965.

Grumel, R.P.V. "L'Illyricum de la mort de Valentinien Ier (375) à la mort de Stilicon (408)." *Revue des études byzantines* 9 (1951), 5–46.

———. *Les regestes des actes du patriarcat de Constantinople.* Vol. I, fasc. 1. Constantinople, 1932.

Gryson, R. *Le ministère des femmes dans l'église ancienne.* Recherches et synthèses, Section d'histoire no. 4. Gembloux, 1972.

Guilland, R. *Etudes de topographie de Constantinople byzantine.* Berliner byzantinische Arbeiten, vol. XXXVII: 1, 2. Berlin and Amsterdam, 1969.

―――. *Recherches sur les institutions byzantines.* Berliner byzantinische Arbeiten, vol. XXXV: 1, 2. Berlin and Amsterdam, 1967.

Guldan, E. *Eva und Maria: Eine Antithese als Bildmotiv.* Graz and Cologne, 1966.

Haacke, R. "Die kaiserliche Politik in den Auseinandersetzungen um Chalkedon (451–553)." *Das Konzil von Chalkedon,* ed. A. Grillmeier and H. Bacht. Vol. II. Würzburg, 1953. Pp. 95–177.

Haehling, R. von. *Die Religionszugehörigkeit der hohen Amtsträger des römischen Reiches seit Constantins I. Alleinherrschaft bis zum Ende der theodosianischen Dynastie.* Antiquitas ser. 3, vol. XXIII. Bonn, 1978.

Heintze, H. von. "Ein spätantikes Frauenbüstchen aus Elfenbein." *Berliner Museen* 20 (1970), 51–61.

―――. "Ein spätantikes Mädchenporträt in Bonn: Zur stilistischen Entwicklung des Frauenbildnisses im 4. und 5. Jahrhundert." *Jahrbuch für Antike und Christentum* 14 (1971), 61–91.

Hermann, A. "Mit der Hand Singen: Ein Beitrag zur Erklärung der trierer Elfenbeintafel." *Jahrbuch für Antike und Christentum* 1 (1958), 105–8.

Hoffmann, D. *Das spätrömische Bewegungsheer und die Notitia dignitatum.* Epigraphische Studien vol. VII: 1–2. Düsseldorf, 1969.

―――. "Der Oberbefehl des spätrömischen Heeres im 4. Jahrhundert n. Chr." *Actes du IXe congrès international d'études sur les frontières romaines, Mamaïa, 6–13 septembre 1972.* Bucuresti-Cologne-Vienna, 1974. Pp. 381–97.

Holder-Egger, O. "Die Chronik des Marcellinus Comes und die oströmische Fasten." *Neues Archiv* 2 (1877), 50–109.

Holtzinger, H. *Die altchristliche Architektur in systematischer Darstellung.* Stuttgart, 1889.

Holum, K. "Family Life in the Theodosian House." *Kleronomia* 8 (1976), 280–92.

―――. "Justa Grata Honoria and the Scepter of Empire (Priscus frg. 15)." (Forthcoming).

―――. "Pulcheria's Crusade and the Ideology of Imperial Victory." *Greek, Roman and Byzantine Studies* 18 (1977), 153–72.

―――, and G. Vikan. "The Trier Ivory, *Adventus* Ceremonial, and the Relics of St. Stephen." *Dumbarton Oaks Papers* 33 (1979), 113–33.

Honigmann, E. *Le couvent de Barsauma et le patriarcat jacobite d'Antioche et de Syrie.* CSCO, Subsidia, vol. VII. Louvain, 1954.

_____. "Juvenal of Jerusalem." *Dumbarton Oaks Papers* 5 (1950), 209–79.

Hopkins, M.K. *Conquerors and Slaves: Sociological Studies in Roman History, Volume I*. Cambridge, 1978.

_____. "Eunuchs in Politics in the Later Roman Empire." *Proceedings of the Cambridge Philological Society* n.s. 9 (1963), 62–80.

Hubaux, J. "La crise de la trois cent soixante cinquième année." *Antiquité classique* 17 (1948), 343–54.

Hunger, H. "ΦΙΛΑΝΘΡΩΠΙΑ: Eine griechische Wortprägung auf ihrem Wege von Aischylos bis Theodoros Metochites." *Anzeiger der Österreichischen Akademie der Wissenschaften, Philosophisch-historische Klasse*, Jahrgang 1963. Pp. 1–20.

_____. "On the Imitation (ΜΙΜΗΣΙΣ) of Antiquity in Byzantine Literature." *Dumbarton Oaks Papers* 23–24 (1969/70), 15–38.

Hunt, E.D. "Palladius of Helenopolis: A Party and Its supporters in the Church of the Late Fourth Century." *Journal of Theological Studies* n.s. 24 (1973), 457–80.

_____. "St. Silvia of Aquitaine: The Role of a Theodosian Pilgrim in the Society of East and West." *Journal of Theological Studies* n.s. 23 (1972), 351–73.

Jalland, T. *The Life and Times of St. Leo the Great*. London, 1941.

Janin, R. "La banlieue asiatique de Constantinople." *Echos d'Orient* 22 (1923), 182–98.

_____. *Constantinople byzantine*. Archives de l'Orient chrétien no. 4a. 2nd ed. Paris, 1964.

_____. *La géographie ecclésiastique de l'Empire byzantine*. Part I, vol. III: *Les églises et les monastères*. 2nd ed. Paris, 1969.

Jones, A.H.M. "The Career of Flavius Philippus." *Historia* 4 (1955), 229–33.

_____. "Collegiate Prefectures." *Journal of Roman Studies* 54 (1964), 78–89.

_____. *The Later Roman Empire 284-602: A Social, Economic and Administrative Survey*. 3 vols. Oxford, 1964.

_____. "Numismatics and History." *Essays in Roman Coinage Presented to Harold Mattingly*, ed. R.A.G. Carson and C.H.V. Sutherland. Oxford, 1956. Pp. 13–33.

_____, J.R. Martindale, and J. Morris. *The Prosopography of the Later Roman Empire*. Vol. I. Cambridge, 1971. Vol. II. Cambridge, 1980.

Jugie, M. *La mort et l'assomption de la Sainte Vierge*. Studi e testi no. 114. Vatican City, 1944.

_____. *Nestorius et la controverse nestorienne*. Paris, 1912.

Kabiersch, J. *Untersuchungen zum Begriff der Philanthropia bei dem Kaiser Julian*. Klassisch-philologische Studien no. 21. Wiesbaden, 1960.

Kaegi, W. *Byzantium and the Decline of Rome*. Princeton, 1968.

———. "The Fifth-Century Twilight of Byzantine Paganism." *Classica et mediaevalia* 27 (1968), 243–75.

Kahrstedt, U. "Frauen auf antiken Münzen." *Klio* 10 (1910), 261–314.

Kantorowicz, E. "On the Golden Marriage Belt and the Marriage Rings of the Dumbarton Oaks Collection." *Dumbarton Oaks Papers* 14 (1960), 1–16.

———. "Oriens Augusti: Lever du Roi." *Dumbarton Oaks Papers* 17 (1963), 119–77.

Karayannopulos, J. "Der frühbyzantinische Kaiser." *Byzantinische Zeitschrift* 49 (1956), 369–84.

Keil, J. "Die Familie des Prätorianerpräfekten Anthemius." *Anzeiger der Akademie der Wissenschaften in Wien, Philosophisch-historische Klasse* 79 (1942), 185–203.

Kelly, J. N. D. *Jerome, His Life, Writings, and Controversies.* New York and London, 1975.

Kent, J. P. C. "'*Auream monetam . . . cum signo crucis,*'" *Numismatic Chronicle* ser. 6, 20 (1960), 129–32.

———. "Gold Coinage in the Later Roman Empire." *Essays in Roman Coinage Presented to Harold Mattingly*, ed. R. A. G. Carson and C. H. V. Sutherland. Oxford, 1956. Pp. 190–204.

Kidd. B. J. *A History of the Church to A.D. 461.* Vol. III. Oxford, 1922.

King, N. Q. *The Emperor Theodosius and the Establishment of Christianity.* London, 1961.

Kleiss, W. "Neue Befunde zur Chalkopratenkirche in Istanbul." *Akten des VII. Internationalen Kongresses für Christliche Archäologie, Trier, 5–11 September 1965.* Vatican City and Berlin, n.d. Pp. 587–94.

Kollwitz, J. *Oströmische Plastik der theodosianischen Zeit.* Berlin, 1941.

Kornemann, E. *Doppelprinzipat und Reichsteilung im Imperium Romanum.* Leipzig and Berlin, 1930.

Krautheimer, R. "The Constantinian Basilica." *Dumbarton Oaks Papers* 21 (1967), 115–40.

———. *Early Christian and Byzantine Architecture.* Baltimore, 1965.

Kruse, H. *Studien zur offiziellen Geltung des Kaiserbildes im römischen Reiche.* Paderborn, 1934.

Labourt, J. *Le christianisme dans l'Empire perse sous la dynastie Sassanide (224–632).* 2nd ed. Paris, 1904.

Lacombrade, C. *Synésios de Cyrène, hellène et chrétien.* Paris, 1951.

Laffranchi, K. "Nuovo aureo di Licinia Eudossia e il corpus numismatico di questa Augusta." *Rassegna numismatica* 28 (1931), 251–56.

Lechner, K. *Hellenen und Barbaren im Weltbila der Byzantiner.* Munich, 1954.

Leipoldt, J. *Die Frau in der antiken Welt und im Urchristentum.* Leipzig, 1954.

Lemerle, P. *Le premier humanisme byzantin: notes et remarques sur enseignement et culture à Byzance des origines au Xe siècle*. Paris, 1971.

Leroy, F. *L'homilétique de Proclus de Constantinople*. Studi e testi no. 247. Vatican City, 1967.

Liébaert, J. *DHGE*, XV (1963), 561–74, "Ephèse (concile d'), 431."

Liebeschuetz, J. H. W. G. *Antioch: City and Imperial Administration in the Later Roman Empire*. Oxford, 1972.

Lippold, A. *RE*, suppl. XIII (1973), 837–961, "Theodosius I."

———. *RE*, suppl. XIII (1973), 961–1044, "Theodosius II."

———. *Theodosius der Grosse und seine Zeit*. Stuttgart, 1968.

Littlewood, A. R. "The Symbolism of the Apple in Byzantine Literature." *Jahrbuch der österreichischen Byzantinistik* 23 (1974), 33–59.

Loofs, F. *Nestorius and His Place in the History of Christian Doctrine*. Cambridge, 1914.

L'Orange, H. P. "Nochmals die spätantike Kaiserin im Norwegischen Institut in Rom." *Acta ad archaeologiam et artium historiam pertinentia* 6 (1975), 57.

———. "Statua tardo-antica di un'imperatrice." *Acta ad archaeologiam et artium historiam pertinentia* 4 (1969), 95–99.

———. "Ein unbekanntes Porträt einer spätantiken Kaiserin." *Acta ad archaeologiam et artium historiam pertinentia* 1 (1962), 49–52.

Luibheid, C. "Theodosius II and Heresy." *Journal of Ecclesiastical History* 16 (1965), 13–38.

MacCormack, S. *Art and Ceremony in Late Antiquity*. Berkeley-Los Angeles-London, 1981.

———. "Change and Continuity in Late Antiquity: The Ceremony of *Adventus*." *Historia* 21 (1972), 721–52.

———. "Roma, Constantinopolis, the Emperor, and His Genius." *Classical Quarterly* n.s. 25 (1975), 131–50.

MacIsaac, J. D. "'The Hand of God': A Numismatic Study." *Traditio* 31 (1975), 322–28.

MacMullen, R. "Roman Bureaucratese." *Traditio* 18 (1962), 364–78.

Maenchen-Helfen, O. J. *The World of the Huns: Studies in Their History and Culture*. Berkeley-Los Angeles-London, 1973.

Malingrey, A.-M. Jean Chrysostome. *Lettres à Olympias*. Ed. with introduction, translation, and notes by A.-M. Malingrey. Paris. 1968.

Mango, C. "Antique Statuary and the Byzantine Beholder." *Dumbarton Oaks Papers* 17 (1963), 55–75.

———. "Autour du Grand Palais de Constantinople." *Cahiers archéologiques* 5 (1951), 179–86.

———. *The Brazen House: A Study of the Vestibule of the Imperial Palace of Constantinople*. Det Kongelige Danske Videnskabernes Selskab: Arkaeologisk-kunsthistoriske Meddelelser vol. IV, no. 4. Copenhagen, 1959.

Marique, J. F.-M. "A Spanish Favorite of Theodosius the Great: Cynegius, Praefectus Praetorio." *Classical Folia* 17 (1963), 43–65.

Marrou, H.-I. *Histoire de l'éducation dans l'antiquité*. 7th ed. Paris, 1965.

Martin, T. O. "The Twenty-Eighth Canon of Chalcedon: A Background Note." *Das Konzil von Chalkedon*, ed. A. Grillmeier and H. Bacht. Vol. II. Würzburg, 1953. Pp. 433–58.

Martindale, J. R. "Note on the Consuls of 381 and 382." *Historia* 16 (1967), 254–56.

Marx, B. *Procliana: Untersuchungen über den homiletischen Nachlass des Patriarchen Proklos von Konstantinopel*. Münster, 1940.

Maslev, S. "Die staatsrechtliche Stellung der byzantinischen Kaiserinnen." *Byzantinoslavica* 27 (1966), 308–43.

Mathews, T. F. *The Early Churches of Constantinople: Architecture and Liturgy*. University Park and London, 1971.

Matthews, J. F. "Olympiodorus of Thebes and the History of the West (A.D. 407–25)." *Journal of Roman Studies* 60 (1970), 79–97.

———. "A Pious Supporter of Theodosius I: Maternus Cynegius and His Family." *Journal of Theological Studies* n.s. 18 (1967), 438–46.

———. *Western Aristocracies and the Imperial Court*. Oxford, 1975.

Mazzarino, S. *Stilicone: la crisi imperiale dopo Teodosio*. Rome, 1942.

Meyer-Plath, B., and A. M. Schneider. *Die Landmauern von Konstantinopel*. Vol. II. Berlin, 1943.

Michel, A. *Die Kaisermacht in der Ostkirche (843-1204)*. Darmstadt, 1959.

Mueller-Wiener, W. *Bildlexikon zur Topographie Istanbuls*. Tübingen, 1977.

Murray, C. "Art and the Early Church." *Journal of Theological Studies* n.s. 28 (1977), 303–45.

Murray, R. "Mary, the Second Eve, in the Early Syriac Fathers." *Eastern Churches Review* 3 (1971), 372–84.

Naumann, R., and H. Belting. *Die Euphemia-Kirche am Hippodrom zu Istanbul und ihre Fresken*. Berlin, 1966.

Neumann, C. W. *The Virgin Mary in the Works of St. Ambrose*. Freiburg, Sw., 1962.

Nicolas, M.-J. "La doctrine mariale et la théologie chrétienne de la femme." *Maria: études sur la Sainte Vierge*, ed. H. du Manoir. Vol. VII. Paris, 1964. Pp. 341–62.

Ommeslaeghe, F. van. "Jean Chrysostome en conflit avec l'impératrice Eudoxie: le dossier et les origines d'une légende." *Analecta Bollandiana* 97 (1979), 131–59.

———. "Que vaut le témoinage de Pallade sur le procès de Saint Jean Chrysostome?" *Analecta Bollandiana* 95 (1977), 389–414.

Oost, S. I. *Galla Placidia Augusta: A Biographical Essay*. Chicago and London, 1968.

———. "Some Problems in the History of Galla Placidia." *Classical Philology* 60 (1965), 1–10.

Palanque, J.-R. "L'empereur Maxime." *Les empereurs romains d'Espagne.* Colloques internationaux du Centre National de la Recherche Scientifique, Sciences Humaines, Madrid-Italica, 31 March–6 April 1964. Paris, 1965. Pp. 255–67.

———. *Saint Ambroise et l'Empire romain.* Paris, 1933.

Papadopulos, J. "L'église de Saint-Laurent et les Pulchérianae." *Studi bizantini* 2 (1927), 59–63.

Pargoire, J. "Les débuts du monachisme à Constantinople." *Revue des questions historiques* n.s. 21 (1899), 67–143.

———. "Un mot sur les Acémètes." *Echos d'Orient* 2 (1898–99), 304–8, 365–72.

Paschoud, F. *Cinque études sur Zosime.* Paris, 1975.

Pavan, M. *La politica gotica di Teodosio nella pubblicistica del suo tempo.* Rome, 1964.

Pearce, J. W. E. "Gold Coinage of the Reign of Theodosius I." *Numismatic Chronicle* ser. 5, 18 (1938), 205–46.

Petit, P. "Les sénateurs de Constantinople dans l'oeuvre de Libanius." *Antiquité classique* 26 (1927), 347–82.

———. "Sur la date du «Pro Templis» de Libanius." *Byzantion* 21 (1951), 285–310.

Philipsborn, A. "La compagnie d'ambulanciers «parabalani» d'Alexandrie." *Byzantion* 20 (1950), 185–90.

Pieler, P. "L'aspect politique et juridique de l'adoption de Chosroès proposée par les Perses à Justin." *Revue internationale des droits de l'antiquité* ser. 3, 19 (1972), 399–432.

Quasten, J. *Patrology.* Vol. III. Utrecht and Antwerp, 1966.

Rahner, H. "Die Gottesgeburt: Die Lehre der Kirchenväter von der Geburt Christi im Herzen des Gläubigen." *Zeitschrift für katholische Theologie* 59 (1935), 333–418.

Rampolla del Tindaro, M. *Santa Melania Giuniore senatrice romana.* Rome, 1905.

Ramsay, A. M. "The Speed of the Roman Imperial Post." *Journal of Roman Studies* 15 (1925), 60–74.

Rauschen, G. *Jahrbücher der christlichen Kirche unter dem Kaiser Theodosius dem Grossen.* Freiburg i. B., 1897.

Reisch, E., F. Knoll, and J. Keil. *Die Marienkirche in Ephesos.* Österreichisches Archäologisches Institut: Forschungen in Ephesos vol. IV, no. 1. Vienna, 1932.

Richard, M. "L'introduction du mot 'hypostase' dans la théologie de l'incarnation, II." *Mélanges de science religieuse* 2 (1945), 243–70.

Rist, J. M. "Hypatia." *Phoenix* 19 (1965), 214–25.

Ritter, A.-M. *Das Konzil von Konstantinopel und sein Symbol.* Göttingen, 1965.

Robert, L. *Epigrammes du Bas-Empire.* Hellenica vol. IV. Paris, 1948.

Roey, A. van. *DHGE*, XVI (1967), 87–91, "Eutychès."

Rooijen, J. W. van. *De Theodosii II moribus ac rebus politicis*. Leiden, 1912.

Rubin, B. *Das Zeitalter Justinians*. Vol. I. Berlin, 1960.

Runia, David T. "Another Wandering Poet." *Historia* 28 (1979), 254–56.

Ste. Croix, G. E. M. de. "Suffragium: From Vote to Patronage." *British Journal of Sociology* 5 (1954), 33–48.

Salis, J. F. W. de. "The Coins of the Two Eudoxias, Eudocia, Placidia, and Honoria, and of Theodosius II, Marcian, and Leo I, Struck in Italy." *Numismatic Chronicle* n.s. 7 (1867), 203–15.

Sauerbrei, P. "König Jazdegerd der Sünder, der Vormund des byzantinischen Kaisers Theodosius des Kleinen." *Festschrift Albert von Bamberg*. Gotha, 1905. Pp. 90–108.

Schemmel, F. *Die Hochschule von Konstantinopel vom V. bis IX. Jahrhundert*. Berlin, 1912.

Schneider, A. M. "Die Blachernen." *Oriens* 4 (1951), 82–120.

————. "Sankt Euphemia und das Konzil von Chalkedon." *Das Konzil von Chalkedon*, ed. A. Grillmeier and H. Bacht. Vol. I. Würzburg, 1951. Pp. 291–302.

Schnitzler, T. "Das Konzil von Chalkedon und die westliche Liturgie." *Das Konzil von Chalkedon*, ed. A. Grillmeier and H. Bacht. Vol. II. Würzburg, 1953. Pp. 735–60.

Schwartz, E. *Cyrill und der Mönch Viktor*. Sitzungsberichte der Akademie der Wissenschaften in Wien, Philosophisch-historische Klasse vol. CCVIII, no. 4. Vienna and Leipzig, 1928.

————. "Die Kaiserin Pulcheria auf der Synode von Chalkedon." *Festgabe für Adolf Jülicher*. Tübingen, 1927. Pp. 203–12.

————. *Der Prozess des Eutyches*. Sitzungsberichte der Bayerischen Akademie der Wissenschaften, Philosophisch-historische Abteilung, Jahrgang 1929, Heft 5. Munich, 1929.

————. "Über die Reichskonzilien von Theodosius bis Justinian." *Zeitschrift der Savigny-Stiftung für Rechtsgeschichte, Kanonische Abteilung* 11 (1921), 208–53.

Seeck, O. *RE*, VI (1909), 2431–33, "Aelia Flaccilla Augusta 3."

————. *RE*, II (1896), 1137, "Arkadia 5."

————. *RE*, II (1896), 1137–53, "Arkadios 2."

————. *RE*, VI (1909), 917–25, "Eudoxia 1."

————. *Geschichte des Untergangs der antiken Welt*. Vols. V–VI. Stuttgart, 1920.

————. *RE*, VI (1909), 925–26, "Licinia Eudoxia 2."

————. *Regesten der Kaiser und Päpste*. Stuttgart, 1919.

————. "Studien zu Synesius." *Philologus* 52 (1894), 442–83.

————, and G. Veith. "Die Schlacht am Frigidus." *Klio*, 13 (1913), 451–67.

Sellers, R. V. *The Council of Chalcedon: A Historical and Doctrinal Survey*. London, 1953.

Sickel, W. "Das byzantinische Krönungsrecht bis zum 10. Jahrhundert." *Byzantinische Zeitschrift* 7 (1898), 511–57.

Sirago, V. A. *Galla Placidia e la trasformazione politica dell'Occidente*. Louvain, 1961.

Smith, M. "The Manuscript Tradition of Isidore of Pelusium." *Harvard Theological Review* 47 (1954), 205–10.

Soffel, J. *Die Regeln Menanders für die Leichenrede in ihrer Tradition dargestellt, herausgegeben, übersetzt und kommentiert.* Beiträge zur klassischen Philologie no. 57. Meisenheim am Glan, 1974.

Speck, P. Review of P. Lemerle, *Le premier humanisme byzantin. Byzantinische Zeitschrift* 67 (1974), 385–93.

Spira, A. "Rhetorik und Theologie in den Grabreden Gregors von Nyssa." *Studia patristica* 9 (1966) = *TU*, XCIV, 106–14.

Stein, E. *Histoire du Bas-Empire*. Ed. J.-R. Palanque. Vol. I. Paris and Bruges, 1959.

———. "Untersuchungen zur spätrömischen Verwaltungsgeschichte." *Rheinisches Museum* 74 (1925), 347–94.

Steinwenter, A. "ΝΟΜΟΣ ΕΜΨΥΧΟΣ: Zur Geschichte einer politischen Theorie." *Anzeiger der Akademie der Wissenschaften in Wien, Philosophisch-historische Klasse* 83 (1946), 250–68.

Stiernon, D. *Bibliotheca sanctorum*, X (1968), 1245–56, "Pulcheria."

Straub, J. *RAC*, VI, fasc. 46 (1965), 864–75, "Eugenius."

———. *Vom Herrscherideal in der Spätantike*. Stuttgart, 1939.

———. "Parens Principum: Stilichos Reichspolitik und das Testament des Kaisers Theodosius." *Nouvelle Clio* 4 (1952), 94–115.

———. "Die Wirkung der Niederlage bei Adrianopel auf die Diskussion über das Germanenproblem in der spätrömischen Literatur." *Philologus* 95 (1943), 255–86.

Straubinger, J. *Die Kreuzauffindungslegende*. Forschungen zur christlichen Literatur- und Dogmengeschichte vol. XI, no. 3. Paderborn, 1912.

Strube, C. "Der Begriff Domus in der Notitia Urbis Constantinopolitanae." *Studien zur Frühgeschichte Konstantinopels*, ed. H.-G. Beck, Miscellanea byzantina monacensia, vol. XIV. Munich, 1973. Pp. 121–34.

Sutherland, C. H. V. "The Intelligibility of Roman Imperial Coin Types." *Journal of Roman Studies* 49 (1959), 46–55.

Sydow, W. von. *Zur Kunstgeschichte des spätantiken Porträts im 4. Jahrhundert n. Chr.* Antiquitas ser. 3, no. 8. Bonn, 1969.

Szidat, J. "Die Usurpation des Eugenius." *Historia* 28 (1979), 487–508.

Thompson, E. A. "The Foreign Policies of Theodosius II and Marcian." *Hermathena* 76 (1950), 58–75.

———. *A History of Attila and the Huns*. Oxford, 1948.

———. "The Isaurians under Theodosius II." *Hermathena* 68 (1946), 18–31.

———. "Olympiodorus of Thebes." *Classical Quarterly* 38 (1944), 43–52.

Tiftixoglu, V. "Die Helenianai nebst einigen anderen Besitzungen im Vorfeld des frühen Konstantinopel." *Studien zur Frühgeschichte Konstantinopels*, ed. H.-G. Beck, Miscellanea byzantina monacensia vol. XIV. Munich, 1973. Pp. 49–120.

Toynbee, J. M. C. *Roman Medallions*. American Numismatic Society: Numismatic Studies no. 5. New York, 1944.

Treitinger, O. *Die oströmische Kaiser- und Reichsidee*. Jena, 1938.

Ulrich-Bansa, O. *Moneta Mediolanensis*. Venice, 1949.

Vasiliev, A. A. *Justin the First*. Cambridge, Mass., 1950.

Vincent, H., and F.-M. Abel. *Jérusalem, recherches de topographie, d'archéologie, et d'histoire*. Vol. II, fasc. 4. Paris, 1926.

Vries, W. de. "Die Struktur der Kirche gemäss dem Konzil von Chalkedon (451)." *Orientalia christiana periodica* 35 (1969), 63–122.

Walden, J. W. H. *The Universities of Ancient Greece*. New York, 1909.

Weber, W. "Studien zur Chronik des Malalas." *Festgabe für Adolf Deissmann*. Tübingen, 1927. Pp. 20–66.

Wenger, A. *L'assomption de la t. S. Vierge dans la tradition byzantine du VIe au Xe siècle*. Paris, 1955.

———. "Notes inédites sur les empereurs Théodose I, Arcadius, Théodose II, Léon I," *Revue des études byzantines* 10 (1952), 47–59.

Wessel, K. "Römische Frauenfrisuren von der severischen bis zur konstantinischen Zeit." *Archäologischer Anzeiger* (1946/47), 62–76.

Wrede, H. "Zur Errichtung des Theodosius-Obelisken in Istanbul," *Istanbuler Mitteilungen* 16 (1966), 178–98.

Zakrzewski, C. *Le parti théodosien et son antithèse*. Eus supplementa vol. XVIII. Lvov, 1931.

INDEX

This index does not repeat information given in the list of illustrations.

apple-of-discord legend, on Eudocia's fall, 176–77

Manuel, archimandrite, 196

Marcella, *cubicularia*, 180

Marcian, Emperor: origins, marries Pulcheria, 208–9; coronation, 208; respects Pulcheria's vow, 209; in apple-of-discord legend, 209; marriage solidus of, 209; convokes Council of Chalcedon (451), 212–13; transfers it from Nicaea to Chalcedon, 213; absent during preliminaries, 213; appears before it, 215; saluted as "New David," "New Paul," "New Constantine," 215–16

Long-Cross solidi of, 221; correspondence with Leo the Great, 222, 225; orthodoxy questioned, 223; with monks of Palestine, 223

Marcion, correspondent of Synesius, 84–85

Maria, church in Constantinople, 157*n*

Maria, consort of Honorius, 49

Marianai, palace of Eudoxia, 76

Marina, Empress, 31

Marina, sister of Pulcheria: birth, 53; vow of virginity, 93; in Hebdomon inscription, 110; properties, 131–32, 134; devotion to Virgin Mary, 143; receives treatise from Cyril of Alexandria, 159; "Bride of Christ," 159; death, 196

Marriage solidus: of Valentinian III and Licinia Eudoxia, 209; of Marcian and Pulcheria, 209

Marsa, friend of Eudoxia, 64

Mary, Virgin: in works of Atticus, 138–41; paradigm for female ascetics, 139, 141–42; and dignity of women, 140–42, 145, 155–56; as New Eve, 141; churches of, in Constantinople, 142–43, 157*n*, 221, 227; relics of, 142*n*, 227; and Pulcheria's *basileía*, 142–43, 145–46, 227; popularity of, 145; cult of, in Constantinople, 145; in works of Proclus, 155–57; churches of, at Ephesus, 164, 166, 201; cult of, at Ephesus, 164; and Council of Ephesus (431), 164; honored by procession at Ephesus,

166; deposes Nestorius, 170; in *Homerocentones*, 220; alliance with emperors, 227. See also *Theotokos*

Maximian of Constantinople, bishop, 172, 179–81

Maximus, Magnus, usurper, 9, 44–46

Melania the Younger, ascetic, 183–86

Meletius of Antioch, bishop, 17*n*, 18*n*

Memnon of Ephesus, bishop, 164, 166, 167–68, 171

Mesē, thoroughfare in Constantinople, 11, 80, 107

Messalianism, heresy, 135*n*

Miracle: and the Battle of the Frigidus, 21*n*; at the Hebdomon, 188–89

Monasticism: urban phenomenon, 70; revolutionary character, 134–36

Monaxius, *magister officiorum*, 101*n*

Monks: antagonistic toward Nestorius, 149–50, 158, 168; reject Eutyches, 201; clash with Eudocia, 217–18; of Palestine, reject Chalcedon, 222–24, 225; petition Pulcheria, 223

Muses: in Senate House of Constantinople, 41; sanctuary of, in Antioch, 186

Nebridius, brother-in-law of Flaccilla, 22–23, 71

Nebridius, nephew of Flaccilla, 23*n*

Nectarius of Constantinople, bishop, 71

Nestorius of Constantinople, bishop: origins, training, 147; selected, enthroned, 148–49; views on Virgin Mary, 148; his orthodoxy, 149; antagonizes monks, 149–50, 157–58; inspires legislation against heresies, 150; policy on women, 152; conflict with Cyril of Alexandria, 151–52, 158; conflict with Pulcheria, 152–54, 182, 204, 215; proposes title *Christotokos*, 154; objects to *Theotokos*, 154–56; claims imperial support, 158–59; writings sent to Rome, 158; Celestine of Rome finds heretical, 161; urges council, 162; at Council of Ephesus (431), 166, 171; deposed, 166, 171; "Jew,"

Praepositus sacri cubiculi, office of
eunuchs, 60–61; in *cubiculum* of
empress, 131
Prefect, city, office, 13
Prefect, praetorian, office, 13
Priscus of Panium, historian, 2, 4
Procession: celebrating relics, 56–57,
90, 137; at Ephesus, celebrating
victory of Virgin Mary, 166
Procle, disciple of John Chrysostom, 71
Proclus of Constantinople, bishop:
praises Pulcheria, 137–38; and the
sermons of Atticus of
Constantinople, 141; sermons on
Theotokos, 141, 155–57; on
Eve–New Eve antithesis, 141;
candidate for episcopacy, 148;
opposes Nestorius, 155; Pul-
cheria's ally, 155–57, 192;
selected, enthroned in episcopacy,
182–83; and relics of John Chrysostom, 184; and the liturgy, 188;
death, 197
Procopius, *magister militum*, 95, 122
Proculus, city prefect, 14–15
Promotus, *magister militum*, 52–53
Pronubus, on marriage solidi, 209
Pulcheria, daughter of Flaccilla and
Theodosius I, 22, 53
Pulcheria, Empress: birth, 53; childhood, influence of Eudoxia, 80;
education, literacy, 81–82;
precocity, 90; quarrel with
Antiochus, 90–91; as *epitropos* of
her family, 91; educates
Theodosius II, 91–93; vow of
virginity, 93–96; coronation, 97;
not recognized in West, 128;
policies of her government, 97–98,
98–100; promotes barbarian
generals, 101–2, 207; breaks with
traditionalists, 98–104, 107–11;
attitude toward Hellenes,
100–101; toward Jews, 98, 188;
inspires war against Persia, 102–3,
109, 111; in legend of Eudocia's
marriage, 113, 120; conflict with
Eudocia, 121, 130–31, 175–76,
192, 222
in Chalcedonian era: interest in
Christological question, 199;

supports Formula of Union (433),
199–200; resists Eutyches, 201,
204; alliance with Leo the Great,
203–4, 216; correspondence with
Leo the Great, 203–4, 205, 211–
12, 222, 225–26; legate of Apostle
Peter, 204; letter from Deacon
Hilary, 204; returns to power,
207; alliance with Aspar, 207–8;
reigns alone, 208; marriage,
208–9; in apple-of-discord legend,
209; "Second Eve," 209; crowns
Marcian, 208–9; directs ecclesiastical policy, 211; in acclamations,
211, 214–16; plans ecumenical
council, 212; issues imperial letter,
213; in arrangements for council,
213–14; appears before council,
215; receives petition from monks
of Palestine, 223; defends orthodoxy, 223; letter to Bassa, 225;
illness, 226; death, funeral, burial,
226
Christian virtues: philanthropy, 91,
196, 225; vow of virginity, 93–96,
110–11, 138, 209; and relics of
Stephen Protomartyr, 103–4,
107–9, 196; association with ascetics, 134–36, 196, 201, 223, 225;
and relics of Lawrence, Isaiah,
Forty Martyrs of Sebaste, 137;
paralleled with Stephen Protomartyr, 138; counseled by Atticus
of Constantinople, 139; embraces
Virgin Mary as paradigm, 141–42,
174; and relics of Virgin Mary,
142*n*; piety of her court, 143–44;
and cult of Virgin Mary, 143,
145–46, 227; as holy woman,
144–45; robe used as altar covering, 144, 153; image above altar
of Great Church, 144–45, 153;
dines in episcopal palace, 144,
153; "Bride of Christ," 153, 159;
views on *Theotokos*, 156; and
relics of John Chrysostom, 184–85;
"Jeanne d'Arc" of papacy, 203,
216; praised for opposing heresy,
215–16; "New Helena," 216;
sainthood, 226–27
between Ephesus (431) and

Designer: Sandy Drooker
Compositor: Freedmen's Organization
Text: EditWriter Garamond
Display: EditWriter Garamond
Printer: Maple-Vail Book Mfg. Group
Binder: Maple-Vail Book Mfg. Group